Right to Revolt

Right to Revolt

THE CRUSADE FOR RACIAL JUSTICE IN MISSISSIPPI'S CENTRAL PINEY WOODS

Patricia Michelle Boyett

UNIVERSITY PRESS OF MISSISSIPPI • JACKSON

www.upress.state.ms.us

The University Press of Mississippi is a member of the Association of American University Presses.

Copyright © 2015 by University Press of Mississippi
All rights reserved
Manufactured in the United States of America

First printing 2015

∞

Library of Congress Cataloging-in-Publication Data

Boyett, Patricia Michelle, author.
Right to revolt : the crusade for racial justice in Mississippi's Central Piney Woods / Patricia Michelle Boyett.
    pages cm
Includes bibliographical references and index.
ISBN 978-1-4968-0430-3 (cloth : alk. paper) — ISBN 978-1-4968-0431-0 (ebook) 1. African Americans—Civil rights—Mississippi—Piney Woods (Region)—History—20th century. 2. Civil rights movements—Mississippi—Piney Woods (Region)—History—20th century. 3. Race discrimination—Mississippi—Piney Woods (Region)—History—20th century. 4. African Americans—Mississippi—Piney Woods (Region)—History—20th century. 5. Piney Woods (Miss. : Region)—Race relations. I. Title.
    F347.P63B69 2015
    323.1196'07307625—dc23
                                        2015019357

British Library Cataloging-in-Publication Data available

TO MY PARENTS, BONNIE AND BOB BUZARD, FOR GIVING ME WINGS, AND to my husband, Ricky Boyett, for traveling with me on this journey as I sought to trace a courageous struggle of men, women, and children who revolted against injustice. This book is dedicated to them too, to those named in these pages, and to the far too many unnamed freedom fighters.

Acknowledgments

A BOOK IS A PILGRIMAGE IN SEARCH OF SOME TRUTH, AND MINE TOOK me deep into a southern landscape filled with an array of intriguing people whose stories captivated me. It led me into libraries, courthouses, and government buildings that held scattered pieces of racial struggles tucked neatly away in boxes by dedicated archivists and civil servants, and it brought me into university offices filled with devoted professors who became my guides across unknown terrains as I sought to reconnect the fragments of the past into the mosaic they once made. I have not enough space here to name each person who helped me in my endeavors, but I am deeply grateful to all of them.

I wish to thank first the men and women who opened their homes and offices to me and shared their experiences in Mississippi's racial struggles. They continue to move and inspire me. I would never have had this opportunity to convey their stories were it not for the assistance of so many people and institutions. Thus, I wish to express my deep gratitude to the University Press of Mississippi, particularly Craig Gill, for believing in my manuscript and for guiding me through the process of transforming it into a book. Thanks also to an amazing group at the press, including Anne Stascavage, Katie Keene, John Langston, Courtney McCreary, Steven B. Yates, Kathy Burgess, Clint Kimberling, and Kristin Kilpatrick. I am also grateful to the readers of my manuscript, Jason Morgan Ward at Mississippi State University and Charles L. Hughes at Oklahoma State University, for their insightful critiques and their wise counsel. Thank you also to Michael Levine for his meticulous and graceful copyediting. I am deeply appreciative to the University of Southern Mississippi for providing me with the Washam Dissertation Award and the William D. McCain Fellowship, which helped me develop the first wave of research. I am a grateful recipient of the RAND Gulf States Policy Institute Scholars Award (2007) and the Mississippi Historical Society's Franklin L. Riley Prize (2012), which helped me with the middle and latter stages of my work. A special thanks goes to

Rachel Swanger at RAND and to Charles Bolton, James Pat Smith, and Jane Elliott Crawford of the Mississippi Historical Society's prize committee for considering my research worthy of support. Thank you also to Rosemary James and Joe J. DeSalvo of Pirate's Alley Faulkner Society in New Orleans for their faith in my manuscript.

I was blessed to encounter so many wonderful educators on my circuitous journey toward becoming a historian. At University City High School, Susan Vreeland cultivated in me a love for the art of writing; at Arizona State University, theater professors David Vining and David Barker guided me toward a deeper understanding of the human experience; at Mississippi Valley State University, Larry Chappell, Ellen Singh, Robert Waters, the Thomases, and all of my professors and fellow students opened a world of knowledge to me about racial struggles in America. While at the University of Southern Mississippi, Bradley G. Bond allowed me freedom of exploration in my research and writing, which he tempered by coloring multiple drafts with red ink and by teaching me with great wit and wisdom how to sculpt raw ideas into narratives. Neil R. McMillen opened his home and his brilliant mind to me long after he retired. Curtis Austin, Louis Kyriakoudes, Andrew Wiest, William Scarborough, and Marjorie Spruill all read various drafts and offered thorough critiques. My peers also encouraged me with thoughtful evaluations at our beloved Hattiesburg joints.

Many scholars, archivists, and librarians provided me exceptional assistance. Yvonne Arnold, Jennifer Brannock, Diane Ross, Danielle Bishop, and Peggy Price went out of their way to help me sift through new unprocessed collections at McCain Library and Archives. Curtis Austin, Louis Kyriakoudes, Linda VanZandt, Stephen Sloan, Charles Bolton, and Stephanie Scull-DeArmey helped me mine through a treasure trove of oral histories housed at the Center for Oral History and Cultural Heritage at the University of Southern Mississippi, and they provided me with equipment, contacts, and wise instruction when I conducted my own interviews. Christa Cleeton at the Seeley G. Mudd Manuscript Library and Joyce Dixon-Lawson and William L. Thompson at the Mississippi Department of Archives and History went above the call of duty to locate vital sources for me. Many city, county, and state employees graciously aided me in my research, especially Gwen Wilks and Debbie Benardo. Thank you also to Danielle McGuire, Michele Coffey, Crystal Feimster, Marjorie Spruill, and Ted Owenby for their advice during conference sessions. I am grateful to all of my colleagues at Loyola University New Orleans for their guidance and fellowship as I worked toward the publication of my manuscript. And I am moved by a constant source of inspiration: the many magnificent students whom I have had the privilege of working with in my career; their curiosity and passion drive me to continue seeking new understandings of the past and of the struggles of our own era.

My family and friends have been a constant source of unwavering support. Becky and Donnie Boyett, the Highlanders, the Kiehls, the Brians, the Riccis, the Temples, my most cherished lifetime friends from San Diego, particularly Annette Scuderi, Kim Beck, Whitney Punches, Diane Sheehan, Kari Kruesi, and Julia Walsh, my college friends, and the mother's club extended fellowship and encouragement. My parents have been a wellspring of love and influence. My mom, Bonnie Buzard, inculcated in me a reverence for human struggles by coloring my childhood with literature and theater; my dad, Robert Buzard, taught me to seek truth and justice by his outstanding example. My sisters, Cindy Kiehl and Jenny Highlander, both exemplary educators, listened patiently to my research findings and ideas and supported me like best friends do. Thanks to T. L. Boyett who gave me joy when I needed it most. I wish also to thank my grandmother, Teresa Temple, because she believed in dreams and never doubted mine. I am eternally grateful to my husband, Ricky Boyett, whom I fell in love with at the University of Southern Mississippi and who became my fellow traveler; he listened to every thesis and narrative development of my work, repaired my technical disasters, made me laugh in my darkest hours, and endured with uncommon patience the long hours and the long years I devoted to this book. He is my sanctuary, my compatriot, my North Star.

I am in wonderment of all of the people whom I came to know in my travels. I am indebted to the freedom fighters who sought to build a true promised land in America. And I am grateful for the journey.

Right to Revolt

PROLOGUE

Roots of Revolt

NEAR 2:30 A.M. ON JANUARY 10, 1966, KLANSMEN AIMED THEIR SHOTguns at a burning farmhouse in Forrest County, Mississippi, and fired repeatedly. They intended to kill the black family with fire or bullets. It made no difference to them as long as they silenced the troublemaking "nigger" Vernon Dahmer. Inside the burning home, Dahmer slid his shotgun out of the partially opened front door and returned fire. His wife Ellie rushed their ten-year-old daughter, Bettie, toward the only way out—a window at the back of the house. But it was jammed shut. The fire roared down the hallway toward them. Bettie saw no signs of her brothers, whose bedrooms were at the other end of the ranch-style house. "We're not going to make it out of here," she sobbed. Flames licked the ceiling and dripped onto her arms. Her father inhaled burning embers. Her mother yanked at the window. Screams pierced through the raging fire outside and startled the youngest Klansmen. He looked at his leader in horror. The dark-haired preacher fixed his sharp blue eyes on his underling and said, "Ah hell let him die."[1]

Hours later, at the headquarters of the White Knights of the Ku Klux Klan in adjacent Jones County, Imperial Wizard Sam Bowers, who had ordered the attack, promised his men that even if arrested, Mississippi jurors would not dare convict them.[2] Bowers failed to realize that he had made a grave error. Dahmer, a beloved local civil rights leader, had worked closely with Department of Justice officials on voter discrimination for over a decade. The attack enraged them. Special Agent in Charge of Mississippi Roy Moore moved the core of the FBI's war against the Klan into Forrest and Jones Counties. He selected an ideal place from which to launch a major offensive because Jones County was the command center of the Invisible Empire and Forrest County was the home of one the most powerful civil rights movements.

Jones and Forrest Counties are located in the southeastern quadrant of Mississippi in the heart of the Piney Woods region. The area acquired its name because of its dense forests abounding with longleaf pines from the Pearl River in the west to the Alabama border in the east. They are referred to jointly as the Central Piney Woods because they are the hub of the Piney Woods region in terms of geography, population, and economic growth, and they became the nucleus of south Mississippi's racial conflicts. Yet this Deep South community has not received its rightful place in history. Several narratives of the movement and the FBI's war against the Klan capture important images of the Central Piney Woods, but like scattered puzzle pieces, they form an incomplete and, at times, deceptive picture. Most reflect the myths constructed by local leaders in Forrest County that their land was a bastion of moderation in a state notorious for its racial extremism. The myths also suggested that neighboring Jones County served as the heart of southern Mississippi's white supremacist pathology. However, behind this façade lies a dark racial history linking Jones and Forrest Counties in violent trajectories that routinely paralleled each other and often intersected in brutal paths toward wretched ends. During the turn of the century, both counties earned a reputation for racial violence, but the Forrest County seat of Hattiesburg was known as the hub of "nigger lynchings."

The story of the Central Piney Woods is in many ways a tragedy of a Deep South community wracked by mob lynchings, malicious prosecutions, police brutality, and Klan terrorism that culminated with the attack on the Dahmers. Yet it is also a saga of redemption, for in response to racial terrorism, locals launched one of the most powerful racial revolutions in the South. In the Central Piney Woods, the black liberation movement developed in three stages. First, a black vanguard organized and developed a phase of dissent during the 1940s and mobilized much of the black citizenry in the 1950s. Because blacks faced such violent resistance from whites, they could not launch a full-scale revolt. Still, sometimes white brutality backfired as it forced intermittent federal intervention. When the local struggle exploded onto the national scene in 1964, it became a crucial beachhead of the Civil Rights Movement. During this second, revolutionary phase, racial battles escalated federal intervention and spurred watershed developments in racial justice; yet inequity persisted. So the struggle moved into its third, post–civil rights crusade. The nexus of all the forces emerging from within the Central Piney Woods and converging upon it from without take center stage in this tripartite crusade. For it is through their clashing and coalescing that progress finally began; and it is in that nexus that the scattered images of the Central Piney Woods weave together to form one of the most tortured and transformative historical tapestries of the black liberation movement.[3]

The quest for liberty in the Central Piney Woods passed down the generations from the earliest settlers of darker hues who knew something of freedom in the anarchist wilderness and dreamed of building a promised land in the heart of Mississippi. As those first black migrants trickled into the feral forests with their masters and settled upon the Choctaw lands ceded to the United States in 1805, they discovered a landscape unencumbered by the rigid racial mores that defined most of the South. Vernon Dahmer's roots stretched back to those days; he was the great grandson of one of the first settlers, John Kelly, and one of Kelly's slaves, Sarah. Kelly established a 640-acre plantation on the banks of the Leaf River in an area originally part of Greene County and then Perry County and finally the northern edge of Forrest County.

Some of Kelly's fellow pioneers exalted the virgin forests as "majestic," while others condemned the inhospitable woods, overgrown thickets, and dark swamps teeming with predators as "no man's land." These settlers lived in a state of nature beset both by the horrors and hopes inherent in anarchies, a condition perhaps best described by two seventeenth-century English political theorists, Thomas Hobbes, who viewed such an existence as one of constant violent conflict, and his greatest critic John Locke, who perceived such a circumstance as a state of freedom in which humans sought to realize their natural rights to liberty and equity. Surely the Central Piney Woods settlers struggled in a Hobbesian state of war as limited resources pitted settlers both against each other and the wilderness, and life was, as one historian notes, "truly nasty, brutish, and not infrequently short." Yet they thrived too in the Lockean state of freedom as the sparsely populated settlement lacked a stable governing body to enforce racial mores. Most frontier settlers rebelled against the emergence of any authoritative force, whether a ruling class of the few planter elites, a church board, or a yeomanry republic, because they perceived them as a threat to their independence. Like most frontier societies, the dearth of white women led some white men to take slaves and Indians as lovers. Sarah had several mixed-race children with Kelly and his son Green. As the frontier lasted longer in the Central Piney Woods than in many places, interracial affairs proliferated and produced substantial mixed-race societies. Although similar developments had occurred in New Orleans and Natchez, the proliferation of steamboats between 1814 and 1850, which accelerated the pace of delivering commodities to world markets, entrenched the plantation economy and the resulting racial caste system deep into the roots of cities on the Mississippi River. In contrast, the Central Piney Woods remained isolated from the ports, and the plantation economy grew slowly. Such realities neither produced racial equality nor black liberty; however, it did birth racial revolutionaries who fought for such goals.[4]

Jones County was home to Newton Knight, one of the most significant radicals in the Central Piney Woods. When the Civil War erupted, he considered it his duty to protect his homeland and volunteered. He changed his mind in 1862 after the Confederacy passed the Twenty-Negro Law, which exempted slaveholders owning twenty persons or more from conscription. Knight deserted. When Confederate troops hunted deserters, Knight formed an army composed mostly of yeomen, declared his county the Free State of Jones, and led a revolt against the Confederacy in which he promised to free the slaves. Several slaves, including Rachel, a mixed-race slave owned by Knight's grandfather, aided the rebellion by serving as spies and by furnishing the Knight Company with provisions. Colonel Robert Lowry condemned the Knight Company as a band of traitors and hanged those who were captured. After the Civil War, Knight built two homesteads in Jones County, one with his white wife, Serena, and one with his concubine, Rachel, where he raised two sets of children on prosperous farms.

To the south of Jones County in the Kelly Settlement, mixed-race families also flourished. During the war, Kelly freed Sarah and her black and mixed-race children. Several of her descendants married whites. After the war, many of them acquired land in the Kelly Settlement through homesteading acts and established thriving farms. In the heydays of Reconstruction, the future for persons of mixed-race and black heritages seemed promising, particularly after the passage of the Thirteenth, Fourteenth, and Fifteenth Amendments, which respectively emancipated slaves, guaranteed blacks citizenship and legal protection, and granted suffrage to black men. Yet as white resistance to Reconstruction hardened and the white population in the Central Piney Woods grew, black freedoms receded.[5]

Most Jones County whites embraced the revolt against Reconstruction and determined to salvage their marginalized status produced by the Knight rebellion. In the late 1860s, after a black man allegedly raped a white woman, a mob led by the woman's husband hunted down the suspect with hounds and "skinned him alive." A Mississippi newspaper applauded the lynching and celebrated Jones County as a new bastion of white supremacy. Throughout Reconstruction, white radicals terrorized blacks with spontaneous lynchings and organized violence perpetuated by the Ku Klux Klan. Although founded in 1865 in Tennessee as a social group, the first grand wizard, Confederate general Nathan Bedford Forest, transformed it into a paramilitary brigade bent on eradicating Republican rule and subjugating blacks. Jones County Klansman William B. Martin boasted that he and his brethren hanged many "niggers" to save whites from the reign of Yankees and "Negroes." Although Republicans passed several bills, including the Enforcement Act (1870) and the Ku Klux Klan Act (1871), under which federal prosecutors convicted scores of Klansmen, few of the convicted served prison sentences. Republicans abandoned blacks in the Compromise of 1877: in exchange for the termination of Reconstruction, Democrats conceded the contested 1876 presidential election to Republican candidate Rutherford B. Hayes. The compromise included an understanding that if Hayes assumed the presidency, Republicans would support federal land grants and loans for the Texas and Pacific Railroad and federal subsidies for the reconstruction of the Mississippi river levees. In 1881, Colonel Lowry became governor of Mississippi after a zealous, race-baiting campaign. From the ashes of Reconstruction arose the Leviathan of white supremacy.[6]

Railroads speeded the entrance of white supremacist rule into the Central Piney Woods just as it had been advanced by the waves of steamboats into port cities some sixty years earlier. Trains terminated the landscape's geographical isolation from the rest of the state, causing an explosion in population, a revolution in economics, and a surge in the power and reach of the white ruling class. A lumberman and civil engineer, Captain William H. Hardy, initiated the transformation in 1882 when he took over the small settlement of Gordonville in the Central Piney Woods that he renamed Hattiesburg after his wife, Hattie, as a way station for the Gulf and Ship Island Railroad in Perry County. Within three years, workers constructed the first rail through Hattiesburg to New Orleans via Meridian, and over the next few decades, they built rails to Jackson, Natchez, Gulfport, and Mobile, rendering Hattiesburg the railroad center, known as the Hub City. The portion of Perry County that would become Forrest County, a flat, somewhat fertile prairie surrounded and penetrated by rivers and creeks, flourished as part of the thriving commercial nucleus of south Mississippi. Its northern neighbor, Jones County, a terrain of rolling and rough uplands surrounded by streams and waterways that slope softly down to the bottom lands, burgeoned into a booming industrial center. Rail lines from Hattiesburg ran through Jones County's two seats, Laurel and Ellisville. The state of nature existence receded quickly as moguls seized virgin terrain; lumberjacks cleared forests at record rates; barons turned Laurel and Hattiesburg into the world's lumber capitals; laborers transformed raw materials into products and shipped them on trains to the market; speculators sold property to the constant flood of migrants; merchants opened storefronts in towns carved out of the woodlands; and white supremacists, with an evangelical zeal, purged the landscape of racial heretics.[7]

Wealthy white families like the Chisolms, the Rogers, the Gardiners, and the Tatums dominated the budding towns just beyond the mills, gins, and manufacturing plants. The Jones County courthouse in Laurel, a Grecian-Romanesque structure made of clay colored bricks, stood like a sentry at the center of town, lording over the storefronts surrounding it. But the true center of power lay with Laurel's moguls, who built their mansions upward from the courthouse on the sloping hills of Fifth and Sixth Avenues, where lines of oak trees formed awnings over the streets. Hattiesburg tycoons sculpted their charming and vivacious downtown on the lowest terrace ridge of the Leaf River. Entrepreneurs and professionals rushed to open their offices, boutiques, haberdasheries, cafes, and hotels in red brick buildings that blended diverse architectural styles, including Colonial Revival, Italian Renaissance, and Victorian, into a classical New South town. Trolleys transported citizens from nearby residential areas to downtown Laurel and Hattiesburg. Many blacks also prospered in these boom towns. Black entrepreneurs, dentists, and pharmacists capitalized on the needs and desires of the rising black population to develop successful businesses and services, but they lived under the constrictions of a white supremacist state.[8]

Mississippi leaders built the political and legal foundations of their racial order in the state constitution of 1890 and through state legislation. They disfranchised blacks with a poll tax and registration exams, which white clerks administered in a discriminatory manner, and passed laws that forbade miscegenation and that segregated schools and public transportation. The US Supreme Court abetted their efforts with a series of rulings that so weakened the coverage of the Fourteenth Amendment's privilege and immunities and equal protection clauses that it divested blacks of federal protection. *Plessy v. Ferguson* (1896) delivered the final blow, with the court ruling segregation constitutional as long as it provided equal benefits. But separate would never be equal. Patriarchs bolstered their rule with a white supremacist theodicy: a combination of scientific racism, which argued that natural selection chose white men to subjugate all others, and the "segregationist theology," which portrayed the serpent in Genesis as a black man, miscegenation as "the original sin," and segregation as the only means to prevent the "integrated apocalypse." Fictional works like Thomas F. Dixon's *The Clansman* (1905) and D. W. Griffith's film adaptation, *Birth of a Nation* (1915), popularized white patriarchy by portraying Reconstruction falsely as an era of black rule and federal tyranny in which black Jezebels lured all men to their beds and black beastly men raped white women. White females, ascribed the roles of maidens or Madonnas, renewed the cause of southern sovereignty through a virtuous devotion to white men; Klansmen, depicted as knights of southern honor, defended white female purity by restoring white rule.[9]

The confluences of these laws and myths formed a white supremacist orthodoxy that assumed the force of a religious doctrine and stirred an evangelical articulation and zealous fervor in its believers. Elites venerated the restoration of white southern rule by calling it Redemption and its architects Redeemers. Klansmen emerged in southern lore as glorious knights, crusaders, who saved the South. When the city fathers of Hattiesburg seceded from Perry County in 1908, they named their new county Forrest after Confederate general Nathan Bedford Forrest, the Klan's first grand wizard. To maintain the "closed society," as it was later dubbed, disciples proselytized the "faith" and inculcated its tenets in successive generations. Ubiquitous signs marked "white" and "colored" and daily rituals that subordinated blacks perpetuated the racial hierarchy. Blacks had to enter white homes through the back door, sit at the back of the bus, step off the sidewalk to let whites pass, request service in public places only after all whites had been served, and respond to white reprimands like docile children. Deviations from this deferential dance assumed the specter of heresy.[10]

Pierre L. van den Berghe terms these postbellum "regimes" "*Herrenvolk* democracies" and defines them as "democratic for the master race but tyrannical for the subordinate groups." The Redeemers had created a society based upon black subjugation in which laws and customs rendered blacks noncitizens without the right to vote, petition their leaders, or seek redress for racial injustices. Black status had been elevated only slightly, from slavery to outcast. As the ascribed subjugated race, blacks suffered the most, but whites only enjoyed their privileges as the designated master race if they conformed. After Redeemers linked Republicans with blacks, Yankees, carpetbaggers, and scalawags, the party virtually vanished from the South for nearly a century, and Mississippi Democrats drove nascent third parties like the Populists from the landscape. As the Democratic-ruled South became a one-party region, citizens lacked the liberty intrinsic in democracies to challenge the political order. Dissenters confronted personal and professional ruin and even violence. The new southern regimes were far from democratic. And so began the epoch of southern life known as the age of Jim Crow.[11]

Statutes, customs, and rituals established white supremacist rule, but violence and injustice enforced it. Terrorization of black bodies and psyches most readily evinced itself in lynchings, rapes, police beatings, false prosecutions, and executions. Mississippi had the worst lynching record in America: the "most total lynchings, the most multiple lynchings, the most per capita, the most female victims, the most victims taken from police custody, the most lynchings without arrest or conviction of mob leaders, the most public support for lynchings." Between 1882 and 1946, Mississippians lynched over five hundred blacks. At the turn of the century, the Piney Woods attracted larger mobs than any other region. Laurel's newspaper described Hattiesburg as the town most famous for "nigger lynchings." Laurel also earned a reputation as a "town of lynchings and hangings." In 1885, a Jones County Klansman, William B. Martin, drunk and in search of amusement, hunted a black boy and hanged him for sport. He never expected anyone to punish him. To his indignation, that September a local jury found him guilty and sentenced him to death by hanging. Over a thousand enraged whites rushed to his defense; they signed a petition demanding Governor Lowry pardon him. Martin reminded Lowry of his service to the Democratic Party during Reconstruction when he and his Klan brethren lynched "niggers" and saved the South. So why would he execute him for hanging just one "nigger"? Lowry commuted Martin's sentence to life imprisonment because he feared setting a precedent in which Mississippi would hang a white man for killing a "nigger." Martin served less than five years of his life sentence. On April 1, 1890, Governor John M. Stone, the governor who called and presided over the Constitutional Convention of 1890 that disfranchised African Americans, pardoned Martin.[12]

Martin's case revealed the varied racial mentalities battling for control of the Central Piney Woods during Redemption. Local jurors had punished Martin, revealing a moderate if not a progressive racial mindset among some residents. Yet as Redeemers crushed the vestiges of Reconstruction and established a white supremacist state, lynchings and support of lynchers like Martin proved the norm. The Central Piney Woods became as violent as the South's most notorious landscapes, but the area developed with greater complexity. It emerged from Reconstruction fettered with dichotomies of Old South nostalgia and New South imagination, savage in its racist violence, but driven too by dreams of economic progress that begged for biracial harmony. Although conservatives and moderates advanced programs for black uplift that aided white-owned industries and supported the emergence of black businesses that buttressed segregation, they opposed challenges to the racial hierarchy. Whenever shifts on the regional, national, and global stage threatened white rule, conservatives initiated or supported violence to reinforce the white supremacist order. Sometimes the brutality garnered global attention and troubled the conscience of moderates. Still, since they were devoted to the racial order and thus reticent to criticize the means to enforce it and because the federal government refused to intervene to protect the constitutional rights of blacks, Mississippi sustained a nearly uncontested reign of white supremacist rule for decades. Moderates prevented several lynchings, but when mobs succeeded, authorities refused to punish them. Since blacks lacked suffrage, civil liberties, and judicial protections, they could not protest and survive. In August 1903, when Hattiesburg blacks gathered to protest a lynching in which a white mob murdered a black man by dragging him through the streets and hanging him from a pole, that same mob forced them to disperse.[13]

Nothing inspired more lynchings in the Central Piney Woods than actual or imagined black male violations of the sexual color line because such relations threatened the white supremacist patriarchy. Whites often accused black men of "assault" or "attempted rape" when they violated gender/racial mores, which prohibited them from meeting a white woman's eyes or making gestures or expressions suggesting flirtation. Forrest County whites lynched George Stevenson in 1890 after accusing him of attempted rape, Henry Novels in 1899 for assault (a common denotation for rape or violation of racial/gender mores), and William Oatis in 1899 for an "indecent proposal to a girl." In 1895, whites lynched Samuel Wilson in Jones County and Tom Johnson in Forrest County on charges of rape and murder. During Johnson's ordeal, the mob selected a committee to hold a makeshift trial led by the local judge. The committee lynched Johnson by firing squad before a thousand townspeople.[14]

To stave off threats to their lives, most blacks had to assume the roles, wear the masks, and memorize the script of black deference, moving in perfect step across the Jim Crow theater. Yet rather than becoming passive victims, many blacks subscribed to the accommodationist doctrine articulated by Booker T. Washington, the president of the Tuskegee Normal and Industrial Institute in Alabama. Washington urged blacks to use segregation to create a cohesive society that achieved black uplift and eventually liberty through the acquisition of education and practice of black capitalism. Blacks in the Central Piney Woods had ample opportunity to practice Washington's principles.

The dearth of laborers forced lumber and railroad barons and moguls of new industries, including sawmills, turpentine stills, bottling plants, fertilizer factories, and cotton mills, to recruit blacks across the South with better wages and conditions. The lumber industry in the Central Piney Woods, like its counterparts in North Carolina, Alabama, and Louisiana as revealed in William P. Jones's *The Tribe of Black Ulysses* (2005), offered greater opportunities for blacks than agricultural work. Black lumber workers in the Central Piney Woods dominated the timber industry workforce and made five times that of the Delta sharecropper. Many moguls like W. F. S. Tatum in Hattiesburg and Eastman Gardiner in Laurel built company towns that provided their workers with homes, schools, and commissaries. Jim Crow imperatives insured that black workers made five to ten cents less a day than their white counterparts, reserved supervisory positions for whites, and maintained separate "colored" and "white" quarters with whites granted superior facilities. Still, opportunities abounded for blacks in these new industries, and companies often sold land to their employees, who developed small farms.[15]

Two mixed-race clans constructed some of the most prosperous farming communities in the Central Piney Woods. In Forrest County's Kelly Settlement, mixed-race descendants of John and Green Kelly and Sarah continued to expand their farms. The area became a refuge for people of various skin hues. Henrietta, a white baby born out of wedlock, was given to the McCombs, a black family in the Kelly Settlement. Henrietta married Warren Kelly, Sarah's mixed-race son by John. They had eleven children, including Ellen, who married George Dahmer. George was white. George's mother, Laura, had become pregnant out of wedlock at age fourteen by a traveling German salesman, Peter Dahmer. Laura's humiliated parents sent her to a black family in Covington County. Laura married a former slave, Charlie Craft. After Craft angered local whites, the Crafts fled to the Kelly Settlement where they raised George and their ten mixed-race children. After George and Ellen married, they established a 340-acre farm and reared twelve light-skinned children, including Vernon, born in 1908. In Jones County, several of Newton and Rachel's mixed-race children married into the Indian/black/white Musgrove family, and some of Newton's white children married Rachel's children born of previous relationships. As racial categorizations hardened, whites defined mixed-race persons and whites who married persons with black heritages as black. Most residents of the Kelly Settlement identified themselves as black, whereas Knight's descendants, known as White Negroes, isolated themselves from the binary black and white worlds surrounding them. The refuges in the Kelly Settlement and the Knight enclave were still circumscribed by the white supremacist world; however, their ownership of lands allowed them to prosper.[16]

Even many blacks working as servants had better opportunities than their counterparts across Mississippi because the shortage of blacks willing to serve forced whites to offer better pay and conditions. Laurel patriarchs built a black neighborhood on Fourth Avenue for their employees so that they could walk to the mansions of their bosses on Fifth and Sixth Avenues. Many of these moguls of the New South, like the plantation owners of the

Old South, assumed paternal and maternal roles in which they perceived themselves as benefactors to the servants they adored but considered inferior. They aided their workers when they needed loans, health services, or jobs for their children; they vouched for their character and helped them avoid problems with other whites; their children played with their servants' children until they reached puberty, when fears of miscegenation led white parents to enforce the color line.[17]

Ironically, because the color line prevented blacks from acquiring many of their needs and desires in white businesses, black professionals and entrepreneurs thrived. The most vibrant section of black Hattiesburg, the Mobile-Bouie community, emerged between 1895 and 1910. Nestled in the northeast corner of the city between the Bouie River, the manufacturing and commercial area, and the railroad depot, it became the heart of black life. Beauty salons, barber shops, cafes, motels, pharmacies, funeral homes, and juke joints lined its main artery, Mobile Street, from the river to the depot, and homes sprung up all around it. Microcosms of Mobile-Bouie like Palmers Crossing popped up across Forrest County. In Jones County, on the black side of the railroad tracks, Front Street became the hub of black Laurel and its professionals and entrepreneurs emerged as the Front Street Establishment. Persistent black migration led to the proliferation of communities, including the KC Bottom, Kingston, Queensburg, Southside, Harvest Quarters, and Warren Quarters. Some black migrants used their earnings as laborers to open businesses. Others, like Benjamin Murph, a dentist who became a significant civil rights leader, arrived in town with an education and grand expectations.[18]

To perpetuate black prosperity, the black bourgeois developed an educational system for black residents. Segregation offered opportunities for black educators because its separate school systems opened jobs for black administrators and teachers. In Hattiesburg and Laurel, blacks used accommodation tactics to convince whites that education would deter black crime and inculcate a work ethic in black children. Through black fundraising and white paternalism, black schools proliferated and included two high schools—Oak Park in Laurel and Rowan in Hattiesburg. On the Knight lands, Anna, a descendant of Newton and Rachel, donated a portion of her land for a school. Residents helped her harvest her cotton crop to build a schoolhouse. In the Kelly Settlement, Warren Kelly donated two acres of his land upon which the community built a schoolhouse. With the support of white and black benefactors and fund-raising, blacks also built churches and hired preachers. Although the black bourgeoisie achieved financial success, they could not escape the larger Jim Crow landscape that circumscribed their lives. Farmers had to rely on white-owned industries and brokerages to refine and purchase their crops at fair prices. Farmers, professionals, and entrepreneurs depended on a myriad of white-owned companies to sell them equipment and supplies and on white-owned banks for loans. Teachers fell under the direct auspices of whites because whites controlled the school districts.[19]

Moreover, black success often enraged whites and triggered violence. Between 1890 and 1907, middling and poor white farmers suffered from surplus production that caused a decrease in price and thus profit, preventing many of them from paying back their loans. Bankers and merchants foreclosed on their lands and hired black farm hands or tenants to work on their new acquisitions. Some angry whites, particularly dispossessed farmers in the southeastern Piney Woods counties, formed whitecap organizations. Certain that a dearth of black labor would circumvent future foreclosures, whitecappers drove black laborers off the lands by beating thousands of black people, shooting into black homes, and killing at least twelve blacks. As they also considered blacks with economic independence and education a threat, they set fire to black-owned farms, destroyed black-owned livestock, and burned down black schools. In 1902 someone, likely whitecappers, burned down Anna Knight's school in Jones County. During the economic recession in 1907, whitecappers pressured the three major lumber companies in Hattiesburg to stop employing blacks, but only one company complied with their demands. Many moguls fought back against whitecappers because they needed the black labor force. They threatened a mass exodus from Mississippi unless Governor James P. Vardman terminated whitecapping. Vardman, though a virulent racist, encouraged authorities to save Mississippi agriculture and industry. State and federal juries sent whitecappers to jail, though most of them later received pardons.[20]

The suppression of whitecapping and the growing economic power of the black bourgeois combined with national developments between 1907 and 1919, including the Great War, inspired black hope. In 1917, the federal government constructed Camp Shelby Military Base in Forrest County, which housed soldiers from all over the nation. Many blacks answered the call of W. E. B. DuBois of the National Association for the Advancement of Colored People (NAACP), who argued that if blacks fought to liberate Europe from oppression abroad, they would foster their liberation at home. Other blacks left the South to work in wartime industries in the North. The Great War and the Great Migration contributed to the rebuilding of a national and international stage upon which black activists struggled to illuminate the persistence of black oppression and revive the dialogue of liberation that had largely been silenced since the end of Reconstruction. Word of shifts toward racial progress in the North reached blacks in the Central Piney Woods through packinghouse agents who recruited workers for northern industries; from porters on the Chicago-bound trains; and from the *Chicago Defender*, the most popular black-owned newspaper in the black South. On Saturdays, black customers gathered at Robert Horton's Barbershop in Hattiesburg to purchase and discuss the *Defender*. Eventually, Horton led forty people to Chicago, where he opened the Hattiesburg Barber Shop at which he and other migrants launched campaigns to encourage their relatives and friends to join them. Blacks referred to the migration as the exodus; when 147 migrants from Hattiesburg crossed the Ohio River, they knelt in prayer and sang, "I done come out of the land of Egypt with good news." Perhaps most telling, one migrant wrote that that since his arrival in Chicago, "I just begin to feel like a man." Some 5,000 blacks from Laurel migrated. So many blacks migrated from the Hub City that whites accused the *Defender* of "ruining Hattiesburg." Desperate to stem the tide, white employers raised black wages.[21]

Yet the close of the war caused a regression in racial relations because whites feared that returning black soldiers would start a race war. Whites lynched so many blacks across America in the summer of 1919 that NAACP leader James Weldon Johnson referred to it as Red Summer. Jones County whites initiated their bloody summer on June 16 after a white woman accused a black man, John Hartfield, of raping her. During the ten-day hunt for Hartfield, the posse beat numerous blacks accused of helping Hartfield escape, killed one black man for refusing to surrender a weapon, and shot another misidentified as Hartfield. James Street, a sixteen-year-old Jones County resident working as a correspondent for the *Times Picayunne* of New Orleans, covered the story. The hunt deeply disturbed him and would inspire him to become a great critic of racism in his future writing career. When the posse caught Hartfield, nearly ten thousand people gathered on picnic blankets to witness a mob sever Hartfield's fingers and toes for souvenirs, hang him from a sycamore tree, shoot him, and burn him to lumpy ashes. Days later, a mob lynched a black man for discussing the lynching. The NAACP demanded that Congress pass antilynching legislation proposed by Republican representative Leonidas Dyer, which would allow the federal government to prosecute lynchers and local officials who permitted lynchings. The House passed the bill, but a southern filibuster in the Senate killed it.[22]

The Central Piney Woods also experienced a revival of the Klan. Membership ran the gamut from powerbrokers to police officers to lumber camp workers. One lumber worker who joined the Klan, Hulon Myers, praised the hooded order as "the only thing that kept the raping down." In 1922, some five thousand Klansmen from across the state held a parade in Hattiesburg. Local Klansmen harassed progressive whites like the Reverend L. G. Gates because he publicly opposed lynchings. When Klansmen visited him at his church, they informed him that they supported "the protection of home and purity of womanhood." Another group of Klansmen stormed into a restaurant located on the white side of town that served a mostly black clientele. They warned the owner, M. Letow, to cease serving blacks or move his restaurant to the black quarters. A group of whites, possibly Klansmen, threatened to kill a black man, Mack Holiman, when in 1927 he complained to the national NAACP that the Jones County registrar refused to allow him to vote in the primary election. On the advice of the NAACP, he retained a local attorney. Soon Holiman received multiple threats. Although Holiman desired to persist with his case despite the dangers, the NAACP advised him to withdraw his complaint as the organization considered the environment too perilous to Holiman and decided that the case would prove futile. Holiman fled the state before whites could lynch him.[23]

Occasionally, moderate whites publicly opposed racial violence. In 1920, a white man, Sharpe Welborn, murdered Stewart Knight, one of Rachel's mixed-race sons, by hacking his body with an axe and shooting off part of his head. Authorities claimed that Welborn killed Knight while trying to rob him. However, gossip abounded that Welborn killed him because Knight violated racial mores by intervening in an incident on behalf of a white woman. An all-white jury convicted Welborn, but only of manslaughter. Several Hattiesburg whites tried to prevent the lynching of a well-liked black mechanic, Manual McCallum. In November 1928, McCallum offered to help whites involved in a car accident. One of the men pointed a pistol at him. McCallum grabbed the gun, hit the man on the head with it, and fled. Rumors spread that the men he had tried to assist planned to hang him. McCallum's boss, Charles Ross, secured a job for him in Alabama, and with the aid of Sheriff Joe Gray, Ross helped him flee town. In December, McCallum returned to Hattiesburg because he missed his family. Near midnight on December 26, seven white men dragged McCallum from his home in front of his wife. The next day, a constable found McCallum hanging from a tree and remarked, "He's a good Nigger now." Mrs. McCallum identified the lynchers, but lawmen claimed that they lacked evidence to arrest anyone.[24]

The lynching of McCallum proved a significant event in Mississippi because five hundred whites, including many prominent citizens, passed a resolution that called upon Circuit Court Judge Robert Hall to convene a grand jury, Sheriff Gray to arrest the lynchers, and Governor Theodore Bilbo and state law enforcement to provide resources to bring the murderers to justice. The Reverend Joseph Smith of Main Street Baptist Church delivered the most passionate appeal for justice: "I am painfully tired of these perfunctory verdicts of the coroner's juries stating that the deceased came to his death at the hands of parties unknown . . . there are people in this city who know who committed this dastardly crime. I want the cowardly cringing, white-livered yellow-blooded scoundrels arrested and convicted." The Chamber of Commerce raised a $20,000 reward with large donations from elites. It was the first time in Mississippi that so many white citizens condemned a lynching and demanded an investigation. On January 7, 1929, Judge Hall ordered a grand jury investigation but stressed that if jurors handed down indictments on weak testimony that led to acquittals, it would harm Mississippi. On January 10, jurors condemned the killing as a "stain upon the fair name of Forrest County" but claimed that they lacked the evidence to deliver indictments. Most whites considered the McCallum slaying "a bad lynching" because he had not committed a crime, but the Hartfield murder a "good lynching" because they believed him guilty. Yet even participants in "bad lynchings" rarely had to fear punishment because an indictment proved rare, a conviction practically impossible, and an appropriate sentence never.[25]

The greatest shifts in the racial struggle occurred in northern urban centers, where growing white progressivism, black suffrage, a dual party system, and racial, ethnic, economic, ideological, and cultural diversity fostered protest. The Harlem Renaissance and the rise of Marcus Garvey's Universal Negro Improvement Association (UNIA) galvanized blacks and enlightened some whites about black grievances. Growing numbers of academicians debunked "scientific" racism. Black organizations railed against Italy's genocidal conquest of Ethiopia and compared colonialism and fascism to Jim Crow. President Franklin Delano Roosevelt, however reluctantly, began to open political arenas to racial issues because of pressure from progressives, including First Lady Eleanor Roosevelt and New Dealer Harold Ickes, and from the new alliance leaders of civil rights, labor, socialist, and communist organizations. In the famous interracial rape trials of the Scottsboro Boys in Alabama and the lesser-known interracial murder trials of Arthur Ellington, Ed Brown, and Henry Shields in Mississippi, the US Supreme Court ruled that states must recognize the constitutional rights of defendants to adequate counsel and a jury of their peers and deemed coerced confessions inadmissible. The NAACP capitalized on the nascent shifts to convince the justices to order the University of Missouri to admit a black man to its all-white law school.

However, southern judiciaries tended to evade Supreme Court precedents. Dissent trickled into the South but remained more vibrant outside of Dixie. Scattered chapters of the UNIA formed across Mississippi, but none of them launched significant protests, and not a single chapter was opened in the Central Piney Woods. The NAACP opened its first Mississippi branch in 1918 and several others over the next few years, but they collapsed quickly. No branch opened in the Central Piney Woods. The National Negro Congress and the Southern Negro Youth Congress made inroads into the South, but not in Mississippi. Blacks were more successful when they formed self-help groups like the Mississippi Federation of Colored Women's Clubs and the Committee of One Hundred, which presented black grievances to white leaders and negotiated programs to advance black uplift. Blacks in the Central Piney Woods achieved some economic gains via employment with the New Deal's the Works Progress Administration (WPA) located at Camp Shelby and with the Civilian Conservation Corps (CCC), building roads and prefabricated houses with the Green Lumber Company in Laurel; however, management chose white workers first and gave the leftover jobs to blacks. The NAACP's efforts to force the federal government to investigate discrimination on the Mississippi Flood Control Project, which President Herbert Hoover developed after the disastrous 1927 flood, forced an inclusion of black levee workers in its new federal standards that guaranteed a minimum wage and set maximum work hours. Yet as state and local politicians administered all New Deal programs, racial discrimination persisted.[26]

Most blacks suffered from the Depression more than their white counterparts, particularly after many whites accepted the lower-paying jobs historically reserved for blacks. A common saying at the time, "why should niggers eat while whites starve?," reflected the negative racial tenor. Blacks who managed to keep their jobs also faced hardships. Joe Griffin, a black laborer at the Hercules Plant, was only permitted to work two weeks a month. He and his wife had a shotgun house provided to them by the plant, but they had twelve children. Only eight of them survived to adulthood.[27]

However, some blacks in the Central Piney Woods managed not only to survive the Depression, but spent the later 1930s laying the foundations for their subsequent prosperity. Although his light skin would have allowed him to pass for white in the North like his siblings, Vernon Dahmer loved his community and determined to prosper in Mississippi. At the age of twenty-one in 1928, Dahmer married eighteen-year-old Warnie Laura Mott.

When they divorced in 1938, Dahmer retained custody of their sons, Vernon Jr., Martinez, and Caroll. Later he married Ora Lee Smith, with whom he had three sons, George, Alvin, and Harold. Over the next two decades, Dahmer bought a tractor, expanded his farm, and opened several prosperous businesses, including an ice house, a gas station, grist and lumber mills, and a grocery stocked with vegetables and fruits grown on his land and meat from his farm-raised hogs and cows.[28]

The pervasiveness of white violence during the Depression reminded the Dahmers that their refuge was fragile. In the mid-1930s, mobs in Florida and Mississippi took their victims across state lines prior to lynching them, a violation of the Lindbergh Kidnapping Act. But US attorney general Homer Cummings refused to investigate. In Jones County in December 1936, "a football-crazed crowd," holding a "pre-Christmas celebration," tied a black teenager, J. B. Grant, to the back of a car and dragged him through the streets packed with cheering crowds. The car stopped intermittently "so that little children, using their parents' firearms, could pump lead into the inert form." The lynching received little press and no federal attention. Anti-lynching bills died in the Senate under southern-led filibusters. Despite the South's diminished political and economic isolation, the white supremacist state survived.[29]

Black children who grew up in the Central Piney Woods during these years experienced "baptisms" into Mississippi's harsh racial order. Daisy Griffin's initiation came at the hands of police. Born in 1931 as the fifth of twelve children, she considered her father, Joe, a Hercules Plant worker, indomitable until police barged into her home in the middle of the night, accused him of stealing a bicycle, and ordered him out of bed. Her father protested his innocence but, to Daisy's shock, he also obeyed officers "like a little child." When police received word that another officer had apprehended the suspect, one of the officers snapped, "Boy, you can go back to bed." As Daisy came of age, she often saw white officers beat black men in her neighborhood. Her brothers so feared becoming targets of the white system that they all left Mississippi as soon as they had the means.[30]

James Nix's parents tried simultaneously to teach him the disparate values of internal racial pride and external racial subservience. Nix recalled that while riding a bus with his father, he noticed a pretty white girl and remarked to his father, "Daddy, isn't that nice, pretty, long hair?" His father whipped him. Later, Nix understood that the script of white supremacy prohibited him from uttering such words, and he realized that his father had to punish him to protect him. In contrast, Maddie Jones Austin Scott so feared whites that she taught her children to become, not simply act, subservient to whites. Scott worked as a cook for Quitman Ross, a prominent attorney. He empathized with the plight of blacks, but Scott feared him. She was twelve-years-old when the mob lynched Hartfield, and she never recovered from those lynching years. Once she became a mother, she repeated the story of the lynching to her three daughters often. Scott's daughter Gladys accepted segregation and later recalled, "We understood that there were things for blacks and there were things for whites and it did not bother us because it was a way of life. . . . Well, we couldn't have gone to the places to eat because we didn't have any money to eat with."[31]

Like blacks of the Civil War and Reconstruction generations who had suffered when the black freedom struggle, betrayed by the North and obliterated by the South, had ended in tragedy, southern blacks of the Great War and Depression generations despaired when a global war to liberate the oppressed abroad and progressive legislation to uplift the impoverished at home failed to unshackle them from their Jim Crow chains. Yet the story had not concluded. As the tumult of World War II spread across the globe, recurring acts of racial brutality and swelling voices of black protest cast a light upon the shadows of American oppression. And from those shadows emerged beacons like Vernon Dahmer, and later Daisy Griffin Harris and James Nix, who became important forces in the black liberation movement birthed in the rages of this global war between tyranny and freedom.[32]

CHAPTER 1

— Monsters, Mockingbirds, and Morality Plays —

NEAR MIDNIGHT ON OCTOBER 16, 1942, ONE HUNDRED WHITE MEN CONverged on the Jones County jail in Laurel. They intended to lynch Howard Wash, a black man sentenced to life that afternoon for the murder of his white boss, Clint Welborn. The sentence failed to satisfy. Rumors that Wash might have killed Welborn in self-defense failed to deter them. Sheriff J. Press Reddoch, flanked by Deputies Louis Welch and Inmon O. Fowler, stood at the top of the stairs leading to the jailhouse and aimed his rifle at the mob. Undaunted, it swarmed around him. "We want that d[amn] nigger," one man yelled. The sheriff responded, "I'll die before I give him up." Someone retorted that his death could be arranged. Sheriff Reddoch implored the men to go home. If they murdered a man, they would regret that sin for the rest of their lives. They rushed the jailhouse.[1]

Inside the colored cellblock, inmates awoke to the sounds of boisterous voices and the footfall of men running up the stairs. Prisoners bolted upright in their beds when the jailer, Luther Holder, unlocked the door and flung it open. Holder warned, "None of you boys get up. Lay still. Get ready Wash. They have come after you." Inmate Lonnie McNair saw two men approach Wash's cage, a short stocky man and a tall man, both of whom had visited the cellblock earlier that day. Are you sorry for your crime? they asked. Yes, Wash responded, but he insisted that he "had to do it." The men yanked him out of his cell and beat him until Holder shouted, "Don't start that up here, wait till you get outdoors."[2]

Outside, Sheriff Reddoch ran toward the police station across the street and called Judge Burkitt Collins. The judge contacted Governor Paul B. Johnson Sr. and informed him that a mob had abducted Wash and that the sheriff had lost control of the situation. Johnson dispatched the National Guard. It was too late. A vehicle transporting Wash arrived on the Welborn property. Allen Welborn Pryor, "excited" about the prospect of murdering the black man who had killed his cousin, savored the moment as the men fastened the rope around Wash's neck, secured the other end to Welborn

Bridge, and shoved him over the edge. Several hours later, state troopers found Wash's lifeless body dangling above the creek.³

In 1942, had America not been embroiled in a war against despotism, the federal government would have ignored the murder of Wash as it had disregarded the lynchings of over five hundred blacks in Mississippi since 1882. As Neil McMillen argues in *Dark Journey* (1990), "Racial injustice would survive in Mississippi as long as the world's oldest republic would tolerate it." World War II instigated a shift in the Republic's level of tolerance, because a lynching amidst a crusade against fascism and Nazism exposed on a world stage America's racial autocracy. The publicity incurred international condemnation, forced federal intervention, and opened a small space for black dissent in the Central Piney Woods, all of which positioned the racial struggle on a circuitous, but transitional, path toward the civil rights revolution. White supremacists determined to abort the birth of a black liberation movement by severing the fragile cord of federal support. Over the next two decades, federal bodies intervened selectively and often reluctantly. Still, their actions furnished the basic conditions necessary for activists to build, mobilize, and launch a revolution.⁴

National civil rights activists initiated the federal shift. Over a year prior to Wash's lynching, union leader and black activist A. Philip Randolph threatened to bring one hundred thousand blacks to march on Washington, DC, in June 1941 unless President Roosevelt abolished segregation laws, terminated discrimination in federal and wartime industries, and insured black suffrage. Randolph accepted a compromise. He terminated the march when Roosevelt created the Fair Employment Practice Commission (FEPC), which outlawed racial discrimination in industries receiving federal defense contracts. Widespread noncompliance mitigated the impact of the FEPC, but it provided a foundation upon which to address racial discrimination. During the war, the newly formed interracial Congress of Racial Equality (CORE) used sit-ins and boycotts to challenge segregation in the North and the West, and the NAACP and southern progressives formed the National Committee to Abolish the Poll Tax.⁵

World War II provided these activists with a powerful context for drawing parallels between Hitler's Aryan dictatorship and the Jim Crow South. Both regimes were one-party white supremacist states that dehumanized the ascribed inferior others, rendered them noncitizens divested of suffrage, civil liberties, and judicial protections, and employed police state tactics to subjugate them. To insure perpetual white supremacist rule, southern authorities and Nazis prohibited marriage between the privileged and oppressed groups. Nazis perceived Jews as parasites who were of no value, but rather of great danger, to Aryans, and thus the Aryans ultimately sought to exterminate them. In contrast, as southern white supremacists perceived blacks as an economic value to exploit, they used violence as a form of racial control rather than as a method of genocide. Despite this significant difference, the war exposed the frightening likenesses between the two societies.[6]

Wash's life and death exemplified the brutalities of Jim Crow. He, his wife Louise, and their eight children resided in a two-room shack on the Welborn Dairy Farm. Wash worked as the Welborns' livestock overseer and Louise as their maid. According to some whites and many blacks, Clint Welborn had a reputation for cruelty. A relative described him as an "overbearing, harsh, task-master." On May 18, Welborn had intended to "run Howard off" his land because he considered him a drunk. After Welborn called for Wash to report to work repeatedly, Wash stumbled into the barn carrying several milk buckets. Members of the Wash and Welborn families overheard Welborn and Wash brawling. After the fracas, Wash fled. Welborn's wife and daughter found Welborn lying in a "pool of blood," making "feeble groans." Lacerations covered his face; blood gushed from his broken nose; and one of his fingers dangled from his hand, the knuckle sliced by Wash's teeth.

While Welborn lay unconscious in the hospital, Sheriff Reddoch led a posse and a pack of bloodhounds to hunt Wash. When Welborn died on May 20, Reddoch arrested seven black people for questioning. In late June, authorities found Wash seventy miles south of Laurel in Poplarville. During his subsequent interrogation, Wash admitted that he "had difficulty" with his boss but insisted that he had never intended to kill him. Wash's attorney, Luther Saul, requested that District Attorney Andrew Curie and County Attorney Paul Swartzfager accept a manslaughter plea because Wash had killed Welborn in self-defense. Prior to killing his boss, Wash had neither a criminal record nor a reputation for violence. Clint's brother, Hillyer, persuaded the state to reject the deal.[7]

On October 12, while the House of Representatives debated passing the anti–poll tax bill in Washington DC, three whites barged into the Jones County jail and demanded that Deputy Welch deliver Wash to them. When Welch refused, the men left. That evening a white mob in Shubuta—forty-two miles east of Laurel—lynched two black fourteen-year-olds, Charlie Lang and Ernest Green, who had been charged, on dubious evidence, with raping a thirteen-year-old white girl. The following day, the US House passed the anti-poll tax bill. Senator Bilbo pledged that he would insure its death in the Senate and conducted a thirty-day filibuster. Senator Rankin railed that northern congressmen were "waging war against the white people of the Southern States." The black press accused the South of starting the war. The *New Amsterdam News* noted that "on the eve of the congressional action on the Anti-Poll Tax bill to 'enfranchise' some 4,000,000 Negroes in eight Southern States, the South opened the first gun of its reprisal by lynching two 14-year-old boys." Southern power brokers in the Senate eventually defeated the bill; however, the intense racial milieu invigorated activists. The NAACP and the Congress of Industrial Organizations (CIO) demanded a federal investigation of the lynchings.[8]

Several days later, Swartzfager and Curie prosecuted Wash on first-degree murder charges. Welborn's daughter was their strongest witness. She testified that she was near the barn when she heard her father firing Wash and then three thudding sounds. Wash testified that when he entered the barn, Welborn cursed him for his tardiness and tried to hit him with a shovel. To protect himself, Wash threw up his milk buckets and theorized that he might have hit Welborn once—an assertion belied by Welborn's multiple wounds. The all-white-male jury convicted Wash of murder, but several jurors refused to vote in favor of execution. Mississippi law stipulated that juror disagreement in capital cases resulted in the lesser punishment—life, which Judge Collins ordered. The sentence enraged the Welborns. They wanted Wash dead. The Welborns and their kin network had a reputation as a "hot-headed" clan with a "vindictive nature." Seven hours after the sentencing, a mob lynched Wash.[9]

At first, it appeared that Mississippi might punish the lynchers. Governor Johnson dispatched state troopers, the National Guard, and Special Investigator John Byrd to Laurel and ordered Judge Collins to convene the grand jury. Sheriff Reddoch identified and arrested three members of the mob: Barney Jones, Nathaniel T. Shotts, and William Johnson. After the arrests, Byrd noticed that Reddoch received several phone calls. When Reddoch agreed to meet with a caller at the Pinehurst Hotel, Byrd followed him and observed him in a heated conversation with powerful businessmen. After the meeting Reddoch, an elected official, stopped arresting suspects and only charged the three men in custody with intimidating an officer. On October 19, the grand jury neglected to mention the lynching.[10]

These Mississippi killings, in conjunction with two other wartime lynchings, the murder of Cleo Wright in Sikeston, Missouri, and Willie Vinson in Texarkana, Texas, gave fodder to the Axis powers, the black press, and activists, particularly as America portrayed the war in Manichean terms in which the forces of goodness—constitutional democracies—would destroy the forces of evil, the Axis dictatorships. President Roosevelt had asserted that "freedom means the supremacy of human rights everywhere" and that America's sons and daughters of all races were fighting "to uphold the doctrine that all men are equal in the sight of God." The Axis's extermination of those whom they considered lesser beings gave Roosevelt the authority to criticize. Yet America responded to the attack on Pearl Harbor on December 7, 1941, by interring Japanese-Americans; fighting the war with a segregated military; and permitting discrimination, injustice, and lynchings to persist at home. Diplomats warned the Roosevelt administration that the Japanese minister in Berlin possessed "evidence concerning the ill-treatment of negroes" and that the foreign office planned to use them as propaganda.[11]

At home and abroad, lynchings undermined America's assertions of moral superiority in its fight against fascism and Nazism. In January 1942, the *Chicago Defender* responded to the Sikeston lynching with the slogan "Remember Pearl Harbor and Sikeston Too: The Fight to Save Democracy" and implored Americans to disprove theories spread in Germany and Japan that "discrimination, segregation and lynching" were "incurable weaknesses of democracy." The *Pittsburgh Courier* launched the "Double V war cry," which summoned blacks to seek "victory over our enemies at home and victory over our enemies on the battlefield." Both newspapers also covered Wash's murder. These editorials gave a global voice to black suffering and underscored the duplicity of American democracy.[12]

Across the South, whites responded with their own double v campaign. They hijacked the language of liberty to portray the South as a victim of federal tyranny, communist plots, and black savagery. They warned that using black soldiers in combat and abolishing the poll tax would lead to interracial rapes, black lawlessness, and race wars. Congressman William Colmer, whose district included the Central Piney Woods, insisted that the Communist Party inspired the anti–poll tax bill to divide America in a time of war and recruit blacks. The NAACP –and the CIO, he claimed, had more "communists than all other groups in the country." Although red-baiting had impugned black movements before the war and would gain power after the war, the moral imperative underpinning the Good War overshadowed such fear mongering. The wartime lynchings further crystalized that imperative.[13]

Groups as different from each other as the Workers Defense League in New York and the Young Women's Christian Association in Ohio castigated the hypocrisy of fighting against tyranny abroad while practicing despotism at home. On October 25, 1942, two thousand blacks and trade unionists attended a mass meeting in Harlem at which the executive secretary for the

Negro Labor Victory Committee implored Roosevelt to condemn lynching as "treason to the nation." Randolph, who had organized the March on Washington Movement, led a protest at New York's City Hall. Joseph Gavagan, US representative from New York, circulated a petition to move the proposed antilynching bill onto the floor. In Mississippi, fifty-nine whites and twelve blacks signed an open letter to Governor Johnson published in the state's most prominent newspaper, the *Clarion-Ledger*, in which they lauded the governor for calling Wash's lynching a "murder" because it conveyed to the perpetrators that their actions violated a person's right to due process and equal protection of the law, assured Mississippians that the South would never become a "bridgehead of fascism in America," strengthened the morale of the allies of "colored races," and damaged the efforts of the Axis powers to use such crimes as propaganda. The *Laurel Leader-Call* insisted that the majority of Jones County residents despised the fact that one hundred men chose to defy the law that so many soldiers died overseas to protect.[14]

Although the lynchings humiliated the federal government, the FBI neglected to fully investigate the Shubuta murders. The infuriated mob had castrated the teenagers, ripped at their flesh with pliers, and rammed a screwdriver into the throat of one of the boys before hanging them. An NAACP investigation suggested that the white girl had been friends with Lang and Green and that persons close to her had lied about the attempted rape to protect her reputation after a white person caught them playing together. The NAACP forwarded Jones's report to the FBI, but it received little attention, likely because the killing involved an alleged rape of a white female by black males, an accusation which, regardless of its accuracy, enraged white America.[15]

Still, desperate to deprive foreign enemies, civil rights groups, and the press of evidence that America tolerated injustice, federal officials responded quickly to Wash's lynching. On October 19, Attorney General Francis Biddle ordered FBI Director J. Edgar Hoover to initiate an investigation. On October 21, Hoover dispatched a team to Laurel, marking the first time that the federal government had intervened in a lynching case in Mississippi since Reconstruction and the fifth time since the turn of the century that federal bodies had interceded in the South. In Alabama in 1904, a federal grand jury indicted several lynchers, but the case was ultimately dismissed. Five years later, in *US v. Shipp*, the Supreme Court cited a Tennessee sheriff, deputies, and citizens for contempt after lawmen permitted a mob to lynch a black inmate whose conviction for rape was under review. During the same year as the Wash case, the FBI investigated the Sikeston and

Texarkana lynchings, but the grand jury refused to indict the accused in Sikeston, and the Department of Justice never sought indictments in Texarkana. The Wash investigation was historic because it occurred in Mississippi, which the NAACP described as the nation's most "hopeless state" and the *Chicago Defender* as "the most brutal community in history." The FBI had entered America's heartland of racial injustice.[16]

As agents spread out across Jones County searching for the killers, they confronted a hostile public. The *Laurel Leader-Call*, which had initially condemned the lynchings, argued that northerners should focus on problems in their own states and emphasized that their interference generated hostility toward the Wash case. Still, agents found a few whites and several blacks willing to speak to them privately. Inmate Lonnie McNair informed agents that Wash never intended to kill his boss; he struck him with the milk bucket because Welborn tried to beat him with a shovel. After Wash received a life sentence, McNair witnessed several white men visiting the cellblock to locate Wash's cell. That evening, he and the other prisoners watched Wash visit with Louise and two of their eight children, two-year-old little Louise and six-month-old Annie Slee. Louise asked her husband if he had been praying; he assured her that he had. He asked her to raise their eight children "the best she could" and said softly "a man wasn't born to live forever." He kissed his baby and bid his family goodbye. Louise fled the jailhouse in tears. Hours after the lynching, Holder returned to the cellblock and told the prisoners, "That was too bad about Wash but I couldn't help it because they had a gun in my ribs." McNair informed agents, "I wish to state that I didn't see the two fellows holding any gun in Mr. Holder's ribs the morning when they took Wash. I didn't see any gun displayed at all." Agents also interviewed the Welborn clan. A person close to the Welborn family, identified as informant T-1, insisted that Welborn's brother, Hillyer, and his widow planned the lynching. On November 25, Allen Welborn Pryor, Clint Welborn's cousin, confessed.[17]

While the FBI built its case, the revival of Forrest County's Camp Shelby army base inspired black dissent. The reconstruction and operation of the base necessitated the hiring of thousands of employees and offered black workers in the Central Piney Woods unprecedented economic opportunities. Soldiers from across the nation flooded in and out of Camp Shelby, which accommodated 55,000 troops and became the second largest army base and the second largest Mississippi city. When Japanese American troops arrived in Hattiesburg, city officials classified them as whites and allowed them freedom of movement in most public spaces. However, they built them a separate USO and a separate school for their children.

Considering the palpable racism toward Japanese Americans after Pearl Harbor, white Hattiesburg's decision to accept them, at least to a degree, in the white world, while still rejecting blacks, revealed the depth of white racism toward blacks. Some Japanese Americans came to the defense of black servicemen. One soldier beat a bus driver who had kicked a black passenger. Many black soldiers objected to the litany of indignities that they confronted. They had to wait hours for buses to transport them to town, doctors treated them like "dogs," and white officers beat and degraded them and sent them to the stockades arbitrarily. The army segregated military police into separate units, and though it armed whites with .45 caliber pistols, it armed blacks only with nightsticks. After black soldiers and black locals protested the disparate treatment, the army gave black MPs pistols and integrated MP vehicles. The presence of black MPs had a profound impact, for local blacks began to imagine a world in which they obtained powerful positions.[18]

These wartime struggles planted the roots that led to Forrest County's becoming a significant beachhead of the Civil Rights Movement decades later. Many locals gained valuable leadership experience by volunteering for the Red Cross, holding war bond drives, and convincing the white establishment to allocate $42,000 to construct a USO building for black servicemen in Hattiesburg, which housed a library and counseling services and hosted dances. Although the structure paled in comparison to the nearly $116,000 spent on the redbrick USO building for whites located on Front Street, few southern cities built USO structures for blacks. The war also helped factory workers as it encouraged labor union leaders to move into Mississippi. However, the movement failed to gain much momentum until after the war. In 1941, union leaders began infiltrating the Hercules Plant in Hattiesburg, one of the largest employers in the Central Piney Woods. Over the next several years, they tried to open more job opportunities to blacks by terminating the unwritten discriminatory policy of white-only jobs. Although they catered to the Jim Crow system by holding segregated meetings of union members, after the meetings, black and white representatives met together with the company liaisons. Some black union members like Richard Boyd helped form the Negro Civic Welfare Association (NCWA) to protest efforts by the all-white Hattiesburg Chamber of Commerce and the all-white real estate board to transform the Robertson Place federal colored housing project into a white project. After the NCWA contacted the War Department repeatedly to complain, the federal government insured that the project remained a black housing facility. The NCWA worked quietly to improve sanitation, police protection, and school crossings in black areas.

However, when blacks challenged Jim Crow, they confronted intense resistance. Because of the massive population influx during the war, congestion on busses forced whites to move toward the back near black riders. When whites complained, drivers ordered blacks to stand in the back. After Chief of Police M. M. Little announced that drivers could remove violators from their busses, a driver killed a black passenger who disobeyed the rules. Police determined the homicide justifiable. These injustices convinced many blacks that suffrage, which would give blacks power to elect officials and serve on juries, was the key to liberty. Vernon Dahmer took his eldest son and namesake to the registrar's office. When they arrived, the registrar, Luther Cox snapped, "What do you want?" Dahmer informed him of his desire to register. Cox handed Dahmer a card containing a section of the Mississippi Constitution. He returned to his desk and ignored him. Finally, Dahmer said, "Sir . . . I'm finished now." Cox returned to the counter. Dahmer explained correctly the meaning of the section. Cox shook his head, "Nah." However, after Dahmer and dozens of black residents like Richard Boyd visited Cox repeatedly, Cox registered Dahmer and fourteen other blacks to deter federal intervention while also sustaining nearly wholesale black disfranchisement. Federal authorities ignored Cox's violation of federal laws, but they moved against Wash's lynchers.[19]

On January 13, 1943, a federal grand jury indicted Barney Jones, Nathaniel T. Shotts, Welborn Pryor, and William Johnson for violating Sections 88, 550, 51, and 52, Title 18 of the US Code by conspiring to induce state officers to deprive Wash of his rights to "due process of law, to deny him equal protection under the law, and to inflict upon him unusual and different punishment because of his race." By murdering Wash, they also deprived him of his rights to appeal. The counts carried a maximum penalty of a $5,000 fine and a ten-year jail sentence. Jurors charged Luther Holder with violating Sections 51 and 52 because while "acting under the color of law," with the aid of the others, he deprived Wash of his constitutional rights to equal protection under the law. The maximum penalty was a $1,000 fine and a one-year prison term.[20]

Most Mississippi whites supported the lynchers. They raised funds to help the defense pay costs of housing witnesses. Politicians, community leaders, and newspapers portrayed the lynchers as victims of an abusive federal government and labeled the investigation an "invasion." At the US Capitol, Mississippi congressman John Rankin compared the Department of Justice to the Nazi Gestapo and condemned authorities for yanking the accused men out of their homes and charging them in federal court for a state infraction. In contrast, the *Pittsburgh Courier* mocked white

Mississippians for their astonishment that "the alleged lynchers were actually brought to trial just as if Mississippi were a free and democratic country where the life, liberty and happiness of all were guaranteed."[21]

In April, the Department of Justice attorneys Frank Coleman and Toxey Hall and Mississippi attorneys Will Watkins, Stewart Broom, and John Savage dropped charges against Shotts and Johnson, claiming a lack of evidence; however, they presented a powerful case against Holder, Pryor, and Jones in the federal courthouse in Hattiesburg. National and local press along with residents flocked to the trial. So many blacks arrived that they had to stand against the back wall. Sheriff Reddoch identified Pryor and Jones as members of the mob and implicated Holder by insisting that the men could not have breached the jail's solid steel door without keys. Holder claimed that the mob had forced him at gunpoint to unlock the door, yet he failed to identify a single member of the unmasked lynching party. Although several black inmates could identify the defendants and declare that Holder led them into the jail, they feared repercussions. The one inmate who testified claimed that the darkness prevented him from identifying the lynchers. When Pryor took the stand, he accused agents of coercing a false confession from him, a charge that resonated with white Mississippians. Their common belief of the dangers of federal despotism instilled in them a distrust of the FBI and all things federal.[22]

The defense team, which included Earle Wingo, Ed Franklin, Andrew Scott, and Ellis Cooper, capitalized on that distrust in closing arguments. Wingo contended that if the jurors set a precedent by allowing the federal government to impinge upon Mississippi's sovereignty, federal officials would use other cases to transfer absolute power over the states to Washington, DC. He also expressed concern about the impact of this trial in Mississippi, a state in which blacks might soon become the majority race. Franklin employed red-baiting tactics, cautioning that a conviction in the case would prove a legal victory for the Communist Party because legal equality, a core principle of communists, would force social and political equality among the races. Scott proclaimed, "We intend to have in the South white supremacy until Gabriel blows his horn." Finally, Cooper and Wingo invoked the white South's historical memory of Reconstruction. Yankees, they reminded the jurors, had forced southerners to adopt the Fourteenth Amendment, which the federal government was trying to use in this case.[23]

In contrast, the prosecutors declared that the lynching of Wash threatened American democracy, and they invoked the contemporary war—the fight against fascism and Nazism—to appeal to the jury. Hall likened the lynching to "Hitlerism." Broom argued that the Axis powers could use it as propaganda against the Allies. Watkins asserted that America would appear hypocritical if it fought to end oppression abroad while it allowed lynchings at home. Hall, trying to deflate the defense's claims of a Yankee invasion, emphasized that Wash was tried in a state court in which local "white men ruled the proceedings, a white judge presided, a white jury tried the Negro and a white Sheriff had him in his charge." Local white jurors, he declared, had sent Wash to prison for life. Lynchers murdered him. The Department of Justice was trying to protect, rather than to usurp, Mississippi's legal process. To win the case, the racist mores that influenced Mississippi jurors compelled the prosecutors to distance themselves from racially progressive sentiments and agree with the defense that "Negro[es]" should forever remain inferior to whites. This concession reinforced the defense's sentiment that blacks occupied "an unequal and therefore unconstitutional place in Southern life" and thus nullified their Fourteenth Amendment argument that blacks had the right to equal protection under the law.[24]

During juror deliberations, one man on the all-white male jury voted to convict the defendants. In the morning, the jurors voted unanimously for acquittal. Surely, the dissenter faced intense pressure to change his vote. The first federal lynching trial in Mississippi since Reconstruction and in the South since the early 1900s ended with a victory for white supremacy. The *Chicago Defender* labeled the verdict "farcical," noting that the jurors winked at the defense attorneys. Some sixty years later, Welborn's son, Clint Jr., noted that whites "wasn't against lynching back in those days." They perceived lynchings as a means of racial control. After the acquittal, the federal government dropped or dismissed cases against law enforcement officers for assaulting and murdering black soldiers in Texas, Arkansas, and Louisiana. Although federal courts convicted a smattering of accused lynchers in Georgia and Illinois, the murderers received an acquittal via an appeal in the former case and received only a fine in the latter. At the least, however, the Supreme Court upheld a federal civil rights conviction of a town marshal in Florida for killing a black prisoner by forcing him to leap off of a bridge. The federal government had retreated, but not abandoned, southern blacks as it had after Reconstruction. Its involvement in the Wash case set a precedent for intervention, for at least federal attorneys had obtained indictments of lynchers. Moreover, global and national shifts would not allow federal officials to ignore racial atrocities, though they would often avoid intervening. Still, that threat of intervention remained, and that very prospect affected the South.[25]

In Mississippi, fear of federal intervention curbed mob lynchings, but it failed to restrain racial violence. As black soldiers returned after the war, they confronted a society determined to remind them that they belonged to a black disfranchised caste in a white supremacist system. Theodore Bilbo, who had become a US senator after his gubernatorial career, encouraged whites to use violence to keep blacks from the voting booth in the upcoming election. In the perilous environment, many black soldiers hid their service from whites. While Henry Murphy's father drove him back to Hattiesburg from Camp Shelby, Murphy changed from his uniform into "overalls and a jumper, the uniform of a field hand." One black soldier from Hattiesburg remarked, "We were fighting for what we didn't have." Still, that fight concerned many whites because it had moved the black vanguard toward dissent and it had invited federal intervention. To refrain from inciting federal attention again, mob lynchings declined as clandestine murders replaced the spectacle. In the Central Piney Woods, conservative whites used their unjust legal system to eliminate apostates of the racial order.[26] That shift began a few months after the end of World War II, when a rape case ignited racial rage across Laurel.

On November 2, the *Laurel Leader-Call* reported that a "Negro" had raped a young white mother on South Magnolia Street. Officers lacked a description of the alleged rapist other than he had "kinky" hair because Willette Hawkins, the alleged victim, claimed that it was too dark to see her assailant's face. Yet Chief C. W. Valentine ordered several arrests, including that of a twenty-nine-year-old delivery man, Willie McGee. According to McGee, when Officer Hugh Herring spotted him near the bus station, he punched him. Several hours and several beatings later, Chief Valentine promised McGee that if he confessed, he would provide him with protective custody ninety miles away in Jackson rather than turn him over to "white people" in Laurel. McGee wanted to tell him that Hawkins was his lover, not his victim, but he feared that the chief would deliver him to a mob. Authorities lacked evidence linking McGee to the rape. But they did not need it. They could rely on racial lore embedded in the white southern mind.[27]

McGee violated miscegenation laws and southern mores when he crossed the color line into the forbidden sexual landscapes of the white world. But he had always resisted rules. Stocky and handsome with intense, alluring eyes and an easy laugh—and known in the black community as Black Dad because of his "dark, smooth" skin and jocular charm—McGee could always find a party and become the center of it; but he could rarely keep a job because he bucked discipline. After he dropped out of school in the seventh grade, he toiled in hard labor and service jobs. In 1935, he married eighteen-year-old Eliza Payton, and within four years, they had four children. He loved his family, but his penchant for gambling, philandering, and drinking lured him away from home many nights. Although Eliza grew incensed over his infidelities, she stayed with him until Hawkins came along. Hawkins, a willowy and coquettish brunette, married Troy, a postal worker in 1934 when she was twenty years old. Over the next nine years, they had three daughters. They lived in a small three-bedroom home in a middle-class white neighborhood bordering the black quarters. As McGee mowed lawns and delivered laundry on her street, he encountered Hawkins frequently.[28]

According to McGee, one August day in 1944, Hawkins stood on her front porch watching him deliver laundry to her neighbors. When McGee drew near, she summoned him inside her home by claiming that she had a job for him. Once she closed the door behind him, she teased him that he "seem[ed] . . . afraid of white folk." He was alone in a home with a white woman, a precarious situation in the Jim Crow South, but he denied her charge. "You must be," she teased, "you look like you are ready to run." She drew him near. Either he forgot his place or railed against it. He slid his arms around her waist and kissed her. "Do you want to love me?," she asked. "My, oh yes," he responded. Their initial tryst led to an affair. They assumed a sexual agency that the white South denied black men and white women; their affair placed them both in peril. Yet often, McGee slipped inside Hawkins's home at night where they made love, even as her husband slept in a nearby room.[29]

Eventually, Hawkins ordered McGee to dump his other lovers, his "Negro whores" as she called them. He obeyed. Although McGee disliked her power over him, he was obsessed with her. But he also loved his wife. He moved to Nevada briefly in hopes that the distance would help him save his marriage. Yet when McGee returned to Laurel, he visited Hawkins. She claimed that she was bearing his child. To escape their dangerous predicament, she insisted that McGee kill her husband; they could use his life insurance money to move to California. Hawkins's plot terrified McGee. He tried to disentangle himself from her. She accused him of not loving her and warned, "I love you too much to let you do me anyway [so] you are going to do what I say or something is going to happen to you bad." McGee stalled, likely to determine if she was pregnant. Eliza moved out. McGee, fearful that Hawkins would expose their affair, "sweet talk[ed] her and ke[pt] her fooled that I was going to bump him off." Then Hawkins set a date for the murder, November 1, 1945. That night McGee tried to find Eliza to reconcile with her. When he failed, he spent the night drinking whisky and gambling. After losing his money in a skin game at Hattie Johnson's home, he gambled away cash collections from customers for the grocery store where he worked as a delivery man. Before dawn, McGee knocked on Hawkins's window. When Hawkins realized that McGee came for love making and money rather than murder, she threatened to commit suicide. He calmed her, and they made love. She gave him a few dollars but not enough to replace the store collections that he had lost.[30]

Several hours later, police took Floyd Nix and several other black men into custody and interrogated them about Hawkins's alleged rape. Certain of Nix's guilt, police transferred him to Jackson to protect him from a mob. Unaware of the investigation, McGee spent the morning trying to pawn a zoot suit to replace the company collections that he had lost. Unable to obtain enough money, he skipped work. Unbeknownst to McGee, Chief Valentine launched a massive search for him on the rape charge. Later the chief claimed that McGee's boss had filed a complaint charging McGee with theft and that during the investigation, police found evidence linking McGee to the rape. Perhaps McGee saw the article in the *Laurel Leader-Call*, which reported that a white woman on South Magnolia Street had been raped by a black man. That afternoon police found McGee rushing toward the bus station in Hattiesburg.[31]

Authorities denied McGee all of his constitutional rights to defend himself and protect his person. Out of public purview, they brutalized him until he signed a confession that they had authored and kept him isolated in the fortified Jackson jail, denying him visitors until the grand jury indicted him on December 3. By the time authorities allowed him two meetings lasting a total of ninety minutes with his court-appointed white lawyers, H. E. Koch and M. W. Boyd, his mind had broken; he lacked the ability to confer with them. Not that it mattered. Boyd and Koch never wanted the case and could not win it. Koch exerted no effort. Boyd expended minimal energy. Any attempt to exonerate McGee was futile and dangerous. They had a part to play: appearing to defend McGee to prevent federal intervention.[32]

The white community played its part too. On November 10, the *Laurel Leader-Call* reported that McGee had confessed—a report that could taint even a nonbiased jury pool. Reporter Raymond Horne reflected the common perception of the white community in Laurel: "I was never aware of a white woman that had a consensual relationship with a black man. . . . I don't find it plausible at all." Jon Swartzfager, whose father later became a significant figure in the McGee case, recalled that "McGee was going to be convicted. You had twelve white males on the jury who have to make a decision: Are we going to believe the white lady or are we going to believe the black man?" A group of white men, including Sam Bowers, who often gathered at John's Café, planned to lynch McGee before he arrived in the courtroom. Finding an unbiased jury in Laurel would prove impossible.[33]

Determined to prevent the federal wrath that a lynching would invite, authorities insured that heavily armed National Guardsmen transported McGee to Laurel, flanking him at all times. Deputies searched the hordes of spectators for firearms, and Judge Burkitt Collins warned them against violating the law no matter "how provoked we are." Blacks flocked to the trial, but fear kept them from testifying in a change of venue hearing, making it easier for Judge Collins to reject the motion. When the defense requested a sanity hearing, Judge Collins corralled twelve white men around the courthouse who, after listening to testimony from nonexperts and deliberating for fifteen minutes, determined McGee competent to stand trial.[34]

District Attorney Homer Pittman and County Attorney Albert Easterling tried McGee that afternoon in a mob-filled courtroom. Hawkins played the role of the violated virtuous mother, but not as well as the prosecutors had hoped. She testified that on the night of the rape, she slept in the front bedroom beside her sick toddler; her other daughters, ages eight and ten, slept in the adjacent room; and her husband slept in the back room. She had left the light on and the window open. When she awoke to the sounds of someone crawling near her bed, the room was dark. Thinking it was Troy, she reached out; she felt "a bushy Negro head. Oh—Well, this is an awful thing, it's a terrible thing to happen to anyone—I said 'What do you want?'" He said, "Miss . . . I want your pussy and I am going to have it." When she cried "No," he ordered her to "shut your mouth, I will cut your throat." She called for Troy, but quietly "because I didn't want to wake the children." When he told her that he wanted to "fuck" her, she thought "if that's all, I can take it." Pittman prodded, "Did he or did he not force you take your clothes off?" She responded, "Yes, yes he did, he stood over, he said 'unbutton them clothes, take them off, take them off, I will cut your throat.'" Pittman said, "You were afraid of him, of course?" Hawkins declared, "I was afraid he was going to wake the children and I didn't know but he would kill all of them, that is my idea, but I could never have gotten away from him." She described him as "that great big old negro." She did not identify McGee as her attacker. According to her testimony, her assailant had "cut" the electricity; thus, she could not see him. Hawkins insisted that no one in the small house awakened during the rape, not even the child at her side.[35]

Hawkins's narrative of the rape and the aftermath contradicted the testimony of many other prosecution witnesses and the confession. She claimed that after the rapist left, she lay still for a few minutes before she "tipped" through the dark house to check on her sleeping children. Then she made her way to Troy and said, "The worst thing in the world that ever happened has happened to me." Troy whisked her to the doctor's office. Contrarily, Troy testified that after his wife awakened him, he lit a match and found his way to the kitchen where he inspected the fuse box and tried to find the problem. Pittman insisted: "You took your wife to a doctor." Troy responded, "Well, it was a good while after that, that we called the doctor down there." According to the confession, McGee drove to a white neighborhood and stumbled around peeping into houses. When he saw a woman lying on her bed in a well-lit room, he entered the home through the front door, strode into the bedroom, and raped her. Hawkins had testified that the doors were locked and that the intruder had damaged the electricity. Neither the confession nor officer testimony suggested that the intruder picked the lock or impaired the electricity. Chief Valentine recalled that when he arrived at the home nearly an hour after the alleged rape, "the lights were on." But Troy had testified that he had not fixed the electrical problem. Like the Hawkinses, but in opposition to the confession, Valentine suggested that the intruder had entered through the window as he found it "open" and "signs as though someone had crawled" upon it.[36]

Neither Koch nor Boyd asked Troy why he tried to repair the electricity rather than call the police, secure his children, and transport his wife to the doctor. Nor did they ask Willette to identify McGee as her rapist or emphasize that her description of her attacker as "big" was inconsistent with McGee's five-feet, seven-inches stature. She was an inch taller than McGee. They neglected to ask Valentine about the inconsistencies between the confession and testimony and failed to challenge the meager physical evidence. When prosecutors asked Dr. Grady Cook if his exam of Hawkins showed that she had been raped, he responded that he had no idea the cause of the "slight injury to the vagina." Although Cook never mentioned that Hawkins was menstruating, Pittman presented McGee's underwear, allegedly stained with Hawkins's menstrual blood. The defense neglected to ask officers if they tested the blood and to question why McGee would still be wearing underwear soiled with his white victim's blood over thirty-three hours after the alleged attack in a town with a history of lynching blacks accused of interracial rape.[37]

Throughout the trial, McGee never uttered a word. He stared like a "zombie" transfixed on nothing; his body jerked involuntarily. He had much to fear. Koch and Boyd neglected to call a single defense witness or present closing arguments; the all-white jury deliberated for two-and-a-half minutes before declaring McGee guilty; without a moment of deliberation, Judge Collins sentenced McGee to death. Within a single day, the court had tried, convicted, and sentenced McGee to die. The judge scheduled the execution for January 7, less than a month away. Hattiesburg elites abetted the court. McGee's mother, Bessie, gave Hub City lawyer Earl Wingo her life savings to appeal the verdict. Wingo never filed an appeal.[38]

Before Mississippi could execute McGee, northern civil rights leader George Marshall procured the services of Forrest B. Jackson, a prominent lawyer from Mississippi's capital city, to appeal the case. McGee gave Jackson a written statement detailing his affair with Hawkins. On January 2, Jackson convinced the Mississippi Supreme Court to grant a stay. That April, Marshall co-founded and became chairman of the Civil Rights Congress (CRC), a left-wing organization with ties to the Communist Party that was committed to civil and labor rights, and established its headquarters in New York. The McGee case became a central focus of the CRC. In July, Jackson persuaded the justices to reverse the conviction and remand the case to the circuit court on the grounds that Judge Collins erred when he refused to grant a change of venue. As the justices enjoyed autonomy from local pressures, they adhered to the law more consistently than their circuit court counterparts.[39]

The reversal enraged local whites. Some of them projected their fury on McGee's family. Two white men in a truck tried to run over McGee's nine-year-old daughter, Della, while she was walking home from school. Eliza decided to relocate to Nevada where her sisters resided. She took her children to the jail to say goodbye to their father. Della saw in her daddy's face that they should not have come. The jailers treated the family with disdain and harassed Willie's only son, Willie Earl. The children tried not to feel anything as they bid their father farewell because no matter the appeals, Mississippi, they knew, would execute their daddy.[40]

The citizens of Laurel knew that, too. However, killing McGee proved difficult. In September 1946, McGee's new Jackson-based lawyers retained by the CRC, Dan Breeland and Dixon Pyles, moved to quash the indictment on the grounds that McGee would not be tried by a jury of his peers; since the registrar drew jurors from voter rolls and had only registered ninety blacks compared to twelve thousand whites, blacks were unlikely to be chosen. They also demanded a change of venue. Although every local black person interviewed by the defense declared that McGee could never receive a fair trial in Jones County, only the Reverend T. W. Patterson agreed to testify to that effect. On the stand, Patterson fell silent, for he feared the mob that filled the courtroom. Judge Collins promised, "You won't be bothered as long as you are in court." Patterson replied, "Judge, I won't be in this court very long." The spectators laughed. Pyles snapped that their response reflected the prejudicial atmosphere. Finally, Patterson stated that McGee could not receive a fair trial in Laurel. Judge Collins denied all defense motions, but he had to recuse himself because his wife had fallen ill. When Judge John Stennis, the future Mississippi senator, took over the bench, he ordered the sheriff to discharge the National Guard in favor of local deputies. The sheriff refused to comply unless Stennis accepted responsibility for McGee's safety. Stennis moved the trial to neighboring Forrest County.[41]

The new venue was not an improvement. Mobs lurked around the courthouse throughout the October trial, a lynching only prevented by presence of the National Guard. When Pyles and Breeland hinted that Willette had a consensual affair with McGee, Troy threatened to murder them. So instead, they tried to prove that Willette had not been raped by noting that Mississippi law defined assaults as rape only if the victim physically resisted her attacker. However, during this trial, Hawkins insisted that she had resisted. At least Pyles discredited the sole physical evidence in the case—McGee's underwear; Chief Valentine admitted that he had never tested the alleged menstrual stain. Nevertheless, an all-white male jury convicted McGee in eleven minutes. Judge Collins, who had reassumed the case, sentenced him to death again.[42]

Devotion to the white supremacist patriarchy also trumped justice in a case that developed less than two months after McGee's conviction. On December 6, 1946, a white man abducted a seven-year-old black girl in Jones County and raped her in the woods. When a doctor examined her, he found her "bleeding profusely from lacerations that indicated rape." Police, acting on a tip from witnesses who had seen twenty-four-year-old Laverne Yarbrough covered with blood stains, arrested him. During the trial in March 1947, defense attorney Jack Deavours stressed that prosecutors coached the victim to identify Yarbrough and that the state had never tested the bloodstains found on his client. The jury found Yarbrough guilty and sentenced him to life. The conviction was not a watershed. Even though the victim was a child, whites failed to react with the same rage that they had displayed in the McGee case. No lynch mobs swarmed around the courthouse. And Yarbrough served a little over sixteen years rather than life in prison; the state released him on parole in 1963. The prosecution's case had its weaknesses, but it was stronger than the case against McGee.[43] Authorities were always more interested in sustaining white patriarchy than racial purity. They grew incensed when McGee received another reprieve.

In 1948, the US Supreme Court ruled in *Patton v. Mississippi* that systematic exclusion of black jurors violated a defendant's Fourteenth Amendment right to equal protection under the law. Pyles and Breeland cited *Patton* in their appeal to the Mississippi Supreme Court and proved that for at least the past thirty years, authorities had not selected a single black person to serve on a Jones County jury. The justices remanded the case. When the new district attorney, Paul Swartzfager, learned that he had to "get a damn nigger on my grand jury," he and other officials handpicked three black men whom they ordered to sit in a corner away from the fifteen whites on the grand jury and raise their hands when instructed. The jury indicted McGee.[44]

Pyles and Breeland withdrew from the case and considered themselves "lucky to get out of it." The CRC hired Bella Abzug, a twenty-six-year-old attorney, who had just passed the New York bar exam, to procure Mississippi lawyers for McGee. After an exhaustive search, Abzug persuaded twenty-three-year-old A. N. London and twenty-five-year-old John Poole to accept the case. Recent Ole Miss graduates and Jackson residents, neither of them understood the dangers of defending McGee. When McGee pled not guilty on February 19, he gazed hopefully at his new lawyers; they seemed determined to exonerate him. Yet once again, Jones County denied McGee a fair trial. Despite *Patton*, McGee faced an all-white petit jury. Apparently the prosecutors determined that having blacks on the grand jury, which indicted him, allowed them to have an all-white petit jury hear the case and determine the verdict. Judge Collins rejected motions to quash it, prohibited the lawyers from asking potential jurors if they would exonerate McGee if they proved the sex consensual, and denied a change of venue motion.[45]

In the final courtroom drama, prosecutors Swartzfager and E. K. Collins, along with the Hawkins's attorney, Jack Deavours, breathed life into the black beast caricatures codified in the canon of southern lore like Thomas Dixon's *The Clansman*. Set in Reconstruction, the tale portrays white southerners as so devoted to the white patriarchy that when a black man rapes a white virgin, she kills herself to protect her family's honor, and the Klan lynches the rapist. Hawkins had played the violated mother of virtue. But she learned that when a white woman had sexual contact, forced or consensual, with a black man, society thrust her into one of the archetypes of the "segregationist theology"—Eve. Hawkins had become intimately familiar with the misogynistic caricature. On the stand, she declared, "It would be better for my family ... if he had just killed me... I don't want to live ... people look at me and say 'That's the woman that Negro man raped' and I can hear them say it." Hawkins would not kill herself, but her society expected her testimony to eliminate McGee.[46]

Hawkins struggled to portray herself as a valiant victim fighting a "brutal beast ... [a] monster." She recalled that when she awakened to find the intruder in her home, he threatened to decapitate her if she screamed. "Of course I called [for Troy]," she claimed, "but he had just—Oh! I was just scared that's all." She tried to push him away, but "he was so big and so rough, he was just a brute and there was nothing I could do." Her daughter cried. The intruder ordered her to "keep that damned brat quiet or I will cut her head open." In the first trial, she had claimed that her toddler slept through her rape. Deavours inquired how her rapist unclothed her; she stammered, "I unbuttoned them, they were jerked off, oh, I don't remember how it was, but I did unbutton them, and I was stalling for time and he—" Deavours interrupted, "Did you do that because the threats he made toward, you?" She responded, "Oh, yes, I was so afraid." In this final narrative, Troy did not rush Willette to the doctor as she had claimed in the first trial nor did he try to fix the electrical outage as he had professed. They both ran out of the home. She "went all to pieces," darted across the street, and banged on a neighbor's window. Troy did not pursue her. Willette stayed in the neighbor's spare room for hours. When the defense pointed out how this testimony contradicted that of the first trial, the prosecution led Hawkins to explain that she confused some details because the doctors put her on medications that affected her memory.[47]

Poole and London presented the strongest defense of McGee to date. The prosecutors never asked Hawkins to identify McGee as her attacker. Poole did. Hawkins admitted that she could not identify him. Poole inquired, "All you know is that he was a big monster of a Negro, that was what you thought?" She replied, "He was a Negro, and he was a beast." Poole asked if the rapist was "a big old Negro, and as you termed it while ago, a monster—" the prosecutors objected and the judge ended the line of questioning. The defense also challenged Hawkins's claims that neither Troy nor their children awoke to her screams or those of their toddler in the small house in which all the bedroom doors were open. To prevent the admission of the confession, the defense sought to prove that it was coerced. Outside the presence of the jury, McGee told a story of police brutality all too familiar to black Mississippians. McGee testified that Officer Hugh Herring punched him during his arrest, and in the Forrest County holding cell, officers took turns pummeling him with "slapjacks" until Chief Valentine arrived with Officer Jeff Montgomery and Highway Patrol Officer Jack Anderson. Valentine ordered McGee out of his cell and shouted into his face, "Get your clothes down, Nigger." As McGee, whose hands were cuffed in front of him, bent over to pull down his pants, Valentine "popped" his face. After the officers examined his clothing, the beatings resumed as they tossed him in the back of the highway patrol vehicle and Officer Montgomery slid in beside him. During his incarceration in Jackson, District Attorney Easterling, Deputy Preston Royals, Officers Montgomery and Herring, and black trustees tortured him. Between beatings, they kept McGee locked in the hot box—a space about the size of the witness chair. Finally, he signed the confession that they had authored because they threatened to "lynch me, hang me on a bridge," and "I was scared to death way they had been treating me and threatening me, and I was tired of them knocking on me."[48]

The prosecution paraded the jailer, the former county attorney, the chief, the sheriff, and several officers across the stand to deny McGee's allegations. Easterling called McGee a "Smart Negro" who was "instructed by somebody to tell you these lies." During Royals's testimony, Poole asked him if he was indicted for beating a prisoner. Jones County had indicted Royals on assault and battery charges for beating a man jailed for drunkenness. Judge Collins instructed Royals not to answer, declared that he had known the witnesses for many years as men with good characters, called McGee's testimony a "prefabricated story," and admitted the confession. So Poole and London showed how it contradicted witness testimony. They also invalidated the sole physical evidence—McGee's underwear, allegedly stained with Hawkins's menstrual blood. Dr. Cook, who had examined Hawkins after the rape, testified emphatically that she was not menstruating.[49]

Poole knew that in closing arguments, he must declare that Hawkins and McGee were lovers, but he also knew that he would not survive if he delivered such a statement. As the trial neared completion, the mobs that circled the courthouse threatened him constantly. On March 6, the defense rested in the mob-filled courtroom without presenting a witness or a final argument. Poole and London excused themselves to use the restroom and slipped out the back door where a secretly arranged police escort whisked them away. Back at the courthouse, the all-white jury deliberated for less than an hour. McGee stood at the defense table alone when, for the third time, the jury found him guilty, and Judge Collins sentenced him to death. London and Poole filed a motion with the Mississippi Supreme Court for a new trial on the grounds that Judge Collins made several procedural errors from failing to change the venue to admitting the false confession. They also claimed that the jury erred in its verdict. Witness testimony, full of lies and inconsistencies, exonerated McGee. In April 1949, the justices rejected McGee's appeal.[50]

Desperate to save McGee, the CRC changed its strategy: it inverted the black beast myth. In a white supremacist America that feared black masculinity, a black male defendant had to appear as pure and as unthreatening as possible. However, McGee's 1945 statement detailing his affair with

Hawkins proved problematic because he admitted that he drank and gambled excessively, cheated on his wife with several black paramours, flirted with Hawkins, and willingly engaged in an affair with her. So the CRC changed the script and turned Hawkins into a rapist. The CRC needed help from McGee's wife. Yet Eliza had divorced him and moved to Nevada. In the spring of 1949, a woman named Rosalee claimed that she was McGee's wife. Journalist Alex Heard argues that Rosalee, a poor country girl who met McGee while visiting her cousin on death row, concocted the story with McGee. It is unlikely that the two acted alone. By 1949, the CRC had a thorough history of McGee, including his marriage and divorce from Eliza. Moreover, William Patterson, a black communist who had assumed the chairmanship of the CRC in 1948, had a pattern of lying in similar cases.[51]

The CRC and Rosalee created their Mississippi morality play in a global publicity campaign that exposed the gaping chasm between America's rhetoric of freedom and its reality of racial terrorism. However, to force white America to acknowledge racial oppression, they felt compelled to create a narrative as rife with caricatures as the black beast myth. They ascribed to Hawkins the role of the white Jezebel who ordered Willie to work at her house so she could rape him. McGee played the hapless Sambo, powerless to resist his sexual subjugation in a world ruled by white supremacists. Rosalee assumed the role of his wife and claimed to have witnessed Hawkins making McGee come to her home. On November 1, Troy found McGee in his home asking his wife for a loan. McGee fled to Hattie Johnson's home where he remained until hours after the alleged rape. Rosalee claimed that Hawkins chased his wife out of their home and "they say her husband was about ready to kill her that night. So I guess to save herself from her husband she figured she would say she was raped and get Willie lynched." Embracing the role of righteous warriors fighting to rescue McGee from death and struggling to liberate the black race from white tyranny, Roslaee and the CRC leaders delivered speeches across the nation. Patterson characterized Mississippi's executions of black men to prevent miscegenation as "genocide, exactly paralleling Hitler's racist mass murder." He also indicted the federal government, declaring that "legal lynchings are perpetrated by the police arm of the government's administration branch, upheld by the legislative branch which refuses to outlaw jim crow terror, and allowed to continue by the judicial branch which declines to intervene." The CRC staged demonstrations outside the White House, led marches into congressional offices, sent delegations to Mississippi, and orchestrated letter-writing campaigns to President Harry Truman and Mississippi governor Fielding Wright. The crusade incited support from the Chinese Communist Party;

European politicians, intellectuals, and journalists; and American luminaries, including Phillip Morrison, Paul Robeson, and William Faulkner.[52]

On the legal front, Poole filed an appeal in circuit court in which he accused Hawkins of fabricating the rape story and charged the prosecution with "procuring perjured testimony" from Hawkins and from law enforcement. In subsequent appeals, Poole and Abzug presented a signed affidavit by Hattie Johnson, who claimed that McGee was in her home at the time of the rape, and others signed by Willie and Rosalee, who contended that Hawkins forced Willie into a sexual affair. McGee's lawyers filed a petition for writ of habeas corpus with the Southern District Court and petitioned the Jones County Circuit Court, the Mississippi Supreme Court, and the federal court for a new hearing. All requests were denied. Finally, Abzug convinced the US Supreme Court to consider hearing the case.[53]

The McGee crusade played out amidst great challenges to white supremacy. With the aid of the CRC, the NAACP sought to remove Senator Theodore Bilbo from office on charges that he violated the Constitution by encouraging whites to use violence to keep blacks from the polls in the 1946 election. During the Senate hearing in Jackson, hundreds of black Mississippians testified against Bilbo. The CIO launched Operation Dixie, an effort to unionize the South across racial lines and established its Mississippi base of operations in Laurel. Thomas Knight Sr., a white employee of Reliance Manufacturing Company in Hattiesburg, became one of the most influential unionists in Mississippi. When Knight became president of the local union in 1948, he bucked his segregationist and patriarchal society and strove to register all workers regardless of race or gender. At the Hercules Plant in Hattiesburg, black unionists like Richard Boyd, and Boyd's white boss and union leader, Huck Dunagin, fought to end job discrimination. On a national level, in two NAACP cases, the Supreme Court ruled that state-supported law schools must create equal facilities for blacks or integrate.

Enraged Mississippi leaders launched counterassaults. Powerful southern senators packed the committee deciding Bilbo's fate with segregationists who exonerated him. Soon afterward, Bilbo died of mouth cancer. Judge John Stennis, who had briefly presided over McGee's case, replaced him. Although Stennis shared Bilbo's white supremacist ideology, he argued that "hell-raising" had only encouraged federal intervention. To nationalize the fight, he fought antilynching legislation, the new anti-poll tax bill, the FEPC, desegregation through conservative interpretations of the Constitution, and red-baiting. Yet his cohorts continued to focus on "southern nationalism." In the summer of 1948, when the National Democratic Party adopted a civil rights platform based on the findings of Truman's Civil Rights Commission,

Mississippi and Alabama delegates founded the Dixiecrat Party and ran South Carolina's Strom Thurmond for president and Mississippi's Fielding Wright for vice president. Those Democrats who found Truman's proposals too conservative formed the Progressive Party. Their presidential candidate, former Vice President Henry Wallace, vowed to dismantle segregation.[54]

The racial passions that flared because of the McGee case, the Bilbo challenge, Operation Dixie, the NAACP cases, and Truman's Civil Rights Commission exploded into a white supremacist firestorm. At the heart of all of these racial battles lay fear of black men. A few years before Bilbo died, he declared that miscegenation would prove more disastrous to the South than any other development: "When there are two streams that flow side by side and the barrier between is removed, they immediately begin to mingle their molecules. No power on earth could sift them out and restore them to their original purity." In 1948 such a mixed stream, created nearly a century earlier by former slave Rachel and her common-law husband Newt Knight, existed in the "White Negro" community on the edge of Jones County. For decades, the community had lived a quiet existence under the radar of Jim Crow.[55]

Recent threats to the Mississippi racial order, as well as renewed interest in the legendary Knight tale, rendered the enclave vulnerable. A son of Jones County, James Street, portrayed the interracial rebellion against the Confederacy as heroic in his 1943 historical fiction, *Tap Roots*, which Hollywood adapted in 1948. Two years earlier, Davis Knight, a mixed-race descendant of Newt and Rachel, had returned from his naval service and married a white woman. Mississippi had never prosecuted anyone under the miscegenation statute until June 22, 1948, when a grand jury indicted Knight. Mississippi law defined persons possessing one-eighth or more African ancestry as legally black. The marriage license, identifying the couple as white, was the only material evidence. Defense attorney Quitman Ross sought to present Knight's military record that classified him as white. But Judge Collins rejected it. Thus, Ross relied on witnesses who considered Knight a white man based on his appearance, namely the clerk who issued the marriage license and Mayor J. M. Powell, who performed the ceremony.[56]

District Attorney Swartzfager also relied on witnesses. Since census records failed to identify the precise racial makeup of many of Knight's ancestors, he could not define Knight's race with genealogical records. To prove that Knight possessed enough black blood, as they said in those days, to render him black, prosecution witnesses characterized Rachel (Knight's great grandmother) as pure African. Six witnesses described Rachel as black because "she had kinky hair, a wooly head . . . she was colored like one." On cross-examination, these witnesses all conceded that most whites considered persons who possessed any degree of "Negro blood" a Negro. Although one witness characterized Davis's grandfather, Early, as "a yellow looking fellow," another defined him as a "Negro" because of his impudent behavior, conduct apparently he believed only black persons exhibited. Despite the lack of evidence, the all-white jury found Knight guilty in fifteen minutes. Judge Collins sentenced Knight to five years.[57]

Whites also used racism to destroy Operation Dixie. When a strike broke out at Masonite, the white establishment used the "lynching spirit" stemming from the McGee case and red-baiting tactics to divide black and white workers. Company executives sent their lackeys to convince black laborers that whites ran the union and only represented white interests, while they persuaded whites that the CIO used unionism as a cover for communism and civil rights reform. To repel such tactics, union leaders purged leftist members, among whose ranks were the only supporters of integration. When the CIO won victories, such as an election for union control of the Masonite plant, white unionists enforced Jim Crow policies. By 1949, the CIO considered its Mississippi successes minor and retreated from the state, leaving behind scattered local unions.[58]

Yet racial liberals achieved stalemates and an occasional victory in these battles. Some union leaders, including Knight, Dunagin, and Boyd, worked quietly in their unions toward opening traditional white jobs to blacks. In the November 1948 elections, both secessionist Democratic parties disbanded after the Progressives failed to win a single state in the 1948 presidential elections and the Dixiecrats only won Mississippi, Alabama, South Carolina, and Louisiana. Truman defeated Republican challenger Thomas E. Dewey in a landslide, and Democrats secured both houses of Congress. As the Dixiecrats and Progressives rejoined and battled for control of the Democratic Party, Ross appealed Knight's conviction to the Mississippi Supreme Court. Noting that a California court in *Perez v. Lippold* found a state statute that nullified interracial marriages unconstitutional, Ross argued that Mississippi's statute violated the equal protection clause of the Fourteenth Amendment. To prevent an appeal to the US Supreme Court that could outlaw miscegenation statutes, Mississippi attorney general Greek L. Rice requested that the justices reverse the decision because the prosecution lacked material evidence to identify Rachel as a "fullblooded Negro" and because witnesses admitted that they characterized all persons with any Negro heritage as belonging to the black race, an assumption inconsistent with Mississippi law. The justices reversed and remanded the case. Prosecutors never retried Knight. But they had ruined his life. Knight's wife divorced him; he lost his business and moved to Texas, where he passed as a white man until 1958, when he died in an automobile accident.[59]

Jones County whites may have mourned their inability to keep Knight in jail, but they remained determined to insure that McGee would not escape their wrath. On July 26, 1950, authorities returned McGee to the Jones County jail to await his execution, scheduled for midnight. Before they could execute him, the US Supreme Court granted a stay pending the Mississippi Supreme Court's response to a new appeal authored by Abzug. By 1:00 p.m., word of the stay spread and drew men to town. Denunciations of the decision developed into talk of lynching. Three hours passed before Deputy Royals arrived, allowing time for an angry crowd to gather. To avoid the mob, Royals and McGee crawled across the catwalk connecting the jail to the courthouse and sneaked out the door. They ran toward Royal's vehicle. A man among the crowd at the jail noticed them and whistled. The mob rushed forward. Just as McGee and Royals reached the car, a man struck McGee on the back of the head. McGee staggered. Royals started the car. McGee flung himself into the backseat. Royals sped away.[60]

The enraged men gathered again. Talk of organizing a lynching party to abduct McGee from Jackson circulated until Swartzfager led the mob into the courthouse to meet with Judge Collins, Mayor Gartin, and Attorney Easterling. He turned the discussion toward plans for combating the communist influence that he insisted had awarded McGee his reprieve. The men formed a citizens' league to fight communism; authorities passed ordinances banning communists from Laurel, prohibiting the circulation of communist literature, and penalizing violators with a one hundred dollar fine and thirty days in jail; and the white establishment disbarred Poole on charges that he worked for the CRC, which the federal government had labeled a communist front. In the US Capitol on July 31, Representative Colmer fulminated against the CRC's "communist invasion" of Laurel. Although Colmer conceded that Mississippi had the smallest percentage of communists of any state, he argued that the party used the McGee case to recruit. Only 43,000 Americans out of 150 million identified as communists, but the Korean conflict, the Rosenberg spy case, and McCarthyism rendered America vulnerable to fear-mongering. That November a federal grand jury indicted CRC chairman Patterson for contempt of Congress when he refused to release the CRC's membership list. The State Department vilified the McGee crusade as a Soviet plot to incite hostilities between America and Western nations. On March 26, 1951, the US Supreme Court refused to hear McGee's appeal. By linking McGee with communism, authorities had turned the case into a battle against the despised Reds and burdened McGee with the double jeopardy of belonging to an outcast race and associating with America's greatest enemy.⁶¹

As a new execution date neared, the CRC intensified its crusade. Leaders recruited citizens across America to the free McGee campaign and convinced the NAACP, which often sought to distance itself from the leftist organization, to join the McGee cause. In April, five hundred protesters assembled in Times Square in New York chanting "Save democracy—free Willie McGee." At a mass meeting in New York City, Rosalee declared, "I am fighting for freedom and justice for all people. And even if they kill my husband . . . I'm going to keep fighting until my blood runs like water." On May 7, the day before the scheduled execution, three hundred supporters marched on Washington, D.C. One group chained itself to the Lincoln Memorial. Down in Mississippi, protesters demonstrated outside the state capital, while Abzug implored Governor Wright to grant McGee clemency. Mayor Gartin, who attended the meeting, responded that the "bestial" McGee was guilty and lambasted McGee's lawyers as evil "communist[s]" who besmirched "the name and honor of a Laurel wife and mother who . . . is fine and noble and pure [with] brazen accusations, conceived in the miasma of some perverted mind [that] are an insult to womanhood and motherhood in general."⁶²

Turned away from the capital, McGee's lawyers filed a civil damage suit charging Mississippi with convicting McGee on perjured testimony. They petitioned Judge Sidney Mize in federal court for a stay of execution pending the outcome of the civil suit and appealed again to the US Supreme Court because it had recently ruled in the Groveland Four interracial rape case in Florida that prejudicial news stories prevented the defendants from receiving a fair trial. Abzug also helped McGee write a telegram to President Truman requesting a pardon. McGee argued that rigged trials were the new lynchings and emphasized that the President's Committee on Civil Rights condemned lynchings as a terror tactic used to sustain the white supremacist order. He also noted that Secretary of State Dean Acheson had admitted America's mistreatment of its minorities generated bad publicity for the nation and stressed that America had agreed to protect the civil rights of all its citizens when it submitted to the United Nations Charter. McGee concluded, "We dare not preach freedom abroad and tolerate its absence at home." Finally, he begged the president to save his life, for he was an innocent man.⁶³

All efforts to save McGee failed. Judge Mize rejected the petition, the Court declined to hear the case, and President Truman refused to intervene. On the evening of May 7, authorities assembled the portable electric chair in the same second-story courtroom where Judge Collins had sentenced McGee to death. Over five hundred whites flocked outside the courthouse to catch a glimpse of the proceedings. The weather was pleasant, and the vigil became a festivity. Townspeople and reporters socialized. Local radio anchors Jack Dick and Granville Walters from WAML and WFOR, respectively, set up camp among the crowd to report the spectacle in a live broadcast. McGee spent his final moments with Rev. T. W. Patterson—the only African American who had dared to testify on his behalf. As midnight neared, guards led McGee across the catwalk connecting the jailhouse to the courtroom. Down below, Jack Dick compared the image of McGee's death march to the circus masters bringing lions from their cages to the arena. When a boy climbed into the branches of a tree, Dick noted, "I say it looks like he's going to see it." Inside the courtroom, one hundred witnesses gathered, including Troy. Willette was absent. As McGee entered the courtroom flanked by guards and Rev. Patterson, he froze. A guard propelled him forward. The executioner strapped him to the chair, secured the metal electrode skull cap to his head, and fastened a leather band over his eyes.[64]

At 12:05 a.m., the executioner discharged a bolt of electricity. McGee clenched his fists as the 2,500 volts coursed through him. The massive generator supplying the electricity to the chair roared like waves of thunder. The streetlights dimmed. Over the rumble, the crowd cheered. At 12:08 a.m., the executioner turned off the switch. Willie McGee was dead. Black undertakers collected McGee, wrapped him in a sheet and transported him down the stairs. Rebel yells coursed through the night air as the hearse carrying McGee's body drove past the mob.[65]

In Harlem, they cried. The thousands who had gathered for an all-night vigil vowed to destroy the "lynch system that killed McGee." McGee's final words, in a letter he left behind for Rosalee, the woman he called his wife in his final years, galvanized their spirit: "tell the people . . . I never did commit this crime. tell them the real reason they are going to take my life is to Keep the Negro down in the south. they cant do this if you and the children keep on fighting. . . . tell the people to keep on fighting." Devastated by McGee's death, Patterson berated the South for replacing "magnolia tree hangings" with legal lynchings. He chastised southern white women who had "their black men and wantonly spill blood when the whim arises." Patterson concluded, "The lessons of anti-Semitism in Germany have not yet been learned in America."[66] Neither had the CRC leaders learned the lessons of the Cold War. They could not save McGee because red-baiting trumped Nazi-baiting. Hitler was dead, the Nazis defeated, and the Soviet Union was America's gravest enemy. But perhaps nothing could have saved him.

The execution consumed McGee's only son, Willie Earl, with an anguish from which he could never heal. He spent most of his life in prison. When his grandniece asked him the story of his father, he broke into sobs and could not speak. The case haunted the Hawkins family, too. Through the law offices of future Mississippi governor Ross Barnett, Willette filed a $1 million defamation suit against the *Daily Worker* because it claimed that she "shouted rape" when caught in her "illicit affair" with McGee. In 1955, the *Daily Worker* settled the suit for $5,000 and admitted that it had not proved its allegations. The settlement failed to validate Hawkins's story; the money was a pittance of her asking price. On March 25, 1967, Troy and Willette perished in an automobile accident. McGee's granddaughter considered the suffering of both families a "curse" from the "unjustified" execution.[67]

Despite its ultimate failure, the McGee campaign advanced the crusade against racial injustice. Although the CRC's white beast parable had peddled inverted racial stereotypes, it also expressed important truths about the intensity of racial oppression in America; thus, it exported powerful analogies between the white supremacist South and Nazi Germany across the globe, exposing the dichotomy between America's rhetoric of freedom and its brutal oppression of its black citizens. By unveiling the myths, injustices, and violence used to sustain the sexual color line, the CRC inspired global outrage, reawakened the national conscious, and galvanized the fiercest attack on southern injustice since the Scottsboro case. These developments rendered it increasingly difficult for the white South to use the gavel as a lynching mechanism. Although white authorities had managed to red-bait the case and portray McGee as a black beast traitor, the Cold War imperative was a double-edged sword. After nations across the globe condemned McGee's execution, some powerful Americans worried about its impact on America's position as the leader of the free world. Senator Richard Nixon argued that it damaged America's Cold War fight for ideological domination and insisted that America must strengthen its resolve against racial injustice because "we can still lose the struggle with worldwide communism for men's minds, hearts and souls."[68]

The global spotlight on Mississippi encouraged activists. The NAACP launched a massive recruitment drive that included the formation of branches in Jones and Forrest Counties founded by members of the black bourgeois like Vernon Dahmer and Benjamin Murph. As these activists became significant leaders in the growing black struggle, they incorporated lessons from the McGee case. To accrue the empathy of a white-controlled nation in a racist era, blacks had to be paragons of virtue like Harper Lee's tragic character, Tom Robinson, in her acclaimed 1960 novel, *To Kill a*

Mockingbird. It appears that McGee was neither a monster nor a mockingbird but a man who suffered the wrath of the white supremacist society for crossing the color line. Yet because the image of a suffering black man with flaws failed to galvanize the white masses to battle the racism within themselves and their nation, the CRC turned the man into a mockingbird.[69]

Similarly, civil rights leaders across the South understood that to dramatize black oppression, they would need to stage a modern morality play in which blacks assumed the role of Christ-like figures. In that play, they struggled for the reconciliation of humanity through loving one's enemy and turning the other cheek to violence. Through their suffering under white terrorism, they turned mockingbirds into martyrs and galvanized the nation to fight for black freedom and for the expiation of racial sins that had violated the laws of Christian brotherhood by separating human from human and humanity from God. Only through the destruction of white supremacy could the races reconcile and only through reconciliation could they find salvation.[70]

The morality play emerged amidst World War II and the onset of the Cold War when America promised to bring its enlightened system of representative democracy to lands controlled by fascism, Nazism, and Stalinism. The Manichean worldview that divided the globe into dark domains controlled by forces of evil and enlightened lands ruled by idealized constitutional democracies allowed activists to articulate their demand for liberation in a lexicon understood by the world. With such language, they carved fissures in Mississippi's iron wall. The forces of freedom slipped through the openings as a stream of promises. Progressive currents permeated the Central Piney Woods and transformed the nature of black resistance. To a people so long suffering from a drought of liberty, most local blacks approached the rivers of revolution tentatively. The boldest members of the black community immersed themselves in the currents and created tributaries of resistance to the racial order. Whites could neither repel the waves of national changes rolling toward them nor contain the swells of protest churning within their lands. Their efforts to stem the tide only strengthened the surge of the rising Mississippi movement.

CHAPTER 2

Massive Resistance and the Making of the Movement

THE ANGRY WHITE MEN GATHERED. ONE MAN SUGGESTED THAT HE could make it look like a railroad accident—the Negro tried to run the tracks, but the train came too fast. Another convinced the rest that they should frame the Negro for a felony and send him to prison instead. Perhaps he opposed murder, or maybe he worried that the killing would attract federal attention. Going to prison for conspiring to kill someone did not appeal to them. Still, they had worked hard to turn the Normal School into Mississippi Southern College (MSC), a respectable institution that attracted commercial wealth to Hattiesburg. They would not watch it collapse because some colored boy wanted an education. Besides, they had warned him. He knew the dangers. But he refused to capitulate.[1]

The white men had no understanding of Clyde Kennard. To them, he was just another troublemaking *Negro*, a heretic to the racial order whom they wanted to put down but settled for putting away. Among blacks, Kennard was a hero, a twentieth-century black philosophe who fought the ignorance of white supremacy with the reason of the black liberation movement. They respected him, and they feared for him. No black person had dared to seek admission to MSC before 1955, when Kennard requested an application. To Kennard, segregation was as illogical as it was evil. MSC was a state-supported college. His tax dollars funded it. When a friend warned him that whites might kill him, he replied, "History is in the making. It's an interesting time to live, and not such a bad time to die." He had no idea yet the suffering he would know before they insured his death.[2]

During the 1950s, Kennard stood at the forefront of the struggle in the Central Piney Woods, but he did not stand alone. He rose to prominence in the Forrest County NAACP, an underground branch that included Vernon Dahmer. The revolutionary spirit was also growing stronger in Jones County, where a dentist, Benjamin Murph, led the NAACP. These reformers were encouraged in their efforts on May 17, 1954, when Thurgood Marshall and his NAACP team won the decisive battle in their legal crusade against Jim Crow education. In the landmark case *Brown v. Board of Education*, Chief Justice Earl Warren declared that the US Supreme Court found segregation in education at every level a violation of the equal protection clause of the Fourteenth Amendment and therefore unconstitutional. The ruling was unanimous. If it had a ripple effect, the decision could dismantle Jim Crow. Eighteen months later, in Montgomery, Alabama, NAACP activist Rosa Parks refused to relinquish her seat to a white person on a city bus. After her arrest, she and fellow activists challenged segregated seating on the city's busses with a boycott that spurred the rise of Martin Luther King Jr. and the formation of the Southern Christian Leadership Conference (SCLC). Although many historians classify *Brown* and the Montgomery Bus Boycott as the launching points for the Civil Rights Movement, in the Central Piney Woods, white resistance to *Brown* proved so violent that it would take a decade before the black vanguard could transform their campaigns against racial oppression into a revolution.[3]

That decade served as transitional era that included the climax to the first phase of the Central Piney Wood's black liberation movement—mobilization and dissent—and the prelude to its second phase—revolution. Local black leaders and their few white allies focused on three powerful fortifications of the white supremacist state: segregation, disfranchisement, and injustice. They blended the Judeo-Christian principles of brotherhood and social justice with the Enlightenment tenets of democracy and merit to articulate a powerful thesis for black liberation and expose the parasitic effects of the white supremacist ideology. In response, white supremacists launched a counterrevolution known as massive resistance to defeat the *Brown* ruling and its likely ripple effect. Massive resistance involved both militant hardliners reminiscent of the Bilbo era and the emerging "practical segregationists" who substituted the crass "rhetoric of white domination for a refined language of states' rights and racial integrity." Although whites sustained enough unity to maintain and reinforce the citadel of white supremacist rule in Mississippi during the 1950s, they confronted a tenacious protest campaign that continued to intensify despite white assaults.[4]

The national NAACP had grown accustomed to white backlashes and had no intention of surrendering its battle to overturn the separate but equal doctrine established by *Plessy v. Ferguson*. Beginning in the 1930s, armed with evidence that with the exception of Meharry Medical College, the South lacked graduate and professional schools for blacks, NAACP lawyers established a history of legislation chipping away at segregation in education. In *Gaines v. Canada* (1938), *Sipuel v. Board of Regents* (1948), and *Sweatt v. Painter* (1950), the US Supreme Court ordered that state-supported law schools must create equal facilities for black students or integrate. In *McLaurin v. Oklahoma* (1950), the Court found that segregation within the university denied black students "equality before the law" and ordered it to integrate. In an effort to develop a case in Mississippi, Medgar Evers among others applied to law school at Ole Miss; all were rejected. Meanwhile, the NAACP gained ground in exposing inequity in primary and secondary education by revealing the disparity in budgets for black and white schools. For example, Mississippi spent five times as much on white schools than on black schools. To stem NAACP efforts, southern states created façades of equalization. Mississippi leaders developed a committee to upgrade black education, but they spent much of the allotted funding on white schools instead. Finally, in *Brown*, Marshall attacked the concept of segregation by arguing that it symbolized the majority's desire to subjugate the minority and thus violated the Fourteenth Amendment's equal protection and due process rights. The victory would not come to fruition for many years, for Mississippi, like many other southern states, had no intention of complying with the ruling.[5]

After *Brown*, Mississippi thwarted the rise of a sustained black revolt in any county until 1960 and in the Central Piney Woods until 1964. Most whites viewed the ruling as tyrannical. The more militant among them joined with some religious leaders and politicians who invoked the old "segregationist theology" to condemn it an evil ruling that would lead to the ever-feared white supremacist notion of an "integrated apocalypse." Pragmatic segregationists focused on constitutional arguments that portrayed *Brown* as a violation of the First Amendment's freedom of association. Both militants and pragmatics red-baited the ruling: the militants because they associated communism with atheism and sin, and the pragmatics because by turning the fight against integration into a national battle instead of a regional struggle in which the South was again rebelling against the Union, they might actually win. Congressman Colmer condemned the decision in fiery speeches that encouraged the hysteria thundering across Mississippi. He asserted that since "a few generations ago the Negro was a savage in the jungles of Africa and only a shorter time past, a serf in bondage," blacks were unprepared for equality and integration. He also warned that if the federal judiciary could regulate its schools—a normal function of the states—it could regulate all state institutions. Colmer joined Senators Stennis and James O. Eastland in support of the Southern Manifesto, which challenged the constitutionality of *Brown*. The state legislature, with

Governor Hugh White's support, passed an amendment to the state constitution that authorized abolishment of public schools to prevent integration. Attorney General James P. Coleman retained one thousand attorneys to work pro bono on desegregation cases. On March 29, 1956, the state established the Mississippi State Sovereignty Commission. Staffed by politicians, former FBI agents, and police, the commission gathered intelligence on activists by spying on meetings, infiltrating activist organizations, and recruiting black collaborators.[6]

On local levels, prominent leaders used their influence to mobilize their communities against all forms of desegregation. In a speech to the Greenwood chapter of the Sons of the American Revolution, Circuit Judge Thomas Pickens Brady condemned May 17, 1954, as "Black Monday." He expanded his diatribe in a ninety-page booklet that became the bible of the segregationist philosophy. Preserving racial purity served as the gospel. Brady claimed God created three separate human "species . . . HomoCaucasius—the Great White Race, Homo Mongolideus—the yellow man, and Homo Africanus—the Negro" and argued that whereas the first two evolved to produce fruitful civilizations, "the negroid man, like the modern lizard, evolved not." Miscegenation violated God's design and would devolve the white race. Brady also employed red-baiting tactics. Communists, he claimed, hoped to use desegregation in America to foment miscegenation, thus weakening the white race and rendering it easier for them to usurp power. He recommended the election of Supreme Court justices, the development of a separate state for blacks, the abrogation of public schools, a national program to indoctrinate the white youth, and the formation of a white resistance political party.[7]

Brady's rhetoric inspired Robert Patterson and other prominent whites in the Delta to form one of the most powerful white supremacists organizations in the South—the Citizens' Council. The organization, founded on July 11, 1954, devoted itself to preventing "the potential flood of negro invasion into our schools, parks, swimming pools, restaurants, hotels, trains, buses, into our very neighborhoods and homes, and into public office." Local councils used their political clout to insure the passage of anti-integration legislation. They printed the names of black residents who participated in civil rights activities in local newspapers and coerced white employers and landowners to fire and/or evict them. To indoctrinate white youth, the councils included scientific racism and a warped Christian theology that supported segregation in their handbooks. They prevented the dissemination of pro-integration information that challenged their theories by screening college lecturers, censoring textbooks, and spying on teachers. By

1956, councils had emerged in every congressional district in the state and membership reached eighty thousand. Many council members supported violence as a form of resistance. As one council member noted, "A few killings at this time would save much time later."[8]

White Mississippians answered the call to arms against *Brown* with such intense violence that the NAACP declared in a pamphlet, "M is For Mississippi and Murder." The most shocking racial murder occurred in the Delta on August 28, 1955, when two white men shot fourteen-year-old Emmett Till in the head and dumped his body in the Tallahatchie River. Till had allegedly whistled at a white woman. An all-white jury acquitted the defendants. The federal government refused to intervene. Its apathy in the wake of the murder strengthened massive resistance. As one black Hattiesburg teenager asked, "What can you do ... when there's no justice?"[9]

Fealty to white supremacy was pervasive, but not absolute. Every region of the state had white progressives who opposed Jim Crow and white moderates who supported segregation but disdained violence. Four MSC students protested the killing of Till, if only anonymously, in a poem published in the *Hattiesburg American* that declared, "When Christians say/ Thou shalt not kill/ They do not think/ Of Emmet Till." Some of the most eloquent protests came from editors and owners of newspapers, such as Hazel Brannon Smith in Lexington and Hodding Carter in Greenville. Both major newspapers in the Central Piney Woods, the *Laurel Leader-Call* and the *Hattiesburg American*, were segregationist sheets, but they opposed violence and occasionally published perspectives from racial progressives. More significantly, P. D. East, a son of the segregated lumber camps in Forrest County and the owner and editor of a newspaper in Petal, a suburb of Hattiesburg, evolved into a fierce critic of white supremacy.[10]

East launched his initial foray against massive resistance in November 1955, when he derided the state amendment allowing Mississippi to close public schools to avoid integration. Attempting to appeal to the Bible Belt conscience of his readers, he used satire to enlighten his brethren when he contemplated the racial arrangement in heaven: "Do they have another Heaven for [the Negro]? Or possibly just a section of Heaven set aside for the Negro's quarters? Are the streets in the Negro quarters paved with gold, too? Do they give him milk and honey, or does he stay too busy mopping the gold streets that run in front of the white area?" Perhaps God forbade segregation in heaven. In that case, he warned his fellow citizens, "It's likely to be thumbs down just when we tell St. Peter we're from Mississippi."[11]

When the Citizens Council became one of the most powerful enforcers of racial control in Mississippi, it became East's favorite whipping boy. In

March 1956, attorneys Earl Wingo and Dudley Connor founded the Forrest County Citizens Council. Wingo had a history of supporting white supremacist causes. He served on the defense team for Howard Wash's lynchers, and he had swindled Willie McGee's mother out of her savings by pretending that he would appeal her son's conviction. Other members included Constable Lee Daniels, registrar Luther Cox, and future registrar Theron Lynd. The *Hattiesburg American* advertised the first meeting on its front page and encouraged whites to join. East announced the council's formation in a full-page advertisement featuring a donkey singing, "Join the Glorious Citizens Clan Next Thursday Night! ... BE SUPER-SUPERIOR." The council, he stated, offered one the liberty to interpret the Constitution as one desired, to shout "Nigger" without guilt, and to "hunt 'Blackbirds' with no bag limit, and without fear of prosecution!" Angry whites telephoned him to call him a "nigger-loving, Jew-loving, Communist son-of-a-bitch."[12]

Over one hundred whites attended the first council meeting at the courthouse. Wingo opened the meeting by asking, "Who is naïve enough to believe that [the NAACP will] stop with integration in the schools? They wish to do away with all laws related to segregation, even those barring marriage between the races." The council, Wingo pledged, would preempt the efforts of the NAACP, "a communist outfit," "to divide [America] with racial squabbles and conquer it." Connor became the president of the local council and helped organize and chair the council's branch in the Sixth Congressional District, which included Forrest, Jones, and six other counties. As the local council grew, East declared that the *Petal Paper* wished to note the positive influence it had on Mississippi. Beneath these words lay a completely blank page. For East's transgressions, he suffered financial ruin and became a public pariah. Still, he had the support of some whites, including, Charles Mantinband, the rabbi of Temple B'nai Israel in Hattiesburg.[13]

Mantinband perceived *Brown* as a divine calling to fight racial injustice and invoked the history of Jewish persecution to encourage his congregation to support the movement. In February 1955, Mantinband helped form and became chairman of the Mississippi Council on Human Relations (MCHR), which sought to place blacks on school boards and police forces. The Citizens Council demanded that the temple board fire Mantinband. Most of the fifty Jewish families in Hattiesburg were prosperous, many of them retailers who collectively owned about half of the businesses downtown. They lived on the white side of town, were respected civic leaders, and understood that their status was contingent upon their acceptance of Jim Crow. Most Jews supported the rabbi's beliefs, if only privately. The board refused to fire him. After a bombing of a Jewish synagogue in Atlanta, a council member informed Mantinband, "I told my boys at the last Council meeting how foolish it was to bomb a synagogue which, after all was lifeless." The rabbi would make a better target. Undaunted, Mantinband persisted in his civil rights work.[14]

Local blacks became the most ardent racial reformers. Kennard took the greatest risk when he responded to *Brown* by seeking to desegregate Mississippi Southern College. By the 1950s, Forrest County whites perceived MSC, located on Hardy Street, as the precious jewel of Hattiesburg—a status its administrators fought to achieve. Between its founding in 1910 and World War II, MSC had suffered from a marginalized reputation as a backwoods teacher's school, known derisively as Hardy Street High. In the mid-1940s, President Robert Cecil Cook transformed the campus into a thriving institution that determined the pulse of the city by successfully lobbying the legislature to fund a massive building expansion and by hosting hundreds of parties to entertain faculty, students, and the city's elite. Administrators also bound whites to the campus by celebrating their devotion to white supremacy. MSC changed the mascot from the Yellow Jackets to General Nat after Confederate General Nathan Bedford Forrest, the first grand wizard of the Ku Klux Klan. Each spring, MSC hosted a minstrel show in which black-faced Kiwanians, garbed in gaudy costumes, performed derogatory parodies of black life. These parodies and Confederate and Klan symbols celebrated a society devoted to a white privileged racial order and represented a heartfelt desire to exclude blacks. MSC, with the exception of its service staff, was an all-white world that glorified white supremacy. From 1955 to 1975, President William McCain, a National Guard general and veteran of World War II and the Korean War, lorded over the institution. He considered blacks inferior and defended segregation to prevent miscegenation. McCain had no intention of permitting Kennard to attend MSC.[15]

Kennard, however, was as determined as McCain. Born on June 20, 1927, Kennard grew up on a small farm in the Kelly Settlement. When Kennard was four, his father passed away. At the age of twelve, he moved to Chicago to help his older sister, who had been incapacitated by an injury. Kennard survived the gang-infested streets there by focusing on achieving high grades and working as a clerk at the Mutual Insurance Company. Between 1945 and 1952, while serving as an army paratrooper that included tours in Germany and Korea, he earned four medals, including the Bronze Star. After his honorable discharge at the rank of sergeant, he returned to Forrest County. While he applied to colleges, he tutored the son of Dave Matison, a Jewish co-owner of the largest department store in town. In 1953 Kennard attended the University of Chicago. During his junior year, Kennard's stepfather fell ill, and Kennard—always the dutiful son—returned home to help his mother run the poultry farm. After his stepfather passed away, he determined that MSC, located miles from his farm, was the most logical place to complete his degree.[16]

Kennard contacted MSC, revealed his race, requested an application, and met with President McCain. When McCain realized that Kennard's record surpassed the academic requirements for acceptance at MSC, he ordered Security Officer John Reiter to conduct an investigation into Kennard's past. Kennard's acquaintances described him as kind and hardworking. Because the family farm failed to produce much of a profit, he toiled as a field laborer and a construction worker and tried his hand at business. But when he started a gardening service, he allowed people to borrow his mowers. While working as an insurance agent for Security Life, he used some of his earnings to keep afloat customers who fell behind in their payments. Finding nothing to use against him, MSC administrators informed Kennard that they could not process his application without five recommendations from MSC alumni. Unable to obtain such recommendations, Kennard suspended his efforts for several years.[17]

During that time, Kennard joined efforts by the black vanguard to mobilize the community. By 1957, Benjamin Murph had recruited 332 members to the Laurel-Jones County branch of the NAACP and had organized a youth council with eighty-five members. Kennard, Vernon Dahmer, and several parishioners tried to form a second Forrest County branch in Bay Springs Church. The Reverend R. W. Woullard excommunicated them, and local NAACP membership dwindled from seventy-one in 1951 to twenty in 1957. Undeterred, Dahmer worked with black pastors in the Ministerial Improvement Association (MIA), a statewide group seeking "political, economic, and social justice." Pastors in the Central Piney Woods dominated MIA membership and leadership. After Hattiesburg police killed a black teenager whom they claimed was trying to break into a white woman's home, the MIA demanded the city investigate the policemen involved. One black resident accused the police of lying about the attempted break-in to cover up their murderous response to the presence of a black teenager in a white neighborhood. Mayor Richard Carlisle had recently fired several officers for beating a white MSC student. The case revealed a pattern of police brutality in the city. Yet authorities refused to investigate Johnson's death. Instead, Sovereignty Commission investigator W. G. Gray spied on the MIA and the NAACP and shared his findings with the police and the Citizens Council.[18]

Because of the danger, during meetings of the Forrest County NAACP held at Dahmer's farmhouse, members parked their vehicles next to his store to appear as if they were customers. Dahmer placed his livelihood and life at risk when he spearheaded the Forrest County struggle. He knew the pain death caused as he had lost his wife, Ora Lee, to an illness. In 1952 Dahmer married a schoolteacher, Ellie J. Davis, and over the next four years they had two children, Dennis and Bettie. Dahmer's businesses and farm continued to prosper. Several of Dahmer's older six children had left for college or the military, but most of them planned on returning to the family business. As Dahmer wanted his children to live in an America that treated them as equals, he became president of the local NAACP and focused on pursuing black suffrage.[19]

Mississippi had cleared its registration rolls in 1949 to remove the few blacks like Dahmer from the rolls. Forrest County register Luther Cox insured that most blacks failed the registration exam by asking them unanswerable questions, including, "How many bubbles are in a bar of soap?" He allowed whites to register without taking an exam. In 1951, Dahmer and several other members of the local NAACP hired T. Price Dale, a northern Mississippi lawyer sympathetic to the black plight, to file a voter discrimination suit against Cox. The Forrest County Bar Association tried but failed to bribe Dale to drop the case. Judge Sidney Mize dismissed the petition. The plaintiffs appealed. On June 21, the US Fifth Circuit Court ordered the plaintiffs to appeal to the board of election commissioners. Instead, the plaintiffs appealed to the US Supreme Court but to no avail. With the aid of Thurgood Marshall, they appealed to the Department of Justice. The field secretary for the Mississippi NAACP, Medgar Evers, and local leaders like Dahmer and Kennard built the case by tracking Cox's persistent discriminatory actions. Between 1949 and 1955, Cox registered 12,417 whites and seventeen blacks. After March 24, 1955, until his death in late 1958, Cox registered one African American, Erlene Beard, because she had a mixed-race heritage and Cox perceived her as white. Dahmer and many other black citizens, including Clarence Magee, a relative of 1928 lynching victim Manual McCallum, made several attempts to register. The Cox story became part of the national NAACP arsenal. At the National Democratic Convention in 1956, Executive Secretary Roy Wilkins, aiming to goad the party into adopting a civil rights platform, presented Cox's soap question as an example of voter discrimination.[20]

Forrest County NAACP leaders, including the Reverend W. D. Ridgeway, bolstered the case against Cox by testifying at congressional hearings in favor of the pending Civil Rights Act of 1957. The bill would create the US Commission on Civil Rights with the power to investigate civil rights violations, establish a Civil Rights Division in the Department of Justice, and allow it to launch lawsuits against persons preventing eligible voters from casting ballots in federal elections. Ridgeway testified that he had resided in Forrest County for thirty years and had abided by the laws and paid his taxes, but not once had the county permitted him to vote. Passing the bill in an era of massive resistance seemed impossible until it received the support of two powerful Democrats from Texas, House Speaker Sam Rayburn and Senator Lyndon Baines Johnson, who worked behind the scenes to secure its passage.[21]

Jones and Forrest County NAACP branches intensified their voter registration campaigns to test the legislation and build a case against recalcitrant registrars. In Jones County, Murph held mass meetings to encourage blacks to flood the registration office until registrar Leonard Caves added their names to the books. When NAACP member Maycie Gore tried to register, a white clerk snarled, "We're not registering any n[iggers] today." Some white progressives helped the cause. When Bob Holifield, a white dentist who despised segregation, learned that Caves had failed his black bookkeeper, Cora Wade-Seals, on the registration exam, he asked Caves, "She is a college graduate and social studies was [her] major, how could [she] fail that test?" On Holifield's insistence, Caves registered her.[22]

Although the Forrest County branch had increased its membership by more than 100 percent in the late 1950s and formed the Forrest County NAACP Youth Council with Kennard serving as president, Dahmer as advisor, and teenagers Dorie and Joyce Ladner as founding members, it had no success with registration. Cox's successor, Theron Lynd, was just as determined as his predecessor to keep blacks off the registration books. The thirty-five-year-old plant manager, avid fisherman, devout Mason, parishioner of Broad Street Methodist Church, and stalwart Citizens Council member mingled with the power elite. After Lynd's election, Kennard and the Reverend John Barnes sought to register. Lynd, his hair cropped short, his 350-pound obese frame spilling over his specially-made white short-sleeve shirts and dark slacks, asked them if they belonged to the NAACP and ordered them to leave. In the spring of 1959, Barnes appeared before the House Committee on the Judiciary to support the Civil Rights Act of 1960. The bill would allow the Civil Rights Division access to voter registration records to build discrimination cases against recalcitrant registrars and would implement penalties for persons seeking to interfere with a citizen's voting rights. Although Congress passed the bill over the virulent opposition of Mississippi legislators, Lynd, with the aid of the Citizens Council, kept blacks off the rolls.[23]

The Council also focused its attacks on Kennard when he resumed his efforts to desegregate MSC. In October 1958, he requested another application. On December 6, in a letter to the *Hattiesburg American*, Kennard revealed the impossibility of achieving a separate but equal society. After blacks and whites completed their separate educations, he asked, "Where do our parallels of separate but equal go? . . . Are we to assume that parallel hospitals are to be built for the two groups of doctors? Are we to build two bridges across the same stream in order to give equal opportunities to both groups of engineers? Are we to have two courts of law as to give both groups of lawyers the same chance to demonstrate their skills; two legislatures for our politically inclined, and of course two governors?" Because the parallel worlds did not and could not exist, separate was unequal. Only integration, he concluded, would solve the race problem.[24]

White authorities remained as determined as ever to sustain segregation. That summer, Governor Coleman confined Clennon King to the state mental hospital after he applied to the University of Mississippi. Whites would also find creative means to eliminate Kennard's heresy. A Sovereignty Commission inspector, Zack Van Landingham, kept tabs on Kennard's activities through his black informant, Rev. Woullard of Bay Springs Church. Citizens Council president Dudley Connor informed Van Landingham that the council could eliminate Kennard; his car "could be hit by a train or he could have some accident on the highway and nobody would ever know the difference." Connor often said that "what Mississippi needed was a real good lynching." Connor received his wish. On February 24, 1959, a black man raped a white resident of Forrest County when her vehicle broke down on a deserted road in neighboring Pearl River County. Police arrested Mack Charles Parker. On April 25, a mob lynched him. An FBI investigation led to the arrest of eighteen suspects, but the grand jury refused to indict them. Outraged, Rabbi Mantinband blamed "the Citizens' Council and Sovereignty Commission [which] more and more resemble the gestapo of the Nazis." This gestapo was watching Kennard, determining how to eradicate the threat that he posed without drawing federal attention.[25]

In late August 1959, Kennard sent a letter to Admissions Director Aubrey Lucas noting that the college should view integration as a positive economic development for the state because it would raise the educational level of black residents. Lucas, a Methodist committed to social justice, empathized with Kennard. But he lived in a world circumscribed by Jim Crow, and he perceived himself powerless to help. On September 7, Kennard informed

President McCain that although the NAACP was not currently involved in his efforts, if the college refused to admit him, he would file a federal lawsuit, which the NAACP had pledged to support. After the meeting, McCain rushed to Jackson to meet with Van Landingham and Governor Coleman. When they examined Kennard's application, they realized that Kennard had resubmitted his December 1958 application with a slight alteration—he had changed the date of his medical exam to 1959. Van Landingham and Director of Security John Reiter visited Charles Smith, a black doctor whose signature appeared on Kennard's exam. They found Smith, a member of the NAACP, unwelcoming. He admitted that he had not examined Kennard since 1958, but he refused their request to serve on a committee to persuade Kennard to withdraw his application. Van Landingham coerced several black educators to serve on such a committee. They expected a favor in return—the establishment of a black junior college in the area. Far more intimidating, the Southern Farm Bureau Insurance Company canceled Kennard's auto insurance because his attempt to desegregate MSC could lead to an "accident," rendering Kennard a financial risk.[26]

When Kennard announced plans to appear on campus on September 16, McCain arranged a meeting with him for 9:00 a.m. Kennard arrived at McCain's office at 9:17 a.m. and advised McCain and Van Landingham that he had rejected pleas by the committee to withdraw his application. On McCain's summons, Admissions Director Lucas handed Kennard a formal letter rejecting his application. Governor Coleman, McCain, and the Sovereignty Commission had devised the contents of the letter, which declared that Kennard lacked morals as evinced by his fraudulent medical examination and that the University of Chicago had denied him readmission resulting in his automatic rejection by MSC. The latter charge was a lie. The University of Chicago had not denied Kennard readmission.[27]

Kennard returned to his locked vehicle at 9:39 a.m. Constables Lee Daniels and Charley Ward were waiting for him and arrested him. While one constable drove Kennard to the Hattiesburg Police Department, the other followed in Kennard's vehicle. During the interrogation, the constables presented a paper bag containing several half-pints of illegal liquor in the dry state that they professed to have found in Kennard's vehicle. They claimed that they had spotted Kennard in his vehicle on the highway after they received a tip that someone fitting his description was transporting liquor in the area. They pursued Kennard, but he sped away. Later, they saw his vehicle at MSC and waited for him.[28] The constables lied.

Kennard had taken back roads to campus rather than the highway as the constables had alleged. He had driven his mother to their potato patch, visited a local minister in Hattiesburg, and transported a family friend to her home. Moreover, the constables could not have seen Kennard's vehicle on campus from the main road. Van Landingham suspected "a frame-up with the planting of evidence in Kennard's car," and his investigation substantiated his theory. A year earlier, Citizens Council co-founder, Dudley Connor, had suggested killing Kennard. After Kennard's arrest, the outgoing district attorney, Daniel W. Dabbs, informed Van Landingham that he suspected that Constable Daniels and Reiter participated in the conspiracy. Constable Daniels knew Connor because he had served as acting secretary of the local Citizens Council while Connor was president of the organization. Sheriff Bob Waller and Dabbs told Van Landingham that Reiter had expressed several "outlandish and radical ideas" about how to prevent Kennard's admittance to MSC. Van Landingham was not surprised because Reiter had told him that whites had approached him about placing dynamite in Kennard's starter or planting liquor in his vehicle. Considering the autocratic atmosphere that pervaded MSC, it is unlikely that Reiter would act on a conspiracy without receiving consent from McCain. It appears that the conspirators ordered the constables to wait for Kennard on the highway, knowing when he would pass because McCain would summon him to arrive on campus by 9:00 a.m. When the constables pulled him over, they were to plant the whiskey and arrest him. Kennard foiled their plans by taking back roads. Unable to intercept him, the constables drove to campus, located his vehicle, arrested him when he approached, and planted the liquor.[29]

The prosecutor in the Kennard case, Jimmy Finch, was a staunch segregationist and a pillar of the white community. A veteran of World War II, he became district attorney in 1948, served until 1951, and had just been reelected. A few whites, all of them Jewish, tried to help Kennard. During a social visit with the Finch family, Lou Ginsberg said, "Oh Jimmy, you know [Kennard] didn't do that. Y'all were just doing that 'cause he's trying to get into Southern.'" Ginsberg had expressed a common belief among local Jews, but her bold articulation to Finch terrified her husband. When he nudged her, she dropped the subject. Jewish businessman Dave Matison and Rabbi Mantinband offered to serve as character witnesses for Kennard. Justice of the Peace T. C. Hobby responded, "You can't help this bird. We're going to throw the book at him." Kennard's few white defenders fell silent. Their fear overwhelmed their hatred for injustice.[30]

The Forrest County NAACP members rushed to Kennard's defense with greater vigor. They hired R. Jess Brown, one of the few black lawyers in the state, to defend Kennard. On September 29, despite the flimsy testimony of the constables, Justice Hobby found Kennard guilty and fined him six hundred dollars. Brown appealed. In early March, Judge Stanton Hall affirmed the conviction. During these court battles, Kennard struggled financially. He had financed his family's poultry farm of three thousand chickens with a loan from the Forrest County Co-op on the agreement that when the chickens produced eggs, he would begin repaying the debt. After his arrest, the co-op terminated Kennard's credit and won a lawsuit that forced Kennard to pay back the entire loan immediately. With loans from friends, Kennard paid his debt. He also kept his farm intact because the co-op sold damaged feed at a discounted price to an employee, nineteen-year-old Johnnie Roberts, who sold it to farmers, including family friends like Kennard.[31]

On September 21, the conspirators must have looked at the front page of the *Hattiesburg American* with dismay. In the lead article, "NAACP Will Attack Mississippi," NAACP chief counsel Thurgood Marshall announced that he had a school desegregation lawsuit in every southern state except Mississippi but planned to launch a case there as soon as a client emerged. After MSC rejected Kennard's application in 1959, Governor Coleman stated, "If Clyde did reapply, there'd be no way of holding him out because his record was sufficient. There'd be no alternative but to close the college." Mississippi law barred convicted felons from attending a state university. On September 25, a grand jury indicted Kennard and Roberts for stealing chicken feed from the Forrest County Co-Op.[32]

Brown filed a motion to quash the indictment, arguing that since Forrest County used discriminatory methods to avoid registering black voters and selected jurors from the nearly all-white registration rolls, it created all-white juries in violation of the constitutional right to a jury of one's peers. During the hearing, Brown questioned several city leaders, including Registrar Theron Lynd and District Attorney Jimmy Finch. Although they testified that Forrest County had registered and selected blacks for jury duty, they could not produce any specifics. Four black witnesses, including Dahmer, testified to the voter discrimination blacks confronted. Dahmer asserted that he had registered once in 1948, but after the county cleared the books he tried unsuccessfully to register five more times. Judge Hall rejected Brown's motion.[33]

In November 1960, *Mississippi v. Clyde Kennard*, like the McGee case, proved nothing short of an inquisition designed to suppress the latest heresy. Under threat from the conspirators, Roberts testified that he stole the feed on Kennard's orders. He arrived at the Forrest County Co-op at 4:40 a.m. on Sunday, sneaked inside the unlocked door, and retrieved multiple sacks of feed, which he transported to Kennard's chicken house. Roberts blundered during his testimony. He claimed that Kennard suggested that he leave the latch locking the warehouse unhitched before he left work at noon on Saturday, which meant the request had to come prior to that time. When Finch inquired the day that Kennard had made that request, Roberts muttered several different days before settling on Saturday night after his workday. Finch, trying to fix the error, stated, "Now, Johnny Lee... was it about a week before you went in on Sunday?" Roberts insisted that he had met with Kennard on Saturday night, and Finch tried to correct him. Despite defense objections, Finch led Roberts to settle on Thursday. Throughout his testimony, Roberts choked back sobs. When Kennard took the stand and denied the charges against him, Finch asked why Roberts would lie. Kennard replied, "Some person probably influenced him to do it." After deliberating for ten minutes, the all-white jury found Kennard guilty. Judge Hall sentenced Kennard to seven years.[34]

The judgment enraged NAACP leader Medgar Evers, who watched the trial from the balcony. In a public statement, he lambasted the verdict as "the greatest mockery to justice." The evidence, he insisted, proved Kennard's innocence, but "in a court room of segregationists apparently resolved to put Kennard 'legally away,' the all-white jury found Kennard guilty as charged in only 10 minutes." Finch had Evers arrested on charges of contempt. During the trial, Evers's lawyer stressed that white southerners condemned the *Brown* decision, yet Mississippi authorities had never found any of those men in contempt of court. On December 2, 1960, Judge Hall found Evers guilty, sentenced him to jail for thirty days, and fined him one hundred dollars. In July 1961, the Mississippi Supreme Court reversed the verdict. The justices characterized Evers's remarks as unprovoked but conceded that he had the constitutional right of free speech. Kennard was not so lucky. On April 3, 1961, the Mississippi Supreme Court denied Brown's motion to quash his indictment despite the state's unconstitutional methods of excluding blacks from the jury. On October 9, the US Supreme Court refused to hear Kennard's appeal.[35] Kennard's seven-year prison sentence stood. The injustice fueled his fellow activists to intensify another battle that he had helped birth—black suffrage.

For over a decade, the Forrest County NAACP had kept meticulous records of the registrar's refusal to register black voters by collecting affidavits from blacks who had attempted to register but were denied that right by Cox and Lynd. After Kennard's unjust conviction, Dahmer and other members were determined to break the white stranglehold that kept blacks from the polls and, thus, the jury box. On July 6, 1961, Department of Justice attorneys John Doar and Robert Owens filed a lawsuit against Lynd that accused him of voter discrimination on the grounds that he arbitrarily rejected qualified black applicants, that he delayed the registration of black applicants, and that he applied lower standards when evaluating white applicants. Attorneys filed similar lawsuits in Clarke, Jefferson Davis, and Walthall Counties, but the case in Forrest County became the most prominent because the strength of the witnesses seemed to insure its success. Members of the black bourgeois and the black working class provided the Department of Justice with a powerful case because they had repeatedly attempted to vote; many of them were highly educated and should have passed the exam; and the black laborers had both experience in struggling for their rights as union members and significant support from white union leaders. Many of the black laborers, including Richard Boyd, came from Hercules. Their white boss, Huck Dunagin, a World War II veteran and union leader, urged them to register and promised them that they would not lose their jobs. Dunagin opposed school integration, but he had grown close to several of his black employees, and he supported their right to vote and to earn jobs commensurate with their skills, even traditional white jobs. In the late 1950s, Dunagin selected Boyd to break the color barrier and moved him into a traditional white job as helper-at-large and later as crane operator. Other whites helped build the case against Lynd, though many unintentionally. Doar, his army of lawyers, including Charles Martin, and FBI agents from New Orleans interviewed whites all across Forrest County and found that most of them had not had to take an exam and/or had considerable assistance in filling out applications and exams. When Doar sent out subpoenas to witnesses, Lynd's lawyer, M. M. Roberts, accompanied by the police chief, arrived at the Hercules Plant and had all the black witnesses called to the office to meet with him. Although he had a right to interview the witnesses, he clearly intended to intimidate them by appearing with the police chief and interviewing them at the plant. However, his efforts failed to deter the activist workers.

In March 1962, Doar presented several black witnesses and sixty-three affidavits from blacks to the US Southern District Court in Jackson. Black witnesses included Dahmer; a grocery store owner; five teachers; three ministers; and six black workers from the Hercules plant, including Richard Boyd. The testimony and evidence revealed that Lynd flunked several educated blacks on the registration exam, including the Reverend James Chandler, who held a master's in theology; Robert Lewis, a science teacher; and Jessie Stegal, a school principal. Doar also presented seventeen white witnesses whom Lynd had registered. Most of them were illiterate and had little or no formal education. Several of them admitted that clerks filled out their applications. When Doar read to them questions from the exam, most could not provide a correct answer.[36]

Lynd testified that he judged black and white applicants equally but admitted that he had only registered two blacks, both of whom had their registration transferred from other counties. He also conceded that he instructed his deputies to refer all "Negro" applicants to him because "the girls didn't want to talk to the Negroes and I wasn't going to force them." The defense infused its case with the black beast subtext when the female deputies described blacks who had tried to register as evincing wanton behavior. Deputy Wilma Waley testified that she refused to communicate with "Negro[e]s" because she had frightening encounters with black applicants. One man, she noted, "looked like he wanted to be friendly—too friendly to suit me." Judge Cox informed Doar, "You don't know how the Negro people are here. You people up North don't know what Lynd was talking about, but I do. The girls didn't want to be associated with that kind of influence." When the defense received a thirty-day recess, Doar requested a temporary injunction ordering Lynd to cease his discriminatory practices. Judge Cox refused. Doar appealed. On April 10, the Fifth Circuit Court granted the temporary injunction and ordered Lynd to register qualified applicants. The decision, though a landmark in the legal history of voting cases in the South, failed to produce a watershed impact because Lynd refused to comply with the order. The Department of Justice asked the court to find Lynd in contempt and enforce the injunction. While the case remained pending for the next year, ten blacks, including Dahmer, filed affidavits against Lynd for failing to register them.[37]

Frustrated with the laborious legal process, Dahmer looked to the burgeoning Civil Rights Movement in neighboring southern states. The Student Nonviolent Coordinating Committee (SNCC) emerged in 1960 after four black college students staged a sit-in at a segregated lunch counter in North Carolina and ignited a chain reaction of student sit-ins across the South. SNCC joined CORE in the 1961 Freedom Rides in which integrated groups of riders protested segregation in interstate travel by sitting together on buses journeying in the South. Upon their arrival in Jackson, Mississippi's new governor, Ross Barnett, incarcerated them in the state prison. To unify these organizations with each other and with NAACP branches, national civil rights leaders formed the Congress of Federated Organizations (COFO). Although blacks had organized sustainable campaigns in Jackson and the Mississippi coast, the majority of the state remained untouched by the national Civil Rights Movement. COFO, CORE, and SNCC tried to establish a greater presence in Mississippi by surreptitiously sending cabals across the state to foster local leadership.[38]

Dahmer invited the revolutionaries to Forrest County. Robert Moses, a recent Harvard graduate and SNCC and COFO staff member, had tried to develop a beachhead in McComb, located seventy-five miles west of Hattiesburg. Although Moses recruited several locals, including Hollis Watkins and Curtis Hayes, a murder of a local black man decimated SNCC's efforts. SNCC needed a new launching point. The Lynd case attracted SNCC's attention to Forrest County, as it provided the ideal opportunity to publicize black disfranchisement. The invitation from Dahmer, the well-liked local NAACP man, bolstered SNCC's hope. In the spring of 1962, Moses sent Watkins and Hayes to Dahmer, who provided them with shelter, food, and his connections. The white establishment tried to prevent SNCC from making inroads in Forrest County by portraying SNCC as a communist organization in the newspapers and pressuring the black middle class, particularly ministers, to repudiate it. Yet many of the black bourgeois ignored the propaganda and welcomed the SNCC men. NAACP member J. C. Fairley provided Watkins and Hayes with an office in his television repair shop. As the struggle grew, Lenon Woods offered the first floor of her hotel on Mobile Street as a COFO/SNCC office. Cosmetic company owner Victoria Gray and Dahmer met with the Reverend L. P. Ponder of St. John's Church in Palmers Crossing who agreed to open his church to SNCC recruitment. During the first meeting, six blacks, including Rev. Ponder, Gray, and three bus drivers, agreed to try to register to vote. Lynd failed all of them on the exam. The city fired the bus drivers.

As the registration campaign progressed, Sovereignty Commission inspectors worked with Lynd and black informant Rev. Woullard to investigate. Undeterred, Hayes and Watkins organized the Forrest County Voters League, which provided voter registration classes, facilitated registration drives, and reported registration results to the Department of Justice. By September 1962, Lynd had registered four of the one hundred blacks escorted to his office. In September, Watkins and Hayes moved to Greenwood to organize the Delta, leaving the future of the Hattiesburg movement in the hands of Victoria Gray, the new COFO project director. Gray visited churches across Hattiesburg, recruiting blacks to her adult education classes at which she taught literacy and citizenship classes and politicized her recruits.[39]

On September 17, the US Southern District Court held Lynd's contempt hearing in Jackson. With great trepidation, NAACP member Earline Boyd, wife of Richard, who had broken the color barrier at Hercules and who had testified already in the Lynd case, congregated inside the basement of the federal courthouse with the other witnesses. The idea of accusing Lynd of a federal crime in a courthouse full of powerful white men terrified her. As Boyd glanced nervously around the room, she noticed that all black witness wore their Sunday best while white witnesses appeared "raggedy, dirty" many of them wearing "flip-flap shoes." She recognized some of them, "the fish lady" and the cookie lady, as blacks called them because they sold their foods in black neighborhoods. The discrepancy was striking in the basement of the courthouse and in the courtroom. Once again the Department of Justice proved that Lynd and his clerks rejected qualified black applicants and registered unqualified white applicants. Yet the justices refused to deliver an immediate verdict. Determined to sustain attention on the case and pressure the federal government to act, activists continued to try and vote in Forrest County.[40]

Throughout 1962, Jones County activism drew an increased influx of visiting civil rights campaigners who moved into Laurel. Moses sent Lester McKinnie, a veteran of the Nashville sit-ins, a founder of SNCC's Jackson movement, and one of the Freedom Riders arrested in Jackson, to organize Laurel. Soon after his arrival, a judge sentenced him to four months in jail for trying to desegregate the bus station restaurant. McKinnie also confronted opposition from Benjamin Murph, who feared that the approach of SNCC would harm the NAACP movement. McKinnie left Laurel without serving his jail sentence. Yet many SNCC/COFO organizers stationed in Hattiesburg recruited Laurel locals, albeit slowly. Local NAACP members like Bertie Mae McGill, a maid in Jones County whose husband worked at Masonite, became an early crossover recruit.[41] Still, efforts to mobilize the community fared better in Hattiesburg.

The mobilization centered on Kennard, a key figure of the local movement who, along with James Meredith, became the eye of the racial storm in Mississippi. In the summer of 1961, after doctors misdiagnosed Kennard with sickle cell anemia, prison authorities placed him on the harshest labor detail—"the sunup to sundown gang." Kennard had endured with grace his imprisonment in Parchman, Mississippi's state penitentiary, which had a reputation for brutality and for working its inmates like slaves. Despite Kennard's ill health, he labored in the fields six days a week. On Sundays, he wrote letters for illiterate inmates, taught literacy classes, and read classics sent to him by Rabbi Mantinband. That same year Meredith, a black Air Force veteran, moved into the spotlight when his efforts to integrate Ole Miss received federal support and national attention. As Meredith's campaign gained momentum, white authorities took their rage out on Kennard.

In early 1962, Dr. Haynes Helep discovered that Kennard had stomach cancer. After removing Kennard's sizeable tumor, Helep requested that Parchman superintendent C. E. Brezeale seek parole for Kennard. Brezeale refused. In June, Dr. M. L. Dalton removed a tumor from Kennard's colon and informed Governor Barnett that Kennard had a 20 percent chance of living five years. Barnett rejected Dalton's request to parole Kennard. Under Brezeale's orders, the guards refused Kennard treatment even as he became so weak that prisoners had to carry him to and from the fields.[42]

In September 1962, President John F. Kennedy ordered Ole Miss to admit Meredith. When Governor Barnett and Lieutenant Governor Paul B. Johnson—a son of Hattiesburg—blocked Meredith's registration, Kennedy federalized the National Guard. Despite a riot that killed two people, Meredith desegregated Ole Miss. In the wake of Meredith's triumph, the NAACP, SNCC, and the *Mississippi Free Press* reminded the nation that Meredith's victory stemmed from efforts by men who, like Kennard, languished in prison. Brown, Kennard's lawyer, initiated new appeals requesting that the Mississippi Supreme Court overturn Kennard's conviction on the grounds that Lynd's refusal to register black voters prevented blacks from serving on jury pools, which denied Kennard his right to a jury of his peers. The justices refused. Brown appealed and petitioned the court to release Kennard to the hospital. The *Mississippi Free Press* castigated state authorities as "inhuman" and beseeched readers to protest. Forrest County natives Dorie and Joyce Ladner, both SNCC activists attending Tougaloo College, led their student body in a national campaign demanding that President Kennedy free Kennard.[43]

In January, Kennard began hemorrhaging again. During Kennard's transit to the prison doctor's office, the guard warned him, "If you mess up this car, I'll kick you out." The guard dumped Kennard in the waiting area. Kennard crawled to the examination room. When the physician examined him, he realized that Kennard was near death. Famous activists, including Martin Luther King Jr., Dick Gregory, and John Howard Griffin, warned Governor Barnett that if he allowed Kennard to perish in prison, they would accuse him of murder. Griffin, a white reporter, had become familiar with Kennard's case in 1960 when he disguised himself as a black man and traveled the South in a social experiment. He considered Hattiesburg a terrifying place and later described it in his classic, *Black Like Me* (1962), as "hell." On January 23, 1963, Governor Barnett ordered Kennard transported to the emergency room. To stem the bad publicity, Barnett claimed falsely that he had only recently learned of Kennard's illness. Brown implored Barnett to pardon Kennard since he had served over three years in Parchman, which "far exceed the statutory requirement to make him eligible for parole." Barnett refused. Instead, he suspended his sentence, "dependent upon his future good behavior."

The cancer spread so quickly. When Griffin visited Kennard in the hospital, he found him trying to hide the pain that wracked his emaciated body. Kennard told Griffin that his suffering would be worthwhile if it "would show this country where racism finally leads." Kennard noted that the racist society had a far worse impact on the guard who had dumped him at the doctor's office than it had on him: "This system has turned him into a beast, and it will turn his children into beasts."[44]

In June 1963, Kennard's crusade contributed to a great shift in the federal arena, but that shift also fueled violence and tragedy. On June 11, President Kennedy called on Congress to pass a civil rights bill ending segregation in public accommodations and schools and declared, "We preach freedom around the world . . . and we cherish our freedom here at home; but are we to say to the world, and, much more importantly for each other, that this is a land of the free except for the Negroes; that we have no class or caste system, no ghettos, no master race, except with the respect to Negroes." Hours after Kennedy's speech, Citizens Council member Byron de la Beckwith shot to death Medgar Evers in his driveway in Jackson. Evers's murder devastated black Mississippians. He was their Dr. King, their Malcolm X, and now he was gone. Less than a month later, on Independence Day, Kennard died in the hospital. Two great giants in the Mississippi movement were dead.[45]

Throughout 1963, the Mississippi movement slammed against a wall of white resistance. The white supremacist state survived the civil rights acts, the Freedom Rides, the Lynd case, the desegregation of Ole Miss, the murder of Evers, and the imprisonment that killed Kennard. Governor Barnett and Congressman Colmer determined to fortify Mississippi's wall by defeating the proposed legislation that became the Civil Rights Act of 1964. They labeled it the Civil Wrongs Bill and claimed its passage would lead to a black Bolshevik revolution. When Paul B. Johnson Jr. opened a gubernatorial campaign office in his hometown of Hattiesburg, Citizens Council leader Dudley Connor introduced him as the man who "showed his personal courage against the armed might of the greatest nation on earth" during the Ole Miss struggle. Johnson embraced the council's support, noting that a leader facing federal invasion needed a citizenry committed to resistance.[46]

Despite these obstacles, developments on the national level infused life into the movement in the Central Piney Woods. In July, the Fifth Circuit Court of Appeals ordered Jones County circuit clerk Leonard Caves to present his voter records for examination. In Forrest County on July 15, the Fifth Circuit Court ordered Lynd to provide blacks and whites the same sections of the Mississippi Constitution for interpretation, to permit federal agents to review his registration records, and to present to the court a signed statement swearing that he would adhere to the court's ruling. It also gave Lynd ten days to register forty-three blacks whose applications the court approved. If Lynd failed to comply, the US Attorney General would arrest him. Lynd filed the ordered statement but with an addendum contending that it could not interfere with his right of appeal to the US Supreme Court. While the appeal remained pending, ten of the forty-three qualified applicants sent affidavits to the court swearing that Lynd refused to register them.[47]

Lynd was the first registrar in the South convicted for voter discrimination under the 1960 Civil Rights Act, a landmark SNCC capitalized upon by sending veteran activists John O'Neal, Lawrence Guyot, and Carl Arnold to Hattiesburg. The town bustled with activity. A constant flow of locals willing to attempt to register moved through the COFO office. In the fall, COFO leaders launched the Freedom Vote campaign across the state, a parallel unofficial election in which COFO ran candidates on civil rights platforms to reveal that blacks would vote if whites allowed them their constitutional right. Aaron Henry, a black man who was the chairman of COFO and state president of the NAACP, ran for governor, and the Reverend Edwin King, a white man who was the dean of students at Tougaloo College, ran for lieutenant governor. COFO brought in white college students to facilitate the election. Police arrested several of them on trumped up charges. Across the state, over 83,000 blacks participated, proving that they harbored a significant desire to participate in the political process. Simultaneously, the NAACP Voter Education Project registered only 28,000 of the 465,620 eligible black voters in Mississippi, the lowest by far in the southern states. Thus, the black vote made little difference in Mississippi's 1963 elections. Johnson defeated his Republican opponent in a landslide for the governor's office. In Forrest County, whites elected Sovereignty Commission inspector W. G. Gray as sheriff. Lynd retained his position. Finch won the district attorney's office again.[48]

Just over two weeks later, on November 22, the symbol of federal "invasion" to many white southerners—President Kennedy—lay dead in Dallas, felled by an assassin's bullet. White children across Mississippi cheered in their classrooms when they heard the news. Many blacks working in white homes overheard their employers declare that Kennedy "needed killing." Conversely, blacks mourned the loss of the president who had supported their struggle far more than his predecessors, though some pointed out his failure to fully embrace the movement. To the chagrin of white supremacists, when Lyndon Baines Johnson assumed the presidency, he strengthened Kennedy's civil rights bill and then pressed for its passage "so that," in his words, "we can move forward to eliminate from this Nation every trace of discrimination and oppression that is based on race and color."[49]

The hopes of Central Piney Woods activists rose even higher on January 6, 1964, when the US Supreme Court refused to hear Lynd's appeal. Still, Lynd refused to capitulate. His lawyers requested that the Fifth Circuit withhold action against him until the US Supreme Court decided in another case if such a case required a jury trial. If the court found juries necessary in such trials, Lynd could appeal because judges rather than juries had handed down rulings against him. SNCC viewed Lynd's intransigence as the perfect opportunity to place the Hattiesburg movement on center stage. For nearly two years, SNCC and COFO staff had worked with NAACP leaders in the trenches, recruiting local blacks to the movement and transporting them to the courthouse to register, supporting federal cases against Lynd, and launching the Freedom Vote. To force the federal hand against white intransigence, the activists needed a massive protest that would sustain the nation's interest. So COFO and SNCC leaders designed Freedom Day in which hundreds of blacks would converge upon the registrar's office at once.[50]

The campaigns of the local black vanguard and the SNCC/COFO revolutionaries had created a crisis in the white supremacist state. At the advent of 1964, the conflict burst toward a full-blown revolution. Many of the children coming of age at this pivotal moment had witnessed white crackdowns that spawned false imprisonments and racial murders, but they also witnessed the rising black protest. They tended to view white supremacists with more anger than fear. Since twelve-year-old Larry McGill could remember, he had heard whispers about racial oppression, including the rape of his aunt, explaining why his cousin was "so light," and the lynching of a cousin in a nearby county because he looked at a white woman. When McGill's mother, Bertie, began taking him to COFO meetings in Laurel and putting him "in the circle" of the racial struggle, he associated manhood with fighting injustice. In Forrest County's Palmers Crossing, fifteen-year-old Jimella Stokes linked womanhood with female civil rights leaders like Victoria Gray. It infuriated her that the public library contained an abundance of books that she could never read because it belonged to whites only and that even the "poor white trash" called blacks "niggers" as if that elevated their status. Stokes never internalized her oppression. Her community had taught her that she was equal to whites, but she wanted an equal opportunity, too. The local struggle had opened a porthole for her into a world beyond Jim Crow, and Stokes determined that she would find her way to the other side.[51] McGill and Stokes and hundreds of other locals became the infantry troops of the revolution.

CHAPTER 3

Freedom Days and White Knights

ON JANUARY 22, 1964, GRAY CLOUDS DARKENED THE MORNING SKY AND the rain fell, but nothing could stop the throngs of African Americans as they marched from the COFO office on Mobile Street toward downtown Hattiesburg to join the Freedom Day demonstration. Hundreds had summoned the courage to protest Theron Lynd's refusal to register black voters. Fifteen-year-old Jimella Stokes could barely contain her excitement when she turned a corner and saw a group of local blacks led by COFO leaders and northern white clergy picketing the Forrest County Courthouse. Stokes had no fear as she joined the Freedom Day revolt.[1]

Black adults like Daisy Griffin Harris, a pretty, thirty-three-year-old mother, had lived under Jim Crow long enough to be afraid, but she had a quiet strength about her. Beneath her slender frame, delicate face, and ready smile burned a passion that drove her into the rainy streets. As she neared the courthouse and saw a horde of policemen, garbed in raincoats and riot helmets, marching like a "platoon" toward the picketers, she froze. She watched police barricade Main Street and take up positions on both sides of the road. A police vehicle roared to a halt near the protesters. Through a blaring loudspeaker, an officer shouted, "People who wish to register, line up four at a time.... All those not registering to vote move off." Instead, fifty more pickets joined. A legion of police lined up beside them, wielding clubs, but they did not arrest anyone. Deputies assumed their positions in front of the courthouse doors. The presence of the officers troubled Harris. As a child, she had witnessed lawmen terrorize her neighborhood and had seen her brave father cower before officers. She understood the fragility of black life in Mississippi, and she had three young sons and a husband to think about. She huddled with dozens of black adults across the street from the courthouse.[2]

Some whites gathering downtown watched the protest unfolding with curiosity, but most of them glowered with rage. From the picket line, Stokes glared back at them and sneered at the "Toms," as she considered the nonparticipating blacks. She could not understand how these adults could bend to their oppression. James Farmer, a stalwart figure in the Civil Rights Movement, was more patient than Stokes and waved over Harris and the others. Inspired by Farmer's courage, Harris crossed the street and into a world of black defiance.[3]

Few of the protesters had raincoats or umbrellas, but all day they marched, sang, and waved signs declaring, "One Man, One Vote," and "Let My People Vote." The national media spread the story across America. Local reporter Elliot Chaze described Freedom Day as "Hattiesburg's first all-out demonstration in the simmering civil rights war." Freedom Day was the first frontal assault on white supremacy in the Central Piney Woods, and it instigated a major turning point in the black struggle. Even though SNCC and COFO staff members—visitors rather than residents—led the charge, organizers recruited an impressive array of locals into the infantry ranks. Together they launched a massive and protracted assault on one of the most powerful citadels of white rule—the registrar's office. They put into practice the nonviolent strategy that had come to define the Civil Rights Movement rolling across the South. To dramatize racial oppression on the national stage, the most powerful civil rights organizations, including CORE, SCLC, SNCC, COFO, and some NAACP branches, were staging a civil rights morality play. Through their suffering under racial oppression, they sought to inspire the nation to join their righteous cause for freedom, for brotherhood, for justice, and for equality under God. In Forrest County, the hundreds of local blacks who joined Freedom Day fought for their political rights, and they fought to force the nation to recognize their humanity. They faced a daunting enemy.[4]

Prior to Freedom Day, the Sovereignty Commission, the Mississippi Highway State Patrol, Mayor Claude Pittman, and local law enforcement gathered intelligence from informants, briefed Governor Paul B. Johnson Jr., and planned their counterrevolution. They decided to appropriate the movement's nonviolent strategy and turn it against the activists. Officers would request that nonresidents leave the courthouse. Lynd would admit prospective voters into the courthouse at a sluggish pace. They theorized that the lack of spectacle would bore reporters and that blacks would not wait in the long lines. Officers would arrest activists who violated the laws, and court officials would convict them, but peacefully and selectively to diminish nationwide media coverage and mitigate federal intervention. Local newspapers would publish the names of Freedom Day protesters so white bosses, landlords, and business owners could fire, evict, and refuse to conduct business with them. The plan was a clever counterreaction because most Americans failed to understand the detrimental impact of nonviolent white supremacist resistance.[5]

Radical whites resolved to launch a far more brutal strategy. That winter hundreds of disgruntled white men formed the White Knights of the Ku Klux Klan and planned to annihilate the Mississippi movement. The emergence of the terrorist legion imperiled the strategy so meticulously planned by the city fathers, as it forced the federal government to intervene, however reluctantly and gradually. At the advent of 1964, the clashing forces of white supremacy, federalism, and civil rights activism hurled the Central Piney Woods into a state of war for the next decade.

COFO and SNCC came well prepared to the revolt. Several weeks before Freedom Day, Sandy Leigh, a black SNCC field secretary, became the new project director in Hattiesburg. Leigh, who had left Yale University to join the movement, had gained valuable experience working projects in Greenwood and in Birmingham, Alabama. When he arrived in Hattiesburg, Vernon Dahmer took him into his home and provided him with his contacts. To galvanize locals and attract national attention, Leigh and other SNCC/COFO leaders cooperated with the United Presbyterian Commission on Religion and Race, the Episcopal Society for Cultural and Racial Unity, and the Rabbinical Association of America to bring to Hattiesburg's Freedom Day one hundred northern, mostly white, ministers and rabbis. COFO/SNCC tied the local NAACP to Freedom Day by working with Dahmer and convincing members, like Dr. C. E. Smith and Jeanette Smith (a descendant of Newton and Rachel Knight), to host clergy. Teenagers recruited hosts outside civil rights circles. On January 21, Douglas Smith and Charles Glen knocked on Daisy Harris's door. That night, four white ministers entered Harris's home as guests. On January 22, Harris joined them in a war against her Jim Crow world. Victoria Gray, one of the most influential activists in Forrest County, convinced many of her relatives to house clergy in nearby Palmers Crossing.[6]

The night before Freedom Day, COFO and SNCC held a mass meeting at St. Paul's Methodist Church. Cardinal leaders of the movement across the South, including Ella Baker, John Lewis, Dave Dennis, James Forman, Bob Moses, Fannie Lou Hamer, Lawrence Guyot, Aaron Henry, and Annelle Ponder, hastened to the Hub City as they hoped that Freedom Day would turn Hattiesburg into one of the state's most powerful beachheads of the movement. Some one thousand people packed into the church pews and spilled into the aisles and doorways. A hush fell over the crowd when the lights dimmed. Out of the darkness a voice sang, "We shall not be moved." A thousand voices joined. As the lights rose, Aaron Henry bellowed from the podium that over a decade after local blacks filed an affidavit with the Department of Justice exposing rampant voter discrimination in Forrest County and two years after the Fifth Circuit Court of Appeals ordered Lynd to register qualified black citizens, city officials remained intransigent. Henry proclaimed that they would march until Lynd complied with federal orders. The crowd cheered. It burst with excitement as Guyot strode to the pulpit and pledged in his sonorous voice that they would fight until they achieved equality. As the rally wound toward its climax, someone shouted "Freedom!" The audience responded "Now!" The chant continued until a voice belted, "We Shall Overcome" and the activists linked hands and sang.[7]

When Freedom Day commenced, Theron Lynd executed Hattiesburg's nonviolent resistance strategy with perfection. As reporters looked on, Lynd, dressed in a black suit, smiled and appeared to fulfill his duties. By noon, Lynd had rejected two prospective voters because they were illiterate, one man had left voluntarily because he was nervous, and sixteen blacks had completed voter registration applications. Lawmen also performed their roles with precision. Jim Forman tested their resolve when he escorted an elderly black woman to the entrance of the courthouse and asked, "Sheriff, will you be a Christian and let this old lady inside?" When Sheriff W. G. Gray ignored him, he asked, "Is there no compassion in Forrest County for a woman seventy-one years old . . . who has nursed white children . . . who has toiled in the fields of Forrest County . . . who now must stand out in the rain because she wants to register to vote?" Still, the sheriff avoided relenting or engaging in a confrontation. Forman considered the interaction a success. As he later noted, "Maybe it seems strange to make a fuss over standing in the rain, but it's exactly in all these little things that the Negro has been made to feel inferior over the centuries. . . . It's important . . . to show the Negroes in Hattiesburg that it is possible to speak up loudly and firmly to a white sheriff as an equal."[8]

It might have been possible, but law enforcement planned to punish the activists when the cameras were not watching. Police arrested several activists, including Oscar Chase, a white, twenty-three-year-old Yale law student. Chase had become a police target a couple of weeks earlier when he tried to desegregate the waiting room at a bus terminal. On Freedom Day, Chase transported blacks to the courthouse. During one of Chase's stops, he hit a pickup truck while trying to park, but after realizing he had not damaged it, he left. Later that day, officers arrested him for fleeing an accident. Two hours after police tossed Chase in jail with eleven other men, the jailer delivered an intoxicated prisoner, Dave Bass, to his cell. A belligerent white man often arrested for fighting, Bass ranted about the demonstrations and asked the jailer "why the jail wasn't full of niggers?" He told Chase that he had served in World War II but that he would rather kill a "nigger lover than a Nazi or a Jap." One of the inmates informed Bass that Chase was one of those "integrationist[s]." Realizing that Bass was "sick enough to kill" him, Chase denied the charges. Bass waved his lit cigarette in front of Chase's face and promised to burn Chase's eyes out. When Bass demanded to know if Chase was "one of them nigger lovers?," the jailer nodded. Bass fixed his gaze on Chase and said, "Now I know why I'm in this jail." Bass punched Chase so hard that he fell on the floor and blacked out. When he regained consciousness, Bass hovered over him. As smiling policemen watched from outside the bars, Bass kicked Chase in the face and chest repeatedly. Finally, Chase heard the clanking of the keys against the lock. The guards yanked Chase off of the floor and shoved him into another cell.[9]

In the morning, activist Howard Zinn and attorneys John Pratt and Robert Lunney paid Chase's bail and rushed him to a meeting with an FBI agent to document his beating, including his crooked nose, swollen face, blood-encrusted eyes, and blood-soaked shirt. The agent never acted on the complaint. The next day, Mayor Pittman commended law enforcement and the citizenry for sustaining peace in the face of the protests. Elliot Chaze reported that the low number of arrests revealed "a record for tranquility" in Hattiesburg and that northern journalists became disappointed with the lack of violence. To the chagrin of the authorities, as word of the attack on Chase spread, it strengthened the resolve of the activists.[10]

Freedom Day transformed into the Freedom Days campaign when the day after Chase's beating, hundreds of activists returned to picket the courthouse. That same day Congress ratified the Twenty-Fourth Amendment, which prohibited federal or state governments from requiring citizens to pay a poll tax to vote in national elections. The legislative victory strengthened the faith of blacks participating in Freedom Days and inspired other locals to join the struggle. When Daisy Harris tried to register, Lynd threw an application at her. He failed her on the exam, but she took the test several more times until he passed her, and she picketed the courthouse daily. During the last week of January, 119 people took the registration exam. Hundreds of teenagers, including Jimella Stokes, fortified the revolt by boycotting their classes to protest Jim Crow education and by joining the picket lines. Freedom Day proved so successful in Hattiesburg that COFO and SNCC introduced it in Canton in February and in Greenwood in March.[11]

The Freedom Day movement grew stronger each week in Hattiesburg. Clergy formed the Hattiesburg Minister's Project, rented office space from

NAACP leader J. C. Fairley in his radio and television shop across the street from SNCC/COFO headquarters, and developed a three-month rotation system that supplied the Hattiesburg movement with a constant presence of northern clergy. By January 27, organizers had established a daily transportation system with ten drivers, including Vernon Dahmer, who picked up locals at multiple stations across the county. Police tried to interrupt the system by arresting drivers on false traffic charges, but staff replenished the losses with new volunteers. Leaders held mass meetings routinely and brought in famous African Americans, such as Dick Gregory, to draw more locals to the movement. By February 11, 299 blacks had taken the voter registration exam. Capitalizing on the explosion of activist energy in Hattiesburg, the staff members developed local leadership. They trained block captains and recruitment committees to convince their neighbors and fellow parishioners to join the struggle and register to vote. They also held evening workshops and "teas for freedom" in which groups of twenty congregated in the homes of block captains to engage in "bull sessions" on canvassing, voting, and protests.[12]

The white establishment fought back with economic repercussions, but activists resisted. When the newspaper published photographs of locals participating in Freedom Day, a regular picketer, Pinky Hall, lost her job as a maid. After Lenon Woods signed a property bond to bail out arrested activists, the North American Insurance Company canceled the policy on a building she owned. To sustain the participation of local activists suffering the wrath of the white establishment, SNCC/COFO formed a welfare and relief committee to provide food and clothing to people like Hall who lost their jobs. Leigh raised funds for the committee with a mass letter-writing campaign to Friends of SNCC. The United Presbyterian Church of the USA intervened on Woods's behalf, as it also used the North American Insurance Company. After church officials threatened to cancel their policy, Woods's policy was reinstated.[13]

Although white authorities responded with divide and conquer tactics in which they tried to turn blacks against each other, they underestimated the determination of local activists and overestimated the ability of black collaborators to suppress activism. When whites stationed a black woman on the courthouse steps to scold the activists, Harris and other picketers sang, "Ain't Gonna Let Nobody Turn Me Round." After the Great Mt. Bethel Baptist Church expelled a teenager who asked church leaders to open their facilities to voter registration activities, protesters staged a kneel-in outside the church, and many congregants joined them. Few blacks retreated or betrayed the struggle in the face of white counterattacks.[14]

Authorities were most adept at using their unjust legal system to suppress Freedom Days even as they faced some setbacks. On January 29, Judge Stanton Hall issued a temporary injunction ordering the termination of Freedom Day demonstrations until March 4, when the court would rule on the legality of the protest. Protesters ignored the ruling and packed the picket and registration lines. Police tried to shrink the crowds by erecting barricades in front of the courthouse where they established a no-picket zone and arrested violators, including Bob Moses. Still, the pickets returned. Officers arrested one black and eight white Presbyterian ministers on charges of disorderly conduct after they refused orders to cease marching in a restricted area.[15]

During Moses's trial, activists challenged Mississippi's segregation laws by sitting in the courtroom in integrated groups. Judge Mildred Norris smiled pleasantly at the crowd and asked the court marshals to "segregate the courtroom." Activist Howard Zinn asked, "Your Honor, the Supreme Court of the United States has ruled that segregated seating in a courtroom is unconstitutional. Will you please abide by that ruling?" After a short recess, Judge Norris declared, "We here in Mississippi have had our way of life for hundreds of years, and I obey the law of Mississippi. I have asked that you sit segregated or leave, or be placed under arrest. We would have appreciated your complying. But since you do not, we will allow you to remain as you are, provided you do not create a disturbance." Judge Norris prevented a public scene while also ensuring that the activists would suffer for their protests. An officer testified that Moses had broken the law by obstructing sidewalk traffic and refusing an officer's orders to disperse. Moses testified that he had a First Amendment right to petition the government. Judge Norris found Moses guilty and fined him two hundred dollars. Moses paid his fine and rejoined the picket line. Police arrested him again on charges of interfering with an officer. Judge Norris fined him twenty-five dollars and sentenced him to thirty days in jail. The picketing persisted, and the activists used the court records in their legal battles against the state's violation of federal laws.[16]

While the nine ministers awaited their trial in jail, Rabbi David Z. Ben-Ami, who had recently replaced Charles Mantinband as the head of Temple B'nai Israel, visited them. He was the only local white religious leader to make such an overture. A survivor of Nazi Germany, Ben-Ami refused to ignore the movement. After Sheriff Gray contacted prominent members of the B'nai Israel congregation, the temple board ordered Ben-Ami to refrain from conducting any further actions that would disrupt the tenuous peace enjoyed by the Jewish community. Ben-Ami disobeyed. He served on the Mississippi Council on Human Rights and the Mississippi State Advisory Committee to the US Commission on Civil Rights. Once again, the Jewish community found itself with a rabbi committed to social justice, a stand they feared. The Jewish community also witnessed with trepidation the Rabbinical Association of America's participation in the Freedom Days campaign. One of the rabbis, A. James Rudin, tried but failed to persuade Hattiesburg Jews to support the movement.

Within the white Christian community, Rudin found a small minority of progressive whites, mainly professors at the University of Southern Mississippi or soldiers stationed at Camp Shelby. They supported integration and political rights for blacks, but most of them remained too frightened to support the movement publicly. At least one white woman donated secretly five hundred dollars to the movement, and a white doctor, Eckard Johnson, encouraged his black employee, Willie Moore, to take time off to picket the courthouse and to make multiple attempts to register to vote. In Palmers Crossing, Victoria Gray drew some poor whites to the COFO/SNCC office when she allowed whites to receive aid from the welfare and relief committee. Sheriff Gray visited the homes of white recipients and ordered them not to participate. One white woman, a Mrs. Newman, defied his orders. Whites called Newman and her family "nigger lovers" and threatened them until they moved.[17]

Most local white Christians were stalwart segregationists who had never questioned the Jim Crow system. Since childhood, they had been indoctrinated in the theology purported by segregationists that God condoned segregation as the natural order. They perceived activists as sinners against God's plan. They insisted that local blacks had accepted the racial system until outsiders disturbed their thinking with their social gospel. If the activists left, they could pacify blacks. *Hattiesburg American* editors argued that the Bible did not support "ministers marching in picket lines" or removing children from school to participate in protests. Local Presbyterian ministers sought to disassociate local Presbyterians from their northern brethren by pointing out that the activist ministers belonged to the United Presbyterian Church of the USA while Hattiesburg's Presbyterian congregation affiliated with the Presbyterian Church United States, known as the southern Presbyterian Church.[18]

On February 3, when the trial of the nine ministers began, County Attorney Jimmy Dukes argued that the defendants had failed to comply with orders from law enforcement officers to move away from the main entrance of the courthouse and return to the barricaded area designated for protesting. The ministers, he declared, must obey laws like every other American citizen. Failure to enforce laws led to anarchy. Defense attorney Diane Gaylor, citing the Supreme Court decision *Edwards v. South Carolina*, countered that the ministers had the right to picket the courthouse. Judge Norris refused to peruse the precedent. She found the ministers guilty of disorderly conduct, sentenced them to the maximum penalty of four months in jail, and imposed two-hundred-dollar fines for each minister. The court released them on appeal bonds. Dukes praised Norris's ruling, noting, "God help us if we have no rules at all."[19]

Tall and pale with a crew cut and a thick accent, Dukes fit the stereotypical appearance of a redneck lawman, but he was more complicated. He never developed a hatred for blacks like some whites in his community. Rather, he expressed an abiding love for his black nanny who raised him, a black man who had taught him how to hunt and fish, and the black men he labored alongside in various working-class jobs during his summer breaks from college. Still, he was a segregationist, who accepted the "existing mores" of the time and perceived white and black activists who demonstrated in the streets as dangerous "radicals."[20] His philosophies and actions would grow more moderate. But in 1964, he used the power of his position to suppress the movement through diligent prosecution of activists.

Most local whites supported Dukes. Resident J. H. O'Kelly condemned the ministers as modern "John Browns and Henry Ward Beechers" and accused them of paying blacks to join the picket lines. O'Kelly used a well-worn paternalistic argument when he asserted that blacks knew "who their real friends are and who came to their rescue when they were victims of flood waters in Hattiesburg." He warned the ministers that they should return home to preach, or "otherwise as far as I am concerned, you also can be hanged to a sour apple tree." To advance the segregationist argument, five white Presbyterians from Forrest County traveled to Illinois to participate in a discussion at Mattoon Presbytery about the involvement of the northern Presbyterian Church in the Hattiesburg movement. At the meeting, lawyer Frank Montague Jr. and the Reverend W. J. Stanway argued that Christ had ordered the separation of political and religious affairs, and thus, the involvement of the activist ministers was unchristian. Montague praised Hattiesburg for responding to the protest in a lawful manner. He declared that neither Hattiesburg citizens nor law enforcement had prevented blacks from trying to vote and that Lynd, working under the auspices of the federal government and answering the dictates of his conscience, had registered voters without racial bias.[21]

To dispel the propaganda, the Reverend John Cameron, a black minister of Faith Baptist Tabernacle in Hattiesburg, demanded an opportunity to speak. Church authorities decided that he might only address the audience after the meeting officially adjourned since his name had not appeared on the formal program. During the postmeeting, Cameron explained that Lynd and white officials had denied black suffrage in blatant disregard of the Constitution and federal court rulings. He stressed that black citizens of Hattiesburg had invited Presbyterian ministers to help them exercise their right to vote. Across the nation, northern Presbyterian ministers responded to reports of the meeting by supporting Cameron. They emphasized their constitutional rights to assemble and petition the government. The Reverend Dr. Eugene Carson argued that as the church considered laws protecting discrimination "serious violations of the law of God," the ministers had engaged justifiably in civil disobedience. The Reverend Robert Moore declared that he and his fellow ministers had traveled to Hattiesburg "in Christian conscience to proclaim liberty to the captives."[22]

Hattiesburg authorities used the power of their courts and law enforcement agencies to expel these racial missionaries, or interlopers as they perceived them, from their lands. On March 9, white authorities persuaded the nine convicted ministers to avoid jail time by pleading no contest to disorderly conduct and by paying their forfeiture bonds and fines. In a press release, the ministers maintained their innocence but explained that the movement organizations should devote their financial resources to the protest rather than their appeal. Authorities considered the plea deal a victory, and they continued to wield the badge and the gavel to suppress the movement. On February 5, officers arrested Sandy Leigh for failing to carry his selective service card and another SNCC staff member on trumped up burglary charges.[23]

Authorities also targeted locals who joined the movement. Policemen maintained constant patrols on the courthouse demonstration. According to local protestor Earlene Boyd, everyone in the black community perceived Chief Hugh Herring as "mean and hateful." Police arrested picketer Rev. Roy Smith on charges of assault and battery when Smith bumped into an officer inadvertently. Judge Norris found Smith guilty, fined him $125, and sentenced him to thirty days in jail. Police arrested picketer Robert Armstrong for shooting with intent to kill. Armstrong had been firing an air rifle at pop bottles. After Luella Haralson became a regular picketer, police tried to intimidate her by kicking down her door.[24]

Policemen sought to diminish the involvement of children by arresting them and requiring their parents to retrieve them. Yet when police arrested Jimella Stokes along with other teenagers for picketing without a permit, Stokes spent her short stint in jail preaching about Mississippi injustices.

While her mother arranged her release with the clerk, Stokes replied to the clerk's questions with the word "yes," omitting the southern courtesy of "ma'am." The clerk barked, "Don't you say yes to me, you say yes ma'am." Stokes replied that the clerk did not deserve such respect. Terrified, Stokes's mother shoved her outside. Still, whenever Stokes's mother voiced her objections, Stokes responded, "I can't let you all stop my freedom."[25]

Many black children and parents showed similar courage. After city leaders passed an ordinance that prohibited nonadults from participating in public protests, four pre-teens, James and Anthony Harris, Horatio Jones Jr., and James Hix, picketed the courthouse in defiance of the law. Infuriated policemen "ripped the signs" from their necks and hurled them into a police car. As the driver sped toward the station, the other officer radioed headquarters and asked, "Have the dogs been fed today? ... We're bringing in fresh meat for them!" At the station, the officers forced the boys to sit on the wet cement floor in the interrogation room. One of the policemen faced the boys, tossed a blackjack between his hands, and snarled, "This is what we use to beat nigger's asses with." Suddenly, the door flew open. Diminutive Daisy Harris entered and ordered the officers to release the boys—two of whom were her children. Harris declared that they could not arrest persons for exercising their constitutional right to assemble and petition their government. To the boys' surprise, the officers released them to Harris, who transported them back to the picket line.[26]

Some locals like Lenon Woods defended their homes, businesses, and the activists whom they hosted. One night, police and firemen shined bright lights into the COFO office, aimed their guns toward the door, and ordered Sandy Leigh to come out with his hands above his head. Before Leigh could comply, he heard the "clack, clack, clack" of Lenon Woods's "Minnie Mouse shoes" descending the stairs behind him. She threw open the front door, aimed a sawed off shotgun at the firemen and policemen and shouted, "Whos' out there? Les, is that you? Now you just get to getting.... Melvin, is that you. You know I know about you. Now just get to getting." Woods continued to call out their names. She knew a little too much about everyone in Hattiesburg. So the men obeyed the skinny elderly woman.[27] As few blacks had such power, the movement needed the aid of the federal government.

To evoke national empathy and pressure the federal government to intervene, COFO and SNCC used the media. In an article published in *The Nation*, Howard Zinn described Oscar Chase's jailhouse beating as representative of the police state in Mississippi. He lambasted federal officials for hiding behind the banner of federalism to justify their apathy in the face of state "tyranny," particularly when the Constitution and federal statutes were designed to prevent the formation of "police states." SNCC and COFO also appealed to the federal government. Staff members sent detailed reports of police misconduct and judicial abuses to the Department of Justice and implored it to "enjoin police from intimidating voter registration workers." They dispatched telegrams to President Lyndon Johnson and Attorney General Robert Kennedy. In response, the Department of Justice sent a few officials to Hattiesburg to investigate. Federal pressure led local authorities to reduce some charges against activists and drop others. With these acts, they hoped to avoid mass federal encroachment while sustaining their resistance against the black revolt. It worked. Federal intervention remained minimal.[28]

Throughout Freedom Days, the Mississippi State Sovereignty Commission kept tight surveillance on the Hattiesburg demonstrations. After commission inspectors emphasized that Guyot and Rev. Cameron were significant leaders, police harassed Cameron routinely and arrested Guyot, charging him with "contributing to the delinquency of a minor." Police claimed that Guyot had encouraged thirteen-year-old Barbara Ann Thomas to participate in Freedom Days without her mother's consent. Although Thomas testified for the prosecution that Guyot had solicited her participation and requested that she recruit her classmates to the struggle, on cross-examination, she insisted that she had never met Guyot. Nevertheless, Judge William Harrelson found Guyot guilty, fined him $1,000 and sent him to jail for a month. After the conviction, COFO discovered that policemen had tried to coerce many children into making false statements against Guyot.[29]

Guyot's friend, Peter Stoner, a well-known white activist in the state, became a favorite target of police. The twenty-five-year-old had joined the movement and become a SNCC staff member while attending Tougaloo College in Jackson. When he arrived in Hattiesburg on January 7, police arrested him on charges of obstructing traffic, illegal parking, failure to carry his selective service card, and possession of narcotics. Prosecutors dropped the last two charges, found him guilty on the rest, and jailed him for six days. On many occasions, Stoner complained to the Hattiesburg Police Department that Officer James Olson had threatened picketers. After the assistant chief removed Olson from the beat, enraged officers harassed Stoner. Stoner's complaints to the FBI proved useless because agents considered him a radical. Instead of probing his accusations, agents investigated him. On February 4, when Stoner tried to visit Guyot at the Forrest County jail, jailer Print Jones ordered him to leave. Stoner declared that he had a right to see the prisoner during visiting hours. Authorities charged Stoner with disorderly conduct, disturbing the peace, and resisting arrest.[30]

Justice of the Peace John Leonard held Stoner's trial in a room behind the jail. Stoner's court-appointed attorney apologized profusely to the court for fulfilling his obligation to represent the activist. Stoner dismissed him as his counsel. County Attorney Dukes called one witness to the stand, Print Jones, who claimed that Stoner barged into the jail after visiting hours and shouted, "I God damn well *am* going to see Guyot." When Judge Leonard asked Stoner if he had any questions for the witness, he replied that as Jones lied throughout his testimony, he had nothing to ask him. Stoner declared that authorities lacked the right to try him on false pretenses and that the trial was a charade. Judge Leonard found him guilty of contempt of court, disturbing the peace, resisting arrest, and profanity. He sentenced him to 120 days in jail and fined him $391.[31]

While Stoner served his time at the Forrest County Work Camp, he suffered multiple beatings. His civil rights ideology and his sluggish work on the various county projects irritated the guard, Les Morgan. One cold workday when Morgan refused to allow Stoner to retrieve his coat, Stoner spat on the ground next to him. Morgan kicked Stoner, threatened to shoot him, and made Stoner work the entire day without his shirt. On February 17, Morgan transported Stoner to a special cell as punishment for his apathetic attitude. Fellow prisoner Bob Moss greeted Stoner by beating him. Stoner used his weekly phone call to report the beating to SNCC. When Morgan overheard the conversation, he punched Stoner, shoved him on the floor, and kicked him repeatedly. SNCC beseeched federal authorities to investigate these attacks, but to no avail.[32]

The abuse continued when authorities transported Stoner to Jackson on April 21 for his appeal. During transit, Forrest County Constable Wilmer Kitchens launched into a diatribe, denouncing blacks as an inferior race. Stoner replied that he found blacks superior to the constable. Kitchens backhanded him. While Stoner spent the night in a holding cell to await his hearing, three inmates, under orders from the jailer, yanked Stoner off of his bunk and beat him. Later that night, one of his attackers tried to rape him. Stoner fought back; the attacker broke his ribs. After Judge Sidney Mize rejected Stoner's appeal, Stoner's lawyer reported these beating to various authorities. Jimmy Dukes and Sheriff Gray promised to investigate. While transporting Stoner back to the prison camp, Dukes implied that if Stoner agreed to leave Mississippi, he would insure Stoner's release. Stoner refused. Within days, FBI agents interviewed Stoner about the beatings but appeared to move slowly on his case. Finally, when Stoner petitioned the Fifth Court of Appeals to release him on the grounds that the repeated beatings proved he was in danger, agents fully investigated his case. On May

21, Sheriff Gray released him.³³ Once again, authorities had succeeded. They incarcerated a vocal activist and facilitated his abuse out of public purview, but when the FBI pursued the case and when Stoner appealed to federal courts, they released him to mitigate federal intervention. All the while, however, radical whites were making plans that endangered the strategy of the city authorities.

Throughout the winter of 1964, radical white men gathered in the woods and in barns to form a secretive and brutal Klan to suppress the black revolt. Many whites shared the Klan's white supremacist philosophy, but some opposed its methods, particularly Governor Johnson, who perceived the Klan as a danger to Mississippi sovereignty. Surprisingly, Johnson's inaugural address, delivered the day before COFO launched Freedom Days, lacked the racial demagoguery so prevalent in his campaign. Instead, he focused on Mississippi's economic and educational development. He concluded that whether or not Mississippians liked it, they were part of America, and "hate, or prejudice, or ignorance will not lead Mississippi while I sit in the Governor's chair. I will oppose with every fiber of my being, and with every resource at my command, any man, any faction, any party, or any authority which I feel is morally wrong or constitutionally in error." After taking office, Governor Johnson notified all Mississippi Highway Patrol (MHP) officers that if they belonged to the hooded order, they must admit their membership and provide his office with their knowledge about the Klan or face termination. Many officers complied and became state informants. Others, including some officers from Laurel, cast their lot with the Klan. Johnson sustained surveillance on the recalcitrant, gathered copious intelligence on the Klan, and provided the FBI with his findings.³⁴

Although Johnson's governorship departed from the vulgar rhetoric that had symbolized his predecessor's reign, he remained as devoted to segregation and as determined to sustain it. An ever-consummate politician attuned to the shifting political climate on the national level, Johnson used, as Joseph Crespino argues, "a calculated moderation" to disempower white extremists and fill that void with pragmatic segregationists. To avoid spectacles that forced federal intervention, he planned to crush the movement nonviolently. He introduced and signed into law bills designed to prevent movement protests, launched legal battles against federal civil rights legislation, and used the MHP and the Sovereignty Commission to spy on activists. Because he also used them to spy on the Klan and cooperated fully with the FBI in Klan investigations, he inadvertently aided some civil rights goals. However, neither the governor nor the FBI proved a sudden champion of the movement and neither fully committed the resources necessary to prevent the rise of the Klan in the winter and spring of 1964.[35]

The FBI conducted its minimal investigation of the Klan out of the bureau's New Orleans office. Since the advent of the movement in the South, FBI agents had often stood at the periphery of violent clashes. They took notes as police or mobs attacked civil rights protesters. When asked to protect activists, the FBI provided the standard response that it was an "investigative" bureau, not a law-enforcement agency. Many agents working in Mississippi hailed from the South, and their empathy often lay with segregationists. Several former FBI agents worked as investigators for the Sovereignty Commission. Even Director J. Edgar Hoover objected to racial equality. When the Klan grew more violent that summer under the leadership of Sam Bowers, the FBI reacted more aggressively, but by then, stopping the violence proved much more difficult.[36]

During the winter of 1963–1964, the FBI learned that Bowers had begun his Klan life as a member of the Mississippi chapter of the Original Knights of the Ku Klux Klan of Louisiana. But he decided to form his own Klan so he could attack comprehensively civil rights uprisings in Mississippi. On February 15, 1964, two hundred Klansmen congregated at Brookhaven, Mississippi, to defect from the Original Knights, form the White Knights, and elect Bowers as the Imperial Wizard. The Original Knights maintained a presence in Mississippi. Other Klan groups developed strongholds in the state, particularly the United Klans of America (UKA), which became the largest Klan in the nation. However, Bowers, an egomaniac who considered himself the most important force against the movement, sought to wield total power over Mississippi. He struggled for control with the UKA in other parts of the state, but he sustained domination over the Central Piney Woods. The handsome, sandy-haired Klan leader had an almost delicate pretty face but for his dark, squinty eyes that hardened his appearance. Over the next several years, Bowers ordered at least nine murders and over three hundred bombings and assaults. No doubt he was, as theologian Charles Marsh describes him, "the animating force behind white Mississippi's journey into the heart of militant rage, the Kurtz at the heart of darkness of the anti–civil rights movement." His rise as Mississippi's Kurtz was deeply rooted in his self-hatred. Throughout most of his life, Bowers suffered from instability, failure, and isolation. During Bowers's directionless and lonely childhood, he grappled to find his purpose, and he craved belonging.[37]

Born on August 6, 1924, in New Orleans to Sam Bowers Sr. and Evangeline Patton Riggs, Bowers experienced an unsettled youth. His father worked briefly as a salesman; he changed occupations and state residences often. At fourteen years old, Bowers experienced further instability when his parents divorced. He tried living with his father and moved with him between New Orleans, Florida, and the Mississippi coast before settling in Jackson with his mother in 1939. Bowers had a brother and a sister, but it seems that he was the only child to live with his strict single mother. Bowers claimed to have a Methodist upbringing; however, an FBI background check revealed that Bowers's parents and siblings had attended a Catholic Church in New Orleans. Agents never located a baptismal record for Bowers.[38]

During his adolescent years and early adulthood, Bowers vacillated between bouts of intense discipline and erratic behavior. As a teenager, he and a friend broke into their school and vandalized the desks of teachers they disliked. Bowers's stint in the navy from 1941 to 1945 inculcated in him an appreciation for discipline. During the long days far from shore, Bowers enjoyed the powerful sense of a brotherhood and belonging that he had often longed for as a child. Although his nation was fighting against fascist powers, he developed an affinity for fascism. According to Bowers, the navy fostered a fascist community because it was "anticommunist," "antihumanist," and "anti-individualistic" and required sailors to place the community and discipline before themselves. In 1945, Bowers obtained an honorable discharge as machinist mate first class. Afterward he studied engineering at Tulane University and received high grades. He befriended Bus Boyd, a Bolshevik, who persuaded him to leave Tulane for the University of Southern California (USC). Later he became a rabid anticommunist. Bowers continued to study engineering, but he received poor grades because he and Boyd spent much of their time carousing. Bowers lost his way again. In the late 1940s, when his father offered to help him open a business, he returned to Mississippi.[39]

After settling in Laurel, Bowers struggled as he opened and closed one failed business after another, but he persevered. Finally, he established his moderately successful Sambo Amusement Company, a pinball machine business. In 1959, Bowers persuaded Robert Larson, a former college buddy from USC, to move to Laurel and join his business. They became roommates and business partners and ran Sambo Amusement and later Magnolia Consolidated Realty out of their residence. Some Klansmen suspected Bowers and Larson were lovers. Bowers showed no interest in dating, and the thousands of FBI files on Bowers make no mention of a female companion.[40] Bowers might have been asexual, or perhaps he embraced an ascetic devotion to his white supremacist crusade. If Bowers was gay, he kept it a secret.

During the 1940s, Bowers, under the influence of his father, Sam Sr., and his mentor, Walter Johnson, embarked upon a journey toward the inferno of white rage that would define him. Among a violent brotherhood of white radicals, Bowers found a sense of belonging that he had enjoyed in the navy. Johnson, as well as Sam Sr., explained to Bowers that good white southerners would not mistreat blacks for sport but must control them by punishing blacks who stepped out of their place. According to Bowers, Johnson joined the mob that abducted a black man jailed for killing a white man and hung him over a bridge. It is likely that Bowers was referring to the 1942 lynching of Howard Wash. Bowers joined a mob that tried to lynch Willie McGee and was disappointed that the state, rather than the mob, executed McGee. He liked the idea of Mississippi defying the federal government, and he supported "lynching of . . . niggers for these horrible crimes" because he considered such acts "part of the war on the federal government." Bowers also turned his violence inward. Plagued with bouts of depression and bursts of rage, he decided to kill himself. Yet according to Bowers, God saved him by calling him to lead a white supremacist Christian crusade. He began studying the Bible with great intensity. A voracious reader, he also immersed himself in studies of Nazism and white supremacist literature, including Thomas Dixon's *The Clansman*.[41]

Bowers struggled to tie his heritage to powerful white supremacist symbols. He boasted that his paternal grandfather, E. J. Bowers, had participated in the Confederate guerilla warfare struggle in the aftermath of the Civil War in which he lynched and exiled Yankees and scalawags. Later, E.J. became a lawyer and politician moving up the ranks of the Democratic Party as a state legislator and a congressman. Bowers's mother was from Illinois and her father, Lincoln James Riggs, a land speculator, became quite prosperous. Bowers disliked the touch of Yankee and carpetbag heritage that threatened to marginalize him, so he emphasized Riggs's marriage to a German American woman, Olive Payton of Virginia, who Bowers claimed was related to Hitler's second-in-command, Rudolph Hess. Nazis were certainly powerful symbols of white supremacist power and bolstered Bowers's sense of his re-imagined self. He had purged himself of his marginalized and purposeless past and exaggerated his white supremacist roots to set the stage for his rise as the pivotal leader in Mississippi's racial war.[42]

As the Imperial Wizard of the White Knights of the Ku Klux Klan, Bowers not only placed himself at the center of the racial war, but he cast himself as the warrior king in his white supremacist version of God's historical crusade against evil. He believed that God had called him, just as he had summoned Christian warriors in biblical days, to massacre heaven's enemies. He perceived the world in Manichean terms, locked into an epic battle since Genesis. Bowers proclaimed Anglo-Saxon Christians the force of light, and he tied his white supremacist crusade to the biblical story of Elijah the Tishbite, in which the false prophets of Canaan led Yahweh's people astray by convincing them to worship "the prophets of Baal." Elijah saved the chosen ones by forcing them to slaughter the false prophets. Bowers vowed to eradicate the persons he considered modern false prophets—Mississippi's racial "heretics"—and he pledged to save his land from the moral ruin of integration and the resulting sin of miscegenation. He identified such "heretics" in his manifesto:

> We do not accept Jews, because they reject Christ, and, through the machinations of their International Banking Cartel, are at the root-center of what we call "communism" today. We do not accept Papists, because they bow to a Roman dictator, in violation of the First Commandment, and the True American Spirit of Responsible, Individual Liberty. We do not accept Turks, Mongols, Tartars, Orientals, Negroes, nor any other person whose native background of culture is foreign to the Anglo-Saxon system of Government by responsible, FREE, Individual Citizens.

Bowers summoned white Christians to forestall a tyrannical communist coup that would place Jews or blacks in charge of America. God's Christian army—the White Knights—must destroy the forces of darkness.[43]

Bowers not only aspired to create a white supremacist army, but a polity that he dubbed the Invisible Empire because of its secrecy and power. Although many Klansmen resented Bowers's excessive control over the Invisible Empire and considered him a dictator, he tried to present himself as a democratic leader in the vein of the early American presidents, and the empire as a republic modeled after the American Constitution—or at least the parts he liked. The Klan Constitution dispersed power among three branches of government—the executive (the Imperial Wizard), the legislative (the Klongress), and the judicial (composed of five Klan Justices). It included a Bill of Rights that provided members with due process and basic liberties; it created a representative democracy in which citizens elected leaders to make decisions, and it provided a procedure for adopting amendments. Similar to America's federalism paradigm, the Klan Constitution established different levels of government: the Klan (state) level, the province (district) level, and the klavern (local) level. It divided the Realm of Mississippi into five Districts. Each local klavern had twelve officers, including the Exalted Cyclops (the President), the Klaliff (Vice President), the Kludd (the Chaplain), the Klarogo and the Klexter (inner and outer guards, respectively), and the Klokan (the Klan Investigator). The Klokan examined proposed attacks on Klan enemies. With the approval of, or under orders from the Imperial Wizard, the Exalted Cyclops oversaw projects assigned to his klavern.[44]

Bowers headquartered his Invisible Empire at his home in Laurel, an austere wood frame structure located on the south end of Fourth Avenue. He barricaded his property with eighteen-foot-high fences reinforced with thick razor wire and boarded all windows that could be seen from the streets. Poorly fed hound dogs roamed the neglected grounds littered with deteriorating pickup trucks. Behind the iron door, Bowers collected volumes of white supremacist materials and stockpiled weaponry. His Klan grew quickly over the winter and spring of 1964 with klaverns popping up all over the state. By May, nearly six thousand whites had joined the empire. Forrest County had established a klavern by the summer with particularly violent members like Mordaunt Hamilton. Jones County formed five klaverns. Early members of the Laurel Klavern included farmer and business owner Lawrence Byrd. The Ellisville Klavern included a preacher, Cecil Sessum, who became one of its most violent members and who later rose to Exalted Cyclops of the Laurel Klavern. White Knights initiated Klansmen deep in the woods before an altar where they placed their hands over a gun and sword crossed on top of a Bible. They devoted their lives to the "Holy Cause of preserving Christian Civilization," and their "Being not only to combat satan but God willing to the triumph over his malignant forces and agents here on earth." They also swore to obey their superior officers and to maintain Klan secrecy. Death was the punishment for violating the oath.[45] While the Klan prepared for its war against its civil rights enemies, authorities stymied the Hattiesburg civil rights movement with nonviolent resistance.

By mid-April, 700 local blacks had taken the voter registration exam. Around 196 registered successfully. The numbers paled in comparison to the 16,738 registered whites. To circumvent black voter registration, terminate Freedom Days, and block protests across the state, Governor Johnson signed into law an anti-picketing statute proposed by a legislator from Forrest County. The bill forbade picketing on "state property, county or municipal courthouses, city halls, office buildings, jails, or other public buildings or property owned by the State of Mississippi or any county or municipal government." After Johnson signed the bill, authorities arrested thirty-seven Freedom Day demonstrators. Picketing continued over the next few days, but it diminished with repeated arrests. On April 15, not a single picketer appeared at the courthouse. With the exceptions of Sundays, it was the first day without a demonstration since the campaign had commenced. Authorities considered the development a major victory because without deploying massive public violence, they had ended Freedom Days.[46]

White leaders also deflected an attack on segregation by John Frazier, a twenty-two-year-old black activist from J. P. Campbell College in Jackson, when he applied to the local college now renamed the University of Southern Mississippi (USM). On March 9, Frazier, accompanied by NAACP president J. C. Fairley and two white activists, arrived on campus to register. Policemen allowed only Frazier to proceed to the registration office. Administrators rejected his application and prevented a sensational scene by barring the media from campus. When police escorted Frazier and his group off campus and ordered them under threat of arrest never to return, Fairley retorted, "This is a free country. Now if we have business on that campus we will be back." Charles Kershner, the editor of the college paper, the *Student Printz*, published an article explaining Frazier's failed attempt to enroll. President William McCain ordered the confiscation of all copies. Security guards removed newspapers from the *Student Printz* office and from a staffer who was delivering them to the bookstore. Guards stopped students across campus to snatch papers from their hands and interrupted classes to seize papers from students and professors. After Frazier read a hidden copy, he wrote Kershner, noting that "the officials at your school may confiscate your paper, but they cannot confiscate your minds and your ability to think for yourselves."[47]

Authorities, activists understood, had managed to control mentalities by controlling access to information and by lying. The movement had to expose these realities to the nation. Thus, in mid-April, when the Department of Justice sought a permanent injunction against Theron Lynd, blacks flooded inside the courthouse. During the trial, the defense claimed that Lynd had complied with federal court orders. Infuriated by the lies, federal attorney John Doar snapped, "I tell this court that the Department of Justice is here because the defendant has flatly refused to register Negroes." Doar presented several black witnesses who testified that despite their ability to interpret the Mississippi Constitution, Lynd had failed them on the exams. The defense paraded educated whites before the court, including two USM professors, who claimed that Lynd had also failed them. Doar knew that these men were planted witnesses. He unveiled the charade when he elicited from his white witnesses that Lynd had registered them even though they could not read. The court withheld judgment while it reviewed the case.[48]

Nonviolent white resistance was working. Despite the Lynd case, the Freedom Day protests, and the massive registration drives across the state in the winter and spring of 1964, the establishment had kept the majority of blacks from registering. As the Southern Regional Council's Second Annual Report noted, Mississippi blacks faced greater resistance via "intimidation and violence" than in all of the other southern states combined. In two years, the Voter Education Project had only managed to add 3,871 blacks to Mississippi voter rolls, less "than the results [the total vote] of a single small city like ... Decatur, Georgia."[49]

Frustrated but undeterred, activists focused their efforts on a new campaign: Operation Freedom Summer. At a SNCC/COFO meeting in November 1963, Bob Moses and Allard Lowenstein had proposed the project in which they would recruit one thousand predominantly white college students to participate in voter registration campaigns, politicize blacks in Freedom Schools, and bring massive national visibility to the movement. The proposal initiated a heated debate. Some staffers feared that inserting whites into the movement on a massive scale would diminish indigenous black leadership. Moses and Delta activist Fannie Lou Hamer responded that segregation within the movement was hypocritical. COFO leader Dave Dennis pointed out that white America had paid scant attention to the murders and beatings of blacks, but if a white student suffered an attack while working for civil rights in Mississippi, the nation would respond. During a meeting in Hattiesburg, the staff voted in favor of the project.[50]

COFO/SNCC staffers planned two venues to attack black disfranchisement during Operation Freedom Summer. They reintroduced the Freedom Vote, a statewide election paralleling the regular Mississippi elections, to prove that eligible black voters would cast their ballots if permitted to practice their constitutional right. And they created the Mississippi Freedom Democratic Party (MFDP), which used official procedures to run civil rights candidates across the state for Congress, including Victoria Gray and Rev. Cameron. When the MFDP kicked off its campaign, Cameron pledged to fight for jobs, improved education, and black rights, and Gray argued that "Unemployment, Automation, Inadequate Housing, Healthcare, Education and Rural Development are the real issues in Mississippi, not 'State's Rights' and 'Federal Encroachment.'"[51]

After the MFDP candidates lost during the spring Democratic primaries, they tried to run as independents, but the Mississippi State Board of Elections denied their request. Determined to have an impact on the political system during the coming Freedom Summer project, the MFDP decided to send a delegation to the National Democratic Convention in Atlantic

City; MFDP delegates would try to unseat the Regular Democrats on the grounds that Regulars had violated the Fifteenth Amendment by denying Mississippi blacks their right to participate in the election. To prove their case, local blacks tried to participate in the Regular Democratic precinct, county, and state conventions. On the eve of Freedom Summer, Forrest County resident Peggy Jean Connor and seven other blacks tried to attend the precinct convention meeting at the Hattiesburg library. Chairman John Wallace refused to allow any of the black attendees but Connor to participate because the others had not paid their poll taxes. Yet the Twenty-Fourth Amendment forbade the use of poll taxes as a requirement for participation in national elections. Moreover, Wallace allowed all white attendees to participate without determining if they had paid their poll taxes. Activists used these incidents of unlawful exclusion to bolster their case in Atlantic City.[52]

The White Knights watched the rising Mississippi movement with rage. Bowers considered Operation Freedom Summer as the pivotal battle in the racial war that would "determine the fate of Christian Civilization for centuries." Before the commencement of Freedom Summer, the White Knights launched a series of assaults. On April 24, they burned crosses in towns and cities all over Mississippi. Klansmen set two crosses on fire in Hattiesburg—one in front of the Forrest County Courthouse where blacks had held their Freedom Day protest and one behind USM, likely because of the recent efforts of Frazier to desegregate it. On May 10, at 1:38 a.m., a bomb exploded at the *Laurel Leader-Call* building. It blew out several windows and damaged paper rolls but failed to destroy the intended target—the paper press. Klansmen targeted the press because publisher J. W. West was not from Laurel, and though a segregationist, he opposed violence. On June 15, Klansmen burned the auditorium of the Holy Rosary Roman Catholic Church in Hattiesburg. Hours earlier, blacks had held a meeting in the church at which they discussed Freedom Summer.[53]

In contrast to the Klan, Governor Johnson and the state legislature modeled their response plan to Freedom Summer after Hattiesburg's public nonviolent resistance and legal repression. They dubbed it the "policed freedom of movement." The director of the State Sovereignty Commission, Erle Johnston, advised people to avoid the Klan and to allow law enforcement to respond to racial activism. Commissioner of Public Safety T. B. Birdsong directed police departments to obtain riot equipment and to share intelligence across state and local agencies about their local movements. The governor, state authorities, and city officials assumed substantial powers to fight the "army of agitators" and terminate the "threatened invasion." Governor Johnson could issue police powers to the MHP to quash racial clashes.

City officials could assign curfews, restrain people's movements, raise fines, extend jail sentences during crises, and send their overflow of prisoners to the state penitentiary. To discourage federal intervention, legislators made it unlawful to file false complaints with federal authorities and punished violations with five years in prison and a $1,000 fine. The *Mississippi Free Press* rebuked Mississippi authorities for creating a "police state."[54] Actually, authorities had legalized a system that already existed.

On the other side of the battle lines, Freedom Summer planners sought to mitigate police state tactics by soliciting protection from the federal government. In early June, they held hearings in Washington, DC, at which parents of volunteers expressed their fears about the protection of their children in Mississippi. The organizers requested that President Johnson dispatch a cadre of federal marshals to the state to protect citizens, implored him to order the Department of Justice to enforce federal laws, and demanded that he meet with Governor Johnson to establish guidelines that would permit activists to exercise their constitutional rights to demonstrate peacefully and to practice freedom of association by living in interracial communities. The federal government responded apathetically.[55]

During Freedom Days, the dearth of federal intervention and the success of Hattiesburg's nonviolent public strategy allowed authorities to portray themselves as peaceful segregationists and their town as moderate on civil rights. Activists knew better. COFO described Hattiesburg as "deep-dyed conservative," noting that despite its proximity to the "moderate" gulf coast cities and the presence of a sizeable university and a strong economic foundation in commerce and manufacturing, the city "feels like a small, agrarian-oriented community." USM had sustained segregation regardless of Kennard's crusade and death and Frazier's attempts to integrate it. Lynd continued to evade court orders to terminate voting discrimination practices. As of June 9, only 15 percent of blacks who had sought to register to vote in Forrest County had succeeded. Still, activists were optimistic. Hattiesburg had become one of the "largest and most active" SNCC/COFO projects in Mississippi, with a powerful core of locals participating. The Freedom Day demonstration, which turned into a nearly three-month protest, made Hattiesburg the center of the Mississippi movement. While nonviolent white resistance had stymied registration and picketing, it also allowed COFO to organize the city with two MFDP candidates, 100 block captains, fifteen citizenship teachers, and numerous protesters. Several ministers opened their churches to Freedom Sumer activities, and residents offered housing for 110 volunteers.[56] COFO determined to make Freedom Summer the decisive battle.

CHAPTER 4

Operation Freedom Summer

ON A SWELTERING JULY DAY IN 1964, TWELVE-YEAR-OLD LARRY MCGILL stifled his fear as he followed five black teenagers into the S. H. Kress department store in downtown Laurel and strode toward the "whites-only" lunch counter. White customers stared angrily at the black youths, as if daring them to stage a sit-in here in the heart of Klan country. McGill tried to calm himself by focusing on his training: if they beat you, curl into the "freedom knot" to protect your head and vital organs. He had practiced the knot many times at the COFO house. He tried to be brave, but he was the youngest of the group. It was his first protest. As McGill and the others approached the counter, the black server "eyeballed" them to warn them away. The young activists ignored her as they quietly arranged themselves on the stools. Within a few minutes, a white man ordered them to leave, but the oldest protestor, shot back, "Leave or what?"[1]

Suddenly, ten Klansmen, armed with baseball bats, rushed from the back of the restaurant toward them. McGill froze. Klansmen yanked his friends off their stools and bludgeoned them with bats. One Klansmen stabbed fourteen-year-old Jessie Arrington. McGill forgot his training; rather than balling into the freedom knot, he rushed for the door sobbing; but a Klansman caught him and started punching him. When McGill wrestled free, another Klansman blocked his path, slammed his bat down against McGill's back, and sneered, "Get out of here you little black monkey and don't come back." As McGill burst outside, downtown Laurel descended into "chaos." Blacks congregated on one side of the street, and whites on the other. Amidst the mayhem, McGill's fear morphed into humiliation. At the precipice of puberty, McGill coveted masculinity. He was ashamed that he had run. Determined to prove his manhood, he organized another sit-in at the store. Throughout July, hundreds of locals launched, as whites perceived it, invasions of whites-only territory in the massive sit-in campaign that exploded across the Central Piney Woods.[2]

Months before the sit-ins, SNCC and COFO had developed two missions for Freedom Summer—mobilize locals into an enduring movement force and compel Washington, DC, to dismantle the white supremacist state. To transform more black locals into freedom fighters with the ability to assume the full reins of the movement, the organizers planned a two-pronged approach. They would persuade adults to participate in registration drives, the Freedom Vote, and the MFDP, which would challenge the white monopoly on power at the Democratic Convention in Atlantic City, and they would establish Freedom Schools to decolonize the minds of black youths and channel them toward revolutionary thinking. To force a federal alliance with the movement, the organizers incorporated nearly one thousand mostly white volunteers into their ranks. They knew that if whites became the victims of violence, the media would give the Mississippi movement the visibility it needed. Their plans laid the groundwork for Freedom Summer to become a significant turning point.[3]

The volunteers brought immediate attention to Mississippi. Descended from the Greatest Generation, the mostly white volunteers understood abstractly the dangers that they would confront in Mississippi, and they prepared to sacrifice, as their parents had in a time of war. Yet they fought their battles inside their own nation as peaceful soldiers armed solely with a belief in the equality of humankind, romantic idealism about the efficacy of their activist generation, an abiding faith in their ability to transform America, and disciplined devotion to nonviolent direct action. Most of the volunteers were politically progressive white college students from elite universities and privileged backgrounds who perceived the Civil Rights Revolution as the moral battle of their era. Volunteer Joseph Ellin found himself drawn to the passionate black community whose love and "intensity" rendered his middle-class experience vapid and "bloodless," and he hoped that by fighting injustice, he would infuse his life with greater value. White guilt and a moral imperative to battle oppression motivated Terry Shaw. Her parents taught her about the evils of racism, which inspired her to join the NAACP at Antioch College in Ohio. David Owen, motivated by his juvenile thirst for adventure and his "social conscience," chose Mississippi over the Peace Corps, despite his parents' protestations, because he could no longer sit among the apathetic white masses while dictatorial oppression existed in his country.[4]

During the last two weeks of June, Owen, Shaw, and Ellin and hundreds of other volunteers converged on Oberlin College in Ohio for Freedom Summer orientation. Although Shaw found many parallels between the

Mississippi project and "a military operation," the Freedom Summer boot camp taught volunteers nothing of weaponry and killing. Rather, as peace soldiers, they acquired training in nonviolent opposition. Veteran activists taught the volunteers how to protect their "vital organs" when attacked and how to respond to the gathering of a mob. They also repeated the rules in the COFO "Security Handbook" until they became mantras: never reveal the address of your host; never congregate in doorways or porches; never sleep near windows; and never travel alone or at night or without informing the COFO office. The veterans struggled to divest the volunteers of their perilous naiveté before they sent them off to battle. Through the intense training, the volunteers became more deeply aware of the dangers that they would soon confront and the sacrifices that they must make to achieve radical structural changes in America. As the session came to a conclusion, the veterans inculcated both vigilance and morale in their new troops, for they perceived the summer as a decisive battle in the racial war. As one COFO worker declared, "The danger now is greater than it ever has been—and so is our hope."[5]

Klansmen were fully prepared to destroy that hope and attack the "invaders" when they began arriving in Mississippi in late June. On June 7, three hundred White Knights flocked to a statewide meeting at the abandoned Old Boykin Methodist Church in Smith County, located some seventy miles north of Hattiesburg. Klan leaders, fearing that law enforcement or other uninvited interlopers might spy on the meeting, implemented intense security measures. Two planes circled above the church while sentries conducted ground watches below. Bowers and his top echelon feared most the Klansmen among them who might be informants. Armed guards prohibited Klansmen from leaving the church until the meeting concluded, and leaders warned that they would punish treason with execution. At least one informant stood among his fellow Klansmen that day, a member of the Laurel Klavern, known in FBI circles as 1257-R. He listened as Sam Bowers ordered Klansmen to track the movements and actions of activists and wait for them to violate Mississippi laws. Such crimes, Bowers declared, empowered Klansmen with the "right to kill them." As of early June, the White Knights had ninety-seven projects planned. During a meeting of the Laurel Klavern, Lawrence Byrd ordered Klansmen, including 1257-R, to find addresses of those locals hosting volunteers and plan drive-by ambushes. No one—not the volunteers, nor the veteran activists, nor the local insurrectionists—would escape unscathed, and some would never escape at all.[6]

On June 21, the terror of Freedom Summer commenced over one hundred miles northeast of the Central Piney Woods when three civil rights workers investigating a church burning in Neshoba County vanished. The case would have generated little attention if James Chaney, a black CORE staff member from nearby Meridian, had been the only man to disappear. Two of the missing men, however, were middle-class whites from New York—Michael Schwerner, a CORE staff member working in the state since January, and Andrew Goodman, a Freedom Summer volunteer who had arrived in Mississippi the day before. The nation reacted with outrage. In response, President Johnson ordered former Central Intelligence Agency director Allen Dulles and director of the FBI J. Edgar Hoover to solve the Neshoba case and received assurances from Governor Johnson that he would cooperate with the investigation. Hoover reestablished an FBI office in Jackson and flooded Neshoba County with agents. President Johnson sent Hoover to Jackson on *Air Force One* to communicate the significance of the Mississippi mission.[7]

To the frustration of activists, Hoover reiterated the long-standing Bureau policy toward the movement. The FBI, "purely an investigative agency," had one task: investigate MIBURN (Mississippi burning) as Hoover called the Neshoba disappearances. Agents must solve a missing persons case, not dismantle Jim Crow. At the least, the disappearances advanced two goals of Operation Freedom Summer: it forced federal intervention, albeit narrow in scope, and it elicited mass media attention. But those developments also insulted many activists. SNCC leader John Lewis noted, "It is a shame that national outrage is aroused only after two white boys go missing." Most Mississippi whites also reacted with indignation. Publisher of the *Laurel Leader-Call* Jay West accused the "invaders," as he called visiting activists, of staging the disappearances to instigate the reversal of Mississippi's racial order. The black beast myth so ingrained in the white Mississippi mind led many whites to perceive Freedom Summer as a part of a grand strategy designed by depraved black males to force a black coup and deliver them the spoils of war, particularly white women. Whites disagreed on how to protect their homeland from the so-called invasion. A Hattiesburg reporter implored whites to support Governor Johnson's policed freedom of movement modeled after Hattiesburg's response to Freedom Days because it avoided sensational media attention and sapped the movement of its strength. The White Knights had other ideas. Klansmen gathered intelligence and developed targets by circling the COFO office and following canvassers in black neighborhoods.[8]

Volunteers grew accustomed to living with fear, just as they adapted to impoverished housing standards. As volunteers drove across the railroad tracks into Black Hattiesburg, they were shocked. Joseph Ellin described it as "a middle-income slum." The quarters lacked street lights, sewers, and drainage systems. Railroad crossings had not a single gate, signal, or bell. Chickens and roosters roamed the streets. Volunteers found Palmers Crossing worse. Three miles outside of the Hub City, the decaying village featured dilapidated homes, churches, a school, and a smattering of businesses all sandwiched between a sawmill on one side and small farms on the other. As few homes had indoor plumbing, volunteers grew familiar with sponge baths and chamber pots. Across the Central Piney Woods, volunteers treaded carefully on rotting porches and among the army of insects, including the "fleets" of mice-sized cockroaches.[9]

Black residents viewed their communities quite differently. Although they resented the city's failure to appropriate equal funding for their public services and roads, they adored their vibrant, tidy neighborhoods. Their bustling business centers on Mobile Street in Hattiesburg and on Front Street in Laurel filled them with pride. They took great care of their homes and gardens, always tending to them and helping their neighbors. Their communities operated like a communal village, and they boasted of their good schools and lovely churches. They had much to teach the volunteers who hailed from communities many of them would have considered austere and detached and who knew nothing of the pride earned by collectively surviving hardships. Freedom School student Cheryl Outlaw recalled that the volunteers taught blacks how to confront the white supremacist state. In return, blacks, who were "survivors," taught the volunteers how to endure the struggle by drawing strength from their close-knit communities that fostered psychic protection from white onslaughts."[10]

Despite the racial and class divides, most blacks welcomed the volunteers by opening their homes, businesses, and lives to these strangers. Some hosts, including Daisy Harris, had participated in the struggle since Freedom Days; some, like Vernon Dahmer, had participated in the struggle for nearly two decades; and for others, their involvement began by becoming hosts that summer. Local activists hoped that the volunteers would help change the tide of the struggle. A host in Palmers Crossing, Mrs. McCullim, had tried unsuccessfully to register five times. She told volunteer Jinny Glass, "We was sure waiting for you." Outlaw adored the volunteers who stayed with her relatives in Hattiesburg because, "it was like they came to our rescue."[11]

Freedom Summer expanded the breadth of local participation tremendously. Arthur Siggers, a teenager that summer, later recalled, "Nearly everybody [in Hattiesburg] was involved in the Movement ... whether openly or clandestinely everybody wanted something better." Siggers's mother, a domestic in white homes, and Jeanette Smith, the wife of a physician, were two of hundreds of locals who fed the volunteers. Blacks like Mrs. Siggers who worked for whites often had to remain in the background to keep their jobs and feed their families. Women like Smith, whose husband depended on black patients for his family's livelihood, took on more public responsibilities, including signing property bonds to bail activists out of jail. Blacks of all classes donated their money to the struggle. During a mass meeting at True Light Baptist Church, the minister asked congregants for donations to house and feed volunteers, whom he described as "angels unawares." The parishioners gave all that they could. Participation was not absolute; many blacks remained outside of the movement for fear of losing their jobs or facing violent repercussions.[12]

In Jones County, volunteers faced great obstacles as COFO, SNCC, and CORE had made few inroads into the area and lacked a strong home base. At the commencement of the summer, organizers had not found blacks in Laurel willing to host volunteers, so volunteers assigned to the Central Piney Woods stayed in Hattiesburg. After a few days, SNCC leaders sent three black activists to Laurel: Lester McKinnie, a SNCC field secretary who had been arrested in 1962 for trying to desegregate a restaurant in the Laurel bus station; Gwendolyn Robinson, a Spellman student; and Jimmy Garrett, a college student from Los Angeles. SNCC staff directed them to operate in a clandestine manner because Laurel was a dangerous town, certainly too dangerous for SNCC to send whites. Robinson found the special protection of whites irritating. The staff had focused on recruiting whites to serve in Mississippi that summer precisely because white America failed to "value black life." Nevertheless, Robinson pursued her assignment vigorously. The threesome visited Susie Ruffin first as they had learned that she was heavily involved with the NAACP. Ruffin sent them to Eberta Spinks.[13]

When Spinks opened the door to Robinson and learned that she was a COFO volunteer, she said, "Girl, I've been waiting on you all my life." From the moment Robinson met Spinks, the Laurel project took flight. Spinks's three-bedroom house became a buzz of activity as dozens of volunteers overflowed from the beds and couches to sleeping bags on the floor. Whenever activists grew discouraged or frightened by white retaliation, Spinks recalled, "We sat here and sang freedom songs 'till we almost got happy." They needed the comfort of solidarity, for they faced retaliation often. Soon after their arrival, McKinney disappeared. With the aid of local black ministers, Robinson learned that police had arrested McKinney on charges of fleeing his 1962 bond. A COFO lawyer secured his release on the condition that McKinney would never return to the county. SNCC appointed

Robinson as project director. Although she had never led a project, she learned quickly. She found housing for twenty-three volunteers, many of whom were white men from Ivy League colleges. Some of them harbored paternalistic mentalities and despised the idea of working under a black woman. They had to change their attitudes because Robinson was not easily intimidated. She called the Laurel struggle the Amazon project.[14]

Robinson confronted many challenges in expanding the Laurel movement. According to local black teenager Jerome Wyatt, most black professionals who worked "inside the system" and blacks working directly under whites avoided the movement because they feared economic repercussions. Still, Robinson and her team managed to draw new recruits to the struggle, including children like Johnny Magee, even though his mother, a maid, had forbidden him to participate in any form of activism. In midsummer, COFO sent Marion Davidson, a white Hattiesburg volunteer, to Laurel to help Robinson establish a permanent COFO office. A minister opened his church to the activists but then expelled them, likely because of white pressure. When the Laurel activists moved their operations to a trailer, Mayor A. S. Scott facilitated their eviction. Finally, a wealthy black realtor rented to COFO a home large enough to house an office, a residence for workers, a library, a community center, and a freedom schoolhouse. The Laurel Project had a base.[15]

In Forrest County, the COFO office located on Hattiesburg's Mobile Street served as the brain center of the movement from which staff and volunteers coordinated and recorded all of the activities occurring in the field, schools, and community centers. Volunteer Terry Shaw worked as the communications coordinator responsible for gathering intelligence, managing the office, keeping activity records, providing law clerk services, and fostering public relations. Shaw also communicated with the FBI, the Department of Justice, local police, and the media. Frequently, she worked fifteen hours a day in the frantic office that overflowed with activists.[16]

The voter registration project became the heart of Operation Freedom Summer. Black suffrage remained the great hope for change. Hattiesburg Project Director Sandy Leigh divided sixteen voter registration volunteers into four groups of canvassers composed of one captain and three team members to work in four precincts—Palmers Crossing, the Library Precinct, Walthall, and Buton. Each volunteer paired off with local recruits, a cleric from the Hattiesburg Minister's Project, and block captains established during Freedom Days. As the summer progressed, COFO expanded voter canvassing to Laurel. Six days a week, canvassers spread out across the main arteries of black communities in Forrest and Jones Counties, and for eight hours a day, they trudged across dusty roads in the thick heat from home to home, imploring locals to register to vote. They also encouraged locals to register in the Freedom Book and participate in the MFDP election of delegates to the National Democratic Convention in Atlantic City in August.[17]

Several canvassers found their work frustrating. As they moved into neighborhoods and backcountry homes untouched by the movement, blacks expressed interest in Freedom Summer, but fear of reprisals deterred many of them from participating. During his first day of canvassing, Owen handed a man a flyer advertising a mass meeting. Although the man pretended to read it, Owen noticed that he was holding it upside down. He also grew despondent as he watched the terror spread over the faces of black children when he drew near. They never looked him in the eye and called him "sir" even though he asked them to use his first name. Owen felt alienated from the world that he had come to change. Joseph Ellin decided that local blacks lacked the education to understand their oppression and, thus, the will to fight it. This view reflected racial, regional, and socioeconomic divides that caused some volunteers to perceive themselves as saviors, and they arrived in Mississippi with a "missionary" zeal reminiscent of the paternalistic racism that they strove to destroy.[18]

The Freedom Summer project could not in such a short time span produce a utopian community void of the racism, elitism, sexism, and regional prejudices so prevalent in America. According to Hattiesburg volunteer Shelia Michaels, women were the core of the movement; however, as men often took credit for their work, public narratives cast males as the lead actors and women in supporting roles. The movement also suffered from ideological divides, with many northern whites viewing the struggle through the lens of Marxism and northern blacks perceiving it through tripartite theories of Marxism, black nationalism, and the Social Gospel; although southern blacks embraced the Social Gospel, for the spiritual concept was deeply rooted in their history, they often disdained Marxism and divided over black nationalism. These ideological divides led to a series of debates over the ultimate effects of integration. Some Marxists argued that integration required acceptance of the bourgeois state, which would lead to the uplift of the black middle class and to the alienation of the black poor. Others disagreed that capitalism caused racism. Many activists and volunteers refrained from voicing publicly their frustrations over the various fractures that emerged within their beloved community because they feared that criticizing the movement meant betraying it.[19]

Still, these clashes, combined with struggles that volunteers experienced in Mississippi, produced vital shifts in mentalities. As the largely middle- and upper-class white volunteers moved into a southern black world, many confronted their racial prejudices and restructured their perceptions. They discovered that because many blacks viewed whites with suspicion, blacks played the accommodationist roles that had allowed them to survive the white supremacist state. A teacher in Laurel, Gladys Austin, refused to speak with the volunteers because she feared that local whites might observe the interaction. Austin had joined the NAACP, but she kept her membership a secret because the state forbade teachers from joining the organization. NAACP president Benjamin Murph protected the identity of members who wanted to remain anonymous. He sneaked to their backdoors at night to collect NAACP dues so that no one would tie them to the movement. Conversely, SNCC's and COFO's interracial groups of volunteers strode to their front doors in daylight. Volunteers had only to survive the summer. Locals would have to endure the repercussions long after the volunteers departed. Owen learned these lessons when COFO sent him to Laurel. Because Laurel volunteers had less access to vehicles, Owen spent many nights playing cards with locals, afternoon breaks tossing a football with children, and Sundays attending church. In these activities, he saw the struggle from the perspective of local blacks. Soon, he along with many other volunteers realized that most local blacks, regardless of their education or literacy, possessed extensive knowledge about the political system and their powerlessness as disfranchised persons, and they harbored a deep desire to vote. But some were afraid.[20]

Heartened by their new understanding, volunteers inspired each other and locals by infusing the tedious canvassing work with symbols of inspiration. Since Palmers Crossing lacked street signs, the canvassers created their own. They named the center road "Freedom Street" and the major street that intersected it "Now Street." They used names of black celebrities and black activists to identify various roads, and they named three small roads that converged in one corner of Palmers Crossing "Schwerner," "Chaney," and "Goodman" after the freedom fighters who had vanished in Neshoba County. When they met people who had tried to register to vote, they recruited them as block captains. They also informed residents about the Freedom Schools and community centers.[21]

A SNCC field secretary, twenty-three-year-old Charlie Cobb, designed Freedom Schools to decolonize the minds of the black youth and to foster indigenous movement leadership. He intended to transform Jim Crow children into freedom children by inculcating in students, through free and critical thinking, a desire to unshackle themselves from the yoke of intellectual darkness and physical oppression. The white-controlled school boards had long insured that textbooks and curriculums excluded black achievement, exalted whites as the master race, and socialized blacks to accept subjugation. Some districts prohibited mention of Reconstruction. Freedom Schools became the inverse of Mississippi's black public schools. The curriculum exposed white supremacist concepts as myths and moved students toward self-realization by teaching them the history of black resistance. Freedom Schools were the soul of the movement, particularly in Hattiesburg, the "Mecca of the Freedom School World." The organizers expected seven hundred children to participate in the entire state. On the first day of registration, six hundred students arrived in Hattiesburg alone, and registration increased steadily over the summer. Blacks of all ages also flocked to the community centers, which housed libraries and offered classes in sewing, arts and crafts, public health, and literacy.[22]

In the first few Freedom School sessions, students and teachers, both a little in awe of each other, crossed racial boundaries constructed centuries before their existence. Students like Cheryl Outlaw and Glenda Funchess had learned to distrust, if not fear, and dislike whites. When Outlaw first stared up at volunteers Lawrence Spears and David Owen, who entered her church, she was not sure how to respond to them. She had grown up believing that "whites didn't like blacks." Owen and Spears dispelled some of her fears when they hugged Willie Moore, Outlaw's grandmother. Funchess experienced a similar epiphany with her teachers Dick Kelly and Paula Pace when she noticed that they considered blacks their "equal[s]." Kelly, Pace, Owen, and Spears dined, worked, socialized, worshipped, and slept in the black community. Through these actions, which expressed the volunteers' faith in the equality and dignity of humans regardless of race, volunteers gained the trust of locals.[23]

Throughout the summer, in church attics and basements and in community centers stacked with books written by or about African Americans, children embarked upon great intellectual journeys of discovery; they learned of the kingdoms and empires in Africa as bastions of intellectual and economic power. Studies of slave revolts, of black protests against Jim Crow, and of black intellectuals, leaders, and businessmen, who—with very little opportunity—had achieved great success, inspired them. Students Larry McGill and Johnny Magee had never seen so many books. They became voracious readers, each sentence opening their minds to worlds of knowledge so long barred to them. As students achieved a new understanding of their oppression, teachers guided them to explore the world of their oppressors. Teachers explained that white elites had created white supremacist myths in the interest of exploiting black labor for greater white profit.

These myths also helped them sustain control over politics by disfranchising blacks and by focusing the attention of poor whites on racial hatred rather than on class oppression. By keeping the poor divided by race, elites preempted an interracial class revolt. Through laws and wealth, white elites determined who had access to jobs, loans, good schools, decent living conditions, and justice and preserved the white supremacist state. In such a state, only one political party could survive. If more than one existed, debate ensued, which caused the monolithic support of the system to crumble. Throughout Jim Crow, elites feared the education of the masses because knowledge inspired revolts.

The volunteers had come to Mississippi to help inspire that revolt. Thus, teachers provided students with the knowledge and tools to challenge racial myths and rebel against their oppressors. They employed a didactic pedagogy and used sociodrama methodologies rather than lectures because questioning and debating led to greater participation, free thinking, and active listening and inculcated in students a sense of a collective purpose and empowerment—all necessary qualities to facilitate intellectual enlightenment, self-realization, and transformation. Joseph Ellin led his students at Priest Creek Baptist Church in Palmers Crossing to create a congressional committee to investigate how the American political system could change Mississippi. Teachers at True Light Baptist Church Freedom School staged mock precinct and county elections. In Sandra Adickes's class, students reenacted a betrayal of a slave revolt as a cathartic exercise to express their outrage at the compliant adults in their community. Years later, activist Daisy Harris noted the most important lesson that her three sons learned in Freedom School: "we're level with other people" and could achieve greatness.[24]

Teachers also helped students transform from pupil to activist by bringing them onto the movement battlegrounds. Canvassing became one of the most important activities for students because it politicized them and because they recruited many adults to the struggle. But they faced setbacks. Some blacks shouted at the students, "Get out of here, y'all gonna get killed." Jimella Stokes, already a veteran activist who had participated in the Freedom Day protests, grew frustrated with her parents, who tried to curb her activism. As Stokes told Adickes, "I'm always fighting for my parents' freedom so I won't be worried about my children's freedom." Students like Stokes obtained the skills necessary to sustain the black revolt once the volunteers departed. Experience in public speaking, public relations, community development, and political organization cultivated student activism.[25]

Students also flocked to the nightly mass meetings with staff, volunteers, and locals that bound them in a collective spirit against the absolutist state.

In the packed churches, activists shared their experiences, announced the latest protest, delivered inspiring speeches, and joined their voices in songs like "This Little Light of Mine" and "Oh Freedom." Each song, drawn from the gospel music so deeply ingrained in black church life, bound blacks and whites in a single purpose—to know the earthly freedom that God endowed upon every human being. Victoria Gray's eleven-year-old niece, Lillie Jackson, savored these meetings. She was filled with pride at the sight of "a church full, just flowing all outside . . . all the black people . . . talking about what we want." Meetings always closed with everyone crossing arms and grasping the hands of their neighbors to sing, "We Shall Overcome." And then, as Daisy Harris recalled, "the fear was just gone."[26]

But fear sometimes paralyzed the struggle. Although as the summer progressed, blacks joined the movement at a steady pace, as of July 19, only twenty-one thousand blacks and a few whites had signed MFDP registration forms. The figure, far short of the two hundred thousand registration goal, could harm the MFDP's argument that blacks would participate in the political process if permitted. Bob Moses directed COFO to focus the majority of its efforts on MFDP registration, on attempted attendance at precinct and district conventions, and mass participation at MFDP's parallel conventions. Victoria Gray devoted herself to the MFDP challenge. White authorities resisted her efforts by providing false information about the date, time, and location of meetings or by refusing to allow blacks to attend. Gray used these incidents to prove that the white establishment denied blacks their constitutional rights to participate in the political process.[27]

Activists even dared to recruit local whites to their ranks, because if they could draw white progressives into the struggle, then they could begin breaking the racial divide that sustained Jim Crow. To that end, the co-coordinators of the Hattiesburg Minister's Project, white Presbyterian minister Robert Beech and local black minister Rev. John Cameron, recruited a few white sympathizers. In general, they confronted substantial resistance from whites. Beech's fellow parishioners at the Westminster Church forced the pastor to expel him. Mordaunt Hamilton, a Klansman who owned a local hardware store, refused to sell Beech a ladder and punched him. Although police charged Hamilton with assault, Judge Norris dismissed the case.[28]

Klan violence exploded in the Central Piney Woods in late June. Around midnight on June 28, a red pickup truck circled the COFO house; the passenger, wielding a rifle, shot into a crowd of blacks but failed to hit anyone. Prior to the summer, only two FBI agents covered the Central Piney Woods. The bureau increased the number to eight by the end of June. Although agents took a detailed report of the attack, which included a description of the truck, no arrests followed. Days later, a black fourteen-year-old, James Smith, rushed into the COFO office and shouted that white men had abducted a black man. Terry Shaw, a volunteer who ran the office, contacted the FBI. The next morning a Hattiesburg police lieutenant summoned Shaw to his office where he informed her that the alleged abductors were "just niggers" playing a joke. Shaw learned otherwise. Several blacks witnessed the abduction, but only Smith signed an official witness statement. Officers took Smith to the police station, where they demanded that he accuse COFO of fabricating the incident. When Smith refused to pedal their lies, officers threatened to take his mother off the welfare rolls. As the FBI neglected to investigate, the case passed into oblivion like so many others. FBI apathy encouraged white supremacists.[29]

Racial hostility intensified after July 2, when President Johnson signed the Civil Rights Act of 1964, which outlawed voting and employment discrimination and prohibited segregation in public facilities, including schools. Governor Johnson implored white citizens to disobey the law until he could test its constitutionality in court. The Forrest County Citizens Council condemned the act as the most oppressive bill since Reconstruction, demanded that white customers leave the counters when blacks sat next to them, and insisted that police use trespassing and disorderly conduct laws to remove black patrons. *Hattiesburg American* reporter Elliott Chaze encouraged whites to express their resistance by refusing to celebrate Independence Day. The Klan expressed its disapproval with terror. After midnight on July 3, a truck hovered near the Greasy Spoon restaurant in Jones County. Within minutes, an explosion blew out all of the restaurant's windows, destroyed the juke box, and damaged the roof. Most whites across the state protested the Civil Rights Act as Chaze had suggested by refusing to celebrate Independence Day.[30]

In contrast, blacks cherished the day. Volunteers, staff, and locals gathered for a Fourth of July picnic on the Dahmer farm where Vernon and Ellie and three of the eight Dahmer children resided in a brick ranch-style home upon a hill overlooking their cotton fields. The Dahmers and their guests celebrated with "explosive joy," singing, chatting, and feasting on "catfish deep-fried in large dome-bottom iron pots." The celebration stopped when a muddy truck drove slowly by the farm. Dahmer and one of his sons retrieved rifles and rushed toward the fence where they knelt in firing positions. The truck passed again, but faster this time. Later, one of the COFO directors informed Dahmer that activists adhered to nonviolence. In a courteous but unyielding manner, Dahmer replied that he would protect his family from "those rednecks who had been terrorizing [them] for a long time." The nuances of the movement and of racial relations began to take shape for many volunteers that day. Dahmer appeared white, owned a farm, several businesses, and a lovely home, but his miniscule black heritage rendered him a member of the oppressed race. Thus, he lacked the power that usually accompanied economic advantage as he remained disfranchised and under the perpetual threat of white assaults. He responded to threats with self-defense, a seeming contradiction of the movement's nonviolent strategy. Soon, volunteers learned that most black Mississippians advocated self-defense and used nonviolence as a tactic, not a way of life.[31]

Most white volunteers were also surprised when local blacks led the charge in testing the Civil Rights Act. Many locals initiated sit-ins without asking organizers or volunteers to join. In early July, Peggy Jean Connor sat down at Owl Drug Store's white-only lunch counter in Hattiesburg. White customers and the staff bolted from their seats and stations. A local white shoe salesman snarled, "Don't you know you're not wanted here?" Connor found his rage almost humorous, for he had on many occasions knelt at her feet to sell her shoes but disdained the notion of eating next to her. When the store owner informed Connor that he refused to serve "Negroes," she sued him for violating a congressional act. Eventually, she won the case.[32]

Black teenagers led the majority of the sit-in protests that summer. In mid-July, six blacks from the NAACP Youth Council and COFO, including eighteen-year-old Garvin Hughes, twelve-year-old Larry McGill, and fourteen-year-old Jessie Arrington, tried to integrate the lunch counter at the Kress department store in Laurel. They informed police and FBI agents of their plans but received no protection. During the melee, in which Klansmen beat them with baseball bats and stabbed Arrington, Chief L. C. Nix watched. Afterward, Nix arrested one of the perpetrators but released him on a twenty-five-dollar bond. He also arrested a black man for saying "G--- d---" and charged him the same bond. That afternoon, when a black man tried to integrate the lunch counter, a group of whites attacked him while police watched. When the defendant in the Kress beatings failed to appear at his trial, the judge dropped the case.[33]

White attacks only fueled black protest. One group of black teenagers decided to integrate the Burger Chef, located on Cook Avenue, the main artery running through the heart of the poorest black section of Laurel, the KC Bottom, without seeking backing from the established movement organizations. Blacks could purchase food at the back window but could not dine inside. Blacks considered the existence of a segregated establishment in their neighborhood a grave insult. When a group of well-dressed black protesters entered the Burger Chef, a group of whites threatened to attack them. Some black adults arrived and threatened to throw bottles unless whites allowed the black teenagers their right to enter the restaurant. Suddenly, hordes of white men, brandishing knives, razor blades, and irons pipes, attacked the teenagers. Police ignored several calls about the confrontations because the callers, out of fear, refused to leave their names.[34]

After word of the attack spread, furious black teenagers across Laurel rushed to the Burger Chef. Police on the scene ordered them to leave. Several teenagers, including Jerome Wyatt, obeyed. Wyatt's parents, both teachers, had ordered him to stay away from the movement, for they feared that they might lose their jobs and face violent repercussions. Other blacks reacted with violent fury. Charles Coleman stabbed a white man, Harrell Stringer. Charles Jordan, wielded a shotgun and threatened to shoot whites. Policemen arrested Coleman and Jordan, but they did not arrest the white perpetrators who attacked black teenagers. Enraged by the biased treatment, groups of blacks retaliated by throwing rocks at whites who drove through the KC Bottom. When a twenty-year-old black man, James Lee Buckley, hurled rocks and bottles at vehicles occupied by white passengers and injured a woman and her baby, authorities charged him with assault and battery with attempt to maim. During these violent conflicts in the Central Piney Woods, urban rebellions exploded in Harlem, Rochester, and Philadelphia.[35]

Surprisingly, Jones County courts did not subject blacks to the usual severity of the Jim Crow judicial system. Prosecutors never indicted Jordon for wielding a shotgun. In September, a grand jury indicted Coleman and Buckley for assault and battery with intent. In early October, Buckley pled guilty, and the court sentenced him to one year in jail. Judge Lunford Casey suspended ten months of the sentence and released him on two years of probation. Although jurors found Coleman guilty of the stabbing, they requested mercy in sentencing. Judge Casey imposed a one-year suspended sentence, placed him on probation, and fined him $750. The *Laurel Leader-Call* referred to Coleman's sentence as "light" but neglected to mention that police refused to arrest a single white person. Likely, white authorities delivered lighter sentences because they feared that if they subjected black defendants to stern punishment while failing to even arrest whites who had assaulted blacks during the protests, they would invite federal investigations.[36]

Hattiesburg teens who led sit-ins also confronted racial injustices and brutality. On July 6, when around twenty black teenagers tried to integrate the By-Pass Inn, a white woman aimed a pistol at the group and ordered them to leave. They complied in a peaceful manner, but police arrested ten of them later that night on false charges of hurling bricks and overturning a vehicle. At the police station, officers forced one of the teenagers into a separate room, ordered him to sit on the desk, and turned out the lights. In the dark, they asked him who led the protest. When he replied that he did not know, one officer punched him in the stomach and called him a liar and a "nigger" while other officers chastised him for acting like a "bad nigger" on the streets but a frightened coward in their custody. When he responded that he "wasn't afraid," four officers took turns punching him. After the beating, they ordered him to "get his black ass out" of the station. With COFO's urging, the Department of Justice filed a police brutality complaint with the FBI, but agents never took any action on the case.[37]

Police harassment and brutality proved a constant form of oppression in the Central Piney Woods. Constables Wilmer Kitchens and Constable Frederick Humphrey earned reputations for "shaking down" black club owners and beating blacks for sport. One night in June, Kitchens made the mistake of assaulting Cloudies Shinall, a young black man with no ties to the movement. When Shinall and his girlfriend stepped out of Bama Madison's pub, Kitchens ordered two lawmen to throw Shinall into his vehicle. The men hurled Shinall face first toward Kitchen's car. When Shinall struggled to his hands and knees, the lawmen beat him. Shinall's girlfriend screamed for Madison to help, but she was helpless against white officers. Shinall fought back. During the struggle he knocked off Kitchen's eyeglasses. In the moment of shock that followed, Shinall wrestled free and fled into the woods. Kitchens and his men pursued him. Shotgun blasts echoed across the landscape.[38]

As Shinall ran from certain death, his mother, Lee Mae, sat up with her daughters canning vegetables and waiting for her son to come home. She had just decided to retire when two white men banged on her door. They demanded to see Cloudies. He's not home, she told them, but they raided her house and searched for him. "You sure he hasn't been here[?]" one of the men asked. Her eyes fell across the blood splatters on their clothing. She insisted that she had not seen her son. One of the men strode out her front door and jumped off the porch. She could hear him talking to someone; she rushed outside. "Oh, it's you Mr. Kitchens . . . what happened . . . is Cloudies into something?" she asked. Kitchens snapped, "He just acted Damn negro" and continued searching around the house. Finding no one, he turned to the others and said, "Well the son of a bitch ain't here" and informed Lee Mae Shinall that "if [Cloudies] don't come you'll find him somewhere because I put a hole in his head you can put an axe in."[39]

Soon after Kitchens and his men departed, Shinall came home in the arms of his friends. His right eye was so swollen it seemed to protrude from his socket; his lips were puffy and bleeding; and blood gushed from a wide laceration in the middle of his head. Shinall would never forget the beating that he had suffered. Blacks in Palmers Crossing whispered of the other reason that drove Shinall's determination to exact vengeance. Kitchens had a reputation for taking advantage of black women; over two years later, a black woman accused him and several white men of gang-raping her; and rumors abounded that Kitchens raped Shinall's girlfriend.[40]

Yet Kitchens believed that blacks adored him. He remarked to a black woman, "You know I'm your friend. Why, if you niggers had to vote, I'd be sheriff." On one occasion, he stopped a vehicle occupied by five white male volunteers and a black female volunteer, Lorne Cress. At first, Kitchens failed to notice Cress. He ordered the driver, Morty Malvain, to present his driver's license and shouted, "If you say anything I'm going to kill you." He proceeded to the passenger side where he called Stan Zibulsky a "beak-nosed motherfucker" and slapped him. When he saw Cress in the backseat, he yelled, "What are you letting them do . . . suck your pussy? Get out of that car." Cress froze. After a horrid silence, Kitchens morphed into her protector. "I don't want to see you again in this car with them," he cautioned. "If you need anything, you just come to me." He followed them to Victoria Gray's home before driving away. COFO complained about Kitchens to Sheriff W. G. Gray. The sheriff did nothing.[41]

Authorities also failed to act against Klan violence. On July 10, Klansmen in a cream pickup truck with no license plate followed white volunteers David Owen, Lawrence Spears, and Rabbi Arthur Lelyveld and two black women, Marjorie Hyatt and Janet Crosby, as they strolled along the railroad tracks toward the Morning Star Baptist Church. Suddenly, the driver swerved his truck in front of the group. In full view of white residents sitting on the porches of their homes near the tracks, the Klansmen, wielding iron pipes, descended upon the truck and rushed toward the activists. The taller, younger Klansman smashed his pipe against Spears's shoulders, face, and head. Spears crouched to the ground and curled into the protective position. As the Klansman kicked and punched him repeatedly, he called him a "nigger lover," "white nigger," "Commie," and "Jew." He grabbed Spears's papers and tried to shove them into his mouth, all while shouting in his face, "Eat this shit nigger lover," and "Get up and run nigger." The older and shorter but more solidly built Klansman, shouting "white niggers" and "Commie," swung his pipe across the back of Owen's head before Owen could protect himself. Lelyveld, lacking in-depth training in nonviolent protection, suffered the most. The Klansman whipped the pipe across the rabbi's face several times, smacked it across his chest and back until

Lelyveld fell to his knees, and struck it across his head. Having completed their mission, the Klansmen returned to their truck. Lelyveld lay prostrate on the ground. Blood poured from multiple lacerations on his head and body. Contusions formed on his chest, arms, and face. As Owen rose to his feet, blood gushed from the back of his head, turning his blond hair red. Not one of the white residents who had witnessed the attack from their porches called the police.[42]

When the activists reported the attack, Chief Hugh Herring promised that if police found the men, he would charge them with "assault and battery with intent to kill." But he did nothing. However, as Lelyveld was one of the most prominent rabbis in the nation, the FBI, under intense pressure from northern Jews, worked the case, which led to arrests in late July. Police charged forty-eight-year-old Clifton Archer Keys and his thirty-one-year-old nephew Kilmer Estus Keys with "assault and battery with intent to maim" rather than attempted murder as Herring had pledged. District Attorney Jimmy Finch promised to prosecute the men "in good faith" and thus deterred a federal prosecution of the Klansmen on civil rights violations. During the August 3 grand jury hearing, Finch insisted that Lelyveld provoked the attack by embracing the black girls before the men assaulted them. Lelyveld replied that no such embrace had occurred. When Finch demanded Spears identify his host family, Spears asked if he could consult a lawyer before releasing their names. Finch shouted, "No! Boy, you realize that you *may* be liable for contempt of the proceedings?" Hyatt infuriated Finch when she requested that he address her as Miss Hyatt rather than "Marge." Finch snapped, "I don't give a God Damn what your name is." After the hearing, Finch gave the Klansmen a spectacular deal: he charged them with simple assault, a misdemeanor, fined them five hundred dollars, and sentenced them to ninety days hard labor, which the judge suspended.[43]

The FBI's apathetic response to nearly every case but the Neshoba disappearances encouraged violence. Over one hundred agents swarmed Neshoba County, infiltrating its towns and backwoods to recruit informants and interrogate suspects. During the search for Schwerner, Chaney, and Goodman, teams found three black bodies in the Mississippi River. One of the men was clothed in a CORE T-shirt, but as soon as agents realized that he was not Chaney, they made no efforts to identify him. Agents identified the other corpses as Charlie Eddie Moore and Henry Hezekiah Dee. Only a handful of agents and local police investigated these murders. The Neshoba investigation remained the only prominent federal case in Mississippi that summer, which left local law enforcement and court officials free to ignore scores of other racial crimes.[44]

Mississippi judges also encouraged lawlessness by dismissing civil rights cases. During the Freedom Days campaign, Hattiesburg civil rights activists filed a lawsuit challenging the state bill that denied demonstrators their constitutional right to picket in front of entrances to public buildings. In late July, Justices Harold Cox, Sidney Mize, and Richard Rives dismissed the lawsuit, contending that there was "no evidence or testimony to show it was the intent . . . of the legislature . . . to suppress, deter or in any manner impinge upon . . . any constitutional right of the plaintiffs to free speech, assembly and the right to petition for redress of grievances." In another case, COFO accused the Klan, the Citizens Council, the Americans for the Preservation of the White Race, and law enforcement of preventing blacks from exercising their constitutional rights through legislation and terrorism. Judge Mize dismissed the case. Soon afterward, on August 4, FBI agents found the bodies of Schwerner, Goodman, and Chaney buried in an earthen dam in Neshoba County. Clearly, the Klan was impinging upon the rights of blacks through terrorism. In the wake of the funeral in Neshoba, despair gripped activists.[45]

Yet these setbacks and tragedies also galvanized locals. In mid-August, Jimella Stokes led five students and their teacher, Sandra Adickes, to the all-white public library in Hattiesburg. Stokes chose the library instead of a restaurant because "it was the house of knowledge. . . . I wasn't going to learn anything to go sit next to a white person in a restaurant." When they arrived and asked for library cards, the "eyes [of the clerks and librarians] nearly bolted from their sockets." The librarian responded that she could not comply with their request. Stokes shot back, "Who told you that, the Whites Citizens Council or the Ku Klux Klan . . . who told you that you couldn't serve us?" When she failed to provide a response, Stokes declared, "If we can't use the library, then nobody else should." Stokes and her group sat down and read magazines. The supervisor alerted the police. Chief Herring ordered the library closed under orders from Mayor Claude Pittman. A few days later, several volunteers and students staged another sit-in at the library. Police shut down the library indefinitely. It was at least a partial victory, for as Stokes had demanded, if blacks could not use the library then neither could whites. Activists also achieved a partial victory in their MFDP challenge in Atlantic City.[46]

The MFDP challenge served as the boldest national campaign of the Mississippi movement. In the Central Piney Woods and across the state, the challenge politicized locals, achieving a core goal of Freedom Summer. Hattiesburg leader Victoria Gray served as national chairwoman. MFDP workers held parallel precinct, county, and state conventions at which delegates selected sixty-eight persons to attend the National Democratic Convention in Atlantic City, including six persons from Forrest County—Helen Anderson, J. C. Fairley, J. W. Brown, and Marie Blalock as delegates and Pinkie Hall and George Harper as alternates—and one delegate from Jones County, Robert Stenson. At the end of August in Atlantic City, the delegates challenged the seating of the Regular Democrats on the grounds that they had used voter discrimination and terror to exclude blacks from the political process. President Johnson was sympathetic to their plight, but he feared losing the southern vote. Despite powerful testimony by legendary figures in the movement, including Martin Luther King Jr. and Fannie Lou Hamer, the Credentials Committee, under pressure from President Johnson, refused to unseat the Regulars. Instead, the committee offered the MFDP two at-large seats.[47]

Some powerful civil rights leaders, including Dr. King and Bayard Rustin, and significant white allies, including Senator Wayne Morse and Joseph Rauh, encouraged the delegates to accept the compromise. They confronted resistance from many of the delegates, particularly three women, Victoria Gray, Fannie Lou Hamer, and Annie Devine, who beseeched the delegates to reject the compromise. Gray declared that the people of Mississippi had risked their lives to support this challenge and expected it to "make a difference. Two seats at-large aren't going to make a difference. So I'm not going back to the people and lie." After similar speeches by Devine and Hamer, the delegates rejected the compromise and left Atlantic City demoralized by the betrayal. Still, it proved a partial victory. It had politicized thousands of black Mississippians, and it drove many of the leading participants, including Gray, to develop new methods to challenge the white ruling class. The MFDP members, though devastated, were not defeated. Over the next several years, the MFDP remained a vital vehicle for black political empowerment in the Central Piney Woods and across the state. Moreover, most of the official Mississippi delegates considered the Democratic Party's recognition of the MFDP as an attack on Jim Crow and left their seats vacant. Governor Johnson and the majority of Mississippi whites ended the summer with a defection to the Republican Party.[48]

The Klan closed the summer with violence. On August 24, Brewell Curie hosted a farewell picnic for volunteers at his farm in Jones County. Volunteers, activists, and freedom students, including Larry McGill, spent the day swimming in Curie's pond and enjoying a picnic. In the evening, they gathered on the banks and sang folk songs. At dusk, Klansmen Cecil Sessum and Pat Dickerson, wielding chains and wooden clubs, emerged from the woods and approached the party. They asked the guitarist, volunteer David

Gelfand, if he knew "Dixie." When Gelfand tried to play it, Sessum grabbed the guitar, heaved it into the pond, and beat him. Thirteen Klansmen "charged out of the woods" brandishing chains, clubs, and guns. Activists ran. Some plunged into the pond and swam toward the farmhouse. Klansmen fired bullets into the water. As activists reached the house, they flung themselves upon the floor to avoid the bullets piercing the windows and splintering the walls. Curie's son grabbed his gun, and shot at the Klansmen. Finally, all of the volunteers escaped inside the house except Gelfand. V. L. Lee pummeled Gelfand until repeated gunfire from the Curie home forced him and his brethren to flee.[49]

Activists contacted federal and local law enforcement immediately. It took the sheriff and his deputies an hour to arrive even though the station was a fifteen-minute drive from the farm. Two hours passed before FBI agents responded. Sheriff Deputy R. W. McMinn claimed that he investigated the incident with great thoroughness, but COFO activists insisted otherwise. McMinn had not even searched the crime scene.[50] The violent conclusion to the summer proved an ominous introduction to the bloody battles to follow, but it also reflected the success of Freedom Summer as local blacks demanded justice.

Throughout Freedom Summer in the Central Piney Woods, the meshing of black and white, indigenous and visitor, the unfree and the free cultivated the local movement into an inexorable force with the strength to outlast the departure of the organizers and the volunteers. The summer had certainly achieved Cobb's goal, for it had transformed many Jim Crow children into freedom children. Student Glenda Funchess perceived Freedom Summer as "a training ground to prepare us to go to the next level." Jimella Stokes considered the summer pivotal to the struggle, for it caused the circle of local black activism to grow exponentially. The night before volunteer Jinny Glass departed, her host, Mrs. McCullim, informed her that Lynd had turned her away that afternoon, but she would try again. Freedom Summer had emboldened her, for as she told Glass, "Now we've seen. Now, there's no turning back." Activists like Daisy Harris, who had become involved in the movement five months prior to the arrival of the volunteers, deemed Freedom Summer a new watershed in the struggle: "The summer opened the doors. Physically and mentally, it opened doors. . . . [We] walked through those doors" and assumed control of the movement. Stokes proclaimed, "I knew that whatever happened, it would never go back. It would never be the same, after the summer."[51]

In late August, as the majority of volunteers prepared to leave Mississippi behind, most of them considered Operation Freedom Summer successful.

Joseph Ellin concluded that activists had fulfilled the mission to organize the black community, to teach locals how to attack Jim Crow, and to help them confront the white supremacist system. Terry Shaw reflected that the volunteers left

> with a great deal of faith in the strength and capabilities of Hattiesburg's Negroes, but a pessimistic view of the obstacles they face. With a knowledge that we have accomplished something during 'freedom summer,' but a feeling that we should have accomplished a lot more. With a combined feeling of hate and love for that beautiful state of Mississippi with the twisted mind, and with a constant ache in our hearts for the fact that such a trivial thing as race has poisoned the spirit of every American citizen and left wounds that will not be healed for many years.[52]

Operation Freedom Summer had not altered instantly the sociopolitical structure of the Central Piney Woods or Mississippi, but it proved even more pivotal to the movement than many believed at the time. Most immediately, the Klan attacks on white activists provided the movement with the national visibility it needed to accelerate federal intervention. Although the FBI investigation in Neshoba County had yet to produce any arrests or temper Klan violence, and the reality that America responded more aggressively to attacks on whites than blacks spread disillusionment among activists, the discovery of the bodies intensified the FBI response. In September, Hoover ordered Special Agent in Charge of Mississippi Roy Moore to implement the FBI's counterintelligence program (COINTELPRO) "to expose, disrupt and otherwise neutralize the activities of the various klans and hate organizations, their leadership and adherents." With that order, Hoover transformed the FBI's mission from an investigation of a missing persons case to a declared war on the Klan.[53]

The electrifying local black protests proved the most enduring and vital development. The Civil Rights Act had yet to force integration, but it allowed blacks to occupy legally the once "whites only" public spaces with sit-ins and to build desegregation cases. Although whites wielded the totality of their power to repel, as they saw it, the black invasion, their violence only intensified black activism. As the national media delivered images into living rooms across America of white adults beating nonviolent black teenagers and children, they exposed violent whites as depraved beasts and peaceful blacks as civilized freedom fighters. The 1963 Children's Crusade in Birmingham had a similar impact when policemen released their dogs on student protesters and firemen assaulted children with fire hoses. The civil rights morality play was working across the South, for these reversals of racial images challenged centuries of racial mythologies and jarred the American conscience. As important, the sit-ins helped shift the local movement from an attack on disfranchisement led by a cadre of veteran activists to a massive local black assault on Jim Crow's white world. In the decade to follow, as the presence of COFO and SNCC staff and volunteers diminished in the Central Piney Woods, black residents fought segregationists on every battlefield, determined to win the war.[54]

CHAPTER 5

Wars of Attrition

"NIGGER, YOU ARE GOING TO GET KILLED," THE KLANSMAN SHOUTED through the phone. The calls came frequently to the Dahmers' home. Many late nights, Klansmen drove slowly by the secluded farmhouse. The Dahmers had begun sleeping in shifts so at least one of them would be prepared to respond quickly if the White Knights attacked. Ellie always answered the door when someone knocked because she believed even a Klansman would not kill a woman. If working into the night, Dahmer carried a gun, and he stopped his cotton picker and switched off the lights whenever a car approached. The Dahmers had reason to worry. Klansmen had placed Vernon on their enemy list. When Freedom Summer ended and the exodus of the majority of the volunteers began, most whites hoped that the local struggle would dissipate. Instead, local blacks reassumed control of the Laurel and Hattiesburg movements. Dahmer remained involved, though he stayed in the background at first. Toward the end of 1965, Dahmer reemerged as a significant leader in Forrest County. Bowers moved him to the top of the Klan's hit list.[1]

Both the white establishment and the Klan sought to crush the movement by launching a war of attrition against it. By persistently attacking it, they hoped to squeeze the life out of the struggle and weaken the will of the federal government; if their plans worked, the federal government would abandon blacks as it had deserted them during Reconstruction. They differed only in their tactics. Whereas the establishment relied on the powerful arm of its police state and its legal and political power, the Klan accelerated its terrorist campaign. Authorities responded in an ambivalent manner to Klansmen. Radicals encouraged attacks on activists. Moderates blamed the Klan as much as they blamed the activists for bringing Washington, DC, into their counties. Eventually, moderates began to cooperate with federal authorities to diminish Klan power and to punish some whites for crimes against blacks. But they moved in that direction slowly and sporadically and thus failed to hinder the explosion of Klan violence that spiraled toward its zenith over the next eighteen months.

Activists fought a war of attrition as well, but from a defensive position of protracted warfare. They could not achieve a decisive battle that would suddenly obliterate Jim Crow. Victory depended on their will to insure the movement's persistence. Their struggle was one of survival and tenacity. Although often unnerved and frustrated by the series of assaults from Klansmen and authorities, activists determined that as long as they stayed the course, they could win. Attritional tactics combined with localization of movement leadership served as the key strategies. The COFO/SNCC activists and the twenty-two summer volunteers who decided to remain in the Central Piney Woods that fall agreed that Freedom Days and Freedom Summer had achieved a significant goal—the empowerment of local people, and they worked toward continuing that trend. COFO promoted local resident Doug Smith from youth coordinator to Hattiesburg project director and to director of COFO projects in the Fifth Congressional District. Hattiesburg native Victoria Gray, ever committed to the MFDP despite its failure to unseat the regular Democrats at the convention in Atlantic City, focused on obtaining black political power. Gray also continued to foster local activism, often working with Freedom School students who viewed the summer of 1964 as their "rite of passage." Under Gray's tutelage, Jimella Stokes became a full-time voter registration worker. When freedom children returned to their high schools, they convinced many of their teachers to approach the once-forbidden topics of black protest and to facilitate open discussions on the movement. These developments assured the movement's longevity.[2]

Yet at the close of Freedom Summer, the local movement's survival seemed precarious, particularly as activists disagreed over future strategies and faced continued backlashes. Throughout the summer, the movement mission centered on obtaining the vote, political power, desegregation, and racial justice. However, some activists began to incorporate a mission to achieve all of those liberties and opportunities that historian Hasa Kwame Jeffries calls "freedom rights." Such rights span a broad gamut and include constitutional guarantees of civil liberties, freedom of movement, due process, and political participation; the right to economic and educational opportunities; and the right to choose one's profession, romantic involvements, friendships, family planning, and housing. To sustain a united mission, Smith requested that activists compose position papers. A registered nurse, who ran the health and welfare program, argued that COFO should organize the movement around the local people's needs, including Freedom

Schools, community centers, and health organizations. Some activists complained about the resulting moratorium on direct action because it stifled local activism. The Civil Rights Act meant little if whites failed to comply with it. Many activists insisted that the movement focus on black suffrage. Yet others worried that if the sensation of Freedom Summer faded into laborious voter registration projects, the dull work would diminish the people's passion and the nation's interest. All of them worried about violence.³

On August 29, some six hundred people gathered around the Jones County Courthouse to witness the trial of V. L. Lee, the Klansman charged with beating David Gelfand at the Freedom Summer farewell picnic a week earlier. Once a mob formed, the court, facing a potentially explosive situation in the streets, postponed the trial. Authorities never tried Lee for the crime. In early September, eighteen-year-old black activist Luther Collins and three of his friends defied the moratorium on direct action protests and sat at the front of a Hattiesburg city bus to test the Civil Rights Act signed two months earlier by President Lyndon Johnson. The driver held a gun to Collins's head and ordered him to move to the colored section. Collins and his friends exited the bus rather than suffer the continued indignities of segregation. The failure of the judicial system to punish white violence encouraged it.⁴

The Mississippi movement lost its momentum that fall as it faced continual setbacks, still suffered deep wounds from the disappointment in Atlantic City, and lost the media attention it enjoyed in the summer. MFDP activists struggled to revive enthusiasm by running five candidates—Victoria Gray, Aaron Henry, Annie Devine, Harold Roby, and Fannie Lou Hamer—for Congress. They confronted nearly overwhelming obstacles. The Mississippi State Board of Elections had refused to place the candidates on the official state ballot, and Secretary of State Herbert Ladner denied the MFDP's appeal. So the MFDP focused on the parallel Freedom Vote election held between October 31 and November 2 in which all eligible voters could cast ballots for the Regular Democrats or the MFDP. Hundreds of activists worked the freedom polls, but because of white violence and intimidation, only sixty thousand voters participated across the state, over 25 percent less than the previous year. The MFDP used white harassment as the basis for challenging the congressional seats of the Regular Democrats. Their zeal notwithstanding, these setbacks harmed morale.⁵

Klan activities also waned because of FBI pressure. When the UKA launched a bombing campaign in McComb in September, the FBI worked with local law enforcement and arrested three Klansmen. Thirty-six miles away in Meadville on November 6, FBI agents and the MHP arrested two members of the White Knights, James Ford Seale and Charles Marcus Edwards, for the murders of Henry Hezekia Dee and Charles Eddie Moore, whose corpses had turned up in a bayou during the search for the Neshoba activists. But authorities neglected to prosecute them for decades. Although a jury in McComb convicted several of the UKA Klan bombers, Judge W. H. Watkins released them on probation. Some Klansmen wanted to respond by murdering federal officials and Klan informants. Bowers considered such a reaction foolish. He warned Klansmen that anyone arrested after executing an unapproved project would have to pay their own legal fees. At a meeting on November 15, he proposed a moratorium on violence for ninety days commencing on December 1. Despite some opposition, it passed.[6]

Before the moratorium took effect, Klansmen in Laurel executed a project against Otis Matthews, financial secretary of the local International Woodworkers union. After the passage of the Civil Rights Act, Matthews attempted to integrate facilities at the Klan-infested Masonite plant in Laurel. At 9:00 p.m. on November 16, Billy Boyd, Henry DeBoxtel, Tommy Thornton, Billy Roy Pitts, and a hefty Klansman known by his ironic nickname—Tiny—abducted Matthews, transported him to a dead-end road, and dragged him out of the vehicle. DeBoxtel yanked down Matthews's pants and forced him to lie face down on the ground. He held his pistol to the back of Matthew's head and informed him, "We [are] the White Knights of the Ku Klux Klan . . . [and] we [are] going to whip [your] ass because [you are] trying to integrate the showers. . . ." Tiny, wielding a Black Annie—a thick leather strap with holes in it—stepped forward to deliver the emasculating lesson. Using all the strength of his 200-pound body, he lashed Matthews fifteen times. Boyd poured horse liniment on Matthews's torn flesh. DeBoxtel warned him that if he reported the incident, they would kill him. Matthews defied their orders.[7]

In response to the assault, as well as a failed attempt by Klansmen to abduct Matthews two days later, sixteen local union officers released a statement in the *Laurel Leader-Call* notifying the Klan that "fear of verbal denouncement, physical assault or even death [will never] deter us from following a reasonable, practical, sound course." They encouraged union members to arm themselves and warned that if Klansmen "wish to turn our community into an armed camp, disregard law and order and soak our soil in blood, we are prepared to help them." In a public harangue, Sheriff Merrill Pickering promised to punish Matthews's attackers "to the full extent of the law." The sheriff made no arrests.[8]

Yet the tide began to turn against the Klan on January 15, 1965, when a federal grand jury handed down indictments against Bowers and seventeen other Klansmen in the Neshoba case for violating the civil rights of Michael Schwerner, James Chaney, and Andrew Goodman. Two of the participants, Doyle Barnett and James Jordan, confessed and became witnesses for the prosecution. Bowers ordered the collection of all Klan fund-raising jugs kept in stores and restaurants. Many Klansmen suspected that he planned to use all funds for his own defense. Forrest County Klansman Mordaunt Hamilton threatened to beat him. Some Klansmen maligned Bowers as a communist. One Klansman castigated him as a "thieving queer." Rumors spread that Bowers had a gay lover, his roommate and business partner, Robert Larson. Bowers fought back. He accused his detractors of becoming FBI informants and expelled some of them. Still, Bowers realized that to maintain control over his Invisible Empire, he had to make concessions. Thus, he pledged a more equitable distribution of funds and reinstated one expelled Klansman. He had quashed an internal revolt, but he confronted a rising tide of state support for the FBI's war against the Klan.[9]

During the late fall and winter, the white establishment remained committed to sustaining white supremacy, but it grew increasingly concerned that Klan violence might imperil Jim Crow as much as civil rights activism. Consequently, pragmatic segregationists struggled to improve their relationship with the federal government. The director of the Mississippi State Sovereignty Commission, Erle Johnston, convinced the Mississippi Sheriffs' Association that to minimize federal intervention, it must solve its criminal cases. On December 8, the association pledged to support FBI investigations. State legislators passed a bill that provided greater powers to the MHP to sustain law and order. Still, most white citizens remained as resistant to black liberation as ever. On November 4, Mississippi—along with the rest of the Deep South—voted for Republican presidential candidate Barry Goldwater because he supported states' rights. In Mississippi, Goldwater defeated Lyndon Johnson 354,459 to 52,538 votes. Forrest County voters favored Goldwater by a 9 to 1 margin and Jones County voters by 6 to 1. Still, Johnson won the presidency in a landslide.[10]

Frustrated but undefeated, white officials turned to the courts. To avoid compliance with *Brown* and the Civil Rights Act, Mississippi officials encouraged school boards to file lawsuits. Section VI of the Civil Rights Act prevented the federal government from denying federal funds to schools involved in desegregation litigation. If white officials lacked the power to stop integration, they could stall its implementation. Governor Johnson persisted in his fight against the desegregation of public accommodations by supporting an Atlanta case challenging the Civil Rights Act in the US Supreme Court. On December 14, the justices unanimously affirmed its constitutionality.¹¹ Although the court's decision doomed public segregation, the law proved meaningless until blacks integrated whites-only facilities.

Determined to enforce compliance with the act, activists across the Central Piney Woods ended the moratorium on direct action protests and launched a series of sit-ins that winter. Their efforts breathed life back into their war of attrition against Jim Crow, but it also ignited the rage of police, white mobs, and the Klan. In mid-December, activists from Laurel and Hattiesburg staged a sit-in at the Travel Inn restaurant in Jones County. The attorney for the Travel Inn, Paul Swartzfager, who had prosecuted Howard Wash, Willie McGee, and Davis Knight, provided local policemen with warrants to arrest the activists. Policemen dragged the protesters out of the restaurant, across the street, and up two flights of stairs to the police station. Authorities charged all of the protesters with breach of peace and two with resisting arrest. In late December, five COFO workers and fifteen locals, including Eberta Spinks, staged a sit-in at the Pinehurst Coffee Shop owned by Swartzfager. When the manager threatened to have them arrested, Spinks responded, "It looks like to me the more you serve, the more money you'd make here and you'd be glad to serve anybody." Police arrested all of the demonstrators.¹²

To protest the unlawful detention of their compatriots, twelve activists gathered in front of the jailhouse on Christmas Day where they lit candles, knelt in prayer, and sang freedom songs and Christmas carols. Police officers shouted, "The Klan is coming." One officer kicked them repeatedly. Another officer drove his vehicle toward them, slamming on his breaks just before hitting them. A crowd of whites surrounded the protesters; one of them shouted, "If I had a shotgun, I'd shoot them damn niggers." Police arrested the activists. On January 14, when fifteen local blacks tried to register to vote in Laurel, a crowd of white men gathered outside the courthouse. As Ed Dubinksy, a white professor from Tulane University accompanying local blacks, exited the courthouse, two white men knocked him to the ground and kicked him repeatedly. Sheriff Pickering, who after the Klan beating of union leader Otis Matthews had promised to preserve law and order, shouted, "Attta boy, get 'em, get 'em." Although Dubinksy never tried to defend himself, officers arrested him.¹³

Violence also exploded that winter in Hattiesburg. On January 21, four white volunteers, in hopes of gathering intelligence on white supremacists, attended a Citizens Council meeting at the Forrest County Courthouse. Halfway through the meeting, a council member recognized them. He and his associates beat the volunteers. Police neglected to make any arrests. Several days later, twenty activists staged a sit-in at Lea's Restaurant. When the owner contacted Mayor Claude Pittman and policemen, they informed him that he had to comply with the Civil Rights Act. Instead, some thirty white men beat the protesters. A few days later, fifteen activists, including two white volunteers, Joseph Schwarz and Richard Kelly, and local black teenager Robert Abrams, returned to Lea's, but the manager refused to serve them. The group remained for an hour until Klansman Mordaunt Hamilton strolled toward the activists and hit Schwarz in the head so hard that he knocked him off of his chair. The group fled; Hamilton followed. He beat Kelly and Abrams. Later that day, when a black busboy with no ties to the movement arrived at Lea's to start his shift, a white man punched him. All of Lea's black employees quit. Although police arrested Hamilton for the beatings, the judge found him not guilty. Hamilton stalked proudly out of the courtroom. When he saw Schwarz, who had just testified against him, he beat him along with his two companions. The court failed to convict Hamilton on any of his numerous battery charges. COFO and SNCC staffers included these incidents in reports to the Department of Justice, which they hoped would help the MFDP's latest project.[14]

On January 4, 1965, Victoria Gray and four other MFDP candidates launched the Congressional Challenge in which they requested that Congress seat them rather than the Regular Democrats. Since Mississippi registrars had refused to register black voters who had not paid their poll taxes, a requirement for state, not federal elections, they had violated the law. Moreover, they delayed certification of black voters to prevent their participation. Thus, the congressmen were elected illegally. Conversely, Freedom Vote registrars allowed all eligible voters to cast ballots. Congress gave the MFDP nine months to hold hearings and collect supporting evidence before presenting its case to the House Subcommittee on Elections in September. In the spring, 150 MFDP-retained lawyers held hearings across the state at which they took depositions from 400 witnesses and generated 10,000 pages of testimony.[15]

Throughout the hearings in the Central Piney Woods, witnesses proved that Forrest County registrar Theron Lynd refused to comply with court orders to register black applicants and that Jones County registrar Leonard Caves had declared publicly that he would never register any blacks connected with the movement. Caves denied the accusations as well as insinuations that he belonged to the Klan or the Citizens Council. He even claimed that "to my knowledge we don't have a Ku Klux Klan." Throughout the hearings, locals, staff, and volunteers testified that mobs, the Klan, and police subjected them to intimidation and beatings when they tried to register, engaged in political activities, and participated in civil rights protests.[16]

The US Civil Rights Commission bolstered the MFDP's findings that spring when it held investigative hearings in Jackson. Commission investigators and one hundred Mississippians, including several Central Piney Woods residents, testified. Investigators stressed that some of the most shocking incidents had occurred in the Central Piney Woods. In Forrest County, after two Klansmen brutalized Rabbi Arthur Lelyveld, Lawrence Spears, and David Owen, local prosecutors staged a rigged trial designed to interrogate the victims and free their assailants. In Jones County, Klansmen had beaten Larry McGill and his fellow sit-in protesters and stabbed Jessie Arrington while Chief of Police L. C. Nix watched. When investigators called Chief Nix to the stand, he described the attack as "routine" and "just an assault." Additionally, he admitted that in December 1964, he had arrested a group of activists who had staged a sit-in at the Pinehurst Coffee Shop. When the commission asked him if he understood that he had made an oath to protect the Constitution and enforce the laws of the land, he insisted that his job required him to enforce state and local laws, not integration rulings.[17]

Pragmatic segregationists mobilized to undermine the commission and MFDP hearings. Governor Johnson led a contingent of officials before the commission to correct the MFDP "lies," tell the real "Mississippi story," and deny that the state discriminated against black citizens. During the MFDP hearings, Senator James O. Eastland, employing his usual red-baiting tactics, accused twenty MFDP lawyers of affiliation with the Communist Party. In the Central Piney Woods, elites fought fiercely to protect their favored son, Congressman William Colmer, from the MFDP challenge. Many lawyers involved in helping Colmer supported white supremacist causes, including E. K. Collins (who had prosecuted Willie McGee), former Laurel mayor Carroll Gartin (who had fought to insure McGee's execution), Jimmy Finch (who had framed Clyde Kennard), and Harold Melvin and Leonard Melvin Jr. (who later defended a Jones County Klansman in a murder trial). Yet some lawyers on the case were, or became, racial moderates. Quitman Ross had defended Davis Knight in his miscegenation case and Charles Pickering and Judge W. O. Dillard became important forces against the Klan.[18]

During these hearings, activism flourished and Klan violence exploded. In Hattiesburg on February 23, the NAACP launched dozens of tests of the Civil Rights Act. Blacks applied for cards at the Hattiesburg Public Library, desegregated Kamper Park and a local motel, and staged sit-ins at fourteen restaurants. At one restaurant, when white servers refused to wait on the group, a black kitchen worker served the delegation. The well-planned protests were the largest Hattiesburg sit-ins to date, and they occurred without violent reprisals or arrests. Activists also continued to stage sit-ins across Laurel. These demonstrations chipped away at Jim Crow's foundations. The Klan responded with a massive resurgence of violence. On February 9, Klansmen fired shots into the SNCC/COFO office in Laurel. A week later, they firebombed the office, demolishing the structure and destroying two thousand library books, a mimeograph machine, and office records. On March 5, the Klan firebombed the home of Brewell Curie because during the Klan attack on the Freedom Summer farewell picnic the previous August, his son had shot back at the Klansmen. Bowers's moratorium on violence was over.[19]

The resumption of Klan violence combined with the Civil Rights Commission and MFDP hearings, which attested to the persistence of voter discrimination in defiance of the federal rulings in the Lynd case, revealed the necessity of comprehensive federal intervention. When the voting rights protest in Selma, Alabama, that March became mired in beatings and murders, it forced the federal government to act. On March 15, President Johnson implored Congress to pass the Voting Rights Act to strike down barriers to black suffrage and to send federal registrars into intransigent southern districts to prevent discrimination. The Lynd case had set a federal precedent forbidding voter discrimination, but persistent appeals had allowed Lynd and registrars across the South to evade the ruling. Johnson concluded his speech by declaring that blacks "have awakened the conscience of this nation ... to injustice ... their cause must be our cause too. Because it's not just Negroes, but really it's all of us, who must overcome the crippling legacy of bigotry and injustice. And we shall overcome." Although many activists applauded his stance and his articulation of the movement mantra—we shall overcome—progressives across the nation demanded stronger federal action. A *New York Post* journalist argued that since Mississippi and Alabama had abdicated control to terrorists, the federal government must develop a "federal police force to deal with violations of civil rights."[20]

In response to the increasing racial liberalism of the national Democratic Party, white Mississippians continued to defect to the Republican Party. On June 8, Hattiesburg elected its first Republican mayor, Paul E. Grady. But their change in loyalties could not stem the national tide toward reform. On June 16, 1965, the Fifth Circuit Court justices delivered a watershed ruling on Lynd's appeal. They ordered Lynd to review 350 rejected applicants and register persons meeting the registration requirements, to assist all prospective voters with the application process, to inform immediately applicants of their acceptance or rejection, and to explain to those who failed the exam the process for reapplying. Applicants rejected by Lynd had twenty days to contest the decision to the court. Lynd had to supply the court and the plaintiffs' attorneys with a written report containing the names and races of each applicant and the disposition of each application. Blacks rushed to register to vote. Lynd, having exhausted all of his legal maneuvers, had to register most of them.[21] Years of protest had finally forced the federal government to begin protecting black suffrage, the most basic right in a democracy. That summer, President Johnson prepared to widen federal responsiveness when he announced his intentions to incorporate blacks into the socioeconomic fabric of the American dream.

On June 4 at the commencement address at Howard University, President Johnson declared, "Nothing is more freighted with meaning for our own destiny, than the revolution of the Negro American.... American Negroes have been another nation: deprived of freedom, crippled by hatred, the doors of opportunity closed ... you do not wipe away the scars of centuries" through enfranchisement and desegregation alone. "We seek not just freedom but opportunity ... not just equality as a right and a theory but equality as a fact." Black hope surged over the next year as Johnson implemented his War on Poverty. He pledged that this war, which included programs like Head Start, which offered free preschools for all children regardless of race, would provide the foundations for realizing the socioeconomic equality of the races.[22]

When the Hattiesburg Board of Education refused to work with the newly created Child Development Group of Mississippi (CDGM)—established under Sargent Shriver's Office of Economic Opportunity (OEO)—to establish Head Start centers in Forrest County, black locals in CDGM worked with the Delta Ministry (an umbrella organization that had subsumed the Hattiesburg Ministers Project) to organize nearly a dozen preschools. Over the next year, Jones County also developed Head Start centers. CDGM provided students with education, tended to their health care needs, and fed them lunch. Designed to uplift poor adults as well, CDGM elected locals to run the centers and opened many administrative and service positions to working-class and impoverished locals. Although CDGM sought to recruit white adults and children, most students were black, and the few white workers were mostly northerners. Black movement veterans dominated the leadership. In the Eaton Precinct in Forrest County, the committee elected as chair Pinky Hall, who a little over a year earlier had lost her job as a maid when she joined the Freedom Day demonstrations. Maycie Gore, secretary of the Laurel MFDP, assumed the duties of leading community organizer for CDGM in Jones County. Peggy Jean Connor, who was involved with MFDP and had staged a sit-in during Freedom Summer, served as organizer. These centers also brought children and adults outside of the movement into the struggle, and soon they joined sit-in demonstrations.[23]

Klan violence also proliferated in 1965 and 1966, with fifty recorded incidents of Klan assaults in Laurel alone, including house bombings, drive-by shootings, store burnings, and serial attacks on the COFO house. On July 1, Klansmen launched the first of their 1965 summer assaults in Laurel by igniting six fires, which destroyed the Big R Drive-In and thirteen houses in a black community—the Newcomers Quarters. The Klan used the fires as a decoy. After drawing all of the fire trucks in Laurel to these fires, Klansmen hit their most important targets: the COFO headquarters, the Laurel Freedom School, and the MFDP office. That same night, the Klan burned crosses in nearly every county in the state. In the Central Piney Woods, the Klan displayed its powerful presence by lighting twelve crosses in Jones County and five in Forrest County.[24]

In response, Jones County district attorney W. O. "Chet" Dillard and Sheriff Pickering warned the perpetrators that the city and county would not tolerate Klan violence. The sheriff hired four men to work undercover; his department worked in conjunction with FBI agents, the MHP, the Mississippi State Marshals, and the Laurel Police Department; and lawmen patrolled the highways to prevent night-riding violence. Civil rights activists had no reason to trust Sheriff Pickering. Seven months earlier, he had cheered on whites while they brutalized voter registration worker Ed Dubinsky. Moreover, the patrols failed to discourage Bowers. During a state meeting held on July 11, he ordered the Klan to execute a violent project every week in a different geographical area of Mississippi. He hoped the explosion of violence across the state would overwhelm the FBI, thus weakening their ability to solve cases.[25]

Nineteen-year-old Norman Cannon perceived the racist lawlessness as providing a permissive atmosphere for assaults against blacks. On July 13, Cannon drove into an impoverished black neighborhood in Hattiesburg. He scanned the rows of dilapidated shotgun houses on Short Francis Street until he found a suitable target, a fifteen-year-old black girl, Rosa Lee Coates, who lived with her grandmother in one of the tiny shacks. Cannon lured Coates into his vehicle under the ruse that he needed a babysitter for his child. Coates grew concerned when he drove away from the city. She asked where he was taking her. He told her to shut her mouth or he would kill her.

Coates opened the door, but Cannon yanked it shut and sped onto lonely country roads. He parked in a clearing in the woods. Coates escaped the vehicle and ran, but she slipped in the mud. As she scrambled to her feet, Cannon grabbed her by her dress. He smacked her on the side of her face and held a knife to her neck, threatening to sever her head from her body if she refused him. He tore off her clothes and threw her onto the ground. As he raped her, he kept one hand on the knife. After he finished, he forced her to lie still on her stomach. He slipped inside his vehicle and sped away.[26]

Cannon misjudged his place in the ambivalent racial atmosphere. He had a criminal record for burglary, and he lacked powerful friends and financial resources. The MHP assisted Sheriff W. G. Gray in the investigation. Within a few days, officers arrested Cannon. Coates identified him as her rapist. Cannon pled innocent. Jimmy Finch, who had prosecuted many activists, including Clyde Kennard on trumped-up charges, and Jimmy Dukes, who also had a long record of prosecuting activists, wielded all of their considerable legal skills to prosecute Cannon. White juries had never convicted a white man of interracial rape in Forrest County. Juries across the state had only delivered such convictions a dozen times. Still, some things had changed in Forrest County, and this teenage victim elicited empathy among many whites. It helped that the Coates family was not involved in the movement.[27]

During the trial, Coates's grandmother, Lillie Beal, stated that she had witnessed Cannon transport Coates out of the neighborhood. When asked to identify Cannon, Beal strode across the room to the defendant table, pointed at Cannon, and said, "That's him." Lawrence Arrington, who later became a famous Klan lawyer, and Arlington Jones defended Cannon. On the witness stand, Cannon testified that he had met Coates prior to the day of the alleged rape, that she had informed him that she enjoyed dating white men, and that they had engaged in consensual sexual intercourse. Coates insisted that she had never met Cannon until the day he raped her. She identified Cannon as her rapist and described his knife and his vehicle in precise detail.[28]

The jurors found Cannon guilty and sentenced him to life in prison. Although the Cannon case sent the message that not all white men could commit crimes against blacks with impunity, the jury's refusal to sentence Cannon to death when that proved the popular sentence for convicted black rapists at the time revealed that a dual justice system persisted in Mississippi. During the same year as the Coates case, Finch and Dukes employed all of their power to deny a black man charged with murder his right to a fair trial.[29]

The killing occurred on a clear spring night in late March 1965. Cloudies Shinall, a stocky, twenty-year-old black man, went out for a night of bar-hopping in Palmers Crossing with James Anderson and Lewis Willie Smith. At Bama Madison's pub, Shinall showed off a gun he had borrowed from a friend until Constables Kitchens and Humphrey entered the bar. Everyone knew about the beating Shinall had received at the hands of Kitchens that past summer. Madison hid the gun, and Shinall kept his back to the door. After the constables departed, Shinall collected the gun and left with his friends. Later that night, Shinall parked in front of the Heat Wave Tavern, but he panicked when he saw Constable Kitchen's vehicle pull in behind him and flash its lights on the Chevy. Shinall drove toward Palmers Crossing Road. Although Shinall had not committed a crime, the constable pursued him. Shinall sped down dark country roads. Smith and Anderson shouted, "Why [are you] running [?]" and "We ha[ven't] committed no ... crime." Shinall never answered as he careened around corners.[30]

In a residential area, Shinall swerved off the pavement onto a gravel road and lost control of the Chevy. As he tried to straighten the vehicle, he crashed into a yard, and the car came to a halt. The constable parked behind the Chevy and shouted for the men to step out of the vehicle. Smith and Anderson complied, but Shinall froze. The constable approached the driver's side, shined his flashlight into the window, aimed his gun at Shinall, and ordered, "Get out you nigger, I ought to kill you." Shinall grabbed his pistol, aimed it at the officer, and shot him in the throat. The force of the bullet knocked the gun from the constable's hand. He cried out for help. Smith and Anderson ran. As they fled into the darkness, they heard two more shots.[31]

After the killing, Shinall visited Mary Jones's Café, where he bragged that after he shot the constable in the throat, he "shot the son of a bitch again in the head." When police arrived at the crime scene crime, they found that the dead constable was not Kitchens, but Humphrey, who had driven Kitchens's vehicle that night. Later, Shinall claimed that he acted in self-defense. Kitchens, he noted, had beaten him before and threatened to kill him. He thought that Kitchens was the driver because he had never seen the driver's face; he had seen only the vehicle, which belonged to Kitchens. Most blacks across Palmers Crossing believed that Shinall had long dreamed of killing Kitchens, not so much because he had beaten Shinall, but because he had allegedly forced Shinall's girlfriend into a sexual relationship. The next day, police charged Shinall with capital murder. The incident horrified most whites, who perceived the black man's audacious killing of a white constable as the gruesome harvest of the movement.[32]

In contrast, many blacks were relieved that one of the constables who had terrorized their community was dead. Children of Palmers Crossing feared the constables because many of them had witnessed their brutality. Freedom Summer student Carol Jackson recalled, "We knew to stay away from [police], not to say anything to them. You could not be seen anymore if you said something." The day after the killing, Jackson's father took Carol and her sister Lillie over to the crime scene. They stared at the bloodstained street. The Jacksons, like most blacks, would not mourn the constable's passing.[33]

Although Shinall never participated in the movement, his case had an impact on the struggle. Police brutality proved one of the most powerful arms of white supremacy. Defense attorneys Jack Young and Jess R. Brown hoped to prove that Shinall lived under a tyrannical white supremacist state in which the constables launched a "reign of terror" against blacks in Palmers Crossing. Brown planned to bring Kitchens and victims of police brutality to the stand. However, Kitchens and some of Humphrey's victims had vanished. Brown moved for a continuance. Judge Stanton Hall, who had long shown his prejudice against blacks in his courtroom, including Clyde Kennard and Medgar Evers, denied the request.[34]

During change of venue motions, witnesses testified for the defense that since racism plagued Forrest County and local reporting had inflamed racial passions, Shinall could not receive a fair trial in Hattiesburg. The newspapers reported that because the FBI regarded the homicide a murder rather than self-defense, agents aided police. Reporter Elliot Chaze created an impression of Shinall as dangerous by describing him as "a muscular Negro who looks like a middleweight boxer" and by claiming that he lacked human emotions because "his face remained blank during arraignment." Chaze also revealed that Shinall had burglarized a store at the age of sixteen, his brother was imprisoned for burglary, and his father had served four years for manslaughter for killing his mistress. He linked Shinall to the movement by noting that Shinall's black lawyers had worked on NAACP cases. City Attorney Frank Montague admitted that whites had antipathy to the "so called civil rights" protests, but Finch invoked the Cannon rape case to counter charges of racial bias. Judge Hall denied the motion for a change of venue.[35]

Judge Hall also denied Shinall his constitutional right to impartial grand and petit juries of his peers even though Young proved that the state systematically excluded black jurors. As of 1960, blacks comprised 25 percent of the Forrest County voting age population; yet no blacks had served on petit juries deciding criminal cases for at least the past twenty-one years.

The exclusion persisted because jurors were drawn from voting rolls, and Lynd had managed, despite federal rulings against him, to prevent most blacks from registering. Although the June ruling in the *Lynd* case added more blacks to the voting rolls, their numbers had only just begun to climb. Consequently, only three blacks appeared in Shinall's jury pool. The prosecution removed all of them with peremptory challenges. Moreover, the judge refused to excuse juror Paul Kinsey for cause even though he was a Hattiesburg police officer, knew the deceased, had arrested many activists, and expressed resentment toward integration. Young and Brown had to use one of their peremptory challenges to remove Kinsey. The language that the lawyers used during the trial also reflected the racist milieu. Prosecutors and defense attorneys addressed white witnesses with courtesy titles including "mister," "doctor," and "sheriff." The defense also addressed black witnesses with courtesy titles with few exceptions, but prosecutors either neglected to address black witnesses by name or referred to them by their first names.[36]

The prosecution presented indisputable evidence that Shinall shot Humphrey three times. One bullet lodged in the base of Humphrey's throat, one behind his right ear, and one in the back of his head. Anderson and Smith testified that Shinall refused Humphrey's orders to exit his vehicle, that Shinall shot Humphrey, and that after they fled the scene they heard two more shots. A fourteen-year-old eyewitness, Andrew Wilborn, testified that he saw Shinall shoot Humphrey. When Humphrey dropped his gun and staggered toward Wilborn's house begging for help, Shinall shot Humphrey twice more. The latter two shots were clearly not fired in self-defense. Moreover, Shinall's friends admitted that Shinall boasted about the killing later that night.[37]

So Young and Brown sought to prove that Shinall acted out of a panicked state of terror and killed Humphrey because he lived in a police state and suffered from a siege mentality after Kitchens had beaten him so brutally the previous summer. Shinall, they insisted, believed that the constable planned to murder him. When Young and Brown called several witnesses to the stand to testify that Humphrey and Kitchens used their power over Palmers Crossing to terrorize local blacks, the prosecutors objected. Judge Hall removed the jury while he determined the relevancy of the testimony. Witness after witness took the stand and accused Humphrey and Kitchens of dragging them out of local cafes and off the streets to beat them, arrest them, transport them to jail, and beat them again. Furthermore, Bama Madison testified that she witnessed Constable Kitchens attack Shinall in June 1964, and Lee Mae Shinall recounted the multiple wounds her son suffered from that beating. As the testimony provided mitigating circumstances, the defense had introduced a reasonable argument to reduce charges against Shinall. The judge, however, excluded all of these witnesses.[38]

Judge Hall could not prevent Shinall from testifying in his own defense. Shinall claimed that he thought Kitchens was the man who had chased him and pulled him over that night because Humphreys drove Kitchens's vehicle. After Shinall crashed in the yard, he recalled hearing a man's voice shouting, "Get out you nigger, I ought to kill you." The constable shined his flashlight into the vehicle; when Shinall turned around, he could only make out a figure approaching with his gun aimed toward him. He continued to believe that the officer was Kitchens. Since Kitchens had beaten him before, he feared that he might kill him. Shinall grabbed his gun and shot. He claimed that he had no recollection of shooting Humphrey two more times. After fifty-nine minutes of deliberation, the all-white jury found Shinall guilty and sentenced him to death. Judge Hall scheduled Shinall's execution for September 2, less than two months away. Blacks in the courtroom cried out in despair.[39]

Shinall's attorneys appealed the verdict to the Mississippi Supreme Court on the grounds that the circuit court had made several errors. It had systematically excluded black jurors and failed to grant a change of venue, even though Forrest County suffered from intense racial prejudice. Judge Hall denied Shinall the right to present testimony imperative to his self-defense plea when he excluded witnesses who could testify that Constables Humphrey and Kitchens had terrorized the black community. Courts had established extensive precedents allowing defendants the right to present evidence to the jury that showed their perspective of potential danger, their perception of the person killed based on previous encounters, and the character of the deceased so that the court could determine the aggressor in the struggle. The justices agreed only that Forrest County had systematically excluded black jurors.[40]

Forrest County retried Shinall the following summer and again denied him a fair trial. During the voir dire examination in which prosecutors questioned potential jurors, the state used five of its challenges to remove all blacks from the jury panel. Brown accused the state of removing the jurors unlawfully based on race and requested that the judge quash the jury panel. Judge Hall refused. Brown tried to root out racist jurors by asking them if they belonged to white supremacist organizations and by eliciting their views on segregation. When Brown inquired of potential juror William Scarborough, a USM professor, his views on school desegregation, Scarborough admitted that he "had feelings regarding it, but I don't think that's an issue in this case." The prosecution objected. Judge Hall prevented the defense from persisting with such questions. Unbeknownst to Brown, Scarborough was a self-described "diehard segregationist" who had joined the Citizens Council while living in Jackson.[41]

When the trial began, the state prohibited Shinall's attorneys from making a case for self-defense. Judge Hall refused to permit black residents from testifying in front of the jury about the brutality that they had suffered at the hands of Humphrey and Kitchens. He also refused to hear from witnesses who, on the night of the killing, had seen Humphrey consuming alcohol at several bars and would suggest that he was intoxicated when he pursued Shinall. Defense attorneys elicited the most important testimony when Brown cross-examined Sheriff Gray. The sheriff testified that Humphrey was elected as constable for beat four, but that he regularly patrolled beat three with Kitchens. Gray conceded that the law prohibited Humphrey from patrolling beat three alone. When the defense inquired if blacks had accused Kitchens and Humphreys of police brutality, the prosecutors objected, and Judge Hall excused the jury. Outside the presence of the jury, Gray admitted that he had received several complaints against Kitchens and that he had requested his dismissal. After Humphrey's death, authorities investigated some of the complaints and forced Kitchens to resign. Citing the *Eaton* and *Bell* cases, Brown argued that the judge must admit this testimony because as human behavior stemmed from past experiences, the defense had the right to present a full picture of the context in which the killing occurred. The court ruled the testimony hearsay and sustained the prosecution's objections.[42]

On August 6, the jury found Shinall guilty of murder and sentenced him to death. In August 1971, after many failed appeals, the case returned to Forrest County because the US Supreme Court found that courts could not exclude jurors on the grounds that they opposed the death penalty. On August 6, the case concluded. Shinall changed his plea to guilty, and the court sentenced him to life. After many years in prison, Mississippi granted Shinall parole under the condition that he never return to the state.[43]

The Shinall case reflected the complex battles wracking the Central Piney Woods in the mid-1960s. It is possible that Shinall shot Humphrey the first time in self-defense. However, he pursued the wounded constable, shooting him in the side and back of the head even though Humphrey had dropped his gun and was running away. Still, the defense had a point that Shinall had not received a fair trial. The judge refused to allow the jury to hear evidence such as the psychological terror that Kitchens and Humphrey had instilled in Palmers Crossing residents. The court also failed to consider that Humphrey had pursued Shinall initially for no reason as he had not committed any crime, that Shinall tried to escape the constable because he feared police, and that Humphrey approached him with a gun and threatened to kill him. For over a century in the Central Piney Woods, white men had used the white supremacist state to control blacks and to emasculate black men. They harassed, unlawfully arrested, falsely convicted, beat, raped, and killed blacks with impunity. Humphrey and Kitchens mistreated blacks and inculcated in Shinall a violent rage toward them. Humphrey was ultimately a victim, but he was never an innocent.[44]

The Shinall case served as a significant battle in the war of attrition because it struck at the heart of the white establishment's ability to oppress blacks via racial injustice. Although Judge Hall had excused the jury from the courtroom when black witnesses testified before the judge that they had suffered from police brutality and when Sheriff Gray testified that he had received numerous complaints from residents that Kitchens had abused them, the court reporter recorded all such testimony in the trial transcripts. Thus, the official court records contain these significant testimonies. Soon afterward, the Civil Rights Commission and the Fellowship of the Concerned Southern Regional Council identified racial injustice as one of the most powerful forces of racial oppression in Mississippi. Because of its pervasiveness, blacks perceived law enforcement officials, judges, and prosecutors as oppressors rather than protectors. When accused of a crime, blacks faced a nearly "all-white" justice system that was hostile toward them. Some southern cities had hired black police officers, but their numbers were miniscule. Blacks comprised an infinitesimal percentage of court officers in municipal, state, and federal courts. The federal judiciary in the South had not a single black judge, clerk, marshal, or jury commissioner. Southern courts excluded black jurors, which denied blacks their right to a "jury of [their] peers."[45]

Moreover, the federal government helped keep judicial power in the hands of white segregationists when in the summer of 1965, President Johnson nominated former Mississippi governor James P. Coleman to the US Fifth Circuit Court of Appeal. Outraged, thirty-two organizations including SNCC, SCLC, MFDP, and CORE condemned the nomination. Many activists considered Coleman the architect of massive resistance. As governor, Coleman had proposed and/or signed into law legislation and issued executive orders to preserve racial segregation in schools and in transportation facilities, had helped prevent Kennard from gaining admission to USM, and opposed black suffrage. President Johnson nominated Coleman to the very court that decided many racial discrimination cases. Despite protests, in July 1965 Congress affirmed Coleman's nomination.[46]

The federal government, the movement's ever capricious ally, followed its retreat with a massive advance against white supremacy. In August, Congress passed the Voting Rights Act. The new bill prohibited seven southern states, including Mississippi, from using voter qualifications designed to disfranchise persons based on their race or color and prevented states from using literacy exams to qualify voters. It also allowed Congress to send federal registrars into states with low voter turnout. Soon after the act's passage, the NAACP received sixty-seven complaints of voter discrimination in Laurel and requested that the federal government send in registrars. Less than a week later, federal registrars took over registration in Jones County. In a few days, they registered 325 people.[47]

Despite the progressive federal action, a month later the federal government used the Voting Rights Act as an excuse for another retreat. In September, the MFDP congressional challenge came before the House of Representatives. Lawyers presented the wealth of evidence that they had collected to prove that voter discrimination had led to the illegal election of the representatives from Mississippi. Victoria Gray testified that when she tried to run for Congress and presented to Lynd the necessary sixty-eight signatures to make her a lawful candidate, he refused to certify fifty-six names because they had not paid their poll taxes. Gray reminded him that the Twenty-Fourth Amendment prohibited states from using poll tax stipulations in federal elections. Lynd responded that he followed Mississippi laws. Colmer called the MFDP challenge a conspiracy and warned that should it succeed, it would undermine the stability of Congress by encouraging challenges by radicals like the Klan and Black Muslims. On September 15, the House dismissed the MFDP's case, claiming that the candidates lacked a "legal basis" to run, that the votes that they had acquired in their parallel political process would not have changed the election results, and that the Voting Rights Act would prevent future discrimination. Yet the Department of Justice had sent federal registrars to enforce the act in only a few counties. Widespread discrimination persisted.[48]

Blacks understood that they would never obtain influence or authority without political power. Whites understood that, too. Thus, as black voter registration increased, white authorities tried to exclude blacks from the political halls on the federal and state levels by creating multimember districts: they either combined districts countywide or combined multicounty districts to insure a white majority; each of these districts voted for two or more representatives. Blacks would never be elected in the residentially segregated and majority-white state unless Mississippi shifted to single-member districts used in nonsouthern states in which counties were subdivided into smaller districts based on precincts, and each district elected a single representative. In October 1965, COFO, MFDP, and the Lawyers of the Constitutional Defense Committee initiated a lawsuit to dismantle discriminatory districting and selected Hattiesburg activist Peggy Jean Connor as the lead plaintiff. Blacks also confronted discrimination on the local level because most Mississippi towns, including Laurel and Hattiesburg, held at-large elections for commissioners rather than single-district elections. Because whites enjoyed a majority in Hattiesburg and Laurel, blacks lacked the power to influence elections. The effort to dismantle this system continued into the post–civil rights era and would not achieve a resolution for over a decade.[49]

The movement also suffered as sensational events diverted America's attention from the South. In August 1964, Congress had passed the Gulf of Tonkin Resolution, which gave President Johnson the right to use conventional military force in Vietnam; as the conflict there escalated, it detracted attention from the movement. In addition, the explosion of a racial rebellion in Los Angeles incited white fear and diminished the movement's support. Despite these diversions and setbacks, in the fall and winter of 1965, the movement achieved some victories in its war of attrition, even though the trudge toward the proverbial mountaintop remained an arduous one. NAACP leaders J. C. Fairley and Vernon Dahmer helped facilitate the desegregation of USM. The university accepted twenty-year-old activist Raylawni Branch and recent high school graduate Elaine Armstrong out of eighteen black applicants. Efforts by the Delta Ministry to organize a maid's union failed because white families used scabbing techniques to hire from the masses of the unemployed. Still, as community organizer Maycie Gore recalled, many domestics escaped "the white folks' kitchen" because CDGM programs hired them as cooks, organizers, and clerks. Although the Hattiesburg Police Department hired four black officers, black residents complained that they acted as lackeys for their white superiors.[50]

In Jones County, Klan violence intensified during the fall of 1965. Under Deavours Nix's orders, Pete Martin, Lester Thornton, Franklin Lyons, and Charles Noble executed a drive-by shooting on the residence of Jones County NAACP president Benjamin Murph. No one was injured and the house sustained minimal damage, but the insurance company canceled Murph's policy. Police investigated but made no arrests. Determined to quell Klan violence, District Attorney William Dillard charged Pete Martin with possession of dynamite and whitecapping. Yet he learned via a Klan informant that Circuit Clerk Leonard Caves, affiliated with the Klan, would protect Klansmen. Caves's duties included selecting grand jurors. On September 16, the grand jury refused to indict Martin. Klansmen continued to attack blacks with impunity. Less than a month later, several Klansmen shot into Brewell Curie's home and set it on fire.[51]

These acts backfired on the Klan because they inspired Dillard and County Attorney Charles Pickering to instigate a shift in the Jones County judicial system. Pickering had helped defend the Regular Democrats during the MFDP challenge, but he opposed racial violence and had begun to question segregation. After Agent Robert Lee provided Pickering with a list of 130 crimes committed by the White Knights, Pickering authored a statement rebuking the Klan, which he and Dillard brought to Mayor Henry Bucklew. Pickering knew the challenges in convincing the mayor to confront the Klan. A diehard segregationist, Bucklew had directed George Wallace's 1964 presidential campaign in three southern cities and served as a member of the Mississippi Sovereignty Commission Speaker's Bureau. Yet Bucklew was a consummate politician who understood that he needed a good economy to win reelection. After the recent wave of Klan violence, three businesses revoked plans to establish bases in Jones County. The Klan was bad for business. Pickering used the economic crisis to convince Bucklew to reassert control over his city. In October, the *Laurel Leader-Call* printed a photograph of Mayor Bucklew, the police chief, the sheriff, and prosecutors signing a statement denouncing the White Knights and listing the victims, dates, and locations of each act of Klan terror.[52]

A few days later, Bucklew intensified his denunciation of the Klan in a live WDAM-TV broadcast shown across most of southeastern Mississippi, but he used a pragmatic segregationist approach. He compared activists to Klansmen and insisted that Laurel must stem "the flood of scum, degenerates, free-lovers, night riders, church burners, home bombers and hooded thugs running loose." At the least, he saved his harshest words for the White Knights: "Those who create such acts of violence are not only Godless . . . they are traitors! . . . These mob fiends who are infecting our city and state are actually demanding that the Federal government move in and take over." He warned, "You . . . or your family . . . or mine might well be their next target." Bucklew displayed photographs of burned homes and bombed vehicles and offered $1,000 for information leading to the successful prosecution of the perpetrators. The following day, Bucklew circulated a petition requesting that people pledge to reject the Klan and to agree to serve on juries. One thousand Jones County citizens and numerous ministers, bank executives, business leaders, and official representatives from the Masonite Corporation signed the petitions. Forty-six churches of the Jones County Baptist Association and the Laurel Kiwanis Club passed resolutions supporting the mayor. Bucklew's office received letters and telegrams from people responding on a fifteen-to-one ratio in favor of his stance against the White Knights.[53]

Yet many whites across the Central Piney Woods evinced their support of Klan activities by supporting both the White Knights and its rival group, the UKA. Thousands of local whites flocked to a UKA rally in Forrest County featuring Imperial Wizard Robert Shelton. In Jones County, Mississippi congressman and Klan attorney Charles Blackwell publicly lambasted Bucklew's speech, which he argued frightened away big businesses by creating the false impression that Laurel suffered from lawlessness. On WDAM-TV, Klansmen claimed that they had never engaged in violence. The local Citizens' Council released a statement declaring that officials "have made a very serious mistake in that they have attacked a symptom and not the disease ... violence is but a symptom. ... If Jones County were free of the NAACP, COFO, CORE, and Freedom Democrat agitators, our problem would be solved." Bowers planned violent projects against whites who had signed Mayor Bucklew's pledge and ordered local klaverns to whip Pickering. When Agent Lee learned of the order, he warned Pickering, who took proper precautions. Despite the bravery of officials like Pickering, the Invisible Empire sustained its chokehold over Jones County because many white authorities supported the Klan.[54]

As the Civil Rights Commission noted in its report to President Johnson and Congress on November 4, racial violence remained the most powerful systematic method to sustain the racial caste system in Mississippi. The core racism of most sheriffs, police chiefs, and prosecutors produced a milieu conducive to violence, particularly as they failed to denounce, investigate, and prosecute racial crimes. The commissioners suggested that Congress increase the punishment for violations of civil rights and that the federal government use the Fourteenth Amendment's equal protection clause to prosecute persons committing racial violence when states failed to punish them. They also requested that Congress make municipal, county, and state governments liable for police neglect and brutality. Finally, they recommended that President Johnson provide federal officers with the powers to arrest persons violating federal laws. Klan activity slowed in November and December, but not because Klansmen feared repercussions. Rather, they watched activists seeking to reinvigorate the Hattiesburg movement and planned their violent response.[55]

Vernon Dahmer became their primary target. Since the close of Freedom Summer, Dahmer had moved into the background of the movement to protect his family, but he reemerged in the fall of 1965 as an important leader. On November 3, he attended a meeting at St. Paul Methodist Church in Hattiesburg at which activists launched the winter voter registration drive in Forrest County. During a meeting on December 19 with delegates from SNCC, SCLC, the MFDP, the NAACP, the MCHR, and the Delta Ministry, Dahmer volunteered to collect poll taxes at his store to make the voter registration process for state and local elections less intimidating. He persuaded Sheriff Gray and Jimmy Finch to give him a poll tax book. Dahmer also planned to launch a massive canvassing campaign.[56]

The renewed voter registration campaign infuriated the Imperial Wizard. Bowers held two meetings, one in October and the other in December, to discuss Dahmer. Referring to Dahmer, Bowers stated, "Something has to be done about this damn nigger down south." Bowers had expected the Forrest County klavern to deal with Dahmer. One of the klavern's most violent members, Hamilton, had suggested murdering Dahmer, but he had failed to initiate a project. So Bowers turned to his klaverns in Jones County. While Klansmen executed dry run attacks on the Dahmer property, the House Un-American Activities Committee (HUAC) sent several Klansmen, including Bowers and Nix, subpoenas to testify about their activities before Congress. Because Bowers considered himself at war with the federal government, he decided to launch a bold strike with a successful kill in Mississippi. At 8:45 on Sunday morning, January 9, 1966, the Reverend Milton Barnes announced on his *Gospel Sunrise* radio show, "Here is one for the NAACP. Be wise, be smart, act. Pay your poll tax now, to vote in the city, county, and state elections." He informed his listeners that they could pay their taxes at several locations and included Dahmer's store in the list. Bowers ordered Dahmer's execution.[57]

On January 10, 1966, Dahmer and his wife, Ellie, lay asleep in their bed. It was the first time in over a year that they decided to terminate their usual practice of sleeping in shifts so that one of them would be awake should the Klan attack. Since they had not received any Klan threats in a couple of months, they thought that the danger had passed. In Jones County, eight members of the White Knights gathered at the home of Exalted Cyclops Cecil Sessum. As they drank coffee and worked the actions on their shotguns, Sessum asked the men if anyone wished to leave a note for their families should something happen to them. No one did. The Klansmen packed into a Pontiac and a Ford and drove toward the Dahmer property. When they arrived, they shut off their headlights. The men in the Ford—Henry

DeBoxtel, Charles Noble, Franklin Lyons, and Lester Thornton—stopped at the store and shot out the windows. Dahmer's aunt, Luranie Heidelberg, who resided in the backroom of the store, awoke to the sounds of gunfire. As Klansmen hurled gasoline-filled jugs into the store and set the place on fire, Heidelberg crawled to the back window and escaped into the woods.[58]

Across the Dahmer property near the ranch-style farmhouse, the Pontiac stopped behind several tall trees. Two Klansmen, Charles Wilson and William Smith, slipped out of the vehicle and began shooting into the house to provide cover for the assault. The initial shots shattered a picture window. Sessum and his guard, Billy Roy Pitts, rushed the house carrying five gasoline-filled jugs. Sessum heaved two jugs through the shards of glass into the home, another two jugs into the carport, and one into the back of the Dahmer's pickup truck. He ignited a gasoline soaked rag wrapped around a forked stick and hurled it through the shattered window. The gasoline burst into flames. Fire engulfed the middle of the house. Wilson and Smith trained their guns on the house again and shot continuously in an attempt to trap the Dahmers in the burning home or to shoot them should they try to flee.[59]

The sounds of the attack yanked Ellie from sleep. She cried, "Vernon get up, I believe they got us this time." Dahmer jumped out of bed, grabbed his shotgun, and yelled, "Get the children out while I hold them off." Three of the Dahmers' eight children were living at home, Dennis and Bettie, aged twelve and ten respectively, and Harold, aged twenty, who had recently returned home from his service in the army. Bettie's room was the only one not blocked by fire. Ellie hurried across the hall, pulled Bettie into her arms, and rushed her out of the room, escaping the steady rain of bullets. All of the window frames in the front were made of aluminum and could not be opened. Flames blocked passageways to the back door. Klansmen would shoot them if they tried to exit the front door. The back window was their only means of escape. But when Ellie tried to raise the window, it stuck. She shoved harder, but it would not budge.[60]

Through the billowing smoke, Bettie saw her father firing his gun at their attackers through a wedge in the partially-opened front door. The flames vaulted toward Dahmer, searing the skin on his arms. Bettie screamed, "We're not going to make it out of here. Lord have mercy, we are going to get burned up." With ragged, frantic breaths, Dahmer sucked in burning embers and black smoke. Outside, Pitts, startled by the tortured sounds of someone inside, raised his eyes to Sessum. The Exalted Cyclops shrugged and said, "Let him die, that's what we came for." Then Smith saw headlights flash at the store and thought it was someone rushing to help the Dahmers.

He fired several rounds in that direction. "Stop it," Pitts shouted, "they're our own men." The bullets had hit the body of the Ford and punctured its left front and rear tires. Certain that they had trapped the Dahmers inside their home, the Klansmen fled.[61]

Inside the burning home, Ellie Dahmer kept shoving the window, trying to force it open. "We're not going to get out this house," Bettie cried. The flames leapt toward them, scurried across the ceiling, and dripped onto Bettie's arms and forehead. Ellie heaved her shoulder against the window so hard that she fell through it onto the ground. Moments later Bettie felt her father's arms take hold of her and hand her through the window to her mother. He climbed out of the window after her. Their bodies were burning. Bettie collapsed, rolled on the grass, and started screaming. At the far end of the home, Dennis woke his brother Harold, and they escaped through their window. Dahmer led his family to the barn, as he feared the night riders might return. Harold rushed to a relative's home for help. Inside the barn, Bettie lay on the ground, sobbing in pain, her arms and forehead badly burned. She looked across at her father and saw with horror that his burned flesh hung from his arms, his "skin like a sleeve . . . hanging off."[62]

Later at the hospital, Ellie Dahmer paced the halls in her bare feet. A black nurse gave her a blanket and brought the Dahmers clothes and shoes. Doctors covered Dahmer's burned flesh with bandages from his waist to his neck and sedated him, but it barely diminished the severe pain. As news of the attack spread across Forrest County, reporters and friends rushed to the hospital. Dahmer said to NAACP president, J. C. Fairley, "Carry the work on. It's worth dying for, and the worst is left to do." He told a reporter, "I've been active in trying to get people to register to vote." In the afternoon, Dennis and Harold arrived at the hospital. Dahmer sat up, tried to speak to them, but then he collapsed in Ellie's arms.[63]

One of Dahmer's sons, Carroll G. Dahmer, lived in Michigan, and four of his sons were serving in the US military: Sergeant George W. Dahmer, stationed in Homestead, Florida; Staff Sergeant Martinez Dahmer, stationed in Sinemya, Alaska; Private Alvin Hulon Dahmer, stationed in Seinfurt, Germany; and Master Sergeant Vernon Dahmer Jr., stationed in Riverside, California. Alvin was listening to the news in Germany to find out if his unit would be sent to Vietnam when he heard a special broadcast that his father had been murdered. Over the past year, Dahmer had been writing Alvin about new farming methods for cotton. After he completed his service, Alvin planned to return to his roots in the Kelly Settlement and join his father in the family business. Instead, he returned home to bury him.[64]

CHAPTER 6

War on the White Knights and the White City

THE KLANSMEN CELEBRATED VERNON DAHMER'S DEATH, BUT THEY worried, too; they had made many mistakes. Thirteen hours earlier, after the Klansmen had driven a few miles away from the Dahmer property, the punctured tires on the Ford blew out and the car came to a halt. The Pontiac slid alongside it, and the panicked Klansmen gathered around the Ford. They considered burning it, but they had used all of their gasoline on Dahmer's home and store. Then Billy Roy Pitts realized that his holster had broken; his gun was gone. We have to go back, he shouted. But it was too late. The place would be crawling with agents soon. The Klansmen abandoned the Ford, crammed inside the Pontiac, and rushed toward Jones County. Pitts looked over at Cecil Sessum and said, "I . . . told [you] I didn't feel things would go right." Sessum said nothing until they reached his house and the Klansmen gathered around him for a debriefing.[1]

The slim, dark-haired leader fixed his piercing blue eyes on Pitts. If you "hadn't lost your gun," Sessum snarled, then glared at Smith, if "you hadn't shot the car up, it would have been a perfect project." Pitts towered over Sessum, but the ruddy-faced Klansmen feared Sessum. Pitts insisted that no one could trace the gun to him. Sessum ordered Henry DeBoxtel to track down Travis Giles, who had lent the vehicle to his Klan brothers for the Dahmer project, and direct him to report the Ford stolen. Before dismissing his men, Sessum warned them to "keep their mouths shut . . . anyone who decide[s] to be a pimp [will] die." When the Klansmen met with Bowers, they found the Imperial Wizard ecstatic about the murder. He scolded them for their blunders, but he assured them that even if the feds managed to bring them to trial, "no jury in Mississippi would convict a white man for killing a nigger."[2]

Bowers failed to realize that his society was changing and the white supremacist foundation upon which he had built his Invisible Empire was shifting and cracking. State leaders, authorities, and the white citizens of the Central Piney Woods responded to the Klan murder with ambivalence. Some demanded justice, and a few even called for the dismantling of Jim Crow. Other voices still cried never and vowed to protest black liberation to the bitter end. There was no immediate move either in Forrest or Jones Counties or in the state to reconstruct the unjust social order, but crucial developments began flowing from this Klan murder that would render Mississippi a more equitable place for all of its citizens.

As news of Dahmer's murder spread across America, black activists demanded a wholesale assault on racial injustice. Roy Wilkins, executive director of the NAACP, described the killing as "part of a war on NAACP frontline branch officers and on the Civil Rights Crusade." He pressured Congress to pass a bill protecting the lives and property of blacks. MFDP chairman Lawrence Guyot insisted that Governor Paul Johnson Jr. mobilize state agencies to terminate the "atmosphere of terror." Local activists rejuvenated the Hattiesburg movement by encouraging blacks to emulate Dahmer's courage. Dahmer was their everyday hero. After his death, he became their martyr. NAACP member Raylawni Branch praised Dahmer's bold stand against the Klan, noting, "He died like a man: he died fighting back."[3]

To many federal officials, this murder was personal, for they had worked with Dahmer on black suffrage cases for over a decade. Attorney General Nicholas Katzenbach pledged that the Department of Justice would employ all of its resources to punish the perpetrators. President Lyndon Johnson sent a telegram to Ellie Dahmer expressing his condolences and lauding Dahmer's registration work. Days later, in his State of the Union Address, President Johnson called on Congress to pass "legislation to strengthen authority of Federal courts to try those who murder, attack, or intimidate either civil rights workers or others exercising their constitutional rights" and to increase the punishment for such crimes. Roy Moore, special agent in charge of the Jackson office, vowed to "get the bastards." He launched the DABURN (Dahmer burning) investigation, moved the center of the federal war against the Klan into the Central Piney Woods, and prepared a siege on the Invisible Empire's headquarters in Laurel. The handful of agents assigned to Hattiesburg reserved the local Holiday Inn to house the army of agents that Moore had dispatched.[4]

State and local leaders pledged to punish the killers, and they received support from many citizens. Governor Johnson characterized the murderers as "morally bankrupt" and rebuked "the cowardly voices of hate and fear which would destroy us." The *Hattiesburg American* described the killers as "terrorists" and declared that "those who oppose terrorism must not rest until justice has been done." Mayor Paul Grady, the County Board of Supervisors, the city commissioners, and the Chamber of Commerce created the Dahmer Family Fund committee headed by the president of William Carey College to rebuild the Dahmer home. Architects, plumbers, and building supply companies offered their services and supplies for free. The local Red Cross sent the Dahmers garments, food, and furnishings donated by locals. Some whites openly expressed their grief. A science teacher at Thames Junior High School told his students that he lived near the Dahmers and that they had become friends. As he spoke of Dahmer as an extraordinary man, tears filled his eyes. A student, Billy McGee, who decades later became the sheriff, watched his teacher in awe, for in his white society, it was "profound for that teacher to be that broken down by a black man.... And particularly to stand up and say that he was my friend. I loved this man ... this is a great man." This outpouring of sorrow and the aid that whites extended to the Dahmers in their time of grief seemed to offer a promising foundation of interracial goodwill upon which a more just society could be constructed. Of course, fifteen months earlier in Laurel, the mayor, officials, and many citizens had denounced the Klan and it had only grown stronger. And most whites in both counties opposed the movement that Dahmer helped birth. Moreover, although Governor Johnson dispatched the MHP to work with the FBI, he also sent it to spy on the Hattiesburg movement.[5]

Reasons abounded for skepticism; however, the local mentality was shifting. From the opening of the investigation, Agent William Dukes, who had worked on the MIBURN case in Neshoba County, found Forrest County authorities cooperative. It helped that prosecutor Jimmy Dukes was his brother. In Neshoba County, several officers were Klansmen involved in the murder, but no officer working on the Dahmer case was in the Klan. And Moore, his agents, and local law enforcement devoted themselves to solving the case. Just after 6:00 a.m. on January 10, 1966, Special Agents Loren C. Brooks and J. L. Martin accompanied Deputy Sheriff T. A. Woodward to the Dahmer farm, where they found neighbors gathered around the charred remains. They found a plethora of evidence, including shotgun shells, three bullet holes in Dahmer's pickup truck, and a white plastic jug containing gasoline. They also found a .22 caliber Magnum Rohm revolver about ten yards from the foundation of the burned home and a Ford hubcap marred with bullet holes. With neighbors' assistance, they found a 1963 light blue Ford parked three miles from the Dahmer property. Its left front and right wheel tires were flat and its frame had punctured markings.[6]

Several of the Dahmers' black neighbors and one white neighbor, Jay Smith, informed agents that between 2:00 and 3:00 a.m. they saw two vehicles, one that resembled the abandoned Ford, pass their homes and head south toward the Dahmer farm. Some twenty minutes later, both cars passed their homes again heading north. The Ford sounded like it had a flat tire. Although Smith admitted that he recognized some of the passengers, he feared divulging their names. The next day, Smith received a phone call from a man warning him to keep quiet. Agents and local investigators had a few names in mind—starting with Bowers. An informant had revealed to agents that Bowers had boasted, "The Laurel group scored a big one." Agents also focused on Giles, the owner of the Ford and a member of the Ellisville Klavern. When agents questioned Giles, he claimed that he had parked his vehicle in the Masonite parking lot at 10:30 p.m. on January 9 and worked until 7:00 a.m. After dining at the Chow House Restaurant across the road from Masonite, he found his vehicle missing and reported it stolen. Agents knew that the manager of the Chow House, Henry DeBoxtel, was a Klansmen. After questioning Giles's family and friends, agents learned that Giles had only used the Ford once, on January 9. He had gone out of his way to track down his wife at a friend's house to swap his truck with her car before rushing to his shift at Masonite.[7]

Giles's vehicle unveiled a porthole into the Invisible Empire. Agents hoped that the gun found on the Dahmer property would illuminate another. The revolver's serial number—6403—led agents to R. A. Mayberry's gun shop in Laurel. According to the shop's paperwork, Mayberry sold a gun with serial number 6403 to Jimmy Jones, who had then sold it to a pawn shop. But Mayberry had mislabeled the guns; agents located Jones's old gun at the pawn shop with serial number 6402. Agents theorized that Mayberry had sold 6403 to either the Klansman who attacked the Dahmer home or to someone who sold it to the Klansman.[8] While FBI agents and officers moved into the White Knights' territory in Jones County in search of the link between the gun and the Klansman, black protests erupted across Forrest County.

On the night of Dahmer's death, local blacks flooded the streets of Hattiesburg, the rage so palpable that police, as Daisy Harris later recalled, were "afraid to come into our area." Harris marched with thousands to St. James Church, where black leaders declared that Dahmer's "sacrifice on the altar of freedom should inspire us to finish the task." After the service, NAACP field secretary Charles Evers led the mourners to the Forrest County courthouse where he encouraged them to launch a boycott and a voter registration campaign: "The only thing the white man understands is the ballot and the dollar. . . . You take away the white man's ballots and his dollars and you remove his power." The president of the Forrest County NAACP, J. C.

Fairley, also rallied the crowd to action: "We won't let his death be in vain. If you haven't paid your poll tax do it immediately. If you haven't gotten down to the registrar's office and placed your name on the book, do it. This is what he died for. The life of a Negro is taken too lightly. When one of us is killed nothing is done about it." Dahmer's tragic death became the rallying cry to revitalize the Hattiesburg movement.[9]

The next night, blacks packed into a mass meeting at St. James Church where Fairley presented the demands that the NAACP and the Delta Ministry planned to submit to officials. The city must open the political system to blacks by creating a biracial government. It must hire black bus drivers, firefighters, and deputies. Law enforcement agencies must terminate police brutality and insure that black and white officers possess equal authority. Authorities must enforce the *Brown* ruling, the Civil Rights Acts, and the Voting Rights Act. To tackle health and safety hazards and infrastructure deficiencies in black communities, the public works department must pave roads and construct lighting and sewage systems and eliminate factory toxins. The impassioned crowd approved the list. But when Fairley announced that they would delay the boycott to give authorities time to implement the demands, the crowd reacted with rage, shouting that the NAACP and the Delta Ministry were not the only groups in town. Evers took the lectern and implored the people to stay united, for the enemy was trying "to split us among ourselves." The divisiveness quelled, the protesters marched to the courthouse and knelt in prayer.[10]

The rage, fear, and anguish remained. Most local activists had always advocated self-defense. After Dahmer's death, some of them began carrying guns in public; others hired bodyguards. Fairley, who had received Klan threats, hired James Nix, a black veteran of the Korean War from Laurel, and several of his friends to provide him with armed protection. During one rally, Evers inferred that blacks should seek vengeance when he shouted, "The sooner we bury some of these Klukkers the sooner we will be finished with this kind of thing." Those winter days were anguishing for the Dahmers as they struggled to cope with the relentless pain of living without Vernon and with the horror of how they had lost him. Alvin found it unbelievable that while he and many of his brothers were serving in the military protecting American freedom and democracy from threats abroad, the Klan murdered their father because he was fighting for those values denied him in America. Dahmer's death nearly broke his youngest children. Ellie recalled, "For years my children didn't laugh and play. They lost their childhood."[11]

The killing terrorized blacks throughout the Central Piney Woods. Former Freedom Summer students Carol and Lillie Jackson attended school with Dennis and Bettie; the murder stunned them as did the scars on Bettie's hands and forehead. Although black men in Palmers Crossing carried guns to mass meetings, stood guard at civil rights events, and protected their aunt, Victoria Gray, they never felt safe again. Laurel schoolteacher Gladys Austin grew so frightened of the Klan that she feared even speaking of Dahmer's murder. Eberta Spinks, however, responded with defiance. A few days after Dahmer's death, a white man strode across Spinks's front lawn, sat down on her porch, and warned her, "Mrs. Spinks ... you know what you're doing? That's what Vernon Dahmer got killed about." She responded as she often did to white threats: "If anybody bothers me.... It's going to be blood running down the street like water."[12]

Racial tension percolated as several whites responded defensively to the movement. The Chamber of Commerce called Dahmer's murder an "isolated tragedy" in Hattiesburg and professed that city leaders had devoted themselves to guaranteeing all persons "their rights and privileges." The owners of WBKH television claimed that without coercion, Hattiesburg had desegregated public accommodations; higher educational institutions had integrated; stores had employed black clerks; and the city had hired black police officers. Although reporter Elliott Chaze conceded that blacks had a genuine grievance against the Klan, he castigated them for linking Dahmer's murder with demands for biracial governance and for threatening to boycott Hattiesburg merchants when the "nightriders" likely came from Jones County. In a letter to the *Hattiesburg American*, a man claimed that since Forrest County had a great record because only one person had died, citizens should "be commended for the way they conducted themselves." A woman complained that the community had never raised monies for other families who lost their homes and who were financially less fortunate than the Dahmers; she asked, "How do we know it wasn't civil rights workers who did it to cause trouble? ... Since the Negroes have equal rights now, it's about time they started looking out for their own." Christos Dumas, a political science professor at USM, asserted that the NAACP's demands that the city grant political offices and law enforcement positions to blacks contradicted "American democracy," which provided equal opportunity, not guaranteed success.[13]

This anti–civil rights rhetoric ignored reality. School segregation, police brutality, and employment discrimination persisted in Hattiesburg. Blacks lacked equal opportunity for advancement because in the interest of maintaining the white supremacist state, the white establishment had denied them political and economic power. Klansmen murdered Dahmer because he had planned to collect poll taxes from blacks who wanted to vote. Unless blacks could elect blacks to positions of power from which they could fight discrimination, their plight would never change. The hiring of a few blacks as store clerks and police officers was tokenism and failed to remedy the vast racial injustices and discrimination that still plagued Forrest County some five months after the implementation of the Voting Rights Act, over eighteen months after the passage of the Civil Rights Act, and nearly twelve years after the *Brown* ruling. Dahmer's murder was not an aberration but rather another atrocity born of persistent racial violence and injustices in Hattiesburg's history, including the many lynchings committed at the turn of the century, the conviction of Willie McGee in a mob-filled courtroom, the false imprisonment of Clyde Kennard, the beating of civil rights activists, and persistent police brutality. Moreover, the FBI would soon find that a Forrest County Klansman had proposed Dahmer's murder.[14]

State and city authorities also persisted in undermining the Hattiesburg movement. Governor Johnson ordered the Sovereignty Commission and law enforcement to spy on activists. On January 16, massive patrols of Dahmer's funeral caused racial tensions to explode. Evers and Fairley led 430 black mourners on a solemn march from St. James Church to the Forrest County Courthouse. MHP officers parked at intersections across the city and prepared to aid police should problems arise. When Officer James Owen noticed an inebriated mourner in the crowd, he pushed Evers, Fairly, and two other blacks off the sidewalk with his nightstick and rushed toward the intoxicated man. Evers halted the march and demanded that Chief Herring impose disciplinary action against Owen. Herring refused. Suddenly a vehicle occupied by three white men careened into the street, grazed one woman marcher, and forced others to rush out of the way. Although a MHP report included a description of the red-and-white '56 Ford and the license plate number, police neglected to apprehend the driver.[15]

Thousands of mourners gathered at Shady Grove Baptist Church for Dahmer's funeral. Four of Dahmer's sons wore their military uniforms. NAACP president Roy Wilkins stated that Dahmer had tried to "help his people take part in what the Constitution says, a government by the consent of the governed. . . . [He] was the kind of man everyone has told the colored man he should be, responsible and self respecting and now he is dead." One pastor declared, "Afflictions have always attended the progress of the cause of right and justice. The fires of persecution have cast their dismal shadows across the centuries, but thank God the voice from heaven says God sees it all and one day will set us free."[16]

Local blacks had no intentions of waiting for God to set them free. They expected immediate justice on earth. Between January 17 and 24, activists held five meetings at St. James Church at which leaders established three major goals: the dismissal of Officer Owen, the mass registration of black voters, and the city's compliance with the NAACP's grievance list. Toward those ends, the NAACP filed a complaint against Officer Owen with the civil service board; launched a voter registration drive; and initiated a series of demonstrations. After weeks of protests, city leaders agreed to enter into negotiations with activists and created a biracial Human Relations Committee. The struggle moved from the streets into the boardrooms.[17]

Throughout the city battles, the FBI made progress on the Dahmer case. Moore worked his army of agents from sunup to midnight six days a week and half days on Sundays. Based on evidence collected at the crime scene, informant reports, and interviews, agents developed thirty-eight suspects. Moore assigned agents to each of these Klansmen. Agents shadowed them, questioned them, and interviewed their relatives, friends, associates, and enemies. When agents gathered intelligence from Klan informants, they leaked that information to DABURN suspects. They hoped that if a Klansman thought that one of his brothers had cooperated with agents or feared that they suspected him as the informant, he would cast his lot with the FBI.[18]

To prevent agents from narrowing down the suspect list, Bowers instructed Klansmen to provide the FBI with false information. If the case ever came to trial, defense attorneys could use inconsistencies to discredit witnesses. This misinformation strategy succeeded in complicating the DABURN investigation as a series of contradictory reports from informants combined with lies and half-truths from suspects rendered it difficult for agents to identify all of the killers. Ultimately, agents developed two hypotheses—the six-man theory and the eight-man theory. The theories overlapped at significant points, which allowed agents to determine several important elements of the case. Bowers ordered the murder. Nix assigned Laurel Klavern leaders to plan the killing. Sessum directed the project. Sessum and DeBoxtel selected their crews. Giles supplied one of the vehicles. But when agents attempted to decipher the identities of the men who participated with DeBoxtel and Sessum in the attack, they found themselves entangled in a web of two contradictory stories. The six-man theory emerged from reports by Delmar Dennis, a Klan informant and a close friend of Bowers. Dennis claimed that Bowers had informed him that

Sessum, Billy Moss, Pete Martin, Charles Lowe, Clifton Lowe, and DeBoxtel participated in the attack and used vehicles belonging to Sessum and Giles. Charles Lowe lost his gun at the scene. Clifton Lowe accidentally shot up Giles's Ford. Informants supporting the eight-man theory suggested that the job required eight men: "one wheel man, one bottle throwing man, and two gun men for each car." The theory placed Sessum, Wilson, Smith, and Pitts in Wilson's Pontiac and DeBoxtel, Noble, Thornton, and Lyons in Giles's Ford. Pitts lost his gun at the scene, and Smith shot out the Ford's tire. It took time before the FBI determined the eight-man theory to be correct.[19]

Agents needed to turn one of the killers into a state witness to break the case. As agents swarmed around the Invisible Empire, those who hailed from the South used their background to gain the trust of Klansmen. Agent William Dukes was raised in Forrest County and his father had joined the Klan in the 1920s. He sympathized with Klansmen because he considered many of them "misguided" poor whites who perceived the movement as a threat to their status in society. Agent Frank Watts had an even stronger weapon. His mother grew up in Jones County and knew Klansmen. Some were friends and others were relatives, which helped Watts obtain interviews. Familiarity with the southern dialect, a shared history, and a seemingly common racial perspective sometimes lured Klansmen to trust these agents and divulge information to them.[20]

Bowers made it clear to his White Knights that betraying the Klan constituted treason, a capital offense in the Invisible Empire. Agents tailing Bowers culled no significant information from him. When Bowers and Nix appeared before HUAC in early February, they refused to answer any questions about Klan activities. Bowers expected the same discipline from his underlings. The Leflore County Bar Association and the Jones County Citizens Council helped Bowers by circulating leaflets across the Central Piney Woods advising that "a citizen is under no legal obligation at any time to answer any questions asked by any investigator about anything [,] except in a court hearing or at a court-connected proceeding." Afterward, agents found it increasingly difficult to draw Klansmen into conversations. They had hoped to interview Mordaunt Hamilton of the Forrest County Klavern because informants insisted that Hamilton had introduced the Dahmer project to Bowers. Ellie and Harold Dahmer informed agents that a few months prior to the attack, Hamilton had stopped by their farm to converse with Vernon about his sawmill. Agents deduced that Hamilton was casing the property for the attack. They knew the difficulties of convincing Hamilton to talk as they had learned about his ferocious temper: he abused his employees and shot at people who trespassed on his property. They tried unsuccessfully to interview him on numerous occasions. Agents encountered similar resistance from Thornton, Lyons, Giles, Pitts, and particularly from Nix.[21]

Forty-two-year-old Nix, who ran John's Café in Laurel, told his fellow Klansmen that "FBI men should be treated just like niggers: don't shake hands with them or let them in your homes." Agents James Ingram and James Awe approached Nix in front of his house and informed him that they knew he had planned the Dahmer project. Nix's reddish-complexion flushed more than usual; he berated them for wasting their time on that "nigger" when they should concentrate on fighting communism; he also accused them of threatening him and yelled at his wife to contact the police. When officers arrived, they refused Nix's command to arrest agents without an affidavit. After the encounter, Nix signed three affidavits charging the agents with using profanity, shouting, trespassing, and disturbing the peace. Three days later, MHP officers arrested Nix on various traffic charges and for carrying a concealed weapon—a chain jack. At the station, Sheriff Gray had to use physical force to restrain the nearly six-foot, 200-pound Klansman and obtain his prints. While Agents Ingram and Awe photographed Nix, he shouted, "You men are fugitives from justice.... I have filed a complaint at Laurel, Mississippi, against you two and there are warrants outstanding for your arrest." In mid-February, after the court sentenced Nix to thirty days in jail and fined him $150, Laurel police tried to arrest an agent on charges made by Nix. Upon orders from Moore, Agent Awe informed Chief L. C. Nix that the FBI considered the warrants an obstruction of a federal investigation. If it happened again, the FBI would arrest the officer.[22]

When Klansmen refused to talk to the FBI, agents penetrated their lives by approaching their families and girlfriends, particularly battered wives and mistresses who had reason to betray their husbands and lovers. Giles's battered mistress Mary Lyons revealed to agents that Giles had hinted of his involvement in the murder and had driven her to the spot where the Klan had abandoned his Ford. Klansmen stalking Lyons burned a cross on her yard, and Giles beat Lyons outside John's Café while he castigated her as a "pimp" for the FBI. The agents could not crack Giles. They had better luck with Pete Martin. The beefy, dark-haired Klansman, who worked as a lift operator for Masonite and as a manager of the Burger Chef, was one of the most brutal members of the Klan. Because Martin abused the women in his life, they spoke to agents. His former wife characterized him as mentally unstable; his daughter noted that she had overheard him discussing Klan activities; and his former girlfriend revealed that he had participated in several Klan attacks. When agents interrogated Martin, he informed them that the Forrest County Klavern had proposed Dahmer's murder, Bowers ordered it, Nix planned it, and Byrd approved it. He speculated that DeBoxtel, Pitts, and Sessum had participated.[23]

Agents obtained a major break in the case on January 25 after two white men abducted Byrd, a forty-four-year-old wealthy farmer and businessman, outside his Radio and TV Service shop in Laurel. They transported him to a swampy area where they and a black man beat him. As soon as FBI Agents Robert E. Lee and Robert A. Connors learned that Byrd was in the hospital recuperating, they visited him. Later, Byrd claimed that the FBI staged the abduction to coerce a confession from him. The FBI has always denied the charges. At the least, agents used Byrd's fear for their purposes. Agents promised him immunity and protection if he became an FBI informant. Byrd furnished them with a signed statement implicating himself and several other Klansmen. Byrd revealed that he, Sessum, DeBoxtel, and Moss had attended a Klan meeting in which Bowers ordered Dahmer's murder. Agents spread the information to other Klan suspects. Nix, unaware that Byrd was the informant, ordered Byrd to find the leak. Instead, Byrd used his investigation to identify for the FBI all Klansmen involved in Dahmer's murder.[24]

Soon, Byrd convinced his best friend Moss to provide agents with a signed statement admitting that he had attended the meeting in December at which Bowers solicited volunteers to investigate a "nigger project"; he decided against participating when he found out DeBoxtel, a burly, black-haired, violent drunk, would play a major role. Agents questioned DeBoxtel repeatedly. Finally, he admitted that he had attended planning sessions and suggested that he had led one of the crews. When agents asked if Moss participated in the killing, DeBoxtel snapped that Moss lacked the "guts" for such a job. He also implied that the killers used Giles's vehicle and that Sessum led a crew. So Byrd arranged a meeting with Sessum under the guise of finding the Klan leak. When they met deep in the woods, Byrd demanded to know who had participated in the attack so he could eliminate the leak. Sessum hesitated: "My neck is in the noose, and I don't trust anybody." Byrd responded that his head "was on the block" with Bowers unless he could find the leak. Finally, Sessum conceded that he and DeBoxtel had selected their crews, but he would only name two participants—Pitts and Noble. When agents questioned Noble, he admitted only that he had met Klansmen at John's Café to discuss the Dahmer project and partook in a reconnaissance mission of the Dahmer home.[25]

Agents Awe and Ingram shadowed Sessum constantly and dug deep into his background. Sessum had dropped out of school after the ninth grade, married his fifteen-year-old sweetheart, Mary, and worked as a salesman for Dixie Distributing and as an amateur fundamentalist preacher. He had a fierce temper and often beat civil rights workers, his wife, and children. Mary left him in late 1964. When agents found her on the Mississippi Coast, she informed them that Sessum had boasted that he had led the attack at Brewell Currie's farm during Freedom Summer. Under intense pressure from agents, Byrd revealed to Sessum that he had become an informant. He noted that the FBI was close to making a case and that Sessum would fare better if he confessed. In early March, Byrd brought Sessum to a late night meeting at his farm with Agents Martin and Dukes. With Byrd's urging, Sessum accompanied agents to their Holiday Inn headquarters where he confessed. His confession corresponded with the narrative in Moss's and Byrd's statements regarding the planning phase of the Dahmer project. In addition, Sessum revealed that Giles had left his keys in his vehicle for the Klansmen to use in the Dahmer project. During the attack, one of the Klansmen shot up Giles's car, but Sessum neglected to identify the shooter. He did note that Pitts had lost his gun at the crime scene. When Dukes typed out the statement, Sessum started crying and refused to sign it.[26]

Five days later, under Bowers's orders, Sessum disavowed his confession in a sworn affidavit. He claimed that FBI agents had abducted him and ordered him to sign a confession. When Sessum refused, a US marshal beat him and agents drove him to the "nigger graveyard" where Dahmer was buried. While Sessum knelt in prayer, the marshal held a gun to his head. When agents released him, they threatened to kill him if he uttered a word of his abduction. Sessum chastised the FBI, which he called the "National Gestapo[, for] picking up white Christians and torturing them in a rage of vengeance . . . to appease the nigger mob leaders." Building on Sessum's affidavit, Bowers launched a propaganda campaign. On WDAM-TV, Nix called the federal government a "national dictatorship" and local officials the tools of tyrants who solicited the black vote to foment a "racial revolution in Mississippi." In a widely circulated affidavit, Nix accused Agents Awe and Ingram of threatening his family and beckoned whites to resist the destruction of "our American institution of equal justice under law."[27]

Through threats and persuasion, Bowers brought many wayward Klansmen back into the fold. Martin produced an affidavit stating that he had not participated in the conspiracy against Dahmer. Moss and DeBoxtel reported to agents that they would never testify for the prosecution. Under Bowers's orders, Klansmen made threatening phone calls to Byrd's home, and a Klansman showed up at Byrd's shop wielding a gun and insinuating that he knew that Byrd was the leak. Days later, Bowers strode into Byrd's shop and ordered him to sign an affidavit claiming that agents had abducted Byrd, battered and drugged him, and coerced him to sign a statement. Byrd refused. Bowers retorted that he knew Byrd had betrayed him and made "an alliance with Satan." Byrd snapped that they would see who would win in the end.[28]

Moore determined that the FBI could win if agents arrested the suspects and pressured them to confess. While Moore sought to convince federal officials to seek indictments, the US Supreme Court on March 24 declared poll taxes as a stipulation for voter eligibility in any election a violation of the equal protection clause of the Fourteenth Amendment. The battle for black suffrage, which Dahmer had spearheaded in the Central Piney Woods and for which Bowers had ordered his execution, edged toward victory. Three days later, the Department of Justice indicted fourteen Klansmen—Bowers, Nix, Sessum, Byrd, DeBoxtel, Giles, Clifton and Charles Lowe, Lyons, Martin, Moss, Noble, Pitts, and William Ray Smith—on charges of violating US Code, Title 18, Section 241, which prohibits persons from engaging in a conspiracy "to injure, oppress, threaten and intimidate . . . any citizen in the free exercise and enjoyment of any of the rights or privileges" guaranteed by the Constitution, and for violating Section 11(B) of the Voting Rights Act of 1965, which forbade the use of intimidation, threats, and/or coercion against a person who is attempting to vote, has voted, or is assisting others in their efforts to vote. On March 28, agents arrested all of the indicted Klansmen except Bowers, who went into hiding. A massive federal search for the Imperial Wizard forced Bowers to surrender on March 31.[29]

Within days of the arrests, federal authorities released the Klansmen on bonds. None of the suspects had confessed. After his release, Bowers confided to Nix that "the clank of the jail door closing . . . was a very frightening sound." Still, Bowers remained optimistic because his misinformation campaign had worked; agents failed to arrest three of the participants in the Dahmer attack—Lester Thornton, William Thomas Smith, and Charles Wilson. They had confused William Thomas Smith with William Ray Smith and arrested the wrong Smith, though both were Klansmen. As Nix told Bowers and Martin, "If everybody keeps their mouths shut, they can't even prove that we had anything to do with the planning of it."[30]

The arrests did not temper Bowers's determination to obliterate the movement, but it forced him to modify Klan methods. Based on his study of guerrilla warfare, Bowers developed a twofold strategy. On the public front, he tried to legitimize the Klan by transforming it into the radical political wing of the Democratic Party. He ordered Klansmen to pressure politicians to support extremist policies through a publicity operation that included telephone and letter-writing campaigns, publication of propaganda in newspapers, and distribution of political materials. Bowers also sought to destroy political enemies, particularly Mayor Henry Bucklew, because of the mayor's campaign against the Klan. In April 1966, prosecutors charged Bucklew with attempted embezzlement for endeavoring to steal $816.05 from the city. Bowers and Jones County Klansmen attended the October trial. When the jury found Bucklew guilty, removed him from office, and fined him, Bowers declared that the Klan deserved credit for the conviction.[31]

In a long-term plan to take over the Democratic Party of Mississippi, Bowers persuaded Klansmen to run for offices and backed the gubernatorial campaign of honorary Klansman Jimmy Swan, who hailed from Hattiesburg. To garner support for Klan candidates, Bowers increased Klan membership. He induced many Klansmen from the rival UKA to defect to the White Knights, held recruitment drives on college campuses, and worked with the White Christian Protective and Legal Defense Fund to hold numerous fund-raising rallies at which the DABURN defendants professed their innocence and denounced FBI agents as communists. Only around one hundred people attended the rallies, but most attendees donated to the defense fund. To increase his appeal to mainstream whites, Bowers converted to the Baptist faith, the most popular Christian sect in Mississippi. He also revitalized the Laurel Citizens Council, but most attendees at the organizational meeting were Klansmen.[32]

Bowers directed more of his energies toward developing the second part of his twofold strategy, the creation of a paramilitary underground, because he perceived violence as his most potent weapon to divert FBI attention away from the DABURN case, pacify Klan enemies, and wear down the federal government until it abandoned blacks as it had during Reconstruction. Since Bowers knew that the FBI had infiltrated his Invisible Empire with informants and hoped to topple the organization by turning his minions against him, he tried to decentralize violent units from the Klan core. He ordered all exalted cyclopses to select leaders within their klavern to form clandestine cells, or "units" as he called them, of five members whose identities were only known to each other. Each of these units would be sovereign entities with the power to determine and execute its own projects. Because the FBI focused on the Laurel Klavern, he ordered a moratorium on all Laurel projects and ordered Jesse White to reorient the klavern into a political vehicle that operated in legal enterprises.[33]

Bowers's overhaul plans for the Invisible Empire signified a major shift. On the political front, the Klan sustained its traditional pyramid structure in which orders flowed from the Imperial Wizard to state and local leaders.

The configuration would sustain Klan unity, yet as a political party rather than a terrorist organization, a disgruntled member could not topple the empire. Underground, the militant arm functioned as small, disconnected, and highly secretive units that executed violent projects. If law enforcement infiltrated one unit, only the members of that unit would be compromised. The dual structure was ingenious, but Bowers failed to implement it well. A megalomaniac, he refused to surrender his power to unit leaders. Bowers maintained total control over the units. In addition, he violated his own orders for the Laurel Klavern to stand down.[34] Bowers found it particularly difficult to avoid violence when a protest in northern Mississippi invigorated the movement.

On June 5, 1966, James Meredith, who had integrated Ole Miss, launched a March Against Fear from Memphis to Jackson. The march garnered little attention or participation until the next day, when Meredith entered Mississippi and a white man shot him. Martin Luther King Jr. of SCLC, Stokely Carmichael of SNCC, and leaders from the MFDP, CORE, and the Delta Ministry resumed the campaign. For three weeks, some ten thousand activists, including many from the Central Piney Woods, marched across Mississippi to protest terrorism and promote black suffrage. Reporters captured images of white mobs as they beat marchers in Neshoba County and of patrolmen as they attacked protesters in Canton. At a rally in Greenwood, Carmichael raised his fist and shouted, "We want black power! . . . Every courthouse in Mississippi ought to be burned tomorrow to get rid of the dirt. . . . What do you want?" The crowd shouted, "Black power!"[35]

The Greenwood protest instigated a transformation in the national black struggle. In theory and practice, activists disagreed over the meaning of black power. Some SNCC and Black Panther leaders linked it with black nationalism, black separatism, and anti-capitalism. As SCLC remained devoted to integration and nonviolence, they interpreted black power as the need for black people to acquire equitable political, judicial, and social power. The NAACP shunned the debate. Yet many white Americans, ignoring these nuances and the causes of black anger, branded black power as militant and racist. Over the next year, the FBI blamed many racial disturbances on black power, and the media shifted its focus from critiques of white supremacist violence to sensational exposes on black militancy.[36]

Mississippi's white patriarchs capitalized on the negative national press to vilify the movement. Governor Johnson maligned CDGM, which had provided so many poor blacks with jobs and black children with a free pre-school education via Head Start, as a corrupt black power organization bent on radicalizing black communities. He also appeared before the US

Senate Judiciary Committee to oppose the Civil Rights Act of 1966, which President Johnson had proposed to address racial violence in the wake of Dahmer's murder. Johnson's bill would have prohibited racial discrimination in federal and state jury selection, provided for federal protection of civil rights workers, enhanced the power of the attorney general to initiate desegregation suits, and forbade racial discrimination in housing, but it died in the Senate. Senators John Stennis and James O. Eastland red-baited CDGM by calling it a communist front that used government money to fund a race war; they also claimed it was a racist organization that excluded whites. On a local level, the *Hattiesburg American* declared that militant black activists chanting "black power" and "white blood" at the Meredith march tried to instigate a violent reaction by whites in order to intensify federal intervention. Blacks had never chanted "white blood." Lies like this advanced white efforts to pillory the struggle.[37]

In the Central Piney Woods, the many organizations still operating in the area, including CORE, SNCC, the NAACP, the Delta Ministry, CDGM, and the MFDP, combined black power and civil rights strategies as they struggled against persistent violence and waning national interest. Mississippi and Alabama led the nation in racial terrorism. As Robert Beech of the Delta Ministry noted, authorities abetted violence in Mississippi. They released Bowers on bail after his 1965 arrest in the Neshoba case, which left him free to plan the Dahmer killing. If the courts had punished Hamilton once during his five trials on assault charges against civil rights workers, he might not have requested that the Klan murder Dahmer. Even after indictments in the Dahmer case, the courts released Bowers and his henchmen on bonds. Despite the massive presence of FBI agents investigating DABURN and pledges by law enforcement to punish racial assaults, violence and racial injustice remained rampant. In one incident, when activist Robert Ivey tried to patronize the Chow House Restaurant, DeBoxtel, an indicted DABURN suspect, yanked him out of his seat and beat him. DeBoxtel's stepfather, also a Klansman, shot Ivey. An all-white grand jury refused to indict them, and the federal government failed to charge them with violating Ivey's civil rights. When activists Susie Ruffin, Eberta Spinks, and Robert Stenson protested in front of city hall, Klansmen Billy Roy Pitts, Deavours Nix, Carl Ford, and Jesse White harassed them in front of apathetic policemen. In response to the violent atmosphere, the Deacons for Defense and Justice, a black self-defense organization founded in Louisiana, provided armed patrols during civil rights meetings.[38]

Despite the danger, activists remained as committed as ever to the struggle. Beech launched a summer project in which volunteers and staff from all of the organizations developed surveys on black life and civil rights, organized youth programs, rebuilt structures destroyed by Klansmen, and participated in movement protests and marches. They also focused on voter registration. Their efforts led to the election of the first black politician in Mississippi since Reconstruction when Robert Lee Williams won a seat on the Jefferson County School Board. Though a small triumph, it was a start. CDGM represented one of the most vital civil rights forces despite constant political attacks and low or nonexistent government budgets. In Forrest County, Chairman Pinky Hall praised the growth of the students: "Those that was crying didn't want to go on the first day. Now they is crying wanting to stay.... They look like flowers blooming in early Spring time they be so happy." Staff and faculty in Jones County recalled how three-year-old Joyce Keller refused to speak when she arrived at the center, but after a few weeks, she sang and counted her numbers. Four-year-old Ernest Ivory, "a manly little boy," constantly fought other children when he arrived at the center, but within weeks, his anger dissipated, he made friends and found solace in nature. Students responded to mealtime lessons about nutrition and etiquette by taking pride in their table manners.[39]

Despite CDGM's success, that October the Office of Economic Opportunity (OEO) revoked CDGM's grant because of its alleged "fiscal irresponsibility" and announced that it would fund instead Mississippi Action for Progress (MAP), which created its own Head Start programs. The NAACP and white moderates supported MAP because its bourgeois leadership appealed to them. In MAP, local officials appointed program directors and hired state-certified teachers. CDGM fought back. After a flood of negative publicity that portrayed OEO director Sargent Shriver as Senator Stennis's lackey, OEO allotted CDGM an $8 million grant that fall and $5 million in 1967, still far short of the $20.4 million requested. In April, CDGM advocates lobbied for greater funding at War on Poverty hearings in Jackson. The Reverend J. C. Killingsworth, a black leader in Clarke County who later became a significant force in Forrest County, testified that CDGM intended Head Start to serve the impoverished, employ the black poor, and foster black uplift while MAP "ignored the poor people." A teacher trainee in Laurel called the CDGM "the best thing that ever happened to the Negro race." Yet because the federal government favored MAP and persuaded some state leaders to support it, MAP subsumed CDGM. A Forrest County CDGM worker responded, "You can't blame 'em for being dumb. They're just a bunch of federal jerks, but you cin blame 'em for bein' a bunch of dirty, dishonorable politicians playin' with us little people."[40]

Blacks also continued to confront dirty political tricks in school desegregation. Over a decade after *Brown*, Mississippi politicians had created the freedom-of-choice plan, which ostensibly allowed parents to send their children to either previously all-white or all-black schools. But it was another scheme intended to subvert integration. Black principals had to authorize the transfers, and administrators warned them that substantial transfers would force the district to fire excessive black staff and faculty. Newspapers identified black applicants and the schools from which they requested transfers, placing them, their families, and principals in danger. In the summer of 1966, Bowers furnished his Klansmen with a list of children planning to attend white schools.[41]

Despite the dangers, dozens of black children crossed the color line in the Central Piney Woods schools. Glen, the son of CDGM organizer Maycie Gore in Laurel, was among them. He made some friends and joined the band. But he faced persistent racism. Many teachers and students referred to the students as "niggers," and the junior high canceled the band's appearance in the Christmas parade because of threats against Glen. Black students in Hattiesburg attending Thames Junior High, including twelve-year-old Anthony Harris, who had been arrested for picketing during Freedom Days, also suffered abuse. Harris resolved to neither retreat nor retaliate in the face of white opposition. A student tested that resolve when he hocked a mouthful of spit on Harris's pants sending white children nearby into gales of laughter. Harris fought the urge to hit the boy because he knew that whites would use the incident to demonize blacks and propagandize the dangers of integration. The next year, a former Freedom Summer student, Glenda Funchess, joined Harris and eight other black students attending Thames. As she recalled, when the black students arrived on campus each morning, "the all-white football team charge[d] into us like we were on a football field." White boys routinely slapped and kicked them. When black students walked the hallways, white students often shouted, "Watch out for that nigger" and climbed on "the wall like we were ... snake[s]" and had to be avoided. Funchess only survived the ordeal without suffering an emotional collapse because of her experiences in Freedom Summer, which had inculcated in her a belief in the righteousness of the black struggle.[42]

Blacks integrating Hawkins Junior High confronted similar mistreatment. Isaac Fairley, a career army man, enrolled his son, Kenneth, in Hawkins. Kenneth never shared with his father how much he hated participating in the desegregation effort because Isaac had inculcated in him a sense of responsibility for black liberation. Many nights he told Kenneth that "the field of play would never be leveled" unless blacks broke racial barriers and excelled in the white world. So as Fairley recalled, when his woodshop teacher tried to prevent him from building a china cabinet by insisting that he lacked the talent and finances to create such fine carpentry, Fairley built it anyway. His teacher conceded that he had built a masterpiece and invited the superintendent and principal to view it. Regrettably, their racism marred the laurels that they bestowed on Fairley. They tried to persuade him to pursue industrial arts over academics, for surely his intelligence paled in comparison to whites. Fairley refused and proved his intellectual abilities to the point that white students requested his help on assignments. One evening, while Fairley tutored a white female student over the telephone, her mother grabbed the phone and asked, "Are you colored?" When Fairley responded affirmatively, she severed the call. Fear of miscegenation among black boys and white girls lay at the root of school segregation. The principle suspended Fairley until Isaac demanded successfully that the principal retract the suspension.[43]

The Klan sustained surveillance on the freedom-of-choice children, but projects against them never materialized because betrayals and the DABURN investigation caused a mass defection from the Invisible Empire. Attendance at klavern meetings plummeted. By August, Noble, one of the indicted Klansmen in the case, severed his Klan connections. Bowers and Nix further destabilized the Klan when they informed defendants that the Klan treasury lacked funds to pay their legal fees. On February 11, 1967, the federal government reinstated the indictments and arrested Bowers and several other Klansmen again.[44]

The arrest fueled Bowers's rage. After he posted bond, he activated his underground army. Under Bowers's orders, Klansman Billy Carr used a car bomb in 1967 to murder Wharlest Jackson, treasurer of the Natchez NAACP chapter. On March 7, a Klan unit bombed the Blackwell Real Estate Office in Jackson because it had sold homes to blacks in white neighborhoods. To show his contempt for the DABURN indictments, Bowers ordered an attack in Forrest County; on March 13, Klansmen hurled explosives onto the front yard of Kenneth Bailey's home. Bailey had replaced Klan gubernatorial candidate Jimmy Swan as manager of WBKH radio. During FBI questioning, Swan theorized that his political enemies had bombed the Bailey residence to frame him and damage his campaign. Agents neglected to pursue the case.[45]

Many DABURN defendants demanded that Bowers use his violent cells to eliminate Byrd. While cutting meat in his restaurant, DeBoxtel jested with fellow Klansmen that he wished he was cutting up Byrd. Bowers insisted it was wiser to draw Byrd back into the fold; he developed a foolish tactic to achieve his goal. On the night of March 4, under Bowers's orders, Pitts and Klan lawyer Travis Buckley forced former convict Jack Watkins into Buckley's vehicle. Pitts sat beside Watkins in the backseat while Buckley drove and ordered Watkins to declare on tape that under the FBI's orders, he and another man had abducted Byrd and beaten him until he signed a false statement in the DABURN case. Watkins refused. Buckley, followed by a Ford Falcon, drove to an isolated clearing and parked. Buckley held a knife to Watkins's throat and Pitts struck him. The men in the Falcon, garbed in white hoods and black capes, rushed to the vehicle, yanked Watkins out of the car, and beat him. One of the hooded men placed a gun to the back of Watkins's head and said it contained one bullet. Another began digging Watkins's grave. The gunman pulled the trigger six times. Still, Watkins refused to obey their orders. The Klansmen returned him to his home and ordered him to keep quiet. Watkins disobeyed. On March 9, authorities arrested Buckley and Pitts. Bowers bonded out Buckley and paid his attorney fees but left Pitts in jail. Distraught that Bowers treated him "as if he didn't exist," Pitts threatened to snitch. But Pitts was too devoted to the Klan to betray it.[46]

More determined than ever to propagate the federal conspiracy theory, Bowers persuaded Byrd to sign affidavits claiming that at the behest of the FBI, Watkins had kidnapped him and forced him to give false statements in the DABURN investigation. Byrd's narrative bolstered claims in Sessum's affidavit released a year earlier that accused federal officers of beating him and threatening to kill him until he delivered a false confession. Nix produced an affidavit that featured a photograph of himself with a large bruise on his back. The photograph was taken after an automobile accident, but he claimed that it was from a beating delivered by Sheriff Gray in the presence of FBI agents. The Klan distributed copies of the affidavits across south Mississippi to poison possible jury pools in the DABURN and Watkins cases. Nix also filed a $1 million police brutality lawsuit against the sheriff.[47]

On March 28, Pascagoula district attorney Donald Cumbest tried Buckley on the obstruction of justice charge in the Watkins case. To the Klan's frustration, Byrd testified that he could not identify his abductors and pled the Fifth Amendment when asked about the affidavit that he had signed. The Klan had better luck with career criminal Roy Strickland. He stated that Agent William Dukes and MHP Officers Steve Henderson and Ford O'Neal promised to drop felony auto theft charges against him if he and Watkins abducted Byrd and coerced a confession from him in the Dahmer case. In rebuttal testimony, Watkins's mother declared that on the night in question, her son was at home with her. On March 29, the jury deadlocked, forcing a mistrial. Later, Strickland admitted to Watkins that the Klan had bribed him to testify in the case.[48]

Pitts and Buckley still faced kidnapping charges, and they confronted a judicial system that had grown hostile toward them. Klan attorneys Charles Blackwell and Carl Ford tried to stymie the prosecution's case by presenting their federal conspiracy theory to the grand jury and by castigating District Attorney Cumbest as a puppet of the FBI. Judge Darwin Maples defended federal and state lawmen and denounced Klansmen as "a disgrace to the state of Mississippi." The grand jury returned indictments against Buckley and Pitts. Klansmen had begun to lose their grip on large swaths of white Mississippians. The White Knights had failed to control Watkins through violence, coerce Cumbest through propaganda, or influence the grand jury with fearmongering. Moreover, in May 1967, US district judge Harold Cox dismissed Nix's lawsuit against Sheriff Gray. The Klan had made a major mistake when attacking a lawman adored by segregationists. Cox, a staunch white supremacist, concluded that when officers "meet a character who thinks he is above the law I think they are entitled to lower him to the level of the law."[49]

The White Knights also evinced signs of self-destruction when they targeted one of their brethren, Truman Rogers. Rogers had joined the Klan in October 1965. He lost his affection for the hooded order when Klansmen tried to force him into projects against his will. After suffering through several illnesses that led to the amputation of his leg, Rogers veered toward a mental breakdown and defied Klan orders to participate in projects. Bowers violated his own strategy to use Jesse White to suppress violence in the Laurel Klavern when he commanded White to punish Rogers for his disobedience. On the night of March 29, White, Carr, and Sessum drove thirty miles west of Laurel to Covington County, where they abducted Rogers and drove him to an isolated road. As the car slowed, Rogers opened the door, rolled out, and tried to flee. "Shoot him," White shouted. Carr obliged. The force of the bullet knocked Rogers to the ground. As he tried to rise, Carr shot him again. Sessum shoved a shotgun in Rogers's face and warned him that if he betrayed them, they would kill him.

After the Klansmen dropped Rogers off at the hospital, he reported the attack to authorities and informed the FBI that he had information on DABURN; he had participated in the planning sessions. In July 1967, the state tried Sessum for the attack on Rogers. Sessum, White, and Carr testified that they had abducted Rogers as part of a citizens' arrest because Rogers had forfeited a bond that White had posted for him. They claimed that

Rogers pulled a toy gun on them, but because they thought it was real, Carr shot him. On July 21, the jury deadlocked. Once again, the state failed to convict a Klansman and freed him to participate in terror campaigns. At the least, however, the FBI was using Rogers to build the DABURN case.[50]

The Klan crimes, indictments, and trials weakened the Klan in Forrest County, but they strengthened it in Jones County. In the spring of 1967, *Hattiesburg American* journalist James Bonney declared that under the pressure of federal, state, and local investigations "the Klan's Mississippi empire is crumbling." Fear of FBI infiltration caused mistrust to fester, which instigated defections. Loss of membership dues led to financial disaster for the Invisible Empire. Yet in the spring of 1967, Bowers reinvigorated support for the Klan in Jones County when a strike broke out at Masonite and black scabs filled once whites-only jobs.[51]

On April 21, employees at the Masonite plant in Laurel violated the no-strike agreement between the International Woodworkers of America and the plant after management fired an employee without cause. On April 23, Judge Shannon Clark ordered strikers to return to work. Over two thousand strikers, many of whom belonged to the Klan, violated the order. Masonite sued the union. In early May, the Mississippi Supreme Court ordered strikers to return to work. They refused. Masonite filed contempt of court charges. Appeals mired Jones County in tumult as some white and many black employees returned to work; many whites remained on strike; and management hired black laborers and white college students to replace strikers. Bowers exploited the rage of white strikers to recruit them into the Klan.

As Bowers conspired with Klansmen Deavours Nix, V. L. Lee, and Norman Lee to launch a terror campaign against the workers who crossed the picket lines, he turned Jones County klaverns into a den of the most active terror units that summer. Strikers established a beachhead across the street from Masonite. Large groups marched in picket lines. Small groups watched the plant to identify strikebreakers and scabs. Alvin Gore Sr., whose wife Maycie served as an organizer for CDGM, had joined the strike but abandoned it once the Klan took over. Safer in numbers, Gore joined carpools in which armed blacks crammed into the back of pickup trucks. One evening, whites followed Gore's carpool. The black passengers aimed their guns at the vehicle, and the driver sped away. Nightriders also targeted whites. Between June 29 and July 10, nightriders shot into the homes of dozens of Masonite employees, injuring many of them. Nightriders dynamited part of the Gulf Mobile and Ohio Railroad Line outside Laurel, a Masonite well, and a United Gas Company line. Klansmen attacked the plant with cherry bombs, released tear gas inside Masonite facilities, and used slingshots to fire metal objects at workers and managers. When Masonite hired security guards, a carload of men fired a volley of bullets toward the security vehicle.[52]

Bowers made a mistake when he targeted white scabs and white employees along with their black counterparts. Several Jones County residents formed a Committee of Concern and passed a resolution that condemned the violence. Fern Bucklew, who had assumed the mayor's office after her husband's incarceration, issued a joint statement with commissioners and fifty civic leaders condemning the violence. At the city's request, MHP flooded into Laurel. The FBI aided local law enforcement in the investigation. Sheriff Merrill Pickering reminded the people that they had the right to defend themselves. So after Deavours Valentine, a striking employee, hurled a bottle at a black employee, Otis Milsaps, Milsap threw the bottle back at Valentine. Yet officers arrested only Milsaps. In August, a group of local blacks sent a letter to Mayor Bucklew, noting "we are humbly asking you to make the people stay away from the Masonite plant threatening the poor working men." The mayor neglected to respond, but she stepped up police patrols of the plant. Her efforts failed to deter the Klan.[53]

On August 14 at 11:00 p.m., the sounds of rapid gunfire exploded across the quiet plant and startled the guards on watch. Bullets punctured the windows of a security vehicle driven by Robert Sparkman. Fragments from the blast wounded his passenger, Sergeant DeFazio. Guards Julian Carr and Robert Anthony Billiot left their posts to determine the location of the shooters. Carr heard a quick succession of shots. Light bulbs shattered. The plant went dark. Carr hit the ground until the shooting stopped. Then he scoured the dark grounds for Billiot. He found him lying on his back over his lit flashlight, his swollen eyes staring into nowhere. Blood poured from holes in his head. Twenty-three-year-old Billiot had returned home after serving a tour of duty in Vietnam with the Green Berets only to be murdered at Masonite by Klansmen.[54]

District Attorney Chet Dillard called the killing a "cold blooded murder." Police started arresting nightriders, including Klansman Lavelle Stockman on charges of beating one worker and shooting into the home of another. Prosecutors presented evidence to the grand jury of numerous assaults, sixteen drive-by shootings, four bombings, and one attempted bombing. The jurors concluded that law enforcement had shown a dereliction of duty. With Judge Casey's urging, jurors returned a series of indictments. The crackdown ended violence at Masonite, but Bowers increased it elsewhere. On September 9, three hooded men beat a white CDGM teacher. To divert attention away from the Central Piney Woods, Bowers ordered his most secret unit, which included Thomas Tarrants III from Alabama and a Mississippi schoolteacher Kathy Ainsworth, to launch a series of attacks against the Jewish population in Jackson and Meridian. On September 18, the unit blew up Jackson's Temple Beth Israel Synagogue.[55]

The Klan members also continued to attack black protesters. But they were not alone in perpetuating violence that summer. During the Masonite strike, on May 28, 250 black youths marched to the Burger Chef located in Laurel's KC Bottom. Despite the Civil Rights Act of 1964 and the multiple sit-ins over the years, the burger joint still refused to allow blacks inside the restaurant. Most of the organizers were not activists trained in nonviolent protest nor had they sought backing from a civil rights group. They were teenagers coming of age in an era of black power, some of them already Vietnam War veterans who, after fighting in Southeast Asia, refused to suffer as oppressed people in their own nation. They honored Malcolm X over Dr. King and listened to the Black Panthers rather than the NAACP. They found new black role models in Laurel, particularly Urban Pugh, a Black Muslim, who owned several businesses in the KC Bottom. Even former Freedom School students like Johnny Magee, flocked to hear Pugh preach about black pride and self-defense. These young blacks rejected gradual change. As one black youth noted, they refused to allow whites to "beat the shit out of them with no baseball bat" without retaliation. "To hell with nonviolence."[56]

When the black teenagers arrived at the Burger Chef, they came in contact with over three hundred white youths who considered the joint their hangout. Klansmen had urged white teenagers to assault any blacks trying to integrate it. Pete Martin managed the place, and his fellow Klansmen regularly patronized the joint. When the protesters tried to enter the restaurant, white youths hurled rocks at them. The black teenagers refused to leave until policemen arrived and forced them off the property. Down the road from the Burger Chef, protesters gathered. They decided that if they could not eat inside the Burger Chef, then whites could not enter their neighborhoods. Those who dared would be considered invaders open to attack. They hurled bottles and bricks at white travelers. In retaliation, whites at the Burger Chef heaved rocks at black-driven vehicles. Police reported that some two hundred people of both races participated in these fracases, but officers only arrested blacks.[57]

The Burger Chef protest reflected the internecine conflicts in Laurel's black community. Most of Laurel's elder blacks feared challenging Jim Crow. Many middle-aged blacks continued to embrace nonviolence and believed in the power of the ballot and nonviolent direct action to bring about change. Many black teenagers and young adults saw themselves as black revolutionaries and argued that they must fight violence with violence if they wished to liberate themselves from white oppression. Some black youths, including Larry McGill, who had been beaten by Klansmen during a Freedom Summer sit-in, found himself caught between his parents' nonviolent revolution and his older brothers' "black power" ideals. Throughout 1967, factionalism stymied the Laurel struggle.[58]

Although some blacks turned to violence in the Hattiesburg movement that summer, the local NAACP, which by 1967 dominated the local struggle, curtailed factionalism. NAACP leaders had spent over seventeen months haggling with city fathers over the list of demands that they had delivered to them in the wake of Dahmer's murder. Through evasion, manipulation, and lies, authorities rejected each demand. They claimed erroneously that all public establishments had complied with federal desegregation laws. They insisted that they lacked the authority to enforce school integration, to compel the sheriff—an elected official—to hire black deputies, or to require private companies to hire black employees. Although they pledged that when positions became available on city and county boards, they would consider all candidates based on their merit, they failed to acknowledge the need to insure black representation on these boards since whites had long used them to oppress blacks. They denied the charges that the HPD's few black officers were used as lackeys to abuse black citizens, and they refused to investigate black and white officers whom had been accused of police brutality. They concluded, "With the help of people of all races and stations in life this progressive city has always lived under and shown respect for the rule of law."[59]

Blacks disagreed, and they prepared to launch a massive protest. On July 18, the new president of the Forrest County NAACP, Dr. C. E. Smith, held a rally at St. James Church and announced that effective July 19, the NAACP would boycott city buses and white-owned stores downtown until the city met all of their demands. The NAACP chose these targets because blacks comprised 30 percent of the patrons in downtown stores and 90 percent of the passengers riding city buses, and yet these businesses only employed a minuscule percentage of blacks. The audience responded jubilantly, and the NAACP kicked off its boycott with a march to city hall. To the thrill of the NAACP, on the morning following the march, busses passed through town devoid of black passengers. By the third day, the black clientele in Hattiesburg stores had fallen from thirty percent to one percent. By using carpools and black taxis, blacks sustained the bus boycott. White women aided it inadvertently by transporting their black domestics.[60]

Although the black insurrection employed nonviolent direct action, some blacks determined violence to be necessary. Many black teenagers, like their counterparts in Laurel, had grown weary of nonviolence. After the march on city hall, several black youths hurled bottles at white-driven vehicles. The next night a black person shattered the glass storefronts of five white-owned businesses located in black neighborhoods. A group of black adults used violence in a more organized fashion against both whites whom they considered threatening and against blacks who refused to honor the boycott. James Nix, a native of Laurel who had provided protection for NAACP leaders since Dahmer's murder, decided that the Hattiesburg movement must become more militant to succeed. He recruited twelve friends and formed the Spirit. They made threatening calls to blacks who violated the boycott. When that failed, they shot out the windows of their homes or vandalized their vehicles. The Spirit also guarded meetings and neighborhoods aggressively. White leaders capitalized on these sporadic eruptions of violence to accuse "trouble-makers" of using the boycott to foment a "revolution" and pointed to black armed guards as signs of an imminent race war. They also used it as an excuse for mass arrests.[61]

The NAACP had plenty of youths to replenish the frontlines because new civil rights leaders in the Central Piney Woods, Rev. J. C. Killingsworth and Father Peter Quinn, brought hundreds of black teenagers into the summer insurrection, including young veterans of the struggle like Jimella Stokes, Glenda Funchess, and Carolyn and Lillie Jackson. Killingsworth, a Methodist preacher, had become a seasoned activist seventy miles northeast of Hattiesburg in the Clarke County movement. Quinn, raised in the Free State of Ireland, empathized with the plight of blacks, for he perceived the black struggle as parallel to the suffering of the Irish still under British rule in Northern Ireland. As the new priest of Holy Rosary, an all-black Catholic Church, he perceived his civil rights work as fulfilling the church's devotion to social justice. Quinn and Killingsworth, both imposing figures physically and emotionally, commanded respect from their charges. After Killingsworth learned that Mrs. Lotts routinely pointed guns at black customers, he led a massive teenage protest outside her store. Based on an affidavit from Lotts, officers arrested picketers for disturbing the peace. That night 550 people attended a mass meeting.[62]

The insurrection nearly spiraled out of control on July 27, when Officer Willie McGilvery and Officer Lawrence Floyd Jr. investigated an attack on a black café. According to police, black resident Lonnie Charles MaGee shouted at them, "Everyone of you ought to be killed." McGilvery tried to arrest MaGee for ridiculing an officer, but MaGee punched McGilvery and tried to retrieve a knife from his pocket. McGilvery shot him in the chest. Mayor Grady, Chief Herring, and Finch declared the shooting justified. Smith accused the city of engaging in a "cover up." During a rally that night at Mt. Zion Baptist Church, black armed guards shot at whites driving by the church. When Sovereignty Commission investigator Leland Cole and Detective Bobby Earl Roberson rushed to the scene to investigate, a black man shot at their vehicle and then melted into the crowd. The next day, 175 blacks marched to the courthouse to protest the MaGee shooting. During the rally, Killingsworth blamed the exploding violence on whites, noting that "we're not the ones wearing white sheets." That night police arrested five blacks for hurling glass bottles at a vehicle driven by a white man.[63]

When police continued to arrest blacks on various charges of unlawful picketing based on signed affidavits by whites, Smith filed a lawsuit against the city on the grounds that the arrests deterred blacks from engaging in their right to petition their government. US district judge Cox upheld anti-picketing laws and even tightened restrictions on demonstrations. He ruled that protesters could not "utter any sounds or make any signs or gestures" while picketing; they could not number more than six; they must remain five feet apart; and they could not picket on private property. Smith appealed. He accused the city of using arbitrary arrests and excessive bail to repress the boycott and police of refusing to arrest white hecklers who verbally abused black protesters and who drove their automobiles through picket lines at perilous speeds. In response to Smith's lawsuits, whites hurled a brick through the window of his office and broke four windows in a Texaco Station where NAACP members often congregated. Authorities failed to respond.[64]

Black-led violence had an ambivalent impact. It allowed authorities to exploit such incidents to falsely portray the entire movement as unlawful. But it also forced unanimous black compliance with the boycott. And it served as a warning to white southerners who understood the power of violence to control human behavior because they had long used it to oppress blacks. Moreover, the violence remained minimal enough that the NAACP could refute white efforts to slander the entire movement. To that end, Smith issued a statement in the *Hattiesburg American* declaring that the NAACP had never condoned violence, that blacks had showed remarkable restraint in the face of white attacks, and that racial hostility would have exploded into race riots had the NAACP not channeled black rage into nonviolent protest. Smith promised to end the boycott when whites responded to black grievances. Privately, he and his wife, Jeanette, worried that the violence would damage the struggle.[65]

On September 14, Smith terminated the boycott after he and other black leaders brokered a compromise with city leaders and business owners. Banks hired black tellers, grocery stores employed black clerks, and the bus company hired black drivers. Yet white authorities still refused to develop a biracial government, enforce school integration, integrate blacks into the county and city governing bodies and law enforcement apparatuses, and dismiss policemen accused of brutality. Smith enraged some blacks when he ended the boycott with these grievances unresolved.[66] But he turned the NAACP's attention to the 1967 elections.

The 1967 election year concerned everyone in Mississippi. The prospect of change terrified most whites, whereas the possibility of stagnation worried most blacks. Political candidates spanned the gamut from Klansmen to MFDP leaders. All of the five leading gubernatorial candidates, William Waller, John Bell Williams, Ross Barnett, William Winter, and Jimmy Swan supported segregation, but only Klan candidate Swan made it the cornerstone of his campaign. Waller, who had unsuccessfully prosecuted Byron de la Beckwith for Medgar Evers's murder, portrayed himself as the law and order candidate, and he promised to punish all acts of violence whether committed by the Black Panthers or the Klan. Beckwith ran for lieutenant governor in a field of six candidates. This Klan favorite proclaimed that if he won, he would establish "absolute white supremacy. . . ." Klan lawyers Charles Blackwell and Lawrence Arrington ran for district attorney in Jones County and Forrest County respectively, and Deavours Nix ran for sheriff of Jones County. Nix portrayed himself as a Baptist, a Mason, a member of the George Wallace for President Club, a business owner, and a lifelong resident of Jones County except for his World War II service. He pledged that if elected, he would insure "that the majesty of the law [be] upheld, that the cause of freedom and local self-government be strengthened, and that the rights to safety of person and preservation of private property shall not be violated." In secret White Knight meetings, Nix promised that the Klan would run Jones County. Bowers ordered Klansmen to intimidate black voters at every polling place.[67]

The MFDP also had great expectations for the 1967 election because it had developed a new strategy of building a local political foundation. Sixty black candidates, supported by the MFDP, ran for local offices as independents. The MFDP platform called for a complete reorganization of Mississippi's educational structure, the destruction of the state's economic system based on black exploitation, and an investigation of the Klan-led Masonite strike. Victoria Gray campaigned for candidates throughout Mississippi and traveled across the nation to solicit financial support. She informed her audiences that though great changes had transpired, Mississippi remained a "police state" in which diehard segregationists, including Stennis and Eastland, still held Senate seats. Yet because federal rulings, like those against Lynd and Caves, had curtailed voter discrimination, black registration had increased to 225,000. With these rising numbers, the MFDP hoped to integrate the political halls across Mississippi.[68]

The election produced mixed results. Blacks voted in record numbers and elected black leaders across the state in counties where blacks constituted a majority. Although white majorities in Forrest and Jones Counties voted largely for Swan, the majority of the state voted for Williams and Winter. Williams won the primary in the runoff election and easily defeated his Republican opponent in November. He modeled his governorship after Governor Johnson, trying to sustain the white supremacist system and mitigate federal intervention by opposing both the Klan and civil rights activism. Beckwith lost his bid for lieutenant governor. Finch defeated Arrington in a landslide election, Nix lost his bid for sheriff, and Blackwell lost his race for district attorney. Whites sustained power over the state, but the MFDP desegregated many political halls across Mississippi, and Bowers's efforts to usurp the political system had failed.[69]

In addition, Bowers was failing to control his Invisible Empire because he had abused his underlings. The Klan's mistreatment of Rogers had led the latter to become the first key witness in the Dahmer case. During the late summer of 1967, Klan informants revealed to the FBI that Pitts harbored a grudge toward Bowers because the latter had bonded out Buckley and paid his attorney fees in the Watkins affair while leaving Pitts to fend for himself. Many Klansmen believed incorrectly that Pitts had become an informant. They discussed eliminating him. Jesse White, who had become an FBI informant because he thought that he could extort cash from agents, lured Pitts into his confidence. He promised Pitts to agents for $15,000. Agents pressured White to deliver Pitts without pay. Pitts was near a nervous breakdown when White suggested that he become an informant. Terrified that his Klan brothers were planning to execute him, Pitts fled to Louisiana to seek guidance from his brother, a pastor, who persuaded Pitts to surrender to the FBI. White arranged the deal—Pitts would talk in exchange for protection.[70]

The FBI hoped that Pitts would help it bring down the Invisible Empire. The DABURN arrests in 1966 and the Neshoba case had cracked the fortress, and the FBI's divide and conquer tactics spread fissures across the empire. Although Bowers's guerrilla warfare strategy was brilliant, he failed to politicize the Klan, and his ego prevented him from allowing his underground units to execute hits untraceable to him. The many insurrections in the summer of 1967 expanded fractures within the larger white society as all of them diminished white power. When Bowers ordered attacks on white workers at Masonite and when he allowed Nix to launch a lawsuit against a white sheriff popular among white residents, he undermined white solidarity. The Masonite terror campaign compelled city hall, the judiciary, and law enforcement to abet efforts to temper Klan violence. On the other side of the color line, white terrorism inspired blacks to launch massive protests and incited some to use violence. Although activists' use of violence divested the movement of its high moral ground in its civil rights morality play, it advanced the struggle. Attacks on blacks who violated the boycott forced unanimous compliance with the Hattiesburg insurrection, which compelled white patriarchs to broker compromises with activists. And black assaults on whites spoke to white southerners in a language that they understood. If authorities hoped to prevent mass racial violence, they had to start punishing white violence, too. Bowers refused to accept it yet, but his power was fading. The summer insurrections propelled the Central Piney Woods toward a decisive battle.

CHAPTER 7

Trials of the Ku Klux Klan

AT 7:40 P.M. ON SEPTEMBER 29, 1967, KLANSMAN BILLY ROY PITTS ENtered room 334 at the Admiral Bendow Inn in Jackson and informed FBI agents Robert Lee and William Dukes that he had murdered Vernon Dahmer. There was no turning back. The tall, ruddy-faced Klansman betrayed his Klan brothers and joined forces with the FBI. Late into the night, Pitts led agents on a bloody trail of Klan attacks and into the heart of the Invisible Empire as he unveiled its secrets, its members, and its power over Mississippi. When Pitts spoke of Dahmer's murder, he revealed facts that agents had spent nearly twenty-one months trying to confirm—the identities and roles of all of the killers.[1]

The turning of Billy Roy Pitts in the DABURN investigation proved even more significant than the turning of Klansmen James Jordan and Doyle Barnette in the Neshoba murders of three civil rights workers in the MIBURN case. Pitts's klavern, located in Bowers's hometown of Laurel, was the headquarters for the Invisible Empire. He had extensive knowledge of the inner workings of the White Knights and knew the crimes of the top echelon. Pitts not only provided agents and local prosecutors with a wealth of evidence to convict Dahmer's killers but also significant information about other cases, including the Watkins kidnapping and the Klan terror campaign at Masonite. Although the MIBURN trial could produce significant federal convictions, to fully dismantle the Invisible Empire, the FBI needed the state to send Klansmen to prison on murder charges. Prior to Pitts's confession, District Attorney Jimmy Finch informed agents that he needed more evidence before he could consider charging the DABURN suspects. Without the testimony of a participant, the Department of Justice also refrained from proceeding with a federal trial, as an acquittal might spur Klan growth. With Pitts's confession, prosecutors had the evidence to develop their case. The recipe for the Klan's destruction needed one more ingredient—local juries willing to return guilty verdicts. With Pitts on board, Finch was confident that he could deliver convictions. The White Knights were about to suffer for one of their worst mistakes—the mistreatment of Billy Roy Pitts—for he betrayed them all, and his confession tore down the walls of the Invisible Empire.[2]

Pitts's narrative of Dahmer's murder was not the only theory circulating. Klan informant Delmar Dennis remained devoted to the six-man theory. The FBI concluded that since Pitts participated in the attack, "it would appear likely that his information would be more accurate than the information furnished [by Dennis] allegedly by Sam Bowers, as it is conceivable that Bowers put out an erroneous story in an effort to confuse the information which was being gathered at the time." Moreover, Pitts's confession corroborated statements from other participants and conspirators and matched the evidence found at the crime scene, including the pistol, which Pitts revealed belonged to him. Federal and local prosecutors built their cases around Pitts's confession. Pitts tried to convince his best friend in the Klan, Charles Lowe, to become a state witness after Bowers turned on him, too, and expelled him from the Klan. Lowe considered it, but his hatred for the federal government deterred him.[3]

Pitts was good enough; he was a wellspring of information. During meetings with Agents Lee and Dukes, Pitts confirmed Jack Watkins's statement of his kidnapping and revealed the identity of the three masked men—Cecil Sessum, Deavours Nix, and Sam Bowers. District Attorney Donald Cumbest in Pascagoula rebuilt the Watkins case. Pitts also informed agents that he had sold explosives to Andre Hendry and Norman Lee, whom he believed blew up bridges and gas lines at Masonite. Agents passed information about the Masonite cases to Jones County prosecutor Charles Pickering and Laurel district attorney Chet Dillard, who hoped to end their last year as prosecutors with convictions in the Masonite cases. They had already suffered one defeat. In early September, jurors found one indicted nightrider not guilty of interfering with the employment of Masonite workers. While Cumbest worked on the Watkins case, Pickering and Dillard built the Masonite cases, and Jimmy Dukes and Finch investigated DABURN, the most publicized Klan case in Mississippi—MIBURN—came to trial on October 9 in Meridian.[4]

More than three years had passed since FBI agents found the bodies of Michael Schwerner, James Chaney, and Andrew Goodman buried in an earthen dam in Neshoba County. Local prosecutors had made no effort to bring the Klansmen to trial on murder charges. But the Department of Justice, with the help of Klan informants, presented a powerful case against Bowers and seventeen other Klansmen for violating the civil rights of the three murdered men. On October 20, an all-white jury acquitted seven defendants and deadlocked on verdicts for four. However, the jurors found Bowers and six other defendants guilty, marking the first time that a Mississippi jury had convicted Klansmen in a federal civil rights case since Reconstruction. Judge Harold Cox allowed Bowers and the other convicted Klansmen to post bond pending the sentencing hearing. A few days later, Judge Cox learned that someone had stolen large quantities of dynamite in Meridian, and that two MIBURN defendants jested about using dynamite in future attacks. Judge Cox warned Klansmen that he would revoke bail of every convicted MIBURN defendant if a single bomb exploded in Mississippi.[5]

Undaunted by Cox's threats, Bowers planned a fall bombing campaign, and he and Nix, certain that Pitts had become an informant, tried to hunt him down. However, Special Agent in Charge Roy Moore had just relocated Pitts outside of Mississippi under federal protection. On November 10, authorities arrested Bowers, Sessum, and Nix on charges of obstructing justice, conspiracy to kidnap, and kidnapping in the Watkins case. The Reverend Allen Johnson, the new pastor of St. Paul's Methodist Church in Laurel, declared that the people could finally sleep now that the White Knights were behind bars. Before moving to Laurel in June 1967, Johnson, a member of the NAACP and MFDP, had spent several years working on black voter registration in Jackson. Enraged by Johnson's comment, Bowers taught the minister that no enemy of the White Knights could ever sleep well. On November 15, while Bowers remained behind bars, a bomb planted by the Klan's secret unit exploded in the carport of the Johnson home. It decimated the family vehicle and collapsed the roof of the house, but no one was injured. The attack on Johnson kicked off the Klan's fall bombing campaign. On November 19, Bowers's secret unit bombed the home of a white Jackson activist; it destroyed only the porch. The next day, authorities released Bowers, Nix, and Sessum on bond. One night later, the unit targeted a rabbi who had hosted integrated meetings at his synagogue; the bomb destroyed the first floor of his home, but it failed to kill him. The *Laurel Leader-Call* reminded the public that Judge Cox had promised to revoke the bail of MIBURN defendants in the event of a bomb-related attack. Cox proved unworthy of his word.[6]

Blacks and some whites across the Central Piney Woods expressed outrage over the attack on Rev. Johnson's home. The local Committee of Concern and the Jones County Ministerial Association condemned the attack; the former developed a biracial organization with black leaders to preempt violence, open lines of communication, and discuss protests. One of the ministers, the Reverend Robert Marsh of the First Baptist Church in Laurel, represented the typical white moderate preacher in Jones County. Marsh had often counseled his ten-year-old son, Charles, that slavery was "evil" but failed to denounce segregation. He considered it a political rather than a spiritual matter, which gave him an excuse to denounce violence but avoid the heart of the conflict. White ministers did not join black Hattiesburg ministers, the Reverends Milton Barnes and J. C. Killingsworth, when they led nearly all of the black ministers in Laurel and one hundred black students from Oak Park High School in a protest march from Johnson's burned home to Laurel's city hall. On the steps of city hall, Killingsworth shouted that Klansmen had attacked Johnson as they had struck Vernon Dahmer, like "dirty dogs who do their cowardly acts under the edge of darkness." Nothing had changed except black patience. Referring to race riots in Michigan, he added, "We do not want a Detroit in Laurel, but we are at the end of our patience." Aware that Chief L. C. Nix and Sovereignty Commission inspectors were monitoring the protest, Killingsworth warned, "We want to live in peace if the white people will let us. We have taken every kind of abuse and turned the cheek three times, but we will not take any more."[7]

Despite such passionate speeches, black activism posed little threat to the white establishment that fall as the Laurel movement continued to decline, and divisiveness sapped the Hattiesburg movement of its power. Several veteran members of the NAACP, particularly J. C. Killingsworth, J. C. Fairley, Ellis Fluker, and Daisy Harris, grew frustrated with Dr. C. E. Smith's conservative leadership. They had opposed Smith's decision to terminate the summer boycott because the city had refused to comply with many of the demands, including the improvement of infrastructure in black communities, the formation of a biracial government, the firing of police officers accused of brutality, and the full integration of blacks into public safety departments. The foursome insisted that the NAACP initiate direct action projects until the city acquiesced to all of the demands. When Smith refused, they formed the Forrest County Action Committee (FCAC) and launched a boycott of several merchants. As only a few hundred blacks participated, it proved ineffective and ended after six days. Nevertheless, Smith and his wife, Jeanette, perceived the FCAC as a threat. In a report to the National Executive Committee, Smith accused the foursome, all of whom remained NAACP members, of embracing black militancy, usurping NAACP projects, and seeking to radicalize the movement. After a hasty January hearing, the NAACP expelled them. The divisiveness stagnated activism.[8]

Simultaneously, the Klan experienced discord, particularly as attacks from local authorities against the White Knights inspired more mutinies.

Soon after Pitts provided agents information about the Masonite terror campaign, a Klansman telephoned Dillard to report that he had some information about the murder of the Masonite security guard, Robert Billiot. The caller asked Dillard to meet him in a funeral home parking lot and ordered him to come alone. Pickering was at Dillard's home on the night of the call. When Laurel police refused to provide backup, Pickering borrowed an officer's pistol, accompanied Dillard to the funeral home, and hid near the window. To Pickering's relief, the meeting proceeded peacefully, and the Klansman gave Dillard information about the murder.[9]

On October 7, police arrested V. L. "Dubie" Lee and Andre Hendry for the murder of Billiot. At the preliminary hearing, Pickering and Dillard played a tape of Hendry discussing the killing with Klan informant Jesse White. Hendry told White that he planned to shoot the guard's "brains out, and Dubie said, 'Shoot at the legs.' I said 'Hell no. I'm gonna shoot his ____ brains out.'" When White asked him if he had any qualms about the murder, Hendry responded, "Naw, it didn't bother me a fucking bit." Lee and Hendry were among the most violent Klansmen. During Freedom Summer, Lee had beaten David Gelfand at the Brewell Curie farm. In the fall of 1967, the grand jury indicted Lee and Hendry. While building the Billiot case, Pickering and Dillard pursued other Masonite cases. In late November 1967, Henry West pled guilty to shooting into the home of a Masonite employee. Judge Lunsford Casey, who had earlier implored the grand jury to indict the Klan terrorists in Masonite cases, issued a light sentence for West—a five-year probation. West's co-conspirator, Lavelle Stockman, pled not guilty. During Stockman's trial, West, then a prosecution witness, testified that he drove a truck past the target residence while Stockman shot into the home. On December 7, the jury found Stockman not guilty. Pickering left office. The new prosecutor dismissed some of the pending Masonite cases, passed others to the files, and procrastinated on the Billiot case. On December 8, the union and Masonite reached an agreement. A few days later, the Mississippi Supreme Court found the union and five of its leaders guilty of contempt of court injunctions against striking, but none of these charges touched the Klan. Strikers returned to work. Klansmen believed that they had won the Masonite battle.[10]

But the DABURN and MIBURN cases remained a powerful threat. In late December, Judge Cox sentenced the seven convicted men in the Neshoba case. Only Bowers and Alton Wayne Roberts received the maximum of ten years. Again, Cox permitted Bowers to post bond pending an appeal. Upon his release, Bowers instructed his secret units to launch a winter bombing campaign. In early January 1968, Thomas Tarrants's group bombed two black churches in Meridian. But finally, more than two years after Dahmer's murder, the FBI war against the White Knights in the Central Piney Woods approached its decisive battle as authorities began bringing the Jones County Klansmen to trial. The alliance between the FBI and Mississippi authorities produced its first victory in a case peripheral to the DABURN investigation. In mid-January in Covington County, a jury found Billy Carr guilty for assault, battery, and attempted murder of his fellow Klansman, Truman Rogers. Newspapers claimed it was the first finding of guilt against a Klansman on state charges in Mississippi. There had been others, but they were rare, and none had occurred during the Civil Rights Movement.[11]

A week after Carr's conviction, the state delivered murder and arson indictments against twelve Klansmen in the Dahmer case, marking the first time that a Mississippi jury returned capital indictments against Klansmen for an attack on a black civil rights activists since Reconstruction. By Friday, January 26, 1968, the state had arrested and charged Bowers, Buckley, Nix, Byrd, and Giles with arson and Sessum, DeBoxtel, Wilson, Lyons, Smith, Thornton, and Noble with arson and murder. Those men charged with murder were held without bond. On January 27, Nix, Byrd, Bowers, and Buckley posted bond and were released. The indictments stemming from Pitts's testimony in the state cases, save Wilson's, did not shock the public, for all but Wilson had been indicted previously on federal charges or in other Klan cases. But Wilson was a prominent socialite who owned and ran the Laurel Limb and Brace Company and belonged to the country club. The night before his arrest, local Jaycees had honored Wilson with the Distinguished Service Award at the Pinehurst Hotel for his contributions to the Jones County community.[12]

Although the Klan had its sympathizers, *Hattiesburg American* journalist Elliott Chaze reported that most citizens were grateful for the arrests of Dahmer's killers because they believed that the accused men should face more severe charges than federal civil rights violations. Chaze argued that the state indictments revealed a phenomenal development in Mississippi. A few years earlier, such action against Klansmen would have resulted in "political suicide for the prosecutors and public ostracism for members of the grand jury and anyone else connected with pressing the case." Finch echoed Chaze's sentiments: "Mississippi stands ready to defend the rights of its people regardless of the color of their skins."[13]

In early February, the state tested that resolve in the Watkins case. Judge Maples sentenced Pitts to five years in prison for his part in kidnapping, the term to run concurrently with his upcoming federal sentencing in

DABURN. Buckley's case experienced delays because a juror alleged that Buckley tried to bribe him to exonerate him on the kidnapping charges. When the state tried Buckley on charges of obstruction of justice for jury tampering, a biracial jury acquitted him. However, jurors in the subsequent kidnapping case found Buckley guilty. Judge Maples sentenced Buckley to ten years in prison and disbarred him, but he freed him on a $25,000 bond pending his appeal. Finally, on March 8, the Dahmer cases began. Pitts arrived under heavy guard at the Forrest County Circuit Court, where he pled guilty to arson and murder.[14]

National and local media rushed to cover the historic case. A smattering of whites, the Dahmer family, and civil rights leaders, including Father Peter Quinn and Rev. J. C. Killingsworth, packed the courthouse. Sessum, flanked by his lawyers, Percy Quinn and Lawrence Arrington, appeared calm. Racial tensions simmered across Forrest County. The Spirit reinitiated armed patrols. During jury selection on Monday, March 11, Finch, an intense, forty-nine-year-old approached each potential juror, pointed his "bony finger" in their faces, and asked if "any person or group has the right to violate the law of Mississippi just because of their race?" Could they "place no more burden of proof on the state than if the defendant were a Negro and the dead man was white?" The defense used one of its peremptory challenges to strike the only remaining African American on the panel. By Tuesday afternoon, the attorneys had selected twelve white males, most of them working class.[15]

Prosecutors led with emotional testimony from Ellie Dahmer. As she spoke, Sessum, who had remained passive throughout the preliminary proceedings, stopped chewing his gum and stared at her intently. Biting back tears, Dahmer recalled awakening to find her house on fire and under attack by gunmen. She explained how her husband and daughter sustained severe burns as they sought to escape through a jammed window and that her husband had died from respiratory failure in the hospital. After the sad testimony, FBI agents explained the physical evidence found at the crime scene. Then prosecutors began the process of tying Sessum to the murder.[16]

Truman Rogers drew the spectators into the machinations of the Invisible Empire with his dispassionate account of Klansmen gathering in pastures and barns to plan the killing. Rogers identified Sessum as Exalted Cyclops of the Laurel Klavern and testified that he and Sessum had attended fall and winter meetings at which Bowers insisted that "something has got to be done about this damned nigger down south." At the first meeting, Bowers became angry, "fussing and cussing that he wanted . . . the hit . . . done and wanted it done right." The Klansmen argued over whether or not they should kill him. The Klan codified its projects numerically: number one represented harassment, number two a whipping, number three an arson or a shooting, and number four a murder. They decided on a number four. In December, Rogers accompanied Sessum on a dry run of the Dahmer property. On cross-examination, Arrington insisted that Rogers had never belonged to the Klan but had been paid by the FBI to fabricate his testimony. Arrington asked Rogers if he possessed any written record of his membership. Rogers replied, "They don't keep no records, you know that."[17]

Rogers had provided the first glimpse into the Invisible Empire in which Klansmen conspired to murder Dahmer. Prosecutors introduced Sessum's confession to place him at the center of that conspiracy. The defense tried to prevent its admission by claiming it was coerced. Outside the presence of the jury, Sessum accused Agents William Dukes and J. L. Martin of abducting him from Byrd's farm and Dukes of beating him with his fists and a blackjack. The testimony matched the affidavit he had signed two years earlier with one change: in his affidavit, he had claimed that a marshal had beaten him. According to Sessum, when he still refused to confess, Dukes said, "We'll have to kill him." Agents, Sessum claimed, drove him to Dahmer's grave, where they held a gun to his head and threatened to shoot him unless he confessed. Finally, they released him, but they threatened to kill him if he mentioned the incident to anyone.[18]

During cross-examination, Finch asked Sessum, "What doctor did you go to for treatment after this beating you took?" Sessum replied that he had decided against visiting a doctor as he feared that agents would kill him. Finch pointed out that despite this alleged brutal beating from a two-hundred-pound agent, Sessum was well enough to work the next day as a traveling salesman. Finch also inquired, "If you were so afraid why did you publish and distribute all over the country this purported affidavit that your lawyer referred to?" Sessum responded that after a few days, he "gained courage to publish it." Finch emphasized to the court that Sessum claimed that agents had threatened to kill him if he accused them of mistreatment; yet Sessum was still very much alive. The lawyers met with the judge off the record. After the meeting, Finch withdrew his request to admit Sessum's confession.[19] But prosecutors still had a strong case.

When the twenty-one US Marshals rushed the star witness into the courtroom, Arrington commented that Billy Roy Pitts was "worth a lot to them—alive." Smooth and calm on the stand, Pitts delivered chilling testimony as he explained the plans to murder Dahmer, identified Sessum as the Exalted Cyclops who "quarterbacked" the project, and detailed the hit. Pitts's testimony served as the most important element of the state's case. As a former Klansman who had participated in the attack, Pitts identified all of the perpetrators. His testimony matched Rogers's rendition of the planning sessions and corroborated the evidence and accounts by other witnesses. Pitts testified that the Klan had used gasoline jugs from Sessum's service station to set the fires. Ellie Dahmer recalled seeing a gasoline jug in the bed of the family pickup truck; agents and investigators recovered the jug. Pitts noted that he had dropped his .22 caliber magnum revolver in front of the picture window; agents found his pistol in that exact area of the crime scene. The location of the shotgun shell casings at the crime scene matched Pitts's description of the position of the shooters. Pitts testified that Smith shot the tires out of Giles's 1953 Ford, forcing the Klansmen to abandon it on Monroe Road. The FBI found the vehicle where Pitts recalled leaving it with a flat tire and the body riddled with bullet holes. A white neighbor of the Dahmers, Jay Smith, helped solidify Pitts's testimony. Right before the attack, he saw two vehicles full of several white men, including Sessum, heading toward the Dahmer farm. After the attack, one of the vehicles, packed full of men, including Sessum, passed his home again driving in the opposite direction.[20]

The defense hoped to discredit Pitts's compelling testimony by portraying him as "the paid liar of the government" and an unfaithful husband. Pitts admitted that he had received money from the FBI but only enough to relocate his family "so that they wouldn't be murdered" and to pay medical bills. Pitts also insisted that the prosecution never promised him anything in exchange for his testimony. He denied Arrington's accusations that he had a mistress. When marshals escorted Pitts from the room, Sessum turned his head and watched him leave. The state rested after Pitts testified. The defense brought in a series of witnesses who either defamed Pitts's character or contradicted his testimony. Former gubernatorial candidate Jimmy Swan testified that he had attended a defense rally at which Pitts stated that he was innocent of the charges against him. The most important defense witness, Sessum's mother, provided her son with an alibi. She insisted that he left their home at 1:00 a.m. to bring gasoline from the family service station to Ralph Strickland and James Yount, whose vehicle had run out of gas, but that he was at home when the Dahmer attack occurred. Strickland and Yount confirmed her account. On cross-examination, Strickland admitted that he and Younts were Klansmen.[21]

Arrington focused much of his efforts on appealing to the jurors' commitment to states' rights and white supremacy and to their fear of a federal government conspiracy to destroy the white South. During cross-examination of Agent James Awe, Arrington asked him about his background to reveal that the agent hailed from Nebraska, had received his law degree from Georgetown University in Washington, DC, had spent much of his career in Ohio, and had only lived in Mississippi since the latter part of 1964. Awe was an outsider, an invader, not to be trusted. During closing arguments, Arrington demanded that the jurors acquit Sessum if they wanted "Washington DC and the Department of Justice to know how Forrest County feels about running its own affairs." He claimed that the federal government had delayed the proceedings so that defendants were tried during "a presidential election year" to insinuate that it forced the state to prosecute Sessum to curry black votes in the presidential election. He argued that an acquittal would hurt President Johnson in the polls and put George Wallace, "the little man from Alabama[,] in the show." His implication was clear: if the jury acquitted Sessum, Wallace, a southern segregationist, might have a chance to win the presidential election.[22]

The prosecutors also relied on states' rights principles in their closing arguments. Finch declared, "I told the government to back off, that I wanted to try it. I said give me a Forrest County jury. They won't put up with this stuff." With this strategy, Finch sought to deny Arrington's claims that the federal government controlled the case. He stressed that the trial took place in a Mississippi state court, it was prosecuted by native Mississippians, and it was heard by a Mississippi jury. He also appealed to the jurors' pride in Forrest County and their xenophobia when he encouraged them to prevent Jones County Klansmen from usurping dictatorial power over their county and tarnishing their county's reputation. Dukes characterized the case as one of "organized society versus Cecil Sessum."[23]

At 4:50 p.m. on Friday, the jury began deliberations. According to juror Ray William Wells, the jurors knew that Sessum had murdered Dahmer. Still, they struggled over the verdict because they worried that "rednecks" might "come get" them if they convicted Sessum. In addition, Wells, like most Forrest County whites, despised the movement because they feared that it would reverse racial power and lead to miscegenation. As Wells noted, "It wasn't very popular back in them days for a white person to convict a white person for killing a black." Yet many whites, including Wells, considered the murder of Dahmer "a dastardly thing to do, because even though we didn't believe in voter rights for blacks that was beside the point.... [The murder] just wasn't right." Dahmer also enjoyed a different reputation among whites than did most black activists—he seemed more moderate, more reasonable. The turning of white city leaders and some citizens against the Klan also influenced Wells. Finch, described by Wells as a "typical Southern lawyer," prosecuted the defendant diligently, which caused Wells to consider the case seriously. Finch knew how to talk to white southerners, to convince them to choose justice over their fealty to white supremacy. During closing arguments, Finch reminded the jury about Jay Smith's testimony: "Y'all can look at the old man. You know he's honest as the day is long. Now he didn't want to tell on Mr. Sessum but y'all know, y'all know he recognized him, and that he first didn't want to tell on him." Wells had decided that Klansmen were "cruel people."[24]

Convinced of Sessum's guilt, Wells was surprised that only half the jurors voted for conviction. After discussing the case, juror Charles Kroen rose and stated, "This man was killed because he wanted people to be able to vote. They burned his house. Just because I'm Catholic, someone could decide tomorrow to do the same thing and burn my house. Just because you're Baptist, someone could decide tomorrow to do the same thing to you." One of the jurors stated, "Oh, they wouldn't do that," but another juror cautioned, "Remember Hitler." The comment moved many of the jurors, for several among them had fought in World War II. Wells led a prayer: "Lord . . . We believe that we want to know what's right and we want to know what you want us to do." Just before 7:00 p.m., the jury returned to the courtroom. The clerk announced the verdict. Guilty. Spectators' "jaws fell open." Sessum sat passively and chomped on his gum, even as Judge Hall sentenced him to life. The jurors worried about their decision. They feared reprisals, and most of them perceived the verdict as a victory for the "enemy . . . the voter registrations and the civil rights people."[25]

To Bowers's shock, an all-white Mississippi jury had dared to convict a white man for killing a black man. The guilty verdict proved a significant benchmark. Sessum was the first Klansmen ever convicted in Mississippi on state charges of murdering a civil rights activist. As a local journalist stated, the case proved to be a "history making trial." The verdict shook the foundations of the Jim Crow judicial system and weakened white supremacist power. Klansmen could no longer rely on the racism of local whites to insure their immunity; segregationists like Wells decided to place justice above white supremacy. Wells received praise from his friends, boss, and colleagues who commended him for doing "the right thing." Sessum's conviction also convinced Finch and Dukes that they could use the judicial system to destroy the Klan as they had once exploited it to suppress black activism. Judges even punished the state's star witness severely. Pitts received a life sentence for murder, two ten-year sentences for arson, and a five-year federal sentence for violating Dahmer's civil rights. Still, the aftershocks of the verdict failed to bring down the Jim Crow judicial system. As Wells stated, it "still was hard to convict a white man against a black in the courts." And the Klan remained a threat. After the trial, someone sprayed acid on a juror's carport. A man repeatedly telephoned another juror to castigate him as a "nigger lover."[26] Civil rights activists understood that the war might be reaching a turning point, but unconditional victory eluded them.

The day after Sessum's conviction, Martin Luther King Jr. arrived in Jones County at the invitation of Rev. Allen Johnson, the minister whose house Bowers's secret unit had bombed the previous November. Johnson hosted King in his renovated home and delivered him to speak to hundreds of people gathered at his St. Paul Church. Johnny Magee, a former Freedom Summer student, escorted his mother to church, but he refused to listen to "that handkerchief-headed preacher" who, he believed, called on blacks to "roll over." Years later, he regretted not attending, but at the time, like many black youths, he decided that only a militant approach could dismantle the white supremacist state. During the service, King called on the overflowing crowd to fight the racism and poverty that accompanied hatred and exploitation. They must change America where the privileged resided in houses of "wall to wall carpet" and the exploited in homes of "wall-to-wall rats and roaches." Referring to the upcoming Poor People's March, he promised that "we're going to Washington to demand—not to beg—that something be done immediately to improve the lives of our poor people." After his sermon, his motorcade transported him to Hattiesburg's Mt. Zion Baptist Church, where seven hundred blacks waited for him. Armed black men, including Spirit troops, protected King during his speeches and guarded Father Quinn's Holy Rosary Church where he spent the night.[27]

Several weeks later, on April 4, 1968, James Earl Ray assassinated Dr. King in Memphis. Urban rebellions exploded across the nation, leading to the death of forty African Americans and twenty-thousand arrests. As Mississippi blacks mourned, many whites, even children, celebrated. At Thames Junior High School, Anthony Harris stared down at his desk and fought to control his rage as he heard his all-white classmates applaud the assassination. One student shouted, "The King is dead. Yeah!" Another chided, "Hey Wick. Nice Aim. Good shot. How did you get from Memphis so quickly?" Even young children found King's death a reason for merriment. At Mason Elementary School in Laurel, Charles Marsh heard his classmates declare that the "nigger asked for it." One boy chimed in that his daddy thought "it's a good thing he's dead." Another white boy worried that race riots may erupt in Laurel and carried a knife to school so that "those niggers won't mess with me."[28]

Civil rights activists across the Central Piney Woods responded to the murder of their beloved Dr. King with marches rather than violence. They launched a massive boycott of schools and white-owned business and a three-day work stoppage. On April 8, 1,500 protesters marched to Hattiesburg's city hall for a prayer service and continued to the Forrest County Courthouse. Marchers ranged in ages from elementary school children to the elderly and included a smattering of whites. Some protesters linked arms. Others waved signs reading, "Don't Burn. Boycott," "King is Gone, but will stay on," and "He was our Moses and we are his People. Black Power." Many activists in Mississippi, including Killingsworth, struggled to continue King's fight by joining the Poor People's March on Washington that Dr. King had organized to fight for economic equity.[29]

The response of President Johnson disappointed many activists. A little over a month earlier, the Kerner Commission, which Johnson had directed to study the causes of urban rebellions, declared, "White racism is essentially responsible for the explosive mixture which has been accumulating in our cities since the end of World War II." The commission recommended that Johnson initiate a massive urban renewal and fair housing program, desegregate and improve educational facilities, and develop work training programs to address racial inequities. The commission identified significant problems, but its solutions for the job force proved problematic. As William P. Jones argues in *The Tribe of Black Ulysses*, the commission leader, Senator Daniel Patrick Moynihan, relied too heavily on Franklin E. Frazier's research, which contended that most blacks oppressed by racism developed dysfunctional families that led to a cycle of poverty. Frazier failed to understand that many working-class blacks, via union and civil right efforts, had climbed out of poverty, and many had stable families. However, industrial mechanization would soon eliminate their positions. They needed job training in the rising new electronics and aerospace industry. Perhaps it would not have mattered because Johnson neglected the commission's recommendations. The Vietnam War had diverted his attention and funding from his Great Society; it had also led Johnson to break with King, and to some extent with the movement, when King came out against the war. Finally, it had also broken his spirit, and he decided not to run for reelection. At the least, he made one last attempt to advance his civil rights agenda. Amidst the marches in Hattiesburg and the urban rebellions spreading across the nation, Johnson signed the Civil Rights Act of 1968, which fulfilled some of the movement's goals and included part of the legislation that Johnson had proposed in the wake of Dahmer's murder. Included in the broad legislation, Congress prescribed penalties for persons using violence and intimidation to prevent others from exercising their federal rights.[30]

After King's death, many whites were certain a race war was imminent. During a speech on May 6, USM president William McCain proclaimed, "If the people of the United States should ever descend into total racial warfare, there is not the slightest doubt about which side would win. If the police and National Guard ever really lose control, informal white armies will arise." Bowers considered his White Knights the only vigilante group with the power to prevent "Negroes, Jews, and Communists" from usurping power in Mississippi. He was convinced that the FBI and Judge Hall had "rigged" the jury in Sessum's case. King's assassination lifted his spirits. He and several Klansmen gathered at John's Café for several nights to celebrate. Some Klan informants speculated that Bowers might have ordered the hit as he insinuated to them that he was responsible. According to another informant, Bowers stated that the assassination occurred at an inopportune time and theorized that the "Feds" murdered King. As the spring and summer progressed and the Dahmer trials continued, Bowers launched into a stream of diatribes, calling Hoover the "antichrist" and the "enemy of the white race" and his men "unchristian agents of Communism." He even ranted about killing Roy Moore, but he never issued such an order.[31]

Klan bravado aside, the conviction of Sessum frightened many White Knights, and the mistrial in the DeBoxtel case in late March failed to soothe them. They wanted exonerations. So Klansmen tried to tamper with the juries in at least three cases, and Bowers sent his secret unit on a bombing mission, in part to frighten jurors in the upcoming trials into acquitting Klansmen. On May 22, authorities charged Pat Massengale, a reputed Klansman, with obstruction of justice for tampering with the jury in William Thomas Smith's case. A witness for the prosecution, Harvel Smith, testified that one of his employees, Jerry Wayne Shirley, was in Smith's jury pool. Massengale impressed upon Smith that "a conviction would break the back of the Klan," and "if they break the grip of the Klan they will break the back of Mississippi." Massengale implored Harvel Smith to find out Shirley's opinion on the case. Instead, Smith contacted authorities. The jury deadlocked nine to three for acquittal of Massengale, forcing a mistrial.[32]

In mid-May, Klansmen also tampered with the jury in Bowers's trial for arson. The state presented a strong case that included testimony from Rogers and Pitts that Bowers ordered the attack. As he had in Sessum's trial, defense attorney Lawrence Arrington sought to discredit Pitts's testimony by impugning his character, but he had more evidence this time. Despite his life sentence, Pitts was residing not in prison, but at a motel under the guard of US marshals. Arrington showed photographs of Pitts dining at expensive restaurants and swimming in a pool with his pretty blond mistress, Laura

Welborn. Still, the evidence overwhelmed Pitts's questionable character. When the twelve white men gathered in the jury room, all of them declared their intent to find Bowers guilty. Yet after collecting written ballots, the foreman announced that someone had voted not guilty. The puzzled men voted several more times. Each oral vote resulted in a unanimous guilty verdict, and each secret ballot resulted in one not guilty vote. Several of the jurors suspected Donald Butler as the holdout and began to question him. He admitted that he had voted not guilty, but he refused to explain why. Judge Hall declared a mistrial and released Bowers. The Klansmen's new strategy worked, though the result was closer than they thought. Although Butler denied that the Klan influenced his vote, a Klan informant learned from Bowers that the White Knights had contacted three of the jurors, including Butler. Only Butler voted not guilty, but it only took one man.[33]

Free again, Bowers mobilized his secret unit. On May 28, the unit bombed the Temple Beth Israel synagogue in Meridian. For months, agents had worked with the Anti-Defamation League and Jewish communities in Meridian and Jackson to find Bowers's secret unit. The league raised $80,000, which agents gave to two Klan informants after they notified agents of the next target. On June 29, agents and police caught Kathy Ainsworth and Tarrants trying to bomb a Jewish man's home in Jackson. The subsequent shootout left Ainsworth dead and Tarrants and an officer wounded.[34] The destruction of the terror unit combined with shifts on the political horizon advanced the Mississippi movement.

At the National Democratic Convention in the summer of 1968, the MFDP achieved a major victory when the credentials committee accepted the MFDP delegation over the Regular Democrats, and the MFDP delegates were seated. Finally, the tenacity of the MFDP had turned the federal political tide toward their side. Activists hoped that the Klan trials in the Dahmer case would continue to turn the judicial tide toward racial justice. Black registration had skyrocketed in the Central Piney Woods. As whites were the majority population in both Jones and Forrest Counties, blacks lacked the numerical power to affect elections. Still, suffrage had increased dramatically the number of blacks in jury pools, which could have a powerful impact on the Dahmer cases.[35]

Three blacks and nine whites served on the jury for the mid-July trial of William Thomas Smith, a slightly balding, thirty-two-year-old bachelor. Smith was the only DABURN defendant to take the stand in the state trials. He admitted that he had joined the Klan in November 1964, but he claimed that he had severed his Klan ties several months prior to the attack on Dahmer. Smith declared that Charles Wilson, his employer, had persuaded him to join the White Knights. He also inadvertently corroborated Rogers's testimony by revealing that the Klan classified its violent missions under four project numbers. During closing arguments, his attorney opined that "if [Smith] was guilty do you think he would have taken that witness stand and looked you in the eye and given testimony? . . . Don't find this man guilty just because you are a member of the NAACP and the defendant is a member of the Ku Klux Klan." On a July morning in 1968, the jury found Smith guilty. Judge Hall sentenced Smith to life.[36]

The following week, Finch and Dukes hoped to convict the most prestigious suspect—Charles Wilson. The wealthy entrepreneur had hired several lawyers—Leonard Melvin Sr., Leonard Melvin Jr., Harold Melvin, and Sarah Entrekin—to defend him. For the most part, the defense sought to exonerate Wilson with alibi testimony from his wife who swore that her husband was sleeping next to her on the night of the attack. The defense also presented eighteen witnesses—all from privileged backgrounds—who attested to Wilson's honorable character. During closing arguments, Melvin Jr. argued, "Pitts says he had a change of heart and that's why he decided to confess and turn state's evidence. I say that the only time he will have a change of heart is when they quit paying him." Finch countered that Pitts had received a life sentence, and asked the jury, "How much of your liberty would you sell for $3,300?" Finch failed to convince enough jurors that the wealthy, elegant man from Laurel had committed murder. The jury deadlocked. Judge Hall declared a mistrial, but he refused to release Wilson on bond.[37]

In a series of Klan trials that fall and winter, juries refused to acquit a single Klansmen. After jurors deliberated for twelve minutes, they found Byrd guilty of arson. Judge Hall sentenced him to ten years. A few days later, the jury in Lyons's case deadlocked six to six, leading to a mistrial. A state court sentenced Tarrants to thirty years in prison for his part in one of the Klan bombings. Finch and Dukes prosecuted Wilson a second time, and after six hours of deliberation, the jury found him guilty; Judge Hall sentenced him to life. The Klan trials devastated the White Knights. Klansmen began a mass exodus from the Invisible Empire because of the dire legal consequences of membership. It seemed that even the Imperial Wizard might finally face prison when a grand jury indicted him for murder.[38]

FBI agents, however, had grown increasingly concerned about their star witness, Billy Roy Pitts, as he edged toward a nervous breakdown. Pitts spent most of 1968 isolated in motel rooms in Texas and New Orleans under the constant guard of US marshals. Agents permitted Pitts weekly one-hour visits with his wife, his two young sons, and his father, but they reduced his contact with his mistress, Laura Welborn, to short telephone calls. Marshals supervised all visitation sessions and refused Pitts's request for private conjugal visits with his wife. Pitts lacked access to a television, and he had little interest in the few books authorities had given him. Hours seemed to stretch on endlessly. Pitts's interactions with the marshals depressed him, for many of them treated him with disdain; one marshal derided him as a "$75 a week pimp for the FBI." In their presence, his ninth-grade education made him feel inferior. His few telephone calls left him anxious, as they were consumed by his wife's complaints about their poverty and his lover's despair over their separation. With little activity to divert his attention from his circumstances, Pitts vacillated between bouts of boredom, relentless depression, and an anxious dread for his future.[39]

On December 29, 1968, marshals guarding Pitts heard a shot and rushed into Pitts's room, where they found him face down on the floor in a pool of blood. Pitts had tried but failed to shoot himself in the heart. The bullet penetrated his chest and left a four-inch wound, but he lived. He had written a note before he shot himself to declare that he had told the truth in court and that he hoped God would forgive him. While Pitts recovered, he sent Agent Benjamin Graves a letter begging him to send money to his family and to allow him to see Laura. He apologized for trying to commit suicide, but he declared that he could not "live without Laura." Pitts also wrote numerous letters to agents, to his mistress, and to his father ruminating about his living conditions and the prospect of spending his life in prison despite his tremendous aid in bringing down the Klan. Plagued with insecurities and loneliness, Pitts yearned for the approval of agents. He noted that as he lacked an education, he had difficulty expressing himself, but it hurt him when some agents called him a "sorry" person. Agents also received many letters and telephone calls from Pitts's family and mistress. Pitts's testimony had brought down some top officers in the Klan, and agents and state authorities still held out hope that he could hand them the wizard. So agents arranged for Pitts to see Laura, and his father purchased a television for him. The FBI struggled to keep Pitts alive and sane and his family and his mistress calm as Bowers's murder trial began.[40]

Throughout the trial in January, the Imperial Wizard appeared unconcerned and smiled often, even though the jury pool included blacks. A moment of humor relieved the tension in the courtroom during Pitts's testimony. Under cross-examination, Pitts revealed that Nix's office in John's Café had served as the center of Klan business and that most people who entered the space were Klansmen. Arrington said, "Well, I've been in that office and I'm no Klansman." Pitts responded, "I don't know that." At 3:45

p.m. on January 24, the jury began deliberating. Two jurors declared Bowers innocent but refused to review the evidence. The other ten spent hours trying to convince them of Bowers's guilt.[41]

As Bowers's fate lay in deliberation, at 4:15 a.m. on January 25, a freight train derailed in Laurel. Sixteen boxcars transporting twenty-three thousand gallons of petroleum exploded. Busted cars catapulted into neighborhoods and created a firestorm that demolished two blocks in the black community of Kingston. A mile from the crash, civil rights activist Maycie Gore and her husband, Alvin, awoke to the deafening explosion that picked their bed off the floor. They gathered their children and rushed outside into the freezing night where their panicked neighbors had flooded the streets. Another explosion rocked Laurel as another boxcar flipped off the rail, flew into homes and businesses, and exploded into flames. Those residents without cars ran from the successive explosions, which turned the sky crimson, and from the fiery smell and sudden heat penetrating the cold air. The Gores packed into their car and joined hundreds of vehicles fleeing Jones County. Five hours after the train derailment, Judge Hall declared a mistrial in Bowers's case because the foreman informed him that jurors were deadlocked ten to two for conviction. According to a Klan informant, Klansmen had coerced three jurors to vote for acquittal, but one of them "turned yellow." Although an investigation declared the train derailment accidental, many blacks and some whites, including Rev. Robert Marsh, considered it a Klan hit. The fires killed two and injured thirty-nine, all blacks, demolished forty-six homes and businesses, and damaged eighty-five properties over a ten-block radius, most of them black-owned. Tampering with the rails was not beyond Klansmen's skills or protocol, as they had bombed them during the Masonite strike.[42]

Marsh and other white pastors joined forces with black leaders to aid blacks left homeless by the fires. They helped these victims find shelter and provisions and clear the vestiges of their belongings from their burned-out homes. Several white men offered the service of their companies to reconstruct homes and businesses. For several months, Marsh and a number of ministers held weekly interracial prayer meetings. Marsh's son, Charles, marveled at the interracial bonding as white and black youths joined hands and sang, "We are one in the Spirit, we are one in the Lord. We pray that unity may be restored. They will know we are Christians by our love." Yet as the younger Marsh recalled, in the still divided and angry landscape of Laurel, racial harmony could not last.[43]

One Sunday morning, a black girl attended Rev. Marsh's First Baptist Church in Laurel. Many white congregants demanded that Marsh make her leave. He refused. One parishioner declared that he would not "sit down with niggers" and left the church. Over the next several months, blacks attended Marsh's church periodically, and the interracial meetings for rebuilding black neighborhoods continued. Eventually the meetings and the move toward church integration dissipated as the adults and teenagers of both races returned to their segregated worlds. Charles Marsh recalled, "No white people asked black Laurelites forgiveness for the sins of racism, drafted a confession of guilt and reconciliation, [or] discussed the topic in one of our think-ins."[44] Still, the Klan trials served as a forum for reckonings and penance by forcing the Central Piney Woods into a racial purgatory; some whites retreated from the white supremacist battle lines, while others dug into the trenches, sure that their side was right and victory still not unfathomable. Racial relations remained tense as the federal trial approached.

The last major federal stand against the Invisible Empire commenced in April 1969, when the Department of Justice prepared to try the sixteen men that the federal grand jury had indicted in DABURN: Bowers, Sessum, DeBoxtel, Byrd, Giles, Lyons, Nix, Noble, Smith, Thornton, Wilson, Charles and Clifford Lowe, Martin, Hamilton, and Moss. Department of Justice attorneys dropped charges against Martin, Hamilton, and both Lowes for lack of evidence, and Judge Dan Russell granted Moss a continuance after his lawyer proved him too ill to stand trial. In mid-April, Judge Russell ordered the trial moved to Meridian because the federal court facilities in Hattiesburg could not support such a large proceeding. Still, he ordered the jurors selected from a Hattiesburg jury pool despite motions by defense attorneys that the media had prejudiced locals against their clients. A team of seven lawyers represented the defense, including former gubernatorial candidate William Waller, who represented Wilson. In late April, the attorneys selected a jury of twelve whites. During the selection process, Bowers jotted down the names of all of the jurors on his notepad. After Judge Russell received anonymous threats, the judge sequestered the jury, and US marshals guarded the jurors and witnesses. Marshals shackled and linked the eleven Klan defendants and shepherded them to and from the courtroom in chains. The US Attorney for the Southern District, Robert Hauberg, and the Deputy Assistant Attorney General for the Department of Justice's Civil Rights Division, Robert Owen, tried the case in a quiet courtroom as few spectators other than the friends and families of the defendants and "a handful of the curious" bothered to attend.[45]

The quiet courthouse seemed eerie to Ellie Dahmer. Marshals brought her into the witness room occupied by the eleven Klansmen as they awaited the trial's commencement. She had testified eighteen times in state trials and before grand juries, and she held out hope that she could help bring the men before her to justice for killing her husband. On the witness stand, Ellie's voice shook and tears spilled from her eyes as she explained how her husband had died. To lay the groundwork for the Klansmen's motive, J. C. Fairley testified that Dahmer was involved heavily in voter registration activities. Owen and Hauberg tied the defendants to some or all phases of the murder conspiracy through the combined testimony of Pitts and Rogers and through several of the defendants' confessions. In addition, agents testified that Noble had admitted to them that he had participated in a dry run of the Dahmer attack; DeBoxtel had revealed that after Bowers handpicked him for the Dahmer job, he arranged for the vehicles used by the Klansmen; and Sessum had confessed to leading the attack. Sessum took the stand to refute his alleged confession. He claimed that agents had forced him to give a false confession by beating him. Judge Russell asked, "Have you ever been in a mental institution? . . . That's the most fantastic tale I have heard in four years on the bench, and you a preacher. It's fortunate you're being judged by a jury and not by me." Judge Russell granted a mistrial for Byrd because hearsay statements in the testimony regarding Sessum's confession implicated him.[46]

Throughout the trial, defense lawyers employed a two-pronged strategy. They presented alibi and character witnesses for as many defendants as possible and tried to impeach the testimony of Pitts and Rogers. The wives of Wilson, DeBoxtel, Noble, and Thornton and the mothers of Bowers, Sessum, and Smith all provided alibis for their accused husbands and sons respectively. Several witnesses took the stand to testify to the good character of the defendants, including Merrill Pickering, the sheriff of Jones County at the time of the Dahmer attack. Other witnesses testified to the poor character of Pitts and Rogers. Defense attorneys showed compromising photographs of Pitts and Wellborn and referred to him as a paid liar. Wilson was the only defendant to admit his Klan membership—a strategy that backfired on fellow defendant Smith in the state trials. Wilson claimed that he had terminated his affiliation with the Klan prior to December 1965 but reestablished his Klan connections after the arrests in the Dahmer case to raise money for the defendants. Wilson accused Pitts of testifying against him because he had refused to sign a bond for him in the Watkins's case.[47]

In closing arguments, Owen conceded that the government's witnesses were "not Sunday school teachers," but he noted that their testimonies corroborated the evidence. Carl Berry, who represented Smith, sought to appeal to racist and xenophobic sentiments by accusing the federal government of fabricating evidence against the defendants in their efforts to eliminate the Klan—an organization with a "long history in the South." On May 10, after deliberating for over eleven hours, the jury acquitted Giles, Lyons, and Thornton and deadlocked on verdicts for Nix, Bowers, DeBoxtel, Noble, Sessum, Smith, and Wilson, resulting in seven mistrials. Sessum, Wilson, and Smith returned to prison to serve out their state sentences for their recent murder convictions. The rest were released.[48]

The Dahmers clung to the hope that Bowers would face punishment when a grand jury indicted him for Dahmer's murder again. During the trial in late July, as Ellie Dahmer later recalled, Bowers "kept that silly little grin on his face all the way through as if he knew nothing was going to happen to him." The eight white and four black jurors deadlocked eight to four for conviction. Judge Hall declared a mistrial. Bowers escaped justice in the Dahmer case, but on February 27, 1970, after an exhaustive appeals process in the Neshoba case, the US Supreme Court denied Bowers's petition for a writ of certiorari; it would not hear his case. On April 2, federal marshals transported Bowers to McNeil Island Penitentiary in Washington State to serve his ten-year federal sentence. At last, the Imperial Wizard was behind prison bars, even if only for a little while.[49]

After the Dahmer cases, Judge Hall claimed that "the people of Jones County have told me on several occasions—that's the greatest thing that ever happened for the people of Jones County—when we broke up the Klan." His claims notwithstanding, the Masonite Klan cases that went to trial in Laurel in 1969 produced disappointing results. In mid-June 1969, District Attorney Harold Odom and Jones County attorney Robert Sullivan prosecuted Andre Hendry for the murder of Masonite security guard Robert Billiot. They presented thirty-four witnesses and substantial evidence, including a tape recording of Hendry admitting to the murder. After the prosecution concluded its case on a Friday afternoon, Judge Casey granted the defense's motion to recess until Saturday to give lawyers time to develop their trial plan. However, when court resumed Saturday morning, the defense rested its case without calling a single witness. The jury deliberated an hour before returning to the packed courtroom and acquitting Hendry. Cheers broke out from the majority of the spectators. Few noticed Billiot's young widow weeping.[50]

The next Monday, the district attorney prosecuted another man charged in the Masonite cases—John Holifield. The state charged that in the summer of 1967, Holifield had shot into Unit Three of the Masonite Plant, occupied at that time by laborers. Although defense attorneys Carl Ford and Lampkin Butts did not produce a single witness to rebut the state's case, the jury acquitted Holifield in less than twelve minutes. In both trials, the defense never tried to impeach the state's cases. Deliberations were so short that the jurors could not have properly considered the prosecution's case. Prosecutors decided against pursuing other Masonite cases.[51] Not a single Klansman or striker working with the White Knights ever suffered punishment for their many attacks during the Masonite strike. Far too many Jones County whites still perceived Klansmen as the guardians of their white supremacist society.

The Mississippi Supreme Court and lower courts outside of Jones County produced better results, save one. In February 1969, the Mississippi Supreme Court upheld Carr's conviction for assault and battery against Rogers. In January 1970, White received a five-year sentence for his participation in the attack on Rogers in Covington County. In 1969 and 1970, the Mississippi Supreme Court rejected appeals by Sessum, Wilson, and Byrd in the Dahmer cases. Yet the justices reversed Buckley's conviction on kidnapping charges in the Watkins case on the grounds that the lower court should have prohibited Pitts from revealing to the jury that he "pled guilty in the same case."[52]

Transition rather than watershed best defines the impact of the Dahmer cases on racial justice. Four state convictions, six state mistrials, eight federal mistrials, and three federal acquittals revealed a justice system still struggling with racial bias. At the least, juries sent to prison all of the men who attacked the home—Pitts, Sessum, Smith, and Wilson. Perhaps jurors and judges were more inclined to punish those Klansman who had caused the death of Dahmer directly. Jury tampering was an important factor in several of the mistrials. Ultimately, twelve of the sixteen Klansmen indicted in the Dahmer case escaped justice.

Still, the DABURN case, in conjunction with other Klan cases, devastated the White Knights. The pressure exerted upon the Invisible Empire through the DABURN, MIBURN, Watkins, Rogers, Tarrants, and Masonite investigations caused an internal panic among the Klansmen. Self-preservation proved stronger than the bonds of white supremacist brotherhood. Collectively, the cases triggered a mass defection from the Invisible Empire, strained the Klan's fiscal resources, and fostered internal and external betrayals. The Tarrants case destroyed the Klan's bombing campaign. The Neshoba case sent the Imperial Wizard to prison. The four state convictions in the Dahmer case and the convictions in the related Watkins kidnapping and the Rogers assault cases delivered the mortal blow because they proved that local authorities would no longer tolerate Klan violence. The White Knights could not survive internal mutinies and external assaults. The empire cracked and imploded. By 1970, the FBI had won the war against the

Klan. That feat proved a significant watershed in the fight against white supremacist violence. Although racial injustice persisted, never again would the Klan rule the tortured racial landscape of Mississippi.

CHAPTER 8

Stalemate

A FIGHT BETWEEN A BLACK AND A WHITE STUDENT SET OFF THE "powder keg" of racial rage churning at Watkins High School in Laurel in 1970 and exploded into a riot. Classroom doors flew open. Students flooded into the corridors. Some of them joined the mayhem while others, including Larry McGill, fled as the violence spread across campus. Teachers tried to intervene, but they could not stop the melee that erupted just weeks after the district integrated. Policemen rushed to the scene with attack dogs and arrested black students. At that moment and for most of his days at Watkins High, McGill hated white people. Six years earlier, McGill had joined the Freedom Summer sit-ins and fought for integration. However, the achievement of that movement goal had still failed to produce equality because whites clung to the dying Leviathan of Jim Crow and lashed out at the emerging victors of the racial revolution to stymie, as they perceived it, the final invasion of their segregated world.[1]

During the late 1960s and early 1970s, the final battles of the civil rights revolution delivered stalemates. Some groups suffered definitive defeat, but no one group achieved unconditional victory. The Klan, though decimated, clung to survival in its march toward marginalization. Although Klan violence fell out of style, its racial ideology endured. As the Invisible Empire collapsed, local officials assumed the full reins of white supremacist resistance. Moreover, the Vietnam War, the antiwar protests, countercultural revolts, and racial clashes outside the South diverted federal resources and national attention. Between 1969 and 1975, fracases in the Central Piney Woods spiraled painfully toward a wounded peace.[2]

Many of the last battles revolved around school integration, one of the civil rights goals most feared by whites. A year before the Watkins High School riot, white leaders mustered all of their powers to prevent integration. If the home and the church functioned as breeding grounds for white supremacy, the schoolhouse served as the training camp. It took young minds rooted in racism and socialized them into patriots of white rule. If the federal government forced whites to share responsibility for the education of their children with black educators, whites could not prevent the exposure of their children to teachings that challenged white supremacy. Whites also understood that if their children mixed with black students, miscegenation might result and undermine their racial caste system. Mississippi had avoided the *Brown* ruling for fifteen years through massive resistance and its freedom-of-choice policy. Although the 1968 US Supreme Court ruling in *Green v. County School Board* found freedom-of-choice unconstitutional and its 1969 decision in *Alexander v. Holmes* ordered immediate integration, most school districts in Mississippi, including those in the Central Piney Woods, maintained all-black schools and contained the desegregation of white schools to a minimal black presence. On November 7, 1969, the Department of Health, Education, and Welfare (HEW) ordered Mississippi schools to comply with the court ruling using an HEW plan. In response, Senator John Stennis introduced a bill that would apply HEW plans uniformly to every state in the union. He hoped that his colleagues in nonsouthern states would oppose integrating their mostly segregated districts and force the federal government to retreat. In case that plan failed, Citizens' Councils opened white-only academies, which they characterized as "lawful opposition to the racial revolution."[3]

Most whites grew irate with the Hattiesburg school board when it voted to comply with the HEW plan and promised to integrate the faculty and extracurricular activities, form biracial faculty and student-faculty committees to oversee integration, and incorporate black history into the curriculum. To preserve segregation in public schools on a local level, USM professor William Scarborough, along with Charles Wade and Ray Davis, founded the Committee for Local Control of Education (CLCE). CLCE leaders red-baited HEW and employed a nonviolent white resistance campaign to oppose the ruling. During a meeting held at the USM auditorium, Davis denounced HEW as "communistic" and initiated a countywide boycott of Forrest County schools. On December 11, most white students in Forrest County complied with the CLCE boycott, and their parents picketed in front of the schools with signs that declared, "We Want Public Schools, but not run by HEW." Seventy-three teachers endorsed a letter to the *Hattiesburg American* that denounced the HEW plan as unconstitutional since it denied the people's right to choose their children's school. Using the same argument, seven hundred students signed a resolution against the HEW plan. The few white parents who sent their children to school received threats. Although County Attorney Jimmy Dukes disagreed with the court ruling, he warned the public that he would not tolerate threats.[4]

On January 3, 1970, Governor John Bell Williams declared that Mississippi had lost its nearly sixteen-year war against school desegregation. Standing before television cameras, the governor announced that the "arsenal of legal and legislative weapons have been exhausted." Rulings by "revolutionaries" and its "fawning Federal Administration" had defeated the state's freedom-of-choice policy. Williams refused to abolish public schools to prevent integration. Instead, he encouraged whites to send their children to private academies and proposed a bill allotting families $150 in state government loans for tuition and allowing people to direct up to $500 in state taxes to a private school.[5]

In the spring of 1970, many school boards throughout the South refused to comply with the HEW regulations. As of July 13, the Department of Justice had initiated 189 desegregation lawsuits in 11 Southern states—45 of them in Mississippi. School districts not in full compliance included Hattiesburg and Laurel. Not a single white student attended the historically black schools in the Hattiesburg Municipal, Laurel Separate, and Jones County districts. Blacks comprised 130 of the 2,803 students in the Laurel Separate District, 129 of the 1,672 students in the Jones District, and 453 out of the 3,527 students in the Hattiesburg Municipal District. Laurel's white school district preserved its all-white faculty, and of the 148 faculty members in the black school district, only 3 were white. The Jones County District maintained wholesale segregation of its faculty. The Hattiesburg Municipal District employed 3 black teachers out of the 115 in white schools, and 12 white teachers out of 216 in black schools.[6]

During these final battles, the minority of black students attending white Hattiesburg schools under the freedom-of-choice plan suffered as white rage exploded. Anthony Harris had grown intimately familiar with racial prejudice during his movement activities and as one of the first black students to integrate Thames Junior High. Harris suffered continued mistreatment when he and dozens of other blacks attended Blair High during the 1969–1970 school year. Harris had determined that only by enduring the insults and remaining on campus could he conquer white supremacy and advance integration. Still, Harris found it impossible to remain silent in the face of some disparaging remarks. During one history class session, Harris's teacher grew enraged as he read from the textbook an assertion that slavery was an inhumane and exploitative institution. He slammed the book down on the desk and launched into a rant defending slavery as a perfect system because Africans lacked intellectual capabilities to pursue other endeavors. The slave trade, he claimed, rescued blacks from the barbaric continent of Africa where they lived in squalor, and it introduced them to the civilizing influence of Christianity. Slavery was a benevolent system, and slaves were grateful to their masters. Unable to contain himself Harris shouted, "You are wrong and slavery was wrong." The teacher ordered Harris to never contradict him again. Harris gathered his belongings and left, but he returned the next day, determined to defeat racism and segregation through his presence.[7]

One of Harris's fellow black classmates, Kenneth Fairley, was also a seasoned soldier of desegregation as he spent the previous two years under freedom-of-choice at Hawkins Junior High. Yet nothing prepared Fairley for the racism that he confronted in the high school. According to Fairley, when he and four other black students tried out for the all-white football team, most of the coaches and players terrorized them. Soon, black athletes started quitting. When the fourth black athlete turned in his equipment, Fairley decided to quit, too, because he feared suffering the daily tortures alone. He struggled with his decision because his father had never allowed him to quit any team until he completed the season. As he approached the coach's office, he overheard him say to a trainer, "Four niggers down and one to go." The racial slur reminded him that his suffering had meaning. It would help facilitate integration and black liberation. He would not quit. Most of the coaches and white players were as determined to force Fairley off the team. On the practice field, the coaches ordered Fairley to stand alone on special teams, and when the kicker punted the ball to him, the entire team tackled him. In the locker rooms, most of his fellow athletes treated him like a pariah. When he entered the shower, his teammates rushed out. Many of them found it hilarious to urinate on his clothes and equipment. Throughout the season, the team traveled across Mississippi and patronized restaurants that, despite the Civil Rights Act of 1964, refused to serve blacks. So Fairley sat alone on the bus while his teammates dined.[8]

Cruelties piled on top of each other until one day during a practice session, Fairley reached a breaking point. The team practiced at the junior high field located a few miles away. On this day, the bus broke down, and the coaches ordered the players to carpool to the field. Fairley did not own a vehicle, and though he begged his teammates to transport him, they all refused. One boy responded, "No nigger, walk." Fairley ran the few miles to the field. When he rushed down the steps to the complex where the coach and the team waited, the coach slapped a wooden board across his hand and asked, "Boy, where have you been?" Fairley responded, "I tried to get a ride over and I just ran over." The coach turned toward the team, "Did he ask any of you all for a ride?" "No sir," the players lied. He ordered Fairley to assume the position. He delivered ten licks. Fairley stifled his tears as he hurried to the locker room to change into his practice clothes. He determined that he would never let them see him cry. For the first time in a while, he contemplated quitting.[9]

One of Fairley's teammates, Steve Kelly, entered the locker room, sat next to him, and said, "I have had enough of it . . . today it's going to change." Fairley had often seen Kelly read his Bible before practice and he considered him one of those white Christians who practiced Christ's teachings. Kelly had treated Fairley decently. When Fairley returned to the field, the coach, as usual, ordered him to retrieve the kickoff alone. As soon as the coach blew the whistle, Kelly shouted, "The seniors versus the sophomore," and he punched one senior and then another. A massive brawl erupted. When the coaches broke it up, Kelly shouted that "enough was enough." He would no longer allow the coaches or the team to mistreat Fairley. When they laughed, he threatened to expose their actions to the media. The coaches ran Kelly after practice, but the cruel treatment of Fairley began to diminish. Still, Fairley held out hope that the federal government would fully integrate Blair High School to mitigate his suffering.[10]

During the fall of 1970, most Mississippi schools integrated under court orders. In Hattiesburg and Laurel, however, school boards forged a compromise with HEW. They would desegregate on the secondary level but maintain segregated elementary schools. On September 16, Judge Harold Cox barred the state of Mississippi from providing tuition loans for private schools. Most white parents in the Central Piney Woods were infuriated; some staged protests, but most decided against paying to send their children to segregated academies in aluminum buildings with poorly trained teachers. To soothe the transition to integration in Jones County, Laurel mayor Bill Patrick and Rev. Robert Marsh held a public meeting at which white parents and children could express their concerns. Many parents feared for their children's safety because they had heard stories about black students attacking white students in integrated schools in other states. Children were afraid, too. Twelve-year-old Charles Marsh became terrified about the prospect of desegregation when a white friend planning to attend a segregated academy informed him that he was "crazy to be going to school with niggers" as surely they would harm him. Regrettably, white authorities across the Central Piney Woods rendered a peaceful transition impossible because they insured that integration transpired in a discriminatory manner: these authorities kept whites in the top supervisory positions and demoted blacks so that whites could sustain control over the schools. In the high schools, these supervisors permitted the white faculty, staff, and students to discriminate against their black counterparts. Furthermore, during the

1970–1971 school year, Hattiesburg maintained a degree of segregation in its high schools by gerrymandering neighborhood district lines so that blacks would comprise only twenty-five percent of the Blair High School population and Rowan High School would remain nearly all-black.[11]

For the first time in years, Fairley looked forward to the opening of the school year. But most black students treated Fairley like an Uncle Tom. They believed incorrectly that he had chosen to attend white schools under freedom-of-choice because of his fealty toward whites. Fairley determined to prove that he was a devoted civil rights activist. So when black students and the leaders of the Forrest County branch of the NAACP launched demonstrations against the persistence of racial prejudice in the administration of the desegregated schools, Fairley tried to become a student leader. Black anger over the racist implementation of school desegregation exploded into rage in the winter of 1971 after the city appointed two white men to Hattiesburg's school board vacancies. Clarence Magee, a teacher and the new president of the Forrest County NAACP, castigated the city fathers for reneging on their 1966 promise to consider a black candidate when a position on the board opened. NAACP member Rev. Ervin E. Grimmett condemned the appointments as "a deliberate attempt to maintain the status quo . . . a denial of the principle of Christian brotherhood. It is tantamount to taxation without representation."[12]

The outrage expressed by the NAACP inspired black students. In March 1971, three hundred black students from Blair and Rowan High Schools, including Fairley, staged a walkout, both to protest the failure of the city to appoint a black member to the school board and to dramatize demands students had given to school officials. Magee joined them. Many of the student demands included provisions that the Hattiesburg school board had included in its HEW plan but had failed to implement. The board must hire more black teachers, coaches, staff, and a black counselor; insure proportional representation of blacks on school committees, pep squads, and the school newspaper; incorporate a black studies curriculum; and form a biracial student-faculty committee to oversee the transition to integration. Finally, as many black students had grown weary of discriminatory treatment by white administrators, teachers, and staff, they demanded that the board develop a biracial disciplinary committee comprised of students and faculty to insure equitable treatment. The protest revealed a powerful desire by black students to have a voice in their academic lives. At Blair, they wanted to be treated as an integral part of the campus rather than as unwanted interlopers in a hostile environment. At Rowan, they wanted more control over their school, which was still mostly black. In response, Judge Stanton

Hall handed down a temporary injunction to prohibit further protests on Hattiesburg school property, public buildings, streets, and sidewalks.[13]

The following year, federal intervention forced authorities to fully integrate the high schools by sending all of the sophomores in the city to Rowan and all of the juniors and seniors to Blair. The new arrangement balanced the black administrative, teacher, and student population in the schools. However, the white establishment diminished the power of blacks in the schools by demoting black administrators, staff, and faculty. Rowan boasted one of the premier athletic programs in the state, and yet not a single black coach became a head coach at Blair High. Rowan's football coach, Ed Steele, was demoted to coordinator of recreation even though he had won four championships in seven years and had the best record of all coaches in the state. Administrators also deprived black faculty and staff of power commensurate with their white counterparts. The white establishment denied black educators their rightfully earned positions, diminished their ability to serve as role models to students, and divested them of their power to protect black students from mistreatment by white authorities.[14]

Most white administrators, teachers, and coaches disregarded the traditions of black students. As black student Rod Woullard recalled, "They wanted us to assimilate, not integrate." Woullard overheard a football trainer ask a Blair coach if he wanted to use the Rowan jerseys for practice. The coach replied, "You can burn that crap. Our boys will never wear them." Woullard was infuriated, for "these were our game jerseys which we treasured [while] playing at Rowan, and the legacy that Rowan had, and the state championship that they had, that [Blair] had never had. So now they are telling us that none of that has any value where you are now." After facing repeated racial inequities, Fairley, Woullard, and most of the black students staged a walkout. The black sophomores at Rowan joined them. Most of the black students refused to divest themselves of their history, of their culture, of their merit. They chose instead to leave, and in that act, they conveyed that whites must see them as equals with equally meritorious ideas, cultural expressions, and talents. They wanted to integrate, not assimilate.[15]

Black protests brought forth great changes in the schools. On February 14, 1972, the city appointed a black man, Jesse Parker, and a white woman, Eleanor Gerrard, to the school board. Board member Ralph Milloy resigned to help facilitate the appointment of Parker. NAACP leaders Magee and Grimmett praised the black community and the city officials for ensuring this momentous development. On campus, Roscoe Pickett, the black assistant principal of Blair High School, held a forum at which black students discussed their grievances. He selected seven of them, including Woullard and Fairley, to present these complaints to the superintendent. When Pickett mentioned Fairley's name, several students protested that he was untrustworthy because he had been attending school with whites for so long. The rejection wounded Fairley as he realized that, with few exceptions, neither white nor black students accepted him. Pickett defended Fairley. Soon the students realized that Fairley had spent years fighting white racism. They allowed him to serve on the student board and increasingly turned to him for leadership. After a series of talks, the black student board and the administration formed a biracial advisory council comprised of administrators and students to facilitate a transition to a truly integrated campus.[16]

Students also advanced racial progress by excelling in their academic and extracurricular endeavors that disproved myths of black inferiority. Some white teachers and students who rejected the racist mores of their society supported them. The white basketball head coach guided his white and black players to unite as one team. He succeeded, in part, because a black player, Eugene Short, who eventually played professionally, proved so exceptional that he led Blair in an undefeated season and to a victory in its first state championship. White students like Donnie McCleskey cracked racial barriers by befriending blacks. When McCleskey served as a basketball team captain in gym class, he always selected black student Johnny DuPree. McCleskey's friends heckled him for his friendship with DuPree, but McCleskey ignored them. DuPree recalled, "He would always talk to me.... He made me feel like a human being." Students adapted better than adults. As many white administrators and parents continued to fear interracial socializing, they canceled the school prom—at least for blacks. The Hattiesburg Country Club hosted an all-white prom. Blacks relied on their solidarity to partake in traditional school events. They insured the election of a black homecoming queen, Wanda Johnson, by running one black candidate against several white candidates. With the white vote split, Johnson won.[17] Racial relations improved over the year, but tension persisted. In Laurel, the tension over school desegregation exploded into violence.

The white leaders in Laurel set an ugly tone for integration in the summer of 1970 when they sent janitors into Oak Park High School to prepare it for its transition to an elementary school. All Laurel high school students would attend the once whites-only Watkins High. Blacks revered Oak Park. Since the 1920s, it had served as a second home to black children who viewed their teachers, coaches, and administrators as their extended family. Many of its graduates attended college and had prestigious careers as brain surgeons, athletes, entertainers, and military leaders. Leontyne Price, the famous singer, and her brother, Colonel George Price, both graduated from Oak Park. According to Oak Park teacher Larry Coleman, authorities showed their contempt for the school's proud history when in the summer of 1970 they sent white workers to complete Oak Park's transition. On orders from authorities, the workers "stripped" Oak Park bare. They ripped pictures of teachers, graduation classes, sports teams, and academic organizations off the walls and tossed them along with the numerous trophies into trash cans. They hurled the coveted football uniforms into heaps to be burned.[18]

The rape of Oak Park served as the opening assault against black students and faculty. The white leaders could no longer prevent full-scale integration, but they could insure that it transpired in a manner that sustained white power. White authorities demoted black principals and coaches. Oak Park principal Alex Warren became the lowest-ranked assistant principal at Watkins High. The administration sent to the junior high Coach Irving Morrell, who had become an All-American center while playing on the basketball team for Grambling University and who had led the Oak Park High School team to three district championships. White administrators also divested the assistant positions of authority normally ascribed to them. They even limited the authority of black teachers in their classrooms when they forbade them from disciplining white students. By creating a racial hierarchy in which all white employees enjoyed superior positions to their black counterparts and in which black adults had no authority over white children and diminished authority over black students, white administrators insured complete white control over the desegregated schools.[19]

The hundreds of black teenagers sent to integrate Watkins High School and win a significant battle against the Jim Crow system accomplished that victory at great personal sacrifice. As they recalled, they lost their school and their sense of belonging, and when they arrived on the white-controlled campus, most whites treated them like enemies in a hostile land. Administrators canceled all events that would bring white and black students together in an intimate social setting, including the prom, though many blacks believed that whites held their own private prom off campus. Some white teachers segregated their classrooms. In the athletic arena, the white-controlled booster club and white parents expected Coach George Blair to retain all white players in their positions on the football team. Black player Larry McGill recalled that while Coach Blair's "heart was good," pressure from whites forced him to place black players on the second string. After a white assistant coach assaulted McGill, he and several players quit until the black assistant coach persuaded them to rejoin the team. College scouts showed an interest in McGill; he decided that he would not allow racism to ruin his future.[20]

Throughout that first semester, racial tensions escalated until a fight between a black and a white student erupted into a riot. McGill and many other black students who wanted to escape the bedlam rushed toward the parking lot just as police cars sped onto campus. McGill recalled that officers rushed toward the clashing students but only arrested black rioters. In the parking lot, as white parents, who had apparently received telephone calls from the school, arrived to retrieve their sons and daughters, many of them shouted "niggers" at McGill and other black students who were seeking to escape the violence. School officials had not provided black students with an emergency plan. No one contacted their parents. They had to walk home. It was a long journey because the campus was located in a white community, far from black neighborhoods.[21] It was the first of several riots that year.

According to history teacher Larry Coleman, who had been transferred from Oak Park to Watkins High, the mistreatment of blacks by administrators also created an atmosphere conducive to riots. Later that year, the white principal expelled Richard Porter, a black student, when he disagreed with a school policy and argued with the principal. Porter considered the expulsion unfair. When Porter and the principal started shouting at each other in the middle of the campus, students in nearby classrooms left their seats and rushed to witness the commotion. Porter begged the principal to listen to his perspective, but the principal ordered him to leave immediately. Black teachers, including Gladys Austin, in observance of school rules, remained in their classrooms. But Coleman knew Porter and his family and felt compelled to intervene.[22]

Coleman hurried toward Porter, put a protective arm around his shoulders, and beseeched him to leave campus with him. Porter allowed Coleman to guide him out of the school building. They had nearly reached the bottom of the steps when six police vehicles sped into the parking lot and ten officers rushed toward them, aiming their pistols at Porter. Coleman stepped in front of Porter. By that point, a large group of students had gathered around the windows that surrounded the foyer in the front of the school. They stood quietly, watching. Coleman begged the officers to step back and allow him to escort Porter off campus. Policemen inched closer. Coleman pleaded, "I have him ... let him just go home." Coleman never saw the officer who slipped out of the building behind him, but he felt Porter being ripped from his arm so hard that he nearly lost his balance. When the officer threw Porter to the ground on his face, the other officers leapt forward, one jumping on his back and another handcuffing him. Coleman begged them to stop. One of the officers threatened to arrest Coleman if he did not return to his classroom. With great reluctance, Coleman turned away from Porter and reentered the school building. Police escorted Porter off campus.[23]

In the tense moments that followed, as Coleman recalled, "all hell broke loose." Whites and blacks in the foyer attacked each other. The ruckus spread down the halls. Teachers tried to restore order, but it was impossible as the riot spread from the corridors into the classrooms. Someone called the police again. The sounds of students screaming and crying and of bodies banging into lockers rolled across campus. White kids started yelling that the "n[iggers] were going crazy." Black students who wanted to avoid the riot either marched five miles to St. Paul Church where they held a protest or rushed off campus and headed home. Meanwhile, the police returned to campus and attacked and arrested black students involved in the riot. They did not arrest whites.[24]

After the riot, black churches held mass meetings, and the black community arranged conferences with the school board and the principal. Black students refused to return to Watkins High in protest of the mistreatment of black students. The following week, they returned to find that white authorities had stationed armed white guards across campus. Officers carrying riot shields and wielding shotguns patrolled the halls, establishing, as student Johnny Magee termed it, a "police kind of state." White administrators expelled many blacks involved in the fight but refused to expel a single white student. Black students staged a memorial service on the front steps of the school to symbolize their mourning over the loss of black students. When they knelt on the steps to pray, the principal ordered them back to class and officers dispersed them.[25]

Many black students, like Johnny Magee, a former Freedom Summer student, lost all respect for black assistant principal Alex Warren because he never intervened on their behalf. They had feared and respected Warren at Oak Park High and referred to him as "the man." At Watkins, Warren had so few duties that students often saw him picking up trash in the halls. He became so diminished in their eyes that they referred to him as "the janitor." Some black teachers, however, gained the admiration of students like Magee when they dared to buck the rules. Cleeburgh Giles, a relative of Klansman Travis Giles, who had been indicted in the Dahmer cases, disrespected black teacher Gladys Austin in the classroom repeatedly. Finally, Austin threatened to "whup her" if she ever disrespected her or the class again, an admonishment that earned her hero status among black students. They also admired Coleman for risking his job to protect Porter.[26]

Soon after the riot, the principal summoned Coleman. As Coleman recalled, the mayor, the police chief, the assistant police chief, and the lawyer for the Laurel school board had packed into the principal's office, and the principal had a tape recorder on his desk. The chief scolded Coleman for intervening in a police conflict and threatened to arrest him. Coleman insisted that his presence prevented Porter, who had a temper, from fighting police. Had he fought policemen, Coleman said, the officers might have shot him. He insisted that the riot would have paled in comparison to the melee that would have exploded had the police killed Porter. He also blamed the officers by pointing out that the fracas started after they arrested Porter. The officers should have allowed Coleman to finish escorting Porter off campus. Finally, Coleman declared, "I would be less than a man, a black man at this, if I did not come to the aid of this black boy." The principle and city leaders forced Coleman to defend himself repeatedly in meetings before the school board and the superintendent and required him to write a letter to the superintendent defending his position. Eventually, city leaders and school administrators conceded that Coleman had made some valid points and allowed him to remain on the faculty.[27]

As the year progressed, some of the racial tension diminished. Watkins High began to have a winning football season, particularly as Coach Blair allowed his black athletes like McGill to play more often and as he struggled to close the racial divides among his players. Some of the white athletes displayed an interest in becoming "a team" and developed friendships with black teammates. Some black male and white female students even dared to cross the most forbidden lines of Jim Crow and dated, albeit secretly, at least until several white girls gave birth to mixed-racial babies. Many white parents had fought school integration because they feared that it would lead to miscegenation. The exposure of interracial dating terminated racial progress. Over the next decade, the Laurel schools became nearly all-black because many whites removed their children from the Laurel district and sent them to the predominantly white schools in the county or to the private academies that developed over the years following integration.[28]

School administrators and city leaders had decimated an historic opportunity to foster a healthy integrated system because they had insured that integration transpired in a racist manner. The decision by white leaders to tear apart Oak Park and to wrench black students away from the nurturing atmosphere of their beloved school and throw them into the circus of white racism stunted the intellectual growth of many black students.

Large numbers of black students dropped out of school. Others became so angered over the mistreatment that they became apathetic in their studies. Johnny Magee, who had fallen in love with history during Freedom Summer, remained in school and graduated, but he stopped meeting his academic potential and turned away from his dream of seeking a college degree for decades. He refused to take class pictures or attend class night, and he swore never to return to the campus after graduation, an oath he kept until his own daughter attended Watkins High in the 1990s. Although many blacks who integrated Watkins succeeded in their academic careers, they obtained little help from white school authorities. The racist leadership of the white school establishment nurtured hatred in the oppressor and the oppressed and scarred racial relations for decades.[29]

In sharp contrast to the principal of the high school, Joseph Watson, the principal of Watkins Junior High School, fostered a welcoming environment. At the first faculty-staff meeting, Watson stated that he considered all employees professionals and expected them to treat each other in a professional manner. He addressed black and white teachers alike with courtesy titles and treated students equally regardless of their race. Whenever a black and white child fought, he found out who started the skirmish and then punished that individual. Cora Wade-Seals confronted racism from white teachers who refused to acknowledge her and from some students who thought that a black woman had nothing to teach them. However, she determined that by demonstrating her talent and hard work as a teacher and by treating everyone with kindness no matter how they responded to her, she would debunk racial myths.[30]

To Wade-Seals's great joy, many of her students not only divested themselves of their racist views but influenced changes in their parents. Terry Caves, son of the circuit clerk, Leonard Caves, who had blocked black suffrage until the bitter end, was a student in one of Wade-Seals's classes. Only twelve-years-old at the time and small for his age, Terry was nervous. At first, it seemed strange to him to attend school with black students. But Caves found many of the black teachers, particularly Wade-Seals and his physical education teacher, Wilson Terrell, fair and nice to him, and he remained grateful for their presence during those tempestuous times. Wade-Seals had not forgotten that Terry's father had refused her the right to register until her boss had forced him to add her name to the registration book. But she adored Terry because he was intelligent and had a kind disposition. During the Meet the Teachers night, Leonard Caves recognized Wade-Seals and stopped still when he approached her. Wade-Seals smiled and welcomed him. She noticed that the elder Caves soon grew out of his racist attitude because when Terry's sister Tina entered junior high, Caves requested that the principal place her in Wade-Seals's class. Her efforts debunked many racial myths.[31]

Like Terry Caves, Charles Marsh, who attended Gardiner Junior High, found the transition to integration easier than he had feared. He later recalled that as the "sons and daughters of Klansmen and civil rights activists ... of black militants and Citizens' Councilors" sat together in classrooms and played together on sporting fields, they adapted far more quickly than their parents. Integration wiped away many racist myths. A black student, Jerome Johnson, who read unabridged classics by W. E. B. DuBois and Jean Jacques Rousseau, soared to the top of the class. As athletes rejoiced and cried over their victories and defeats, they learned that race was an abstract divide. One of the more surprising interracial friendships developed between two black students, Unkgang Harrison and Flip Freeman, and a white student, Isaac Buckley, the son of Klansman Travis Buckley charged in the Dahmer and Watkins cases. Isaac had always hated school. Too old for his class, dressed in old oversized clothing, disfigured with a scarred face, and constantly smelling of onions, the white kids had treated him terribly for years. Integration changed his life. Black students cared little about his odd appearance, his disheveled clothing, or his strange smell. They liked him.[32]

Despite or perhaps because of these friendships that developed across racial lines, most white authorities and parents in Laurel still opposed integration. With the final implementation of *Brown* through the *Alexander* ruling, civil rights activists achieved an ambivalent victory. The schools had desegregated, but they had not integrated. And desegregation did not last. Over the next two decades, whites fled the city schools in Laurel and Hattiesburg for private academies or schools in neighboring and predominantly white suburbs or counties, leading to a virtual resegregation of most schools.[33]

In the 1970s, white hostility toward blacks grew so intense over school desegregation that the Central Piney Woods faced some significant setbacks in the racial struggle, most notably in the arena of racial justice. State and federal attorneys had promised to retry those Dahmer cases that had resulted in mistrials, and the state planned to try those defendants who had yet to face trial. But prosecutors worried that that the rage stemming from school segregation would make seating a racially unbiased jury impossible. Civil Rights Department attorney Robert A. Murphy insisted that the state finish its cases first. However, Jimmy Finch never tried another Klansmen, and in 1971, he passed the remaining Dahmer cases to the files. On the coast, Donald Cumbest set aside the Watkins kidnapping cases. He never prosecuted

Nix, Bowers, or Sessum, and he neglected to re-prosecute Buckley.[34] Most of the Klansmen responsible for Dahmer's murder evaded justice.

Even those Klansmen sent to prison for their crimes suffered far less than most convicted criminals. On September 3, 1971, Pitts received parole from federal prison, and Governor Williams promised Pitts that as long as he never returned to Mississippi, the state would not incarcerate him for his life sentence in the Dahmer case. In September 1970, Governor Williams commuted Byrd's sentence from ten to five years. Local officials sent a letter supporting Byrd's release to the parole board signed by most of the public officials in Jones County. The board paroled Byrd after he had served less than two years. In the early 1970s, Bowers, Sessum, Smith, and Wilson remained in prison, but they lived well for inmates. Bowers spent his prison time completing a college degree in theology from Pacific Lutheran University. Six days after Wilson arrived at Mississippi State Penitentiary in Parchman, authorities assigned him to work in the hospital, and by April 6, 1970, he had become a trusty. Sessum enjoyed a decent livelihood for a prisoner as he made various leather goods, which Deavours Nix sold in his restaurant. Governor Williams persuaded prison authorities to provide Sessum and Wilson several prison leaves. After his wife fell ill, Wilson received a series of emergency leaves to run the family business, the Laurel Brace and Limb Company. When authorities granted Sessum a two-week leave to visit his ill father at Christmas, he spent his time with his Klan buddies. In March 1971, Sessum received a ten-day release to attend his father's funeral. Before the primary elections in the summer of 1971, Wilson, Sessum, and Smith obtained a weekend pass. The Klansmen spent the weekend campaigning for white supremacist candidates, including Jimmy Swan, who was running for governor again.[35]

To the Klan's chagrin, the political milieu had undergone a transformation. Although Swan punctuated his rhetoric with racist diatribes, neither of the chief gubernatorial candidates, William Waller and Charles Sullivan, campaigned on racist platforms. Waller had defended Klansman Charles Wilson in the Dahmer federal case, but he had also prosecuted Byron de la Beckwith for Medgar Evers's murder. Both Waller and Sullivan promised to spur economic growth by bringing Mississippi into a harmonious relationship with the rest of the nation. As the black vote could swing the election in a close race, candidates appealed openly to blacks. Covert racism continued to influence politics, but the days of open racial demagoguery had passed. After winning the election, Waller promoted programs like the Office of Minority Business and fostered greater diversity in hiring, particularly in the Mississippi State Penitentiary, which ranked first among state prisons in the hiring of black workers. Waller also oversaw the State Democratic Committee's adoption of the state's Affirmative Action Plan.[36]

Yet Waller marred his work toward racial reconciliation when he continued Governor Williams's practice of providing Klansmen convicted of Dahmer's murder with prison leaves. Between March 12, 1969, and April 30, 1972, he granted Wilson, his former Klan client, ten emergency releases for a total of 228 days. *Newsweek* reported that these furloughs allowed Wilson to spend more time out of prison than the FBI spent trying to incarcerate him. The *Delta Democrat-Times* noted that Waller "is reminding us of an old truth . . . justice for the white is not the same as justice for the black." Wilson received his last ninety-day leave on April 30, 1972, and when he returned to prison it was not for long. Waller and state legislators developed a work-release program that allowed prisoners to live in custodial situations while they completed their sentences. Governor Waller placed Wilson in the program nine months before the bill for the program passed the legislature. Authorities housed Wilson at South Mississippi State Hospital in Laurel, where he worked making braces for patients and enjoyed visits with his family.[37]

Ellie Dahmer protested, noting that while Wilson's family enjoyed his presence, "all we have right now is a tombstone and a grave." Mississippi's black leaders characterized Waller's actions as an "abuse of executive power." Waller defended his program and the inclusion of Wilson on the grounds that he had consulted the FBI before approving Wilson's release and that prison reports characterized Wilson as "well-balanced, without psychosis, even-tempered, timid and non-violent." The governor also stressed that eight of the fifteen inmates in the program were black and that many of the participants were serving life sentences for murder. The NAACP on national, regional, and local levels released statements condemning the inclusion of Wilson in the program. Forrest County NAACP president Clarence Magee encouraged local blacks to arm themselves against the former Klansman. The Laurel Interdenominational Ministerial Alliance lambasted Waller, asserting that his actions would cause a regression in racial relations. The editors of the *Hattiesburg American*, which by 1972 had become more progressive on race, noted that although the Klansmen who committed the murder hailed from another county, their crime also defamed Forrest County. The diligent investigation and prosecution and the willingness of local juries to convict Klansmen reflected a shift among the citizenry that laid the foundations for a more just society. Although the editors asserted that they believed in the deliverance of mercy, they disagreed with its application in such a watershed case.[38]

Still, the white establishment in Mississippi and the federal government continued to counteract legal victories against the Klansmen over the remainder of the decade. In April 1973, Assistant Attorney General Murphey moved to dismiss all federal charges against defendants in the Dahmer case because he doubted that he could win convictions. Judge Harold Cox ordered the charges dismissed. On August 19, the FBI closed DABURN. The four Klansmen still behind bars did not stay in prison long. In January 1976, Governor Waller ordered Wilson's release. The state paroled Smith and Sessum in January 1978. Not one of these men served more than ten years of their life sentences. In March 1976, Bowers returned to Laurel, having served slightly less than six years of his ten-year sentence in the MIBURN case. Within a decade of their convictions, these murderers and the thirteen other Klan killers never convicted in the Dahmer case roamed free in Jones County. Black life was still expendable in Mississippi.[39]

Moreover, at least one Klansman got away with murder in the mid-1970s. On June 4, 1974, two young black army reservists, David Windham and Carl Richardson, stopped by the Amusement Center in their hometown of Laurel owned by a fifty-one-year-old Klansman, Maurice Flowers. The Klansman grew irritated when Windham and Richardson engaged in a boisterous game of pool, and he ordered them to leave his establishment. Windham refused. After a heated exchange, Flowers stalked out of the poolroom and toward his grocery store across the street. Windham, with Richardson in tow, followed Flowers into the street and called him a "motherfucker." Flowers returned the insult and then stormed into his store as Windham shouted curses after him. When Flowers strode back out of his store, Windham stood his ground in the middle of the street and engaged in a fiery cursing match with the Klansman. Flowers pulled a pistol out of his back pocket, aimed it at Windham, and pulled the trigger. Windham clutched his chest, took several steps, and fell to the ground. Terrified, Richardson fled.[40]

Word of the shooting spread across the black community quickly, and by the time police arrived on the scene, a large crowd of blacks had gathered around the store. Although police arrested Flowers on murder charges, by 1974 many young blacks in Laurel believed in responding to violence with violence. That night groups of young blacks burned Flowers's vehicle and shattered the picture window of Flowers's storefront. When policemen arrived on the scene to investigate, several blacks shot at the officers and wounded one of them. Officers returned fire. They wounded two people and arrested six persons, but they failed to contain the violence that spread across Laurel over the next four nights. Blacks targeted white businesses in black communities. They shot out windows, vandalized and set fire to buildings, and hurled rocks at whites who dared to enter their neighborhoods. In response, whites attacked black-owned stores. The melee continued, even after policemen arrested a dozen blacks and whites. Chief Herman Aycock and Mayor Bill Patrick appealed to black leaders for help. Reverend Allen Johnson condemned the mayhem, but he empathized with the rage. The White Knights had bombed his home in 1967. Johnson and other black leaders convinced black insurgents to stand down and place their faith in the justice system.[41]

Blacks were hopeful when a grand jury indicted Flowers on first degree murder charges. Initially, Jones County authorities held Flowers in jail without bond, but when he fell ill with cancer, authorities released him. During the trial in November 1974, Flowers was the only defense witness. He testified that Windham followed him into his store and threatened to harm him, so he shot him out of fear for his life. Several of the prosecution's eyewitnesses, including Richardson, testified that Windham had not followed Flowers into the store; neither did he threaten him. Rather, he was standing still in the street with no weapon in his hand when Flowers shot him. During deliberations, the jurors, all whites, engaged in such a heated exchange that people in the courtroom could hear them shouting. After nearly six hours, the jury reported to the judge that it deadlocked eleven to one, which forced a mistrial. During Flowers's retrial in May 1975, the old Klansman again claimed that he had killed Windham in self-defense. The jury deliberated for four hours before acquitting him. Despite the movement victories and the FBI war against the Klan, a Jones County jury failed to convict a Klansman who had wantonly murdered a black man.[42]

Police brutality and the refusal by white leaders to punish rogue officers also reflected the low value many whites placed on black life in the Central Piney Woods. In Forrest County in the fall of 1969, blacks launched a massive protest against the Hattiesburg Police Department after officers beat two black residents, including a Vietnam War veteran. Chief Hugh Herring ruled that in both incidents, the officers had used justifiable force. The Black Coalition, a newly formed local group composed of members of the NAACP, the MFDP, and the FCAC, demanded that the city fire Herring and other racist officers. Herring's reputation for abusing blacks stretched back to the 1940s, when Willie McGee had accused Herring of beating him upon arresting him on charges of raping Willette Hawkins and of torturing him in the Jackson jail until he signed a false confession. The coalition warned that "this problem is of monumental proportions and should be dealt with now before we are confronted with another 'Cloudes Shinall case.'" The invocation of Shinall, who in 1965 had killed a white constable with a reputation for brutality, reflected the depths of black frustration. Blacks leading the coalition also threatened that if Chief Herring did not resign by November 25, 1969, they would implement Black Christmas—a boycott of merchants during Christmas season. They reasoned that blacks should not pay the salary of the chief, via sales tax, when he allowed his officers to "beat our heads." The coalition distributed leaflets that denigrated Herring: "The head is sick, therefore the whole body is afflicted with the disease of racism. For the sake of the well-being of this community, let us get rid of this sickness now." Black residents launched a series of protests. Most activists employed nonviolent tactics. However, after Rev. J. C. Killingsworth led 250 black students to city hall in a protest march in late October, dozens of them vented their rage by hurling bricks at cars.[43]

White authorities and most of the white community supported Herring. On November 11, Mayor Paul Grady and the commissioners issued a public statement that condemned the coalition leaders as "professional agitators who make their living trying to create boycotts, strife, and advocate destruction or violence in the streets." They promised to preserve law and order with all necessary force. Chief Herring brought in white men from Jones County, whom he deputized and whom local hardware stores supplied with guns. A group of white citizens formed the Forrest County Committee to Support Your Local Police and published an "Open Letter to the Citizens of Forrest County" in the *Hattiesburg American* that employed tired red-baiting tactics to claim that communists used professional activists to launch protests and make false allegations of police misconduct to foment unrest.[44]

The Black Coalition leaders battled the white propaganda. The president of the Forrest County NAACP, Dr. C. E. Smith, asserted that the coalition had presented a wealth of evidence via affidavits and witness testimony to the mayor showing that the HPD had still failed to truly integrate. Moreover, the HPD permitted officers to brutalize black citizens, and it implemented discriminatory procedures within the department such as preventing black police from arresting white suspects. Smith also lambasted the latest attempts to red-bait the movement. He declared that the Black Coalition lacked "professional agitators" and that the only outsiders involved in the racial clashes were "those mysterious white men wearing dark glasses, driving cars with mostly Jones County license plates" who harassed and intimidated black citizens. Smith warned that the black protest would continue until the city removed the chief. On November 25, when the city leaders agreed to meet with the black community and negotiate demands, the coalition postponed the boycott. Then the leaders abruptly canceled Black

Christmas when merchants hired more blacks, even though Herring had not resigned.[45]

Problems between the police and the black community persisted. In March 1971, blacks observed five policemen, including Officer Michael Shoemake, rush into their neighborhood and point a gun at John Albert White, a forty-year-old African American. When they ordered him to halt, White stopped and raised his hands above his head. Officers ordered White to back into an alley. White complied, and he and several policemen disappeared behind a row of houses. Seconds later shots echoed through the alleyway. Someone called an ambulance, but according to black witnesses, when the emergency responders arrived, police refused to allow them to attend to White. Instead, police sent them to White's mother who had fainted when she learned of the shooting. While police officers searched White's home, White died in the alleyway. Later, officers claimed that when they tried to arrest White on charges of marijuana possession, he pointed a gun at them and threatened to kill them, which forced Officer Shoemake to shoot him. The local NAACP suspected foul play and conducted an investigation. A black eyewitness told NAACP investigators that White held a radio, not a gun in his hands, which was raised above his head when the officer shot him. Some blacks suspected that officers found White's gun when they searched his house and planted it on his dead body.[46]

Soon after the killing, Officer Shoemake received phone calls from a woman who asked, "How would you like .38 lead in your chest?" On another occasion a male caller warned, "Hey, Pig, we are going to get you, Boy." At 3:00 a.m. one March morning, gunshots echoed across a white neighborhood and bullets shattered Shoemake's front windows. Seconds later, the drive-by shooter sprayed another round of bullets that ripped through three walls. The bullets missed Shoemake. To address the controversy and prevent more violence, authorities requested that the FBI investigate the shooting of White. They also released a statement asserting that the coroner's jury, composed of three blacks and three whites, had found unanimously that Shoemake had fired his gun at White in self-defense, but they decided to ask for an FBI probe because of the rumors of foul play. Mayor Grady suspended Shoemake, but the FBI investigation of White's homicide foundered. And no one was arrested in connection with the shooting on Shoemake's home. Herring remained chief.[47]

In 1972 six black officers, Alvin Eaton, John Smith Jr., Paul Taylor, T. J. Gordon, John Duncan, and Clarence McKinley worked with the NAACP and Douglass Baker, a local black civil rights lawyer, to initiate a lawsuit against the HPD. The officers accused Herring of discrimination and misconduct. They noted that the chief made sure that only one black officer reached a rank above patrolman by sending rookie white officers over experienced black police to training courses necessary for promotions. Herring divested all black officers of their authority by restricting them as often as possible to beats in black neighborhoods. On the occasion that they patrolled white neighborhoods, they had to call a white officer if they needed to execute an arrest. As the chief considered blacks more prone to criminal behavior than whites, he expected the department's arrest sheets to reflect his views, which led to false arrests. The chief and white officers used the term *nigger* habitually, and white police often beat blacks in custody.[48]

In 1975 Judge Dan Russell delivered a watershed ruling when he forced the HPD to implement an affirmative action plan to insure that it reflected the society that it protected and ordered Herring to terminate all racist practices. The case had a domino effect. By December 1977, Laurel had developed an affirmative action plan in its police department. Despite these notable victories, problems persisted. According to a white officer, Wayne Landers, when Arlon Moulds became the new HPD chief, he promoted whites over their senior black officers routinely, and he tolerated racist language and brutality in his department. Landers's bosses used the "n word," and most of the veteran white officers considered black officers beneath them. It would take time for progressive leaders like Landers to move up the ranks and move the HPD away from its racist roots. By that point, grave economic shifts had created deep wounds in historical black communities that led to the formation of ghettos, new racial divides, and deepening fractures between the black bourgeois and the black poor.[49]

Those shifts began to take shape with a natural disaster. On April 13, 1974, the Leaf River crested at thirty-four feet in Hattiesburg and swallowed communities along its banks in Forrest, Jones, and six other counties. It killed eight people, destroyed eight thousand homes, and drowned hundreds of pets. Blacks suffered the most, for segregation had consigned them to reside in the flood zones. After the surge, Kenneth Fairley, one of the first blacks to integrate Hattiesburg schools and now a sophomore at USM, caught a ride on a friend's boat down the watery landscape to survey the damage to his neighborhood. He found his home that he had been building for his fiancée destroyed and that of his parents almost completely submerged underwater. Through the holes in the roof, he stared despondently at his family's prized encyclopedias floating away in the mucky water. In Laurel, the flood wiped out the KC Bottom. Thousands of its residents, including former Freedom Summer student Johnny Magee, were suddenly homeless. When the waters receded on April 20, the Central Piney Woods looked like a combat zone: homes and businesses were torn apart, drenched in mud, and infested with snakes; furniture, appliances, and clothing were strewn across the streets.[50]

In the immediate aftermath of the flood, political officials promised victims federal and state recovery funds. Yet Mayor A. L. Gerrard Jr. of Hattiesburg also warned that a new ordinance prohibited the rebuilding in flood zones unless owners met federal requirements such as structuring homes and businesses on stilts. Poor blacks lacked the financial resources to meet the reconstruction requirements, and they could not afford to purchase homes in nonflood zones, particularly since their properties were so devalued that they could not sell them. Outraged, NAACP leaders, including J. C. Fairley, Clarence Magee, and Susie Ruffin, formed a Flood Victims Committee. On June 20, the committee members, armed with a petition containing thousands of signatures, demanded that local, state, and federal officials distribute emergency funds to victims immediately, provide permanent housing for displaced persons, develop flood prevention plans, and create a new assessment committee composed of flood victims to insure the fair distribution of relief funds and housing allotments for the displaced. The governing bodies ignored most of these requests. Blacks received some government aid, and the US Department of Housing and Urban Development (HUD) provided some homeowners with a low interest loan to rebuild. In general, the government relocated the black poor, like the residents of the KC Bottom, to public housing apartments.[51]

The historically black neighborhoods also became victims of integration, massive economic shifts, and a federal retreat. Farming mechanization, the decline of manufacturing, and the rise and fall of Laurel's oil industry decimated the black working class. When the job training programs of the War on Poverty vanished under the fiscal conservative leadership of the 1970s and 1980s, poor blacks faced perennial unemployment. Simultaneously, the twin developments of integration and the rise of mega-retail devastated black businesses and neighborhoods. Many middle-class blacks moved to higher ground in historically white neighborhoods and flocked to the rising new mega grocery stores and the shopping malls that burgeoned in the suburbs. Locally black-owned businesses suffered more than their white counterparts because their appeal had always been limited to the black population and because most of them were located in flood zones. Business owners whose structures the flood destroyed could not secure loans to rebuild, and the businesses that survived the flood could not survive integration. Within a decade, most black businesses had dried up and closed, and their middle- and working-class employees had joined the growing pool of the jobless. Black capitalism, one of the historic strengths of the black community in the Central Piney Woods, was dying, while black unemployment skyrocketed. Low-skilled laborers, domestics, service employees, and welfare recipients began their descent into an underclass.[52]

By the mid-1970s, the racial war concluded in the Central Piney Woods without an unconditional surrender, a treaty, or racial reconciliation. Blacks had achieved many monumental victories, including two of their primary goals, suffrage and desegregation, and they had received a modicum of racial justice. Despite the early releases of Klansmen, the DABURN and MIBURN cases, in conjunction with several cases tangential to the Dahmer case, had decimated the hooded order. Upon his release from prison in 1976, Bowers found his Invisible Empire in near ruin and efforts to revive it mostly futile. Although he had escaped justice in the at least nine murders and the scores of beatings and arsons that he had ordered across Mississippi, his glory days as the warrior king of the militant counterrevolution had ended. Yet as white men donning robes and pointy hats lost control of white supremacist resistance to white men with suits and badges, blacks realized that the fight to reconstruct the Central Piney Woods had just begun. Moderate whites accepted some changes and progressive whites encouraged them openly; however, conservatives and radicals found new ways to sustain white rule. The Klan faded into the fringes, but police brutality remained rampant. Blacks obtained the vote, but whites dominated the political arena. Federal programs and civil rights acts aided black economic advancement, but discrimination persisted. Schools had desegregated, but whites controlled the administrations. Moreover, the movement enthusiasm faded, and its capricious ally, the federal government, retreated from the Central Piney Woods battlefront. Local NAACP branches survived, but their work slowed as they searched for methods to fight the new amorphous enemy whose racism was more covert.[53]

The flood and the Civil Rights Movement that stormed through the Central Piney Woods drowned an old way of life. But vestiges remained. In the aftermath, as black leaders fought to construct a biracial political system and an interracial community from the wreckage of Jim Crow and from the ruins of the flood, they experienced class breaches within their beloved community and encountered persistent racism. At the dawning of the mid-1970s, Mississippi was polarized still by racial divides and poisoned by racial hate. Yet the forces of resistance that first streamed into the Central Piney Woods during World War II had become vast rivers. The waters of revolution had flooded the landscape and drawn to its banks many whites who dreamed too of finding a road out of racial purgatory. Over the next several decades, a new gathering storm would force reckonings as the races struggled on the ever-winding road toward reconciliation and redemption.

EPILOGUE

Road to Redemption

ON THURSDAY MORNING, MAY 28, 1998, REPORTERS RUSHED FORWARD TO snap Sam Bowers's photograph as investigators pulled the old Klansman from their vehicle and ushered him into the Forrest County Jail. The infamous Imperial Wizard of the White Knights of the Ku Klux Klan, who once had the power to condemn a man to death with a whisper to his minions, now looked frail and a little frightened. Bowers scowled when officers took his mug shot and booked him on charges of murder and arson for the 1966 killing of Vernon Dahmer. Reporters waited for hours in the oppressive heat to photograph Bowers again when three black deputies escorted the seventy-three-year-old, clothed in a red jumpsuit, shackled, and handcuffed, to his arraignment. They also snapped pictures of seventy-two-year-old Deavours Nix as he arrived with a portable oxygen tank to face charges of arson and of fifty-five-year-old Charles Noble, charged with arson and murder. Attorney General Michael Moore noted the irony that Nix, suffering from lung cancer, arrived at jail "complaining . . . that the radiology burned his lungs up. Guess what? That's exactly how Mr. Dahmer died."[1]

The Dahmer family stayed away from the circus of the jailhouse that day, but they spoke with reporters who flocked to their farmhouse outside of town in the Kelly Settlement. As the journalists explored the grounds, they encountered vestiges of the thirty-two-year-old murderous attack scattered across the terrain, each remnant weaving a tale of the tragedy into a torturous memorial: an oak tree bearing burn scars on its trunk from the fire stood like a resilient survivor, a concrete chunk of the burned-down store remained like a statue of the assault, and the burned-out blue Ford deteriorating in the woods still haunted the landscape. Vernon Jr. told reporters that Mississippi's "image still suffers because these cases haven't been solved. . . . This is a big step in the right direction."[2]

The Dahmers had spent nearly three decades imploring a series of district attorneys to reopen the case. Soon after the few convicted Klan killers obtained early releases, a white backlash rolled across the nation. The

Dahmers, like all blacks, confronted the frustrating reality that although the civil rights revolution had guaranteed black suffrage and terminated de jure segregation, it had neither disempowered white supremacists nor vanquished racist mentalities. In the Central Piney Woods, the political and judicial systems remained all-white because the white majority elected white mayors, commissioners, county supervisors, judges, sheriffs, and district attorneys, and these officials selected whites as economic advisors, city and county directors, police and fire chiefs, school superintendents and board members, and investigators. Thus, the majority race still controlled economic development, public services, public safety, justice, and education. Having no dependency on the black vote, white officials ignored black interests. At the close of the movement era, the white establishment replaced the white tyranny with a white aristocracy by limiting the rise of blacks from the disfranchised caste to that of second-class citizen. Blacks rose again to battle white supremacy. During this third stage in the black liberation movement, they had far more white progressives and even some moderates supporting them. Their crusade made the reopening of the Dahmer cold case possible.

At the onset of the post–civil rights era in the latter 1970s, blacks refocused their efforts on breaking the white political monopoly. For fourteen years, COFO, the MFDP, and the Lawyers of the Constitutional Defense Committee had fought in a series of court battles, including nine hearings before the Supreme Court, to end the discriminatory practice of at-large elections for state representatives. They stressed that in the majority white state, white votes diluted black votes and prevented the election of black representatives by using multimember districts. Contrarily, in nonsouthern states, voters elected representatives at the precinct level in single-member districts, which allowed minorities to elect minority politicians to represent them. Finally, in 1979, the courts ruled in favor of the plaintiffs and ordered Mississippi to use single-member districts. That year, Hattiesburg resident Percy Watson became the first African American to represent Forrest County in the state legislature.[3]

Still, racial exclusion in politics persisted at the municipal and county levels. Most Mississippi towns, including Laurel and Hattiesburg, held at-large elections for commissioners rather than single-district elections. Because whites dominated the population in Hattiesburg by 70.9 to 28.8 percent and in Laurel by 60.5 to 30.5 percent, black candidates never won. In 1979, leaders of the Forrest County NAACP collected enough signatures for a referendum to adopt a single-member district voting system, in which each district, rather than the city as a whole, elected representatives in a mayor-council system. The referendum failed. Frustrated, they turned to the judiciary, and Laurel's black leaders joined them. They hired a white lawyer, Elliott Andalman, to sue their cities in federal court. Federal developments aided their cause. In 1982, despite opposition from Mississippi politicians, Congress passed, and President Ronald Reagan signed, a twenty-five-year extension of the Voting Rights Act. The extension included an amendment decreeing that plaintiffs did not have to prove the intent to discriminate but only that the election system had a discriminatory impact. In 1984, Judge John Roper delivered a landmark decision when he ordered Hattiesburg and Laurel to develop mayor-council governing systems. The next year, Hattiesburg elected two black councilmen, Eddie Holloway and Charles Lawrence, and Laurel chose three black council members, Lula Cooley, Viola Malone, and George Gaddy. Blacks levied similar lawsuits against their all-white county governments, which led to the election of black supervisors Jerome Wyatt in Jones County and James Boykin in Forrest County. Yet soon it became apparent that although blacks had a voice, they still had no power. White majorities on the councils (at a ratio of four-to-three in Laurel and three-to-two in Hattiesburg) and on county boards (at a ratio of five-to-one in both Jones and Forrest Counties) continued to privilege white interests and ignore many black demands.[4]

Several black activists in Forrest County, including the Reverend Kenneth Fairley and Fred Burns, determined it time to reinitiate direct-action protests to force the wholesale incorporation of African Americans into the power structures. They focused their first protest on the schools, because white flight to private academies and mostly white county schools had led to the emergence of predominantly black schools in the city while the administration, staff, and faculty remained majority-white. Fairley had never forgotten the suffering he had endured as one of the first black students to desegregate Hattiesburg schools in the mid-1960s. On a Friday afternoon in November 1986, he and Burns led a dozen black men into the Hattiesburg School District Administration building and staged a sleep-in to force the superintendent and the school board to respond to their grievances. Many Hattiesburg blacks supported the sleep-in by picketing the building. On the following Monday, Fairley presented demands to the school board, which included hiring more black administrators, teachers, and staff; funds for after-school programs; increased participation of blacks in extracurricular activities and in college preparatory programs; and the establishment of racial quotas to insure the hiring of black contractors. After a week of protests, the school board conceded to each of these demands. The sleep-in was the first major black protest in the Central Piney Woods since the movement era.

After its success, Fairley and Burns, along with the Reverend Arthur Siggers, businessman Rod Woullard, and civil rights lawyer Douglass Baker, organized a new civil rights organization, the Community Improvement Association of Forrest County (CIAFC), and launched a second movement in Hattiesburg to demand an equalization of racial power. Soon the struggle spread to Laurel. The CIAFC, sometimes working in conjunction with the NAACP in Forrest and Jones counties, led massive protests and boycotts and initiated court battles. Within a few years, blacks assumed positions on city boards and economic organizations and dominated the administration of city schools in Hattiesburg and Laurel.[5]

The CIAFC faced its greatest challenges with the police department. Throughout the 1970s and 1980s, the unbridled racism in the HPD led to unfounded arrests and false convictions of innocent black men. The most glaring injustice began on a Mississippi night in May 1979 after a black man raped a white woman, Eva Gail Patterson, in front of her four-year-old son and then slit her throat. Although Patterson's son Luke insisted that only one man was involved in the crime, police arrested three black men: Larry Ruffin, Phillip Bivens, and Bobby Ray Dixon. Police lacked evidence that any of the three men had actually committed the crime, so officers relied on a common HPD tactic to make a case. They beat Ruffin and Dixon and threatened Bivens until all of the men confessed. Dixon's beating was so severe that he had to walk with a cane for the rest of his life. In the winter of 1980, prosecutors tried Ruffin. On the stand, Ruffin declared his innocence and insisted that he had only confessed because authorities had beaten him. Dixon, as a prosecution witness, began his testimony by affirming the state's case, asserting that he had observed Bivens and Ruffin rape Patterson, watched as Ruffin murdered her, and then helped both men escape. But as the questioning proceeded, Dixon revealed that he was only testifying because he was scared and hoped to receive a reduced sentenced for his cooperation. Then he recanted his confession and declared, "I wasn't there. I ain't never seen the woman. . . . I don't even know how she looks." Frustrated, District Attorney Bud Holmes asked, "Bobby Ray Dixon, did you stand before this court in Hattiesburg and plead guilty to the murder?" Dixon conceded, "Yes, I pleaded guilty." Holmes asked, "And was it free and voluntary?" Dixon retorted, "It wasn't free and voluntary." Despite the weak case, the court found all three men guilty and sent them to prison for life. It would take nearly thirty years to prove their innocence.[6]

During the last decade of the twentieth century, the grind toward equity in racial justice experienced great strides and significant setbacks. A noteworthy leap forward emerged within the policing bodies when law enforcement officers with more progressive racial mentalities took over city and county policing and initiated vital changes in the legal system. Billy McGee, who won the 1992 election for Forrest County sheriff, implemented community policing policies and initiated a no-tolerance policy for brutality. The new police chief, Wayne Landers, an affable family man, was well-liked by most citizens of Hattiesburg, including Reverend Fairley. Landers's critics and his defenders knew that he faced substantial challenges as chief in 1993, but they disagreed on the effectiveness of his response. Less than a year after Landers became chief, gang violence exploded across Hattiesburg.[7]

Since the post–civil rights era, a myriad of developments—including farming mechanization, the decline of manufacturing, the deterioration of black capitalism, and the eradication of job training programs—had created the conditions that fostered gang violence, all of which left many poor blacks perennially unemployed across the nation. Moreover, the War on Drugs insured that the black underclass across the nation descended further into a state that Michelle Alexander has dubbed a black "undercaste" because the drug czars targeted inner cities, even though suburban and rural whites abused and sold drugs at the same rates. The undercaste became cyclical. Born into impoverished neighborhoods, many children of the ghettos turned to gangs for familial ties and to drugs for income.[8]

Within this context, the racial struggle in Central Piney Woods between the police and the black community that erupted in the 1990s had a racist foundation, even though many of its executors lacked racial bias. Blacks had long perceived the badge and the gavel as forces of racial oppression because historically police, prosecutors, and judges had not only failed to protect them but used their power to suppress their liberties. As the drug war ratcheted to its zenith, poor blacks tended to perceive police as an occupying force that invaded their communities to intimidate, brutalize, and incarcerate them. According to Fairley, police brutality proved much more pervasive than the HPD would admit, and he launched a decade-long crusade against the department. On the other side of the color line, many whites considered Fairley a racist and a charlatan who used the race card to draw blacks into his ever-growing Mt. Carmel Baptist Church and enrich his coffers. Most officers of both races perceived complaints as either fabricated or stemming from a misunderstanding of justifiable force.[9]

Hattiesburg's black councilmen, Charles Lawrence and Eddie Holloway, proposed that the council develop an external review panel that would investigate charges of police misconduct and hold town forums to foster a positive relationship between the police and the black community. Holloway argued that the panel's public investigations would prevent the HPD from obscuring facts to protect its officers while also revealing that some complaints were fabricated. The relationships sure to result from the experience would encourage blacks to perceive officers as their protectors, and it would diminish incidents of police misconduct as officers were less likely to abuse persons they knew. According to Holloway, the HPD, Mayor Ed Morgan, and the white council members blocked the proposal because most whites feared that blacks would fill the panel with "radicals."[10]

As whites controlled the mayor's office, the city council, the public service department, the judiciary, and the HPD, CIAFC leaders concluded that blacks would never obtain equal justice until blacks controlled the city. To that end, they convinced Johnny DuPree to run for mayor. A child of Jim Crow born to an unmarried maid, DuPree was intimately familiar with the twin sufferings of poverty and racism. He was also a self-made man. While a manager at Sears and serving on the school board and the county board of supervisors, he received bachelor's and master's degrees in political science from USM and would later obtain a PhD. During the 1997 campaign, DuPree raised $8,000 to Morgan's $100,000, but he had a powerful Bridging the Gap motto and a Ten-point Community Development program to close the abyss between rich and poor, black and white, and police and blacks by improving education, infrastructure, job training, and social services in poor neighborhoods. Although Morgan won the race, DuPree came in a close second. He and Fairley determined that by 2001, persistent white flight would shift the racial demography enough that the black vote could tip the election in their favor.[11]

A conflict between police and the black community bolstered Fairley's determination. On a quiet September day in 1997, Ellis Alford, an ailing black minister, pointed his shotgun at the black and white emergency responders who entered his bedroom. He had not asked his caregiver to call the ambulance, and he refused to return to the hospital. The white EMT fled the house while shouting into his radio that the minister had a gun. Soon dozens of police converged on the scene. Panicked neighbors called Fairley. Alford was Fairley's mentor. When Fairley arrived, the police had formed a perimeter around Alford's home. Snipers stationed on rooftops pointed their rifles at the windows. SWAT teams waited for orders to storm the house from Assistant Chief Charlie Sims, who directed the situation from Alford's carport. As Fairley rushed toward Sims, the black attendant strode out of the house and announced that Alford had put down his gun.

According to Fairley, Sims ordered his men to remain in their positions. Fairley pleaded with Sims, "He's like a father to me, man. . . . I'll bring him out." When Sims failed to respond, Fairley strode toward the house, but Sims blocked his path, smacked his hands against Fairley's chest, and ordered him to retreat. Fairley retorted, "Would you please remove your hand off my chest?" Sims repeated his warning; Fairley again demanded he let him pass. On Sims's order, officers threw Fairley to the ground, handcuffed him, and tossed him in the back of the police vehicle.[12]

Sims remembered the confrontation differently. He recalled that when Fairley demanded to see Alford, Sims responded, "not a problem, Reverend, as soon as we're finished. We just have to secure the scene, make sure everything is safe." Fairley tried to rush the house. Sims claimed that he blocked Fairley's path, and Fairley ran into is hand. Fairley demanded, "Get your hands off me." Sims repeated his command. Fairley scowled and tried to rush the house. Sims arrested him. Sims considered Fairley a shyster. He argued that the reverend levied false accusations of police brutality to acquire power in the black community. Although Sims expressed some sympathy for Fairley as he knew that the reverend had suffered under the Jim Crow system, he insisted that Fairley must realize that the community had transformed.[13]

To Fairley, Officer Sims represented the white southern male ego that he had fought against all of his life. As a teenager desegregating all-white schools in a southern world controlled by white males, he had no choice but to quell the innate instinct to physically fight back when he suffered beatings at the hands of whites. As a man, he reclaimed his masculinity by confronting white authority. His forceful assault against powerful symbols of southern oppression purged the emasculations of his boyhood. To Fairley's dismay, when Landers retired in February 1998, Sims became chief. In response, the CIAFC launched DuPree's 2001 mayoral campaign and spent three years convincing blacks that only when blacks controlled the executive office and the HPD could they "empower the black community" and insure racial justice.[14]

Blacks in Laurel were struggling through similar upheavals. Many of the conflicts stemmed from black frustrations over persistent racial injustices. In 1992, the president of the Jones County NAACP, Manuel Jones, led his five-hundred-strong branch in a protest against the Laurel Police Department's refusal to hire and promote black police officers on par with their white counterparts and against a judge for releasing on an appeal bond a white man convicted of raping a woman in a church while denying bond to a black man accused of selling drugs. During the protests, Klansman J. Dale

Jones threatened Manuel Jones. Although the FBI war on the Klan in the 1960s had marginalized the White Knights, Klansmen sustained a minor presence on the fringes of society. With the help of the FBI, police arrested Dale Jones. A judge forced him to apologize publicly to the NAACP president. Manuel Jones considered the punishment inadequate and reflective of the problems of persistent racial injustice.[15]

The parallel struggles for racial justice in Jones and Forrest Counties intersected over the Dahmer case. In January 1991, District Attorney Glenn White rejected a request by the Dahmers to reopen the cold case. White emphasized that the state no longer had copies of the 1960s trial transcripts and insisted that he would confront a legal albatross if he tried suspects a quarter of a century after the commission of the crime. Mississippi, the Dahmers reminded him, had no statute of limitations on murder or arson. Moreover, a month earlier, a Hinds County grand jury charged Byron De La Beckwith with the 1963 murder of NAACP leader Medgar Evers. White promised to reexamine the possibility, but whenever the Dahmers contacted him, he claimed that he had found nothing to allow him to move forward. Even after Hinds County jurors convicted Beckwith in early 1994, proving that Klan cold cases could be prosecuted successfully, White evaded the Dahmers' request. The Dahmers contacted Rev. Fairley.[16]

On February 8, 1994, Fairley and Douglass Baker formed the Citizens for Justice and amassed substantial biracial support to reopen the case from many organizations and politicians, including the NAACP, the SCLC, the Southern Poverty Law Center, the Center for Democratic Renewal, the Anti-Defamation League of B'nai B'rith, the Hattiesburg Interfaith Alliance, all members of the Forrest County Board of Supervisors, and all of the Hattiesburg city council members. The publicity forced White to open an investigation, but he searched for evidence to dismiss the case. His office focused on the six-man theory, a lead developed in early 1966 after Klan informant Delmar Dennis reported to FBI agents that Bowers ordered six men to murder Dahmer. The six-man theory contradicted vital aspects of Billy Roy Pitts's 1960s testimony that led to four convictions in the case. White sought to prove that since the FBI's contradictory theories rendered it impossible to determine any Klansman's guilt, he could not indict anyone. To White's chagrin, Dennis could not recall the identities of the men whom Bowers had named as the perpetrators, and most of the Klansmen's 1960s statements supported Pitts's rendition. Yet White refused to contact many old Klansmen, including Pitts, and he had neglected to demand access to the entire DABURN file. When the Dahmers and Fairley appealed to Attorney General Janet Reno, she ordered the entire DABURN file sent to the

Jackson FBI office. After a few months, White claimed that the files lacked the evidence needed to pursue indictments. White would not have long to stymie racial justice because 1995 was an election year, and his handpicked candidate lost to Lindsay Carter.[17]

Carter and his team pursued the Dahmer case diligently, and they received substantial federal and state support. Mississippi attorney general Michael Moore sent two investigators to assist in the investigation. Federal judge Charles Pickering approved Carter's request to open sealed federal records. Assistant District Attorney Robert Helfrich devoted himself to the case. As he spent many late nights reading the forty-thousand-page DABURN file, he thought often of Dahmer's youngest son, Dennis, who was twelve years old at the time of the murder. When Helfrich was the same age, he had watched his father die of lung cancer. He knew the anguish of becoming a fatherless child at that age when a boy began the passage toward manhood and needed his father most. Helfrich's mother, like Ellie Dahmer, never remarried. He understood the sadness of a widowed home. For Helfrich, the case became a crusade.[18]

To successfully reinstate the indictments, Helfrich needed proof of jury tampering, transcripts from the 1960s trials, a new witness, and new evidence. Through a meticulous perusal of FBI files, prosecutors found evidence proving that the Klan had tampered with juries in at least two of Bowers's state cases and located reports summarizing the transcripts of Bowers's trials in the 1960s. In hopes of finding a new witness with new evidence, Ellie Dahmer requested help from the public on television. Bob Stringer saw the broadcast. He was in a twelve-step program for gamblers that compelled him to make amends to persons he had harmed. As a teenager, Stringer had worked for Bowers as an errand boy and as a typist and distributor for the *Klan Ledger*. He often attended Klan rallies and hung around John's Café, where he had overheard Bowers ordering Dahmer's murder. His knowledge of the killing troubled him for decades. When he summoned the courage to become a witness for the prosecution, police fitted him with a hidden recorder and sent him to elicit information from Nix's wife, Sybil. During their conversations, Sybil noted that Nix "was lucky he didn't get caught on that Dahmer deal." She said Bowers ordered the execution, and Nix orchestrated it.[19] Early in 1998, Carter searched for Billy Roy Pitts.

Since his release from federal prison in 1971, Pitts had spent his troubled life in Denham Springs, Louisiana. He lost a series of jobs and suffered from heart problems and ulcers. A tortured soul, he mistreated anyone who tried to love him. His first wife, Bonnie, divorced him because he had committed adultery and neglected his children. After a short marriage with Lucille Prine, he had a tumultuous relationship with his third wife, Rachel Smith. He became addicted to pain medication. While in a drug-induced state, he barreled through a glass door and threatened Smith and her mother. He spent weeks in a mental hospital, but nothing cured his broken mind. His past tormented him, for he was haunted by dreams of murdering Dahmer. When the Mississippi Department of Corrections issued a warrant for his arrest because he had never served his state sentence, Pitts sent a statement to Carter in which he promised to testify for the Dahmers, but he reminded Carter that the Department of Justice and local prosecutors had agreed to release him after he testified and served his federal sentence. Pitts feared returning to prison, and upon learning that Mississippi authorities planned to arrest him, he went into hiding. However, his conscience troubled him, and within days he surrendered.[20]

By late spring, the Dahmer team had focused its investigation on Bowers and Nix because they were the ringleaders and Noble because he was the only participant still living who had never faced prosecution. Noble would prove the most difficult to prosecute as he had become a wealthy and well-connected executive of the chicken plant, Sanderson Farms. Conversely, Bowers, a recluse, had few influential friends. Moreover, in an interview in 1994, Bowers romanticized his role in the racial struggle as that of a "warrior priest," leading his crusading soldiers against the civil rights "heretics." He concluded that "when heretics arise, the priests respond with a calculated and confident militancy; for heresy cannot be forgiven, it can only be eliminated." By the 1990s, Bowers inhabited a world in which "heretics" could control his fate. As of 1998, eighteen thousand blacks were registered to vote in the county. Blacks would be in the jury pool and likely on the jury. Moreover, Pitts, who had brought down Bowers's Invisible Empire decades ago, was more than willing to sacrifice Bowers for his expiation. On May 27, 1998, Carter reactivated the 1966 murder and arson indictment against Bowers and Noble and an arson indictment against Nix.[21]

Helfrich worried about seating a racially unbiased jury. White supremacy, though diminished, had not vanished from Mississippi. To weed out racists, prosecutors sent questionnaires to potential jurors and hired juror consultant Andrew Shelton. The prospective jurors had to divulge if they and their family members had affiliations past or present with any white supremacist groups or if they had participated in a verbal or violent racial confrontation. Through questions regarding the backgrounds and associations of prospective jurors, prosecutors tried to seat persons likely to convict Bowers; namely, educated Democrats affiliated with interracial organizations and preferably black. And they sought to remove jurors likely to acquit him: older social and political conservative working-class whites. By evening the attorneys had selected six whites, five blacks, and one Asian.[22]

The trial opened in a theatrical fashion as journalists and spectators flocked to the courthouse under the protection of a phalanx of thirty-five officers and passed through a security system. Although a few white supremacists protested the trial, they hailed from outside the Central Piney Woods and garnered little attention. Journalists from as far away as London hoped to pen dramatic stories of a state facing its tortured history. Helfrich did not disappoint. In a deep and solemn voice, he drew the jurors and spectators into a haunting southern narrative. The Imperial Wizard, Helfrich bellowed, ordered the murder of Vernon Dahmer, a beloved family and community man, because he had fought for black suffrage. A patriot and model citizen, Dahmer had inspired six of his seven sons to serve a total of seventy-eight years in the military. In addition, he was an entrepreneur and a farmer who "believed in the American dream. He built the home they lived in from the timber he cut and he milled right there on his property." On January 10, 1966, Bowers sent the Klan to destroy the Dahmers. The attack was sloppy. Pitts dropped his gun, and the Klansmen had to abandon one of their vehicles after they accidentally shot out its tires. Still, Bowers told his men, "No jury in Mississippi will convict a white man for killing a nigger." Helfrich concluded, "I am proud to say that no matter how long the passage of time, in this . . . state and this country, you do not get away with murder."[23]

Bowers's lawyer, Travis Buckley, lacked the charisma that Helfrich possessed. Certainly, Bowers had made a foolish mistake when he hired Buckley to defend him. During the 1960s, the federal and state governments had indicted Buckley in the Dahmer case and the related Watkins case. Moreover, Buckley's clumsy opening statement set the tone for his weak defense. He reminded jurors that they must base their verdict on the evidence, which required them to judge the defendant's actions, not his beliefs. His strategy was wise, but his execution was flawed. He staged a melodramatic tale of Bowers as a tragic figure, a victim of a federal conspiracy in the 1960s designed to destroy Mississippi sovereignty and a political pawn in the 1990s "media orchestrated and politically driven prosecution—a persecution . . . based on political ambition." The prosecution witnesses, he warned, were paid liars who, like "a fish with a hook caught in his mouth . . . will respond to the pressure that's applied to them." Buckley's arguments harkened back to a bygone era that no longer resonated with most Mississippians. And his efforts to empathize with the Dahmers rang hollow. After Ellie Dahmer detailed the attack on her home, she recalled how her husband died in her arms. Buckley remarked that his wife and son had died recently. He promised that the pain would fade. Dahmer replied that life without Vernon had continued to hurt for thirty-two years. While cross-examining Bettie, Buckley stressed that she never saw the attackers. Bettie responded, "I saw my house burn. . . . I saw the skin hanging off my daddy's arms." Buckley replied, "I know it's painful. . . . It's just like anyone else that had some event happen to their family out of anger, you would be wanting to strike back at them, wouldn't you?" Betty retorted, "No, Mr. Buckley. I just want my daddy to have the same justice that everybody else in America can have." Throughout the Dahmers' testimonies, several jurors bit back tears; others scowled at Buckley.[24]

The prosecution's case hinged on its star witness Billy Roy Pitts. The former Klansman remembered the deed well, and it haunted him. He testified that he had attended several Klan meetings at which Bowers ordered his men to murder Dahmer. Pitts insisted that only Bowers had the power to order murder. As Pitts detailed the attack, he recalled hearing the sound of Dahmer's voice "in distress." The next day, Bowers chastised the Klansmen for their mistakes, but he insisted, "There ain't no jury in the State of Mississippi gonna convict a white man for killing a nigger." Klan informants also implicated Bowers and corroborated Pitts's testimony. Truman Rogers and Bob Stringer testified that they heard Bowers order the killing. Another informant stated that Bowers showed him an article and declared, "Look what my boys did to that Dahmer nigger for me." A Klansman's former wife revealed that she overheard Bowers refer to Dahmer's murder and say "what a good job my boys did."[25]

On cross-examination, Buckley struggled to portray these witnesses as greedy liars who levied false accusations against Bowers for FBI bribes. He depicted Pitts as a man of low character not to be trusted by focusing on his adulterous affairs. Yet several former FBI agents and ballistic experts linked the evidence found at the murder scene to Pitts's rendition of the attack, and agents verified informant reports that revealed Bowers had ordered Dahmer's murder. While questioning Agent James Ingram, Buckley blundered in his attempts to prove that the FBI and the Central Intelligence Agency (CIA) used the Mafia to torture whites until they delivered false statements against Bowers. He claimed that investigative journalist Jack Nelson, in his book *Terror in the Night* (1993), revealed that the FBI and police ambushed Klansmen in a "setup . . . attempt to kill Sam Bowers." Several jurors laughed. Agent Ingram replied that Nelson never made such false accusations. Rather, he proved that Bowers was the Imperial Wizard of Mississippi's Klan.[26]

Buckley made another disastrous move when he called Nix to the stand. Nix admitted that he and several men implicated in the Dahmer murder, including Rogers, DeBoxtel, Lyons, and Thornton, were Klansmen in the 1960s. Buckley solicited this testimony from Nix so that Nix could insist that Bowers was not the Imperial Wizard. But Nix's testimony helped the prosecution because it proved that several people whom Pitts claimed had killed Dahmer were Klansmen. Nix tried to portray the Klan as a charitable organization that engaged in "benevolent work" like delivering fruit baskets to the poor. Buckley also used Nix to advance his conspiracy theory. Nix claimed that on the night of the murder, he was in Washington, DC, because the House of Un-American Activities Committee (HUAC) had subpoenaed him. Buckley inquired, "Do you know what happened to your motel receipts? I believe . . . they had gotten destroyed?" Prompted by Buckley, Nix suggested that the FBI disposed of his receipts and insisted that agents tried to coerce him to frame Bowers for Dahmer's murder by threatening his family and his business. According to congressional records, Nix did not appear before HUAC until February.[27]

During closing arguments, Buckley persisted in this vein with erratic diatribes claiming conspiracy theories. Trying a man four times, he shouted, was not justice, but "persecution." Four attorney generals preceding Moore had refused to retry the case, but "along comes an Attorney General who seeks political advancement. And he decides he has to offer up something to the crowd like throwing meat to hungry lions." As for the prosecution witnesses, most were "old worms" who "crawl out from under the rocks and slime" to present fabricated testimony for informant money while others were brainwashed agents "programmed" to lie. Buckley declared that just as Adolf Hitler, "an evil genius," convinced Germans that their problems were caused by the Jews, the prosecutors used Bowers as a scapegoat "to appeal to the racial prejudice and passion and bias of . . . the voters. And Mr. Bowers is being offered to you as a sacrament to their political ambitions." Buckley insisted that he sympathized with the Dahmers, but he proclaimed that they thirsted for revenge, which was a poor substitute for justice.[28]

As Buckley took his seat, Helfrich rose. "Let's say it's political. Let's talk about everything but what is important. And what is important, ladies and gentlemen is Vernon Dahmer. What did Mr. Pitts say? A man's voice in distress. And yes . . . he was a man. He was a businessman, a farmer, a husband and a father of eight children. His boys served 78 years protecting this country. . . . . [yet] he and Ms. Ellie had to sit up at night to protect themselves from these henchmen." The Fuhrer, Helfrich agreed, was an "evil genius" who ordered the Jewish genocide. "Did Hitler do it? No. His henchmen did it. Was Hitler responsible?" Helfrich reminded the jurors that Nix had called the Klansmen "benevolent gentlemen." Klansmen, Helfrich barked, did "not have a gentle bone in their body. They were night riders. And they were henchmen. And they attacked a sleeping family and destroyed everything they had. And they did it because of one person, a person that had told them to do it over and over and over. . . . A man's voice, ladies and gentlemen, is still in distress. It is in distress because Sam Bowers took his life and took his children away from him. His voice is still in distress because Sam Bowers is still walking the street."[29]

Over three hours later, as the Dahmer family watched from the balcony, the clerk declared, "We, the jury, find the defendant, Sam Bowers, guilty of murder." Judge McKenzie sentenced Bowers to life in prison. Spectators applauded. Tears spilled down Ellie Dahmer's cheeks. When the Dahmers emerged from the courtroom, Dennis stated, "Our father gave his life for a system that he believed in, even though that system wasn't fair to him in his lifetime. We hope today's verdict reflects the fact that we're living in a new South and, more particularly, a new Mississippi." Later that day, as Vernon Jr. stood on the land of his childhood still scarred by the crime that stole his father, he told reporters, "I am going to the cemetery and pray and tell my father that justice finally came and he can begin to rest in peace."[30]

Back in the Forrest County jail, Pitts prayed that he, too, would find peace. He had once admired Bowers and thirsted for his approval. His devotion had led him to commit atrocities, only to have Bowers betray him. The years after the trials of the 1960s were not good to Pitts. Guilt gnawed at his conscience, and his adulterous affairs, violent outbursts, and pain killers failed to numb the anguish. He never believed that he could find redemption, but he dreamed of it. After Bowers's trial, he met with the Dahmers and pleaded for their forgiveness. He told them that he wished that he "could relive his life" and change that day. As he looked at Vernon Jr., who resembled his father, Pitts said, "I woke up many a night to see [his] face. I wish I could somehow erase me out of it." The Dahmers not only forgave him, but they fought for his pardon.[31]

Although the Dahmers would never see Nix face justice because he died on September 19, a month short of his trial, they hoped Helfrich could convict Noble. Noble's lawyer, Sam Joe Owen, proved a formidable opponent. Former district attorney Glenn White provided Owen and his six-member team with his notes on the FBI files of the six-man theory, which purported that neither Noble nor Pitts participated in the crime. Owen won a motion to obtain the entire DABURN file. But then he tried to suppress those files that proved Noble was a Klansman and implicated him in the conspiracy. McKenzie ordered the entire DABURN file admitted. When the trial began in June, the court sequestered a jury of ten whites and two blacks. In his opening statement, Owen declared that six men attacked the Dahmers: Cecil Sessum, Billy Moss, Pete Martin, Charles Lowe, Clifford Lowe, and Henry DeBoxtel. Neither Noble nor Pitts participated in any phase of the Dahmer attack. Noble had never joined the Klan. Pitts lied to the FBI for money and immunity for his participation in another Klan crime—the Jack Watkins kidnapping.[32]

Though Owen's use of the six-man theory was a clever defense, a host of FBI files that he left out invalidated it. Those records revealed that Noble had admitted to agents that he was a Klansmen and that he had participated in a dry run in the Dahmer project. According to FBI interviews with Pete Martin, he, Noble, and several other Klansman attacked the home of Benjamin Murph using the same modus operandi as used in the Dahmer assault. Martin suspected Pitts had participated in the Dahmer attack. He also explained that Klansmen needed eight men for the Dahmer job—a driver, a fire starter, and two gunmen for each of the two vehicles. At one point, Martin confessed to participating in the attack, but that appears to have been part of Bowers's misinformation strategy as Martin's other interviews conform more clearly to the evidence. During Byrd's short stint as a Klan informant, he revealed that Sessum and Moss told him that Moss participated in a dry run of the project but dropped out when he learned DeBoxtel, whom he despised, was second in command. After Pitts confessed, he tried to persuade Charles Lowe to join him as a Klan informant. Lowe admitted to agents that he had peripheral knowledge of the murder and agreed to talk but then changed his mind. If Pitts had lied, as Owen claimed, he would not deliver to agents a man who could contradict his story. Finally, Pitts did not receive immunity in the Watkins case. He received a five-year sentence after pleading guilty, though he did not serve much of any of his federal sentences.[33]

The case for both the prosecution and the defense rested on Pitts's testimony. In a tough cross-examination that lasted three days, Owen proved that Pitts served a short prison sentence, obtained money from the FBI, and received a pardon after Bowers's conviction. Pitts conceded that Governor Kirk Fordice pardoned him a month earlier, but he denied that he had refused to testify without clemency. When Pitts testified that all of the Klansmen participating in the attack carried 12 gauge shotguns, Owen introduced evidence revealing that officers searching the crime scene found only 20 gauge and 16 gauge shotgun shells. Owen had left out FBI files, MHP reports, and testimony by an FBI agent and ballistic expert who proved agents and police had also collected 12 gauge Remington shotgun shells at the crime scene. It was likely that Pitts only noticed the shotguns that the men accompanying him in Giles's vehicle had carried.[34]

During redirect, Helfrich asked Pitts why he turned himself into the FBI. Pitts explained that he had no choice because Bowers, believing incorrectly that Pitts had betrayed him, planned to execute him for treason. Pitts noted that he still feared the Klan. While eating dinner at the Best Western during this trial, Pitts noticed "one of Sam Bowers' right-hand men... Carl Ford" glaring at him, and he worried for his safety. Owen objected and demanded that the court dismiss the charges against Noble because Pitts's testimony could prejudice the jury. Helfrich pointed out that Owen opened the line of questioning when he challenged Pitts's motives. Judge McKenzie refused to dismiss the charges, but he granted a mistrial.[35]

After McKenzie dismissed the jurors, several of them gave Noble a "thumbs up" sign. Later, these jurors noted that they distrusted Pitts's testimony and found the six-man theory convincing. But three jurors remained unsure of Noble's guilt, two believed that Noble was in the Klan, and one thought that Noble had at least participated in the conspiracy. Helfrich insisted that if the trial had continued, he would have proved that the six-man theory was a ruse designed by Bowers to confound the FBI investigation. Helfrich was certain that he could convict Noble in a retrial. However, Pitts fell ill with bladder cancer, which forced the prosecutors to agree to a *nolle prosequi*, meaning they would discontinue the prosecution. Disappointed but resigned, Ellie Dahmer declared, "Charles Noble was guilty from Jan. 10, 1966 and he's still guilty today, and he will always be guilty. I give it up to God. If he can go meet his maker with that on his hands, then let God deal with him."[36]

Despite the failure to convict Noble, the Dahmer cases were among many "little Nurembergs," as journalist David Halberstam labeled the retrying of Klan cold cases in the South. The conviction of men like Beckwith in the Evers case and particularly of Bowers in the Dahmer case reflected the transformation of the racial consciousness of southern prosecutors and citizens.[37] Only Bowers had the power to order the White Knights to murder, and he had ordered at least nine murders in the state. Yet until 1998, he was never convicted of any of them. The significant conviction of the Imperial Wizard furthered the process of unshackling Mississippi from its tragic racial history.

At the dawning of the new millennium, the Central Piney Woods seemed prepared not only to shed its haunting past but to rush forward into a progressive future when it birthed a black political revolution. On July 2, 2001, the inauguration of Hattiesburg's first black mayor proved an historic event in a city that once barred blacks from its political halls. Johnny DuPree had defeated incumbent Mayor Ed Morgan by seven hundred votes. As Mayor DuPree stood before an overflowing, integrated audience, he promised to work with the city council to represent the entire citizenry and to reconcile racial breaches. On the same day, Laurel blacks rejoiced at the inauguration of five black and two white council members, for it initiated a historic shift in their town's racial balance of power. Over the next decade, blacks celebrated other victories. In 2005, Laurel elected its first black mayor, Melvin Mack, and Hattiesburg reelected DuPree. On May 17, 2006, Robert Helfrich, who had become a circuit court judge, delivered a posthumous exoneration of Clyde Kennard, contending that the courts had convicted him to prevent the desegregation of USM. During the proceedings, Johnny Roberts admitted that powerful white men had coerced him into framing Kennard. Yet he failed to identify those men; thus, retributive justice could not occur. At least, the exoneration solidified Kennard's rightful place in history as a martyr of the movement, and it united racial progressives across the color line. On November 4, 2008, civil rights veterans watched in awe as Barack Obama, son of a black father and a white mother, became the forty-fourth president of the United States of America. Few of them ever imagined that they would witness the election of a president born of a relationship over which white men had lynched so many black men. Ellie Dahmer considered Obama's victory proof that "America has changed."[38]

The inauguration of President Obama and the rising political power that blacks enjoy in places like Mississippi certainly reflect the great changes that have transpired across the South and the nation, but a postracial world eludes them both. After the Civil Rights Movement, the racial landscape in the Central Piney Woods continued to evolve as whites with progressive racial mentalities grew in number, while those with radical mentalities became fewer. Yet when the balance of racial power tipped toward blacks in the political halls, some whites feared that black power meant white powerlessness, and some still clung to racist ideologies purporting that blacks were incapable of leading. Other whites considered black leaders to be black supremacists who practiced the very racism that they had condemned. Some black leaders responded that as whites had always ruled in the best interests of whites, it was time for blacks to rule in the best interest of blacks. Fights often divided along racial lines.

Racial hostilities plagued Laurel in the new millennium when Mayor Susan Vincent and the council sought to annex of parcels of white residential areas in Jones County. A group of whites in the area of the proposed annexation sued the city to prevent annexation and avoid becoming part of the town, which had become majority-black in the new millennium. Several black leaders supported the lawsuit because annexation would tip the racial demography of the city from a black to a white majority. The case cost Vincent the mayor's office in 2005. That year Laurel elected its first black mayor, Melvin Mack. To the chagrin of many residents, Mack fought for annexation, a battle he lost in 2009. The combination of white flight, the failure of annexation, and the pressure on Mayor Mack by black leaders to appoint blacks to most of the top city positions led to a predominantly black-run city. The county system was even more segregated with a nearly all-white leadership. Mack sought to foster biracial cooperation in the city, but it proved difficult. In general, citizens in both the city and the county fostered a détente as they accepted their divided racial terrains.[39]

It proved impossible to reach a similar détente in Hattiesburg, where the black and white populations of the city had become nearly equal and the governing body equally divided among the races with three white and two black council members and a black mayor. Soon after DuPree assumed office, he tore apart the nearly all-white city system when he appointed blacks as directors of many departments and insured that blacks dominated the school board for the first time in the city's history. The most controversial divisions centered on David Wynn, the first black police chief in Hattiesburg. Many blacks praised Wynn because he terminated racial profiling and punished officers accused of using excessive force. Most white officers complained that Wynn's militant style, his black supremacist attitude, and his radical policies were destroying the HPD. Droves of whites resigned. White councilmen implored DuPree to replace Wynn. He refused. After DuPree's reelection in 2005, he refused to present Wynn and his other department heads to the council for confirmation on the grounds that like the president of the United States, he should not have to seek approval for his directors confirmed during his first term. The white councilmen sued DuPree. In 2006 Judge Helfrich ruled in favor of the councilmen's lawsuit, and in 2007, the Mississippi Supreme Court upheld his decision. Wynn resigned. DuPree replaced him with Frazier Bolton, a generally well-liked African American who sought to quell the racial storms that had haunted the HPD since the Jim Crow days.

The change brought some peace. Council members and the mayor began to compromise, and in 2009, the voters returned all of the council members and DuPree to office. Furthermore, the march toward racial justice continued. In September 2010, Judge Helfrich reexamined the 1979 case in which police brutalized three black men—Larry Ruffin, Philip Bivens, and Bobby Ray Dixon—to coerce false confessions from them and send them to prison for life for the rape and murder of a white woman. In 2010, attorneys from the Innocence Project presented DNA evidence proving that a man imprisoned for another rape was the guilty party. The court released Bivens and Dixon from jail. Ruffin had died eight years earlier. Between 2010 and 2011, the courts exonerated all three men. Despite such progress, racial divides persisted. In 2013, Councilman Dave Ware, who was white, lost his bid for mayor to DuPree in a controversial election. Although ideological differences rather than racism inspired much of the voting, racial overtones remained part of the election landscape. The root of many racial clashes and divides that persist in the Central Piney Woods stem from the endurance of segregation, though now of the de facto, rather than the de jure, variety. As blacks and whites live somewhat parallel lives, points of intersection often result in confrontation with one side—and thus one race—losing. Segregation, then, still haunts the Central Piney Woods over fifty years after Clyde Kennard asked, "Where do our parallel worlds of separate but equal go?"[40]

Certainly, the Central Piney Woods—like the entire South—has undergone a substantial transformation since Kennard wrote those words. To undervalue the incredible achievements of the black liberation movement insults and misrepresents it. But to ignore the persistence of racial problems and their historical roots inhibits progress. Narratives of the many local racial struggles that coalesced across the South offer a deeper understanding of the roads traveled and the journey ahead. The Central Piney Woods crusade is particularly significant because it chartered watershed paths in the black liberation movement. It offers an ideal place to study how the movement's phases emerged at different times in different spaces and in which to witness how centuries of black resistance gave birth to the revolutionary spirit that drove the modern struggle.

That spirit was always strong in the Central Piney Woods, as was manifested in the first settlers, who in the early 1800s arrived with grand dreams to sculpt towns out of the forests, and who, in doing so, also carved out their histories, some proud and defiant, some cruel and vicious, and all of them telling some truth of the human spirit. The towns emerged from anarchist wildernesses, where whispers of racial egalitarianism during the Civil War spread hope to men and women of darker hues chained in bondage to white masters. The rebellious spirit is reflected, too, in slaves like Rachel and soldiers like Newton Knight who rebelled against the Confederacy.

With the onslaught of Redemption, the towns became white supremacist strongholds where the rope and the gavel replaced the bullwhip and the manacle. Still, hope for liberation never dissipated; it beat in the black underground preparing for the days that revolt was again possible. Many black residents living in the Jim Crow era channeled their energies into resisting their subjugation through the only venue available under the tyrannical racial order—black uplift. These residents sowed the ground for the Central Piney Woods to become one of the most powerful and educated forces of the black liberation movement because they built a sturdy black proletariat by capitalizing on the mass demand for labor in the new budding commercial and industrial centers to obtain higher pay and better conditions; they constructed a significant bourgeoisie by exploiting the segregationist model to build black capitalism; and they perpetuated black uplift by developing excellent schools for future generations.

The first phase of the black liberation movement proved particularly strong in the Central Piney Woods when it was able to emerge during World War II. Racial atrocities forced into motion black dissent, white crackdowns, and federal interventions. All of these exposed on a global stage the dichotomy between America's crusade against fascism and Nazism before and during World War II and Stalinism after the war on the one hand, and its homegrown racial autocracy on the other. That exposure fostered significant developments. The wartime mob lynching of Howard Wash, who had killed his white boss most likely in self-defense, led to the first federal trial of lynchers in Mississippi since Reconstruction. In 1951, the execution of Willie McGee after his interracial rape conviction on dubious evidence inspired national and global protests against the sexual color line. The conspiracy to frame Clyde Kennard for theft in 1960 because he tried to desegregate the local college provoked a national campaign to exonerate him. Although all of these cases ended in tragedy, intermittent federal intervention combined with the international publicity of such barbarities cracked the citadel of Jim Crow and provided the conditions for black dissent initiated by activists like Vernon Dahmer, Clyde Kennard, Benjamin Murph, and Victoria Gray to grow over time from voter registration campaigns and lawsuits, particularly the landmark *US v. Lynd* suit, into a revolution.

During the revolution, black leaders advanced watershed campaigns in the Central Piney Woods that rendered it one of the most crucial battlefields of the Mississippi movement and the national struggle. *Lynd* led to the Freedom Days campaign, which spread across the state; it also shaped the Voting Rights Act of 1965. Hattiesburg hosted one of the most powerful

Freedom Summer projects, including the largest Freedom School in the state; it became a center of MFDP challenges; and along with Laurel, it initiated one of the most powerful sit-in campaigns across the South to enforce the Civil Rights Act of 1964. However, the Central Piney Woods also became the epicenter of white resistance in Mississippi and one of the strongest citadels of white supremacist power in the South. Governor Paul Johnson modeled his police-freedom-of-movement tactics after Hattiesburg's nonviolent resistance strategy. The White Knights, which Bowers headquartered in Laurel, turned Jones County into the heartland of white supremacist terrorism. White violence and injustices inadvertently aided the black liberation movement. They helped form the civil rights morality play by reversing centuries of racial myths; that play cast black activists as heroic, peaceful freedom fighters and white mobs, police, judges, and Klansmen as villains determined to sustain their white southern tyranny through the most brutal of means.

The murder of Dahmer marked a significant turning point. Although the MIBURN case in Neshoba County initiated the war against the Klan, the three state murder convictions and one arson conviction in the Dahmer case, the first of their kind in Mississippi, caused vital shifts in the local judicial system and marginalized the White Knights. Dahmer's murder also inspired President Lyndon Johnson to propose legislation that became part of the Civil Rights Act of 1968 and energized blacks to revitalize crusades against police brutality, economic inequity, and political disempowerment. Although the revolution achieved momentous victories, including the destruction of de jure segregation, the protection of black suffrage, the marginalization of the Klan, a modicum of racial justice, and the advancement of black opportunities, blacks still lacked equity and power. Their status had elevated from the disfranchised caste to second-class citizen.

During the third act, the post–civil rights stage, which is a significant story in its own right, blacks and their progressive white allies, launched a second movement in which they integrated some blacks into the power centers, advanced racial justice, and fomented a black political revolution. In the new millennium, blacks possess more political and economic power in Hattiesburg and Laurel than at any time in history. Interracial cooperation across black and white landscapes in battles for justice and equity has healed some haunted grounds. Still, racial equality and reconciliation eludes the Central Piney Woods as it eludes the nation. The struggle remains unfinished. But the revolutionary spirit simmers still across the Central Piney Woods, an inheritance from the earliest settlers whose whispering dreams of racial egalitarianism have strengthened over the centuries. The lands await the vision of a new generation of activists who believe in their right to revolt against persistent injustices, who have faith in their efficacy to revitalize the roots of hope sowed into the soil by slaves and renegades and cultivated by freedom fighters, and who have the courage to carry the torch onward across the long road of redemption.

Notes

All interviews are recordings by author housed at MOHP unless otherwise noted.

ABBREVIATIONS

AJC	*Atlanta Journal-Constitution*
CA	*The Commercial Appeal* (Memphis, TN)
CD	*Chicago Defender*
CL	*The Clarion-Ledger* (Jackson, MS)
COFO-P	Council of Federated Organizations Papers
CORE-P	Congress of Racial Equality Papers
CPW	Central Piney Woods
CRC-P	Civil Rights Congress Papers
CRMV	Civil Rights Movement Veterans
CSF	Created Subject Files
DOJ	Department of Justice
DW	*Daily Worker* (New York, NY)
FBI-SNCC	FBI Files, Student Nonviolent Coordinating Committee
FBI-MIBURN	FBI Files, Mississippi Burning
FBI-RBH	FBI Files, Robert Helfrich Papers
FBI-Wash	FBI Files, Howard Wash
FCCC-H	Forrest County Circuit Court
HA	*Hattiesburg American* (MS)
HACCR	Hattiesburg Area Chamber of Commerce Records, ML-USM
HAL	Project Historical American Lynching Data
HMR	Hattiesburg Municipal Records
HDUD	Hattiesburg Department of Urban Development, ML-USM
HSF	Helfrich Subject File
JCCC-E	Jones County Circuit Court, Ellisville
JCCC-L	Jones County Circuit Court, Laurel
JCS	John C. Stennis Collection, MML-MSU
JDN	*Jackson Daily News* (MS)
JDWL-UM	J. D. Williams Library, University of Mississippi
KTP	Kenneth Toller Papers
LC	Library of Congress
LLC	*Laurel-Leader Call* (MS)
LF	Leesha Faulkner Civil Rights Collection, ML-USM

LRM	Lauren Rogers Museum, Laurel, Mississippi
MBI	Mississippi Bureau of Identification
MDAH	Mississippi Department of Archives and History
MDPS	Mississippi Department of Public Safety
MDOC	Mississippi Department of Corrections
MFP	*Mississippi Free Press* (Jackson)
MHP	Mississippi Highway Patrol
ML-USM	McCain Library and Archives, University of Southern Mississippi
MML-MSU	Mitchell Memorial Library, Mississippi State University
MOHP	Mississippi Oral History Program, USM
MOHP-D	Mississippi Oral History Program Digital Archives, USM
MS	*Meridian Star* (MS)
MSC	Mississippi Supreme Court
MSSC	Mississippi State Sovereignty Commission
MSU	Mississippi State University
NAACP-P	National Association for the Advancement of Colored People Papers
NARC	National Archives and Records Administration
NPR	National Public Radio
NYT	*New York Times*
NYT-AA	*New York Times* Article Archives
PBJ	Paul B. Johnson Family Papers, ML-USM
PC	*Pittsburgh Courier* (PA)
RBH	Robert B. Helfrich Papers, ML-USM
RD	Radio Diaries, New York, NY
RG	Record Group
SCLC-P	Southern Christian Leadership Conference Papers
SNCC-P	Student Nonviolent Coordinating Committee Papers
SPLC	Southern Poverty Law Center
TGB	Theodore G. Bilbo Papers, ML-USM
TC	Tougaloo Collection
TLC	*The Laurel Chronicle* (MS)
TP	*The Times-Picayune* (New Orleans, LA)
USM	University of Southern Mississippi
USCCRLE	US Commission on Civil Rights Law Enforcement
USvTL	United States v. Theron Lynd Collection, ML-USM
VFD	Vernon F. Dahmer Collection, ML-USM
VF	Vertical Files
VSH	Verner S. Holmes Collection
WCP	William Colmer Papers, ML-USM
WPA	Works Progress Administration, Mississippi
WPA-FC	Works Progress Administration, Forrest County, Mississippi
WPA-JC	Works Progress Administration, Jones County, Mississippi

PROLOGUE

1. First quote, *Mississippi v. Bowers* (1998), 6922 vol. 2, transcript, 9, FCCH; ibid., vol. 2, 14–15, 22–24, vol. 3, 17, 20–23; second and third quotes, *Killed by the Klan*, prod. and dir. Charles Stuart; File vol. 9, #44-1512-373, DABURN-FBI-RBH.

2. Pitts, typed confession, #44-31694-555, 9, Pitts Notebook, RBH.

3. Quoting Editorial, *TLC*, October 14, 1905. Studies, including Payne's *I've Got the Light of Freedom*, Voller's *Ghosts of Mississippi*, Whitehead's *Attack on Terror*, Nelson's *Terror in the Night*, Cagin and Dray's *We Are Not Afraid*, and Hamilton's *Crossroads at Clarksdale*, have placed Jackson, Neshoba County, and the Delta at the forefront of Mississippi's racial struggle. Although Whitehead and Nelson evaluate the Dahmer case as part of the FBI's war against the Klan, neither of them explore it comprehensively. Bynum's *The Free State of Jones* traces the rebellion against the Confederacy. Dittmer's *Local People*, Heard's *The Eyes of Willie McGee*, Adickes's *The Legacy of a Freedom School* and Martin's *Count Them One by One* examine some racial conflicts in Forrest and Jones Counties.

In "The 'Long Movement' as Vampire," Lang and Cha-Jua argue that the revisionists' Long Civil Rights Movement model stretches the racial struggle into an undefined periodization and tends to ignore the variances in different localities and regions. Yet as many revisionists have noted, the movement of the 1950s and 1960s was not a rootless crusade that burst into history for a decade and then vanished as traditional historians have argued. Yet neither is the movement a seamless struggle, indistinct from the battles that preceded and followed it. It developed in significant and defined stages in different localities, see Eagles, "Toward New Histories of the Civil Rights Era"; Lawson, "Freedom Then, Freedom Now"; Hall, "The Long Civil Rights Movement and the Political Use of the Past." In *Race and Democracy*, Fairclough reveals that black protest in Louisiana between the late 1930s and mid-1950s "was the first act of a two act play" (xi). Replacing the terminology the Long Civil Rights Movement with the black liberation movement might convey the distinctions among the different phases of the national struggle, showing that the civil rights era served as the most revolutionary phase and specifying how, when, and if these phases emerged in particular localities. By using Fairclough's conception of different acts of the struggle and by employing Lawson's "interactive model" (see Lawson, "Freedom Then, Freedom Now" [457]), which synthesizes top-down and bottom-up approaches, I found that in the CPW, the black liberation movement developed in three distinct stages.

4. First quote, "Assignment #8," WPA-JC; second quote, *CL*, October 6, 1977, Knight Descendants VF, LRM; third quote, Bond, *Political Culture*, 14–15; ibid., 16–29, 38–41, 133–34. Hobbes, *Leviathan*, 632–33; History, WPA-FC; Bates, *Before There Was a Mississippi*, 6–7. Iola Williams Family Study, in author's possession; Bynum, *Free State of Jones*, 29–48, 59–89, 98–129; 182–83; Locke, *Second Treaties of Government*, 741–42; Hobbes, *Leviathan*, 632–33. For impact of steamboats and sugar on New Orleans, see Johnson, *River of Dark Dreams* and Rothman, *Slave Country*.

5. Bynum, *Free State of Jones*, 98–129. Bond, *Political Culture*, 133–34, 151–82; Bates, *Before There Was a Mississippi*, 24–26.

6. First quote, *Meridian Mercury*, reprinted in *Ralls County (MO) Record*, April 30, 1868; second and third quotes, *NYT*, August 25, 1885. Chalmers, *Hooded Americanism*, 2, 8–14. Bynum, *Free State of Jones*, 131–36, 140–44, 150–51; Addie West, "Reconstruction," WPA-JC; *Federal Civil Rights Laws*, November 1984, 11–14, JCS; Belknap, *Federal Law*, 10–12; Bond, *Political Culture*, 170–82; Foner, *Reconstruction*.

7. Hattiesburg Chamber of Commerce promotion booklet, n.d., 1, HACCR; *Hattiesburg News*, November 29, 1912. Commercial Club of Hattiesburg, *Hattiesburg*, 9, 17, HACCR; Skates, "Hattiesburg," *Hattiesburg*, ed. McCarty Jr., 5, 10; Marda Burton, "Two Centennial Towns: Laurel & Hattiesburg," *Mississippi Magazine*, November/December 1990, Laurel 1990 VF, ML-USM; *LLC*, May 11, 1982, Laurel Founding VF, LRM. History, WPA-FC; History, WPA-JC. Bond, *Political Culture*, 133, 210–11; 224–25; *TLC*, October 14, 1905; *The Lynching Century*, website.

8. Bond, *Political Culture*, 224. *CL*, January 15, 1985; Guy Walker, "Why I Went South," *Manufacturers Record*, February 9, 1928, 8, Laurel Founding VF, LRM. "Assignment #16," WPA-JC; Department of Planning and Community Development, *Historic Hattiesburg*, HDUD; Koch and Wilson

Architects, 1991 Hattiesburg Survey, June 30, 1991, 20-25, HDUD; Synopsis by Secretary of the Commercial Club, Hattiesburg, Mississippi February 1, 1910, HACCR; Payne, *Laurel*; "Hattiesburg Beginnings," *HA*, November 2, 1980, Myrtis Rue Collection, ML-USM.

9. First quote, Flynt, *Alabama Baptists*, 458. Second and third quotes, Dailey, "The Theology of Massive Resistance," Kindle edition. Two delegates from the CPW participated in the convention, but neither played a major role, see *Journal of the Proceedings of the Constitutional Convention, of the State of Mississippi*, August 12, 1890 to November 1, 1890, Jackson, Mississippi. McMillen, *Dark Journey*, 7-14, 23-48; Civil Rights Segregation Laws in Mississippi, JCS; *Plessy v. Ferguson* (1896); Degler, *In Search of Human Nature*; Bannister, *Social Darwinism*; Stokes, *Color of Sex*, Kindle edition; Newman, *Getting Right with God*, Kindle edition; Dixon, *Clansman*, 303-308, 315-74; *Birth of a Nation*, dir. by D. W. Griffith; Cash, *The Mind of the South*, 88-89, 116-20, 131; Hall, *Revolt Against Chivalry*; Cardyn, "Sexualized Racism/Gendered Violence," 765-87, 813-29.Williamson, *Crucible of Race*; Wood, *Lynching and Spectacle*.

10. Quoting Silver, *Closed Society*, 6; ibid., 7-12; McMillen, *Dark Journey*, 23-28. Williamson, *Crucible of Race*, 82; George Watson, "Historical Hattiesburg," 1974, City documents, A-17, #113, HMR; Chalmers, *Hooded Americanism*, 2-3.

11. Quoting van den Berghe, *Race and Racism*, 18; ibid., 126. Frederickson, *The Black Image in the White Mind*; Bond, *Political Culture*, 151-82, 254-95; McMillen, *Dark Journey*, 35-71.

12. First quote, McMillen, *Dark Journey*, 229-30; ibid., 44, 48, 228-51, 394n24; second quote, Editorial, *TLC*, October 14, 1905; third quote, Nix, interview, by Rowe, MOHP-D; fifth quote, *NYT*, August 25, 1885, all other quotes, *NYT*, July 10, 1885, both in *NYT*-AA. For various lynching records, see McMillen; Finnegan, "At the Hands of Parties Unknown," 281-82; Project HAL, *The Lynching Century*, websites. For many of the lynchings and attempted lynchings in the CPW, see *AJC*, July 27, 1895, August 18, 1905, June 13, 1902, and *Special to NYT*, June 23, 1901, July 8, 1907; *NYT*, August 9, 1903, September 8, 1906, all in *NYT*-AA. For stories of lynchings handed down in black families, see, Wade, Clarence Magee, Douglass Baker, McGill, Outlaw, interviews. For Martin's prison record and pardon, see William Martin, Register Mississippi State Penitentiary Convicts, p. 448, Microfilm, Roll 13785, MDAH. For Governor Stone and the Constitutional Convention of 1890, see Bond, *Political Culture*, 246.

13. Williamson, *Crucible of Race*. The author's labels and descriptions of racial mentalities differ slightly from Williamson based on the sorts of white racial mentalities in the CPW. Bond, *Political Culture*; Bynum, *Free State of Jones*; Payne, *Laurel* and *Oak Park Story*; Street, *Look Away*, 11-18, 27-38. Myers, interview, by Caudill, 16-23, 27-28, 3839, MOHP. Austin, interview; Vincent, interview; *TLC*, June 20, 24, July 11, August 22, 1903; *NYT*, March 15, 1904, *NYT*-AA; McMillen, *Dark Journey*, 120-21; *The Lynching Century*; Project HAL; *AJC*, May 16, 1903, August 9, 1903, August 18, 1905; *NYT*, May 17, 1903, August 9, 1903, March 15, 1904, November 6, 1906, and *Special to NYT*, June 23, 1901, July 8, 1907, all in *NYT*-AA.

14. Last quote, Project HAL. All other quotes, McMillen, *Dark Journey*, 235-36; ibid., 202-203, 208-23, 236-40. White, *Rope and Faggot*, 302; Hall, *Revolt Against Chivalry*, 155; Bynum, *Free State of Jones*, 150-51. Wells, *Red Record*, ed. Royster, 78-82, 117-22; Finnegan, "At the Hands of Parties Unknown," 281-82; *AJC*, July 26, 1899; *NYT*, July 26, 1899, *NYT*-AA.

15. Quoting Myers, interview, vol. 349, 27, MOHP; ibid., 16-23, 27-28, 38-39. Nix, interview; Austin, interview; "Assignment #10," WPA-JC; Bond, *Political Culture*, 213-14; McMillen, *Dark Journey*, 8-13,178-79; Hattiesburg Beginnings"; Payne, *Laurel*, 17-37; Commercial Club Synopsis; Skates, "Hattiesburg," 10-11; "Assignment #20," WPA-JC; *LLC*, May 11, 1982, Laurel Founding VF. Jones, *The Tribe of Black Ulysses*.

16. First quote, Bynum, *Free State of Jones*, 144; ibid., 145-76, 182-83, 205-206. Frazier, *Negro Family in the United States*, 164. "Agriculture," WPA-FC; *CL*, December 18, 1994; US Federal Cen-

sus, 1900, Roll: T623 824; 2B; 1910 Roll T624-739, 18A; 1920, Roll T625-875, 17B; 1930, Roll: 1145; 3B, *Ancestry.com*. Bates, *Before There Was a Mississippi*, 19–26, 30; Williams Family Study; Williams, interview; *CL*, October 6, 1977, Knight Descendants VF, LRM. "Assignment #17," WPA-JC; Jeanette Smith, interview.

17. James Jones, interviews.

18. Quoting Payne, *Laurel*, 112; ibid., 25–37, 65–66, 72–73, 89, 172. *HA*, February 12, 26, 2006; "Hattiesburg Beginnings"; Koch and Wilson, "1991 Hattiesburg Survey," 20–25; *Historic Hattiesburg*; Strickland, "Remembering Hattiesburg," in *Remaking Dixie*, ed. McMillen, 149–150; Holloway, interview; Johnny Magee, interview. Williams, interview by Kavan, MOHP. Ariel Barnes, interviews by Walker and Rowe; Constance Baker, interview by Adam; McCarty, interview by Walton, all in MOHP-D.

19. "Hattiesburg Beginnings"; Strickland, "Remembering Hattiesburg," 150. Payne, *Oak Park Story*, 9 and *Laurel*, 65–66, 72–73, 172; Bynum, *Free State of Jones*, 163–64, 167; Koch and Wilson, "1991 Hattiesburg Survey," 20–25; Bates, *Before There Was a Mississippi*, 19–20, 35–37, 40–44; Knight, *Mississippi Girl*, 79–83. Douglass Baker, interview; Barnes, interviews; McCarty, interview; Ellie Dahmer, interview; McMillen, *Dark Journey*, 72–194.

20. Holmes, "Whitecapping," 165–88; McMillen, *Dark Journey*, 120–21. "Mississippi Labor Famine," NYT-AA, March 15, 1904, "Hattiesburg Beginnings."

21. Quoting Scott, *Negro Migration*, PDF-ebook. Grossman, *Land of Hope*, 4, 66–67, 71, 79, 96–97, 109, 155. McMillen, *Dark Journey*, 302–303. "Wars," WPA-FC; Franklin and Moss, *Slavery to Freedom*, 324–36. Bynum, *Free State of Jones*, 164–65. Jones found a similar trend in his study of lumber workers, in *The Tribe of Black Ulysses*, 24.

22. Quoting James Weldon Johnson, in McWhirter, *Red Summer*, 269. McMillen, *Dark Journey*, 303–307. Street, *Look Away*, 11–18, 27–38; Myers, interview, 33–36, MOHP; Hamilton, interview, by Caudill, 18, 1–4, 32, MOHP; Lynchings Report 1919, 7-A-13, NAACP Papers. *HA*, June 16, 23, 25, 26, 27, 1919; Belknap, *Federal Law*, 17.

23. First Quote, Myers interview, 37; Ibid, 34–36; second quote, *The Laurel Daily Leader*, October 20, 1922; Bynum, *The Free State of Jones County*, 164–65; William F. Dukes, interview, by Caudill, MOPH-D. *HA*, October 21, 23, 1922; Correspondence between the NAACP and Mack Holliman, September 1927-January 1928, NAACP Papers, Pt. 4, Reel 2.

24. Quoting *CD*, January 5, 1929. 1928/29 Lynching Report, 7-A-13, NAACP Papers. Bynum, *Free State of Jones*, 275n, 274n, 165–66. *NYT*, March 21, 1921, 13; McMillen, *Dark Journey*, 305–306.

25. First quote, *CD*, January 5, 1929; second quote, Grand Jury Report, January 10, 1929, *Minutes*, vol. 9. 549, FCCC-H. All other quotes, McMillen, *Dark Journey*, 241, 245; ibid., 249–50. Street, *Look Away*, 62; *HA*, January 7, 1929; 1928/29 Lynching Report.

26. Lewis, *When Harlem Was in Vogue*; Cronon, *Black Moses*; Rolinson, *Grassroots Garveyism*; Kluger, *Simple Justice*; McMillen, *Dark Journey*, 278, 302–17. Sitkoff, *New Deal For Blacks*; Lemann, *Promised Land*; Kelley, "'We Are Not What We Seem,'" 75–112; Gellman, *Death Blow to Jim Crow*; Gerstle, *American Crucible*; Gilmore, *Defying Dixie*. *Powell v. Alabama* (1932); Carter, *Scottsboro*; Cortner, *A Scottsboro Case in Mississippi*; *Brown v. Mississippi* (1936). "Wars," WPA-FC; Grantham, *The South in Modern America*, 125; Sullivan, *Lift Every Voice*, 191–92; Mable Fielder, interview by McMillen, 1–3, 83, MOHP. Williams in *The Tribe of Black Ulysses* also finds that the New Deal helped black workers to a degree, see 108–109.

27. Quoting Payne, *Laurel: A History of the Black Community*, 86; Wade interview; Wade "Reminiscences," Wade Papers, ML-USM.

28. Dahmer and Mott, *Marriage Record-Colored*, vol. 13, 130, FCCC-H; Divorce Record Vernon and Warnie Dahmer, *Minutes Forrest Chancery Court*, vol. 18, March 1938-March 1939, Chancery Courthouse, Hattiesburg, Mississippi; Dahmer and Smith, *Marriage Record-Colored*, January 4,

1938-January 25, 1941, vol. 21, 45, FCCC-H; Files vol. 31, #44-1512-2580, 174–77, DABURN-FBI-RBH; *HA*, January 13, 1966; *CL*, December 18, 1994; Jeanette Smith, interview.

29. Quoting *CD* December 11, 1936. Belknap, *Federal Law*, 17–19; McGovern, *Anatomy of a Lynching*; McMillen, *Dark Journey*, 245–50.

30. First quote, Leon Litwack, *Trouble in Mind*, 3; second quote, Wade interview; third quote, Wade, "Reminiscences."

31. First quote, Nix, interview; second quote, Austin, interview.

32. Belknap, *Federal Law*, 17–19; McMillen, *Dark Journey*, 302–18.

CHAPTER 1

1. First quote, Louis L. Welch, statement, #44-661-5, 11; ibid., 10; second quote, Inmon O. Fowler statement, #44-661-5, 17, FBI-Wash.

2. Quoting File #44-661-43, 2; File #44-661-5, 1–2, 34, FBI-Wash.

3. Quoting Pryor, statement, December 1, 1942, #44-661-10, 8; ibid., 7–9. File, #44-661-5, 1–9, FBI-Wash.

4. Quoting McMillen, *Dark Journey*, 317. Ibid., 228–51, 394n. For arguments about the impact of World War II and the Cold War on the movement, see Sitkoff, "American Militancy in the World War II South" and McMillen, "Fighting For What We Didn't Have," both in *Remaking Dixie*, ed. McMillen, 70–110; Hall, "The Long Civil Rights Movement,"1245–48; Dalfiume, "'Forgotten Years' of the Negro Revolution," 90–106; Woods, *Black Struggle, Red Scare*; Dudziack, *Cold War Civil Rights*; Dittmer, *Local People*,1–20; Payne, *Light of Freedom*, 7–66.

5. "8 Point Program: March-On-Washington Movement," TGB. Philip Murray to Colmer, October 8, 1942, WCP; E. E. Benedict to Colmer, n.d., WCP; Wynn, *Afro-American and the Second World War*, 42–48; Myrdal, *An American Dilemma*, 1003–1006; Gerstle, *American Crucible*, 195; Lawson, *Running For Freedom*, 3, 8–13, 16–18, 115; Sullivan, "Movement Building during the World War II Era," *Fog of War*, ed. Kruse and Tuck, Kindle edition; Gilmore, *Defying Dixie*, Kindle edition.

6. Frederickson, *Racism*, 75–138. Sparrow, "Freedom to Want," *Fog of War*; McMillen, *Dark Journey*; Silver, *Closed Society*; Litwack, *Trouble in Mind*; Bond, *Political Culture*, 151–82, 254–95.

7. First quote, File #44-661-13,10, FBI-Wash; ibid., 3–11; second quote, Welborn, interview by Odell, in author's possession; third and fourth quotes, *LLC*, October 16, 1942; fifth quote, *LLC*, June 29, 1942. *LLC*, May 18-21, June 29, 1942. Files #44-661-5, 24–25, #44-661-10, 2–6, FBI-Wash.

8. Quoting Jason Morgan Ward, "'A War for States' Rights' The White Supremacist Vision of Double Victory," in *Fog of War*, Kindle edition; Gilmore, *Defying Dixie*. *Congressional Record*, 77th Congress, 2nd Session (October 13, 1942); *LLC*, October 12, 13, 17, 1942. Anonymous letter to the NAACP, New York, October 12, 1942; CIO to Attorney General Francis Biddle, October 13, 1942; NAACP to President Franklin Delano Roosevelt, October 16, 1942; Governor Paul Johnson Sr. to Vito Marcantonio, October 14, 1942; *HA*, October 13, 1942; and *The Commercial Appeal*, October 14, 1942, all in Pt. 7, Ser. A-II, NAACP Papers, Reel 27.

9. Quoting File #44-661-13, 7, ibid., 4–11; File #44-661-5, 24–25, FBI-Wash. Ward, "'A War for States' Rights,'" *Fog of War*; Gilmore, *Defying Dixie*; *Congressional Record*, 77th Congress, 2nd Session (October 13, 1942). Mississippi Lynchings 1942–43, 7-II-A-27, NAACP-P; *LLC*, October 12–17, 1942.

10. *LLC*, October 17, 19, 21, 1942. *JDN*, October 18, 1942. File #44-661-31, 4–6; File #44-661-15, 3–5; File #44-661-31, 5, FBI-Wash.

11. First quote, Franklin Delano Roosevelt, "The Four Freedoms,"; second quote, Roosevelt, speech, in Maney, *Roosevelt Presence*, 143; third quote, Summaries and Transcripts, The Magic Documents, Reel 1. Dower, *War without Mercy*, 129; Chang, *Rape of Nanking*; Gerstle, *American Crucible*, 4, 191–96, 201–20

12. First, second, and third quotes, CD, March 14, 1942; fourth and fifth quotes, PC, February 14, 1942. PC, January 31, February 7, 1942, May 1, 1943; CD, January 31, March 7, October 31, 1942.

13. Quoting William Colmer, "Anti-Poll Tax Speech," House of Representatives, October 13, 1942, 3, WCP; ibid, 2–10. Sullivan, Days of Hope, 137. See, too, Ward, Defending White Democracy, Kindle edition.

14. First quote, DW clipping, #44-661-8, FBI-Wash; all other quotes, CL, November 14, 1942. Mississippi Lynchings 1942–43. PC, November 14, 1942; LLC, October 19, 1942; File #44-661-9, FBI-Wash.

15. Mississippi Lynchings, 1942–43.

16. First quote White, Rope and Faggot, 171; second quote, McMillen, Dark Journey, 230; Belknap, Federal Law, 1–26; Capici Jr., Lynching of Cleo Wright, 59–60; Waldrep, "National Policing, Lynching, and Constitutional Change," 616–17; US v. Shipp (1909); Files #44-661-2, #44-661-1, FBI-Wash. Indictments, #44-61-20, 1–2, #44-661-11, FBI-Wash. NYT, January 13, April 25, 1943, NYT-AA. "Races: Unusual & Different Punishment," Time, January 25, 1943, 24. JDN, October 21, 1942; LLC, October 20, 1942.

17. First quote, File #44-661-13, 4, 32; ibid., 3, 33; second and third quotes, File #441-661-43, 3. Files #44-661-13, 5, #44-661-10, 7–11, 18–23, FBI-Wash. LLC, October 20, 1942.

18. Quoting letter, McGuire, Taps for a Jim Crow Army, 18. HA, September 14, 1940, February 22, 1941; Schmidt, "The Impact of Camp Shelby," 41–50; Ward, "'No Jap Crow'"; Howard, Concentration Camps on the Homefront, Kindle edition; Strickland, "Remembering Hattiesburg," 147, 152–157. HA, February 22, 1941; Iola Williams, interviews by author and by Kavan; James Jones, interview, October 1, 2008; Austin, interview. Burger, interview, by Pyle, and Boyds, interview, by Bolton, MOHP-D.

19. Quoting Vernon Dahmer Jr., speech, Symposium on Civil Rights in Hattiesburg, recording, ML-USM. HA, February 22, 1941; Richard Boyd, interview. Steven F. Lawson, Running for Freedom, 16–18, 115; Minutes: Camp Shelby, September 7, 1940, HACCR; Burger interview. Iola Williams interviews by author and by Kavan. Austin, interview; E. Hammond Smith, interview and Ellie Dahmer, interview, both by Caudill MOHP-D; Fielders, interview by McMillen, 51, MOHP; Boyds, interview; Strickland, "Remembering Hattiesburg," 147, 150–57. Martin, Count Them, 3, 116–17. For Cox registration of a few blacks, including Dahmer, see Kennard v. Mississippi (1961), 41890, transcript, MSC records, MDAH, 155–85.

20. Quoting File #44-61-20, 1–2, FBI-Wash.; Files #44-661-23, #44-661-11, FBI-Wash. "Races: Unusual & Different Punishment," 24. Kenneth Toller, "Three Are Acquitted," Wash Lynching VF, LRM.

21. First quote, JDN, January 13, 1943; all other quotes, PC, May 1, 1943. File #44-661-42, FBI-Wash. "Races: Unusual & Different Punishment," 24; CA, April 15, 1943, Wash File, LRM.

22. DW, April 22, May 9, 1943; MS, April 22, 24, 1943; LLC, April 21, 23, 1943; CD, April 24, May 1, 1943; CL, April 24, 1943; PC, May 1, 1943; TP, April 22, 1943, Wash File, LRM. For the racial environment in Laurel, see Nix, interview by Rowe; and Austin, interview.

23. Quoting DW, April 25, 1943; MS, April 24, 1943; PC, May 1, 1943; CD, April 24, May 1, 1943. Waldrep, "National Policing, Lynching, and Constitutional Change".

24. First and last quotes, DW, May 9, 1943; all other quotes, CD, May 1, 1943.

25. First quote, CD, May 1, 1943; second quote, Welborn, interview. PC, May 8, 1943. MS, April 24, 1943; PC, May 8, 1943; McMillen, Dark Journey, 252; Zangrando, NAACP Crusade, 7; Belknap, Federal Law, 15–16, 20; Guzzman, Foster, and Hughes Negro Yearbook, 8–9, National Humanities Center.

26. Quoting McMillen, "How Mississippi's Black Veterans Remember World War II," Remaking Dixie, 98–99, 107. Correspondence A. T. Woodruff and Bilbo, May 10, 20, 1944, TGB Papers; LLC, June 24, 1946; McMillen, Dark Journey, 252; Zangrando, NAACP Crusade, 7.

27. First quote, *LLC*, November 2, 1945; second quote, McGee Case Fact Sheet, I-11, CRC-P; third quote, *Mississippi v. McGee* (1948), 1268, transcript, 715–16, MDAH. *LLC*, November 5, 1945.

28. Quoting Bridgette Robinson-McGee, narration, RD. Pyles interview, 355, 359 and London interview, 268, I-11,CRC-P; McGee Statement; McGee and Payton, April 20, 1935, *Marriage Record Colored*, vol. 9, 148, Jones County Clerk's Office, Laurel, Mississippi. Heard, *Through the Eyes of Willie McGee*, 46, 109, 111–12.

29. Quoting McGee Statement, 319–24.

30. Quoting ibid., 320–24. *Mississippi v. McGee* (1948), transcript, 571–77. For examinations of the power white men wielded over the sexual color line, see McGuire, *Dark End of the Street*; Hall, *Revolt against Chivalry*.

31. McGee Case Fact Sheet. Sanders interview and Mills, interview by McGee-Robinson, RD; *LLC*, November 2, 5, 1945; *Mississippi v. McGee* (1945), transcript, 19–23, 34–36, 39, 41–42.

32. *Mississippi v. McGee* (1948), transcript, 715–31. Louis Burnham to George Marshall and Milton Kemnitz, December 26, 1945, II-35; Breland interview, Pyles interview; London interview; Poole interview, I-1; McGee Case Fact Sheet; "The Case of Willie McGee: A Fact Sheet," n.d., II-35, CRC-P. For local report on the trial see, *LLC*, December 6–7, 1945. For other cases, see *Powell v. Alabama* (1932); Carter, *Scottsboro*; Cortner, *A Scottsboro Case in Mississippi*; *Brown v. Mississippi* (1936). For the impact of and lack thereof of these cases on the McGee case, see Zaim, "Trial by Ordeal."

33. Quoting "Willie McGee and the Traveling Electric Chair," *All Things Considered*, NPR, prod. Joe Richman and Samara Freemark, May 7, 2010, NPR. Swartzfager interview by McGee-Robinson, RD. Odell, "Norman Jones: Enemy Territory," *The City Beautiful*, series for *LLC*, 2008, copy in author's possession.

34. Quoting *LLC*, December 3, 1945. *LLC*, December 6, 1945. *Mississippi v. McGee* (December 6, 1945), McGee case file, JCCC-L; "The Case of Willie McGee: A Fact Sheet"; Burnham letter; "Traveling Electric Chair."

35. Quoting *Mississippi v. McGee* (1945), transcript, 7–10. Ibid., 2–6. *LLC*, December 7, 1945. Burnham letter.

36. First and second quotes, *Mississippi v. McGee* (1945), transcript, 10, third and fourth quotes, ibid., 17–18, all other quotes, ibid., 41 and ibid., 2–11, 66–67.

37. Quoting *Mississippi v. McGee* (1945), transcript, 8, 13–15; ibid., 7, 8–11, 15–18, 41–51. Heard, *Eyes of Willie McGee*, 172, 112. For problems with evidence, see, *Mississippi v. McGee* (1948), 593, 596, 644–647, 761–763.

38. Quoting "Traveling Electric Chair." *Mississippi v. McGee* (1945); *LLC*, December 7, 1945; *HA*, December 7, 1945; *Mississippi v. McGee* (1945), 1173, *Minutes*, vol. 11, 511, 516, JCC-L; Burnham letter. For McGee's rendition of events, see McGee Statement.

39. Burham letter. Pyles, interview, 311; Willie McGee Action Bulletin, May 22, 1950, I-10, CRC-P. Heard, *Through the Eyes of Willie McGee*, 55–56. For formation of CRC and involvement with McGee case, see Charles H. Martin, "Introduction," *Guide to the Microfilm Edition of the Papers of the Civil Rights Congress*, ed. August Meir and John H. Bracey Jr. (Bethesda, MD: University of America, 1988), v–x, CRC-P. Petition for Appeal, Order on Appeal, Motion to Remove Defendant, all in McGee case file. *McGee v. Mississippi*, 36166 (1946), 680–84. For analysis of the Mississippi Supreme Court, see McMillen, *Dark Journey*, 218.

40. "Traveling Electric Chair." McGee-Robinson, narration, McGee-Robinson interview, and McGee Johnson interview, RD.

41. Quoting *Mississippi v. McGee* (1946), transcript, 169, 171. Ibid., 104, 140–400; Motions and Rulings, McGee case file; *LLC*, October 16, 19, 1946; "The Case of Willie McGee: A Fact Sheet."

42. Motion for a New Trial, *Mississippi v. Willie McGee*, [?], n.d. I-10; "Execution of Framed Negro Vet Halted," June 3, 1949, II-35; Petition for Rehearing to the Supreme Court, *Mississippi v. Willie*

McGee, [?] (October 1949), II-10; McGee Fact Sheet, May 1950, I-10, all in CRC-P. McGee case file; *McGee v. Mississippi*, 36166 (1946), 680–84; *Patton v. Mississippi* (1948); *HA*, December 7, 1945; *LLC*, October 16, November 12, 14, 1946, February 9, March 5, 8, 1948, April 11, June 3, October 10, 1949. Heard, *Eyes of Willie McGee*, 100–101, 98–99.

43. Heard, *Eyes of Willie McGee*, 135–39. *LLC*, March 10–12, 1947; Observations from Percy Green, n.d., MSSC, PBJ, II-9; The Fellowship of the Concerned, Southern Regional Council, "Dual Justice in the Courts—Unconcerned Community," 2–5, 8–11, Cox Collection, Addendum, 1978, MML-MSU; "A Record of Rape Cases Beginning January 1, 1940 Through March 3, 1965, Compiled from the Records of the Mississippi State Penitentiary, Parchman, Mississippi," Law Students Civil Rights Research Council Papers, Seeley G. Mudd Manuscript Library, MC070, Box 6, Princeton New Jersey; see too, McGuire, *Dark End of the Street*, 171.

44. Quoting Heard, *Eyes of Willie McGee*, 341; ibid., 339–40. *Patton v. Mississippi* (1948); *LLC*, February 9, 10, 16, 1948.

45. Quoting Breland interview, 182; ibid., 180–81; London interview. Zarnow, "Braving Jim Crow," 1014–15; Mills interview; *Mississippi v. McGee*, 1268 (1948), 4–37, 44–139, 365–400; 140–360; 365–400; *LLC*, February 19, March 4, 5, 1948.

46. First quote, Flynt, *Alabama Baptists*, 458. All other quotes, *Mississippi v. McGee* (1948), transcript, 511. Ibid., 534–35. Poole interview, 276–90; London interview, 235–45. Dixon, *Clansman*, 303–308, 315–74.

47. First and second quotes, *Mississippi v. McGee* (1948), transcript, 512, third quote, ibid., 510; fourth and fifth quotes, ibid., 511, sixth, seventh, and eighth quotes, ibid., 514; ninth quote, ibid., 515–16; ibid., 502–17; 534–35. For testimony in first trial, see *Mississippi v. McGee* (1945), transcript, 2–11, 17.

48. First quote, Poole interview, 300; ibid., 299–301; second, third, and fourth quotes, *Mississippi v. McGee* (1948), transcript, 518; all other quotes, 715–16; ibid., 518–33, 555–56, 717–31, 873–75, 902–903; *LLC*, November 2, 5, 1945. London, interview, 235–45, 270. Mills, interview; Poole affidavit, March 1948, I-10, CRC-P; *LLC*, March 5, 1948. For common practice of white authorities coercing confessions from accused blacks in Mississippi, see McMillen, *Dark Journey*, 212–13, *Brown v. Mississippi* (1936), and Zaim, "Trial by Ordeal," 219, 226.

49. First and second quotes, *Mississippi v. McGee* (1948), 755, third quote, 881; ibid., 536–53, 588–97, 637–715, 732–872, 882–91. *Mississippi v. Royals and Holliman* (1948), 761, case file and *Minute Books*, vol. 3, 311, JCC-E. *LLC*, March 25, 1948.

50. Poole interview, 299–301; London interview, 270; Poole affidavit; Motion for A New Trial, *Mississippi v. McGee*, n.d., [?], I-10; George Marshall, "McGee Case—A Crime Against Humanity," *The Liberator*, II-35, CRC-P. *Mississippi v. McGee* (1948), transcript, 908–909; *LLC*, March 5, 6, 8, 1948, April 11, 1949; Mills, interview.

51. According to Eric Rise's study of that Martinsville Seven case, although the defendants were guilty, Patterson "led the CRC to fabricate stories of their innocence," see "Race, Rape, and Radicalism," 489. McGee Statement, 319–25; London, interview, 231; Pyles interview, 313. For Eliza fleeing the state, see Conversations with McGee-Robinson by Richman and Freemark, tape recordings, July 2009, RD. Heard, *Eyes of Willie McGee*, 211–13, 218–19, 273, 345–46.

52. First quote, Petition for Habeas Corpus and McGee Affidavits, *McGee v. Jones*; Johnson Affidavit. Second quote, "Mrs. McGee's Own Story." All other quotes, William Patterson, "The Case of Willie McGee," II-35, CRC-P. For the various protests, see *LLC*, March 16, 26–28, 1951; Roslaee McGee correspondence with CRC, I-10; "A Program of Action to Save Willie McGee," February 22, 1951, II-42; "A Partial Victory for the People," March 19, 1951, Chapter Bulletin, III-2, all in CRC-P. *HA*, April 9, 1951; *NYT*, July 26, 27, 1950, March 16, 1951, October 20, 1952, NYT-AA.

53. Quoting Petition for Writ of Error Coram Nobis, *Mississippi v. McGee*, 1268 (July 21, 1950), 9,

McGee case file. Poole Affidavit, (July 24, 1950), I-11; Chapter Bulletin, March 19, 1951, III-2, CRC-P. Petition for Habeas Corpus, and McGee Affidavits, *McGee v. Jones*; Johnson Affidavit; London interview; *NYT*, March 21, 1951, NYT Archives; *LLC*, July 22, 1950, March 15, 26, 1951.

54. First quote, Ward, *Defending White Democracy*, Kindle edition. Second quote, Woods, *Black Struggle, Red Scare*, 2. For Bilbo, see Resume of Facts, Mississippi Hearing, December 2–5, 1946, ML-USM; Special Committee Senatorial Campaign Expenditures, *Investigation of Senatorial Campaign Expenditures, 1946*. NAACP records of Bilbo case, 18-B-3, 4, NAACP-P. For NAACP efforts to desegregate higher education, see *Gaines v. Canada* (1938); *Sipuel v. Oklahoma* (1948); *Sweatt v. Painter* (1950); *McLaurin v. Oklahoma* (1950); Kluger. *Simple Justice*, 255–84. For union struggles, see Griffith, *Crisis of American Labor*, xii, 22, 62–68; Roper, "The CIO Organizing Committee in Mississippi, June 1946-January 1949", 5–6. Boyds, interview; *LLC*, May 9, 1967, Masonite File, LRM. Knight Sr., interview; Martin, *Count Them*, 124–26. For an overview of the impact of these challenges, see Dittmer, *Local People*, 23–28. For political parties, see "The Conference of States' Rights Democrats Declaration of Principles," May 19, 1948, Jackson, Mississippi, KTP; Sullivan, *Days of Hope*, 273. "Colmer Heads Dixie Group on Civil Rights," *LLC*, March 8, 1948, WCP.

55. First quote, Bilbo, "The War; Constitutional Government; and the Race Issue," Senate: Extension of Remarks, April 17, 1944, 15, TGB; second quote, Bynum, "'White Negroes,'" 252. Ibid., 249–65; Bynum, *Free State of Jones*, 2–3, 158–80.

56. *Mississippi v. Knight* (1948), 646, transcript, 3–9, 82, 111–12, MSC record. Bynum, "'White Negroes,'" 247–65. Bynum, *Free State of Jones*, 1–3, 158–80; *HA*, December 18, 1948. Indictment, Certification of Arrest, Arraignment, Knight case file, JCCC-E.

57. Quoting *Mississippi v. Knight* (1948), transcript, 64, 73. Ibid., 11–12, 47–76. *HA*, December 18, 1948.

58. Quoting CRC, "The Case of Willie McGee: A Fact Sheet." Woods, *Black Struggle, Red Scare*, 91; Martin, "The Civil Rights Congress and Black Defendants," 51; Griffith, *Crisis of American Labor*, xvi, 76. 161; Sullivan, *Days of Hope*, 274; Dittmer, *Local People*, 23–24.

59. First quote, Brief of Appellant, *Knight v. Mississippi*, September 28, 1949, 37, 205, 22–24, transcript, second quote, Brief of the Appellee, *Knight v. Mississippi* (1949), 13, MSC records. Ibid., 14–19; Opinion of the Court, November 14, 1949, case file, JCCC-E; *CL*, October 6, 1977, Knight Descendants VF, LRM. Sullivan, *Days of Hope*, 273; Dittmer, *Local People*, 27–28; *NYT*, November 7, 1948, NYT-AA; Bynum, *Free State of Jones*, 180; Martin, *Count Them*, 116, 124–25, 142.

60. *LLC*, July 27, 1950. Petition for Stay of Execution, *Mississippi v. McGee*, July 25, 1950, and US Supreme Court Order for Stay, *McGee v. Mississippi*, July 16, 1950, US Supreme Court, RG 27, Coleman Papers, MDAH; *LLC*, July 26, 28, 1950); *CL*, July 28, 1950.

61. "Laurel Adopts Ban on Reds," McGee Trials VF, LRM; Colmer, "Communistic Tactics," US House of Representatives, July 31, 1950, Congressional Record—Appendix, A5771 and Wright to Colmer, August 3, 1950, WCP. Whitfield, *Culture of the Cold War*, 2–25. See also *NYT*, August 31, 1947, November 28, 1950, March 27, 1951, April 4, 1952, NYT-AA; "The End of Willie McGee," *Life* (magazine), May 21, 1944, 44; *LLC*, July 22, 27, 28, 1950, March 27, 1951; *CL*, July 28, 1950, CRC Press Release, May 14, 1951, 18-C-7, NAACP-P.

62. First quote, *LLC*, April 2, 1951; second quote, Rosalee McGee, speech, the Abyssinian Baptist Church, New York City, New York, April 1, 1951, 18-C-7, NAACP-P. All other quotes, *LLC*, May 7, 1951. Walter White to NAACP Branches, Youth Councils, and College Chapters, March 7, 1951, and Open Letter to President Harry Truman, n.d., 18-C-7, NAACP-P. *NYT*, April 1, May 3, 6, 1951, in NYT-AA. *LLC*, May 5, 7, 1951; "All Out to Save McGee," May 7, 1951, III-2, CRC-P.

63. Quoting Willie McGee, to President Harry Truman, May 7, 1951, I-10, CRC-P. *TP*, May 8, 1951; *LLC*, May 7, 1951; *NYT*, May 7, 1951, NYT-AA. For Florida Case, see Lawson, Colburn, Paulson, "Groveland," 16–17; *NYT*, April 10, 1951, NYT-AA.

64. Quoting "Willie Mcgee Execution," WAML and WAFL, May 7–8, 1951, recording, MOHP. "Traveling Electric Chair." Order for Execution, Death Certificate, May 8, 1951, McGee case file; Zaim, "Trial by Ordeal," 215–47; CRC News Release, n.d., 18-C-7, NAACP-P. *HA*, May 8, 1951; *LLC*, May 8, 1951, McGee Trials VF, LRM; Odell, "Raymond Horne: Witness to an Execution, Part I," Odell Series.

65. Quoting *CD*, May 19, 1951; Sanders interview. "Willie McGee Execution." CRC News Release; *PC*, May 19, 1951; Death Certificate, May 8, 951, McGee case file.

66. First quote, CRC News Release; second quote, Willie McGee to Rosalee, n.d., Hall Papers, New York State Library. *PC*, May 19, 1951. All other quotes, "Avenge His Murder." *CRC Chapter Bulletin*, May 14, 1951, II-2, CRC-P.

67. First and second quotes, *NYT*, May 6, 1955, 31, NYT Archives. All other quotes, McGee-Robinson, narration. *LLC*, July 3, 1951, McGee Trial VF, LRM; "Traveling Electric Chair"; Heard, *Eyes of Willie McGee*, 22, 112–13.

68. Quoting *NYT*, October 20, 1952, *NYT*, May 9, 1951, NYT-AA. Sullivan, *Days of Hope*; Gerstle, *American Crucible*. Dudziak, *Cold War Civil Rights*; Woods, *Black Struggle, Red Scare*.

69. "No Compromise with Segregation or Discrimination," Annual Report, NAACP Southeast Regional Conference, 1953; Ruby Hurley, Report, May 7, 1951; Hurley to Gloster B. Current, May 5, 1952, 25-A-5, NAACP-P. Gore, interview; Johnny Magee, interview; McGill, interview.

70. For the Christian rhetoric employed in the Civil Rights Movement, see Houck, *Rhetoric, Religion, and the Civil Rights Movement, 1954–1965*, ed. Houck and Dixon; Chappell, *Stone of Hope*; Marsh, *Beloved Community*.

CHAPTER 2

1. Hollander, "How Mississippi Southern Stayed White: The Story of Clyde Kennard," n.d. SNCC, reel 7. MSSC #1-27-0-40-1-1-1, 3-6; #5-3-1-19-1-1-.

2. Quoting Hollander, "How Mississippi Southern Stayed White," 279; ibid., 278; MSSC # 1-27-0-6-32-1-1 through 37-1-1-1, 6-11.

3. *Brown v. Board* (1954). *The Year of the Great Decision, NAACP Annual Report, 1954*, 1, WCP. *Simple Justice*, 396–424; Bartley, *Massive Resistance*; Klarman, "How *Brown* Changed Race Relations," 117–18. Bolton, *Hardest Deal*; Payne, *Light of Freedom*.

4. First quote, Gates, *Making of Massive Resistance*; second quote, Crespino, *Another Country*, 19; ibid., 18–48; third quote, Ward, *Defending White Democracy*, Kindle edition. Bartley, *Massive Resistance*.

5. Quoting *McLaurin v. Oklahoma* (1950). *Gaines v. Canada* (1938); *Sipuel v. Oklahoma* (1948); *Sweatt v. Painter* (1950). Bolton, *Hardest Deal*, 59–60; Kluger, *Simple Justice*, 126–54, 396–424. Eagles, *Price of Defiance*, 69–79. Bartley, *Massive Resistance*, 4–9; *The Year of the Great Decision*, 1.

6. First quote, Flynt, *Alabama Baptists*, 458. Second quote, Dailey, "The Theology of Massive Resistance," in *Massive Resistance*, ed. Webb. Third quote, William Colmer, "School Segregation," Congressional Sidelights, May 26, 1954, WCP. James O. Eastland, "The Supreme Court, Segregation, and the South," speech, Senate, May 27, 1954, 11–14, KTP. September 8, 1954, Mississippi Legislature 1954 Extraordinary Session, *Mississippi Senate Journal, 1954–1955*, 3–10. "Mississippi," 3-C-11, NAACP-P. Bolton, *Hardest Deal*, 69–72; Katagiri, *Sovereignty Commission*, 8–63. Bartley, *Massive Resistance* 118, 121, 116–28. Lewis, "White South, Red Nation" and Badger, "Brown and Backlash," *Massive Resistance*, ed. Webb. Duziack, *Cold War Civil Rights*; Crespino, *Another Country*; Woods, *Black Struggle, Red Scare*.

7. Thomas P. Brady, *Black Monday*, 2nd ed. (Winona, Mississippi: Association of Citizens' Council, 1955), 1–2; 62–77, Erle Johnston Papers, ML-USM.

8. First quote, Association of Citizens' Councils of Mississippi 2nd Annual Report, August 1956, KTP. Second quote, "M is for Mississippi and Murder," pamphlet, 1956, 20-2, NAACP-P. McMillen, *Citizens' Council*, 15-40, 161-88, 237-66.

9. First quote, "M is for Mississippi and Murder"; second quote, Iola Williams, interview. Whitfield, *Death in the Delta*, 15-17, 42-47.

10. Quoting anonymous, untitled poem, in Anna Mantinband, "Time for Remembering" (1979), 74, Mantinband Papers. East, "On the Attainment of Distinction," Vassar College, Poughkeepsie, New York, December 1962, 5, East Collection, ML-USM. Editorials and Articles, 1951–1961, Hazel Brannon Smith Papers, MML-MSU. Hodding Carter, *The Delta Democrat-Times*, 1950s articles.

11. Quoting *Petal Paper*, February 9, 1956, East Collection.

12. First, second, and third quotes, *The Petal Paper*, March 5, 1956; fourth quote, East, *Magnolia Jungle*, 180; ibid., 175-81; *HA*, March 23, 1956.

13. Quoting *HA*, March 23, 1956. *HA*, April 9, 10, 27, May 1, 1956; *The Petal Paper*, November 22, 1956; East, *Magnolia Jungle*, 178-79, 201-202; East, "On the Attainment of Distinction"; Vorspan, "The Iconoclast of Petal, Mississippi," 33; Webb, *The Quiet Voices*, 227-28.

14. Quoting Kreuse, "The Southern Rabbi and Civil Rights," 159-60. Charles Mantinband, "Rabbi in the Deep South," *ADL Bulletin*, n.d.; Charles and Anna Mantinband to friends, December 1954, Mantinband Papers. Webb, "Big Struggle in a Small Town," 214-26; MSSC #2-131-0-3-1-1-1.

15. Quoting Morgan, *Dearly Bought, Deeply Treasured*, 77; ibid., 78-134. *Student Printz*, September 12, 1955, USM Mascot VF, ML-USM; *HA*, April 5, 1951, April 13, 1956, April 6, 1959; Piliawsky, *Exit 13*, 3-20, 76-77; Scarborough, interview; Address by W. D. McCain, Pro-American Forum, Chicago, Illinois, September 9, 1960, MSSC file, PBJ.

16. Hollander, "One Mississippi Negro"; Hollander, "How Mississippi Southern Stayed White," 277; MSSC #1-27-0-6-32-1-1, 11-12, 18-21; Clyde Kennard Timeline, website; Silver, *Closed Society*, 93-94; Dittmer, *Local People*, 79-80.

17. Hollander, "How Mississippi Southern Stayed White," 277-79; MSSC #1-27-0-6-32-1-1 through 37-1-1-1, 6-11, 6-11, 20-21; Branch, interview by Adams.

18. Quoting L. C. Hicks to Ney H. Gore, MSSC #2-3-0-6-2-1-1. For NAACP membership and actions in the CPW, see Annual Report Southeast Region NAACP, 25-A-5, Correspondence and Reports 1950s, Ruby Hurley, Medgar Evers, Gloster B. Current, Lucille Black, and B. E. Murph 25-A-2, 25-A-3, 25-A-5, 25-B-2, 25-D-14, 27-A-10, all in NAACP-P. See, too, Earline Boyd, interview, MOHP-D; Ellie Dahmer, speech, Civil Rights in Hattiesburg, tape recording, ML-USM; J. C. Fairley, interview by Garvey, vol. 375, 12-13, MOHP. For Woullard and the NAACP, see MSSC #s:1-27-0-6-32-1-1 through 37-1-1, pp. 27-29, 35; #2-70-6-1-1-1; #2-3-0-11-1-1-1; #2-3-0-3-1-1-1; #2-3-0-6-1-1-1 to 6-1-1; #2-3-0-9-1-1-1; #2-3-0-1-1-1; #2-70-6-1-1-1; #2-14-0-3-1-1-1; #2-14-0-7-2-1-1; #2-14-0-8-1-1-1 to 7-1-1; #2-14-0-10-1-1-1 through 165-1-1; #2-3-0-5-1-1-1, all at MDAH. For the police shooting, see *HA*, June 2, 1958. MIA to Mayor and City Council, June 3, 1958, SCLC-P, reel 1; Correspondence R. T. Carlisle to HPD officers and commissioners, May and June 1958, HMR. *HA*, June 16-19, 1958. For earlier brutality case, see *HA*, June 15, 1949, HMR, ML-USM.

19. Branch, interview by Adams, Dahmer Jr. interview by Gray, both in MOHP-D; *HA*, January 13, 1966; Adam Cohen, "Widow and the Wizard," *Time* (magazine), May 18, 1998, 72-73; *CL*, August 1, 1995, August 17, 1998; MSSC #1-27-0-6-32-1-1, 10, 20-21.

20. Quoting "NAACP Asks Probe of Mississippi Registrar," May 1, 1952, 18-C-22; Evers, Mississippi NAACP Monthly Reports, October 25, 1956, 25-D-14, NAACP-P. *Peay v. Cox*, 190 F. 2d 123-127 (1951); Plaintiff's Proposed Findings, *US v. Lynd*, (1962) case, no. 1646, S.D. Miss, 9-13, 26-27, USvTL; *Peay v. Cox*, (1951); *HA*, April 12, 1956; Statement by Governor J. P. Coleman, Chicago, August 11, 1956, 11, Coleman Collection, MML-MSU; "Progress and Reaction 1955," NAACP Annual Report, 28, WCP. E. Hammond Smith, interview by Caudill and Burger, interview by Pyle, MOHP-D; Clarence Magee, interview; Martin, *Count Them*, 4.

21. US Senate, *Hearings before the Subcommittee on Constitutional Rights of the Committee on the Judiciary United States Senate, 1957*, 564–565. Martin, *Count Them*, 26; ibid., 23–26; MSSC: #2-5-1-38-1-1-2; #2-2-0-4-16-1-1, MDAH. Evers, Reports, November 14, 1957, February 26, 1957, 25-D-14, NAACP-P; Civil Rights Act of 1957, in *Federal Civil Rights Laws*, November 1984, 14–22, JCS; Lawson, *Running for Freedom*, 58.

22. First quote, Gore, interview; second quote, Wade-Seals, interview. Evers, Report, October 22, 1958, 25-D-15, NAACP-P; MSSC #2-49-0-6-2-1-1; #2-14-0-18-1-1-1; #2-14-0-20-1-1-1; #2-14-0-23-1-1-1; #2-14-0-26-1-1-1; #2-68-0-23-1-1-1.

23. Evers to Current, December 1, 1958; Evers, Report, January 20, 1960; Evers, "Onward to Freedom, Justice, and Equality," 1958, 2-D-15, NAACP-P. Joyce A. Ladner to Haley Barbour, April 5, 2006, Letters of Support, Clyde Kennard website. MSSC #2-3-0-5-1-1-1; US House, *Civil Rights Hearings Before Subcommittee No. 5 of the Committee on the Judiciary House of Representatives, 1959*, 783–801, 957–959; Goldfield, *Black, White, and Southern*, 151. For a description of Lynd, see Martin Jr., *Count Them*, 36–37.

24. Quoting *HA*, December 6, 1958. MSSC # 9-0-0-27-1-1-1, 7.

25. First and second quotes, MSSC #5-3-1-19-1-1-1. Third quote, Webb, "Big Struggle in a Small Town," 219. MSSC #1-27-0-6-32-1-1 through 37-1-1, 6-35; #1-27-0-15-1-1-1; #1-27-0-16-1-1-1; #1-27-0-6-32-1-1 through 37-1-1, pp. 6–33. *HA*, June 6, 1958; James Coleman, Profile of a Man in the News, *Southern Reporting Service*, SNCC, reel 41. For Parker lynching, see Smead, *Blood Justice*, xi, 3–13, 17–23, 52–55, 68–76; Parker Lynching, May 25, 1959, Coleman Collection, RG 27, MDAH. *LLC*, November 6, 1959, January 14, 1960.

26. Quoting MSSC #1-27-0-36-6-1-1. MSSC #1-27-0-36-1-1-1 through 6-1-1; MSSC #1-27-0-31-1-1-1, #1-27-0-29-7-1-1, and 1-1-1 through 6-1-1, #1-27-0-26-1-1-1, #1-27-0-27-1-1-1. Aubrey Lucas, interview.

27. MSSC #1-27-0-40-1-1-1, 1-3, #1-27-0-40-1-1-1, MDAH; *HA*, September 15, 1959. Hollander, "How Mississippi Southern Stayed White," 280.

28. MSSC #1-27-0-40-1-1-1, 3; Hollander, "One Mississippi Negro," 31; *HA*, September 12, 14, 15, 1959.

29. Quoting MSSC #1-27-0-40-1-1-1, 3-6. MSSC #1-27-0-35-1-1-1 and #5-3-1-19-1-1-1; Hollander, "How Mississippi Southern Stayed White," 280–82; Hollander, "One Mississippi Negro," 3. Piliawsky, *Exit 13*, 3–20. For participation by Dudley Connor and Lee Daniels in the Citizens Council, see *HA*, March 23, 1956.

30. Quoting Webb, "Big Struggle in a Small Town," 221. For Jimmy Finch's background, see, *HA*, June 14, 1963. *HA*, March 19, 1995; MSSC #1-27-0-35-1-1-1.

31. MSSC #1-27-0-48-1-1-1, #1-27-0-52-1-1-1, #1-27-0-36-1-1-1, 4, #1-27-0-60-1-1-1, #1-27-0-63-1-1-1. Evers to Robert Carter, September 16, 1959, Pt. 22, Reel 2; Evers, Reports, October 26, 1959, December 20, 1960, 25-D-15, NAACP-P. Hollander, "How Mississippi Southern Stayed White," 283; Memo in Support of Application for Clemency of Clyde Kennard to Haley Barbour, Pardon Docket 06-0005, 20, in TC, MDAH.

32. First quote, *HA*, September 21, 1959; second quote, Hollander, "One Mississippi Negro," 32. Indictment, *Kennard v. Mississippi* (1961), 41890, transcript, MSSC, MDAH; *HA*, September 26, 1960. For proof of Kennard's innocence, see *Mississippi v. Kennard* (2006), 5833, FCCC-H.

33. *Kennard v. Mississippi* (1961), transcript, 78–195.

34. First quote, *Kennard v. Mississippi* (1961), transcript, 209, all other quotes, 353. Ibid., 221–47, 252–54, 265–97, 331–55; Memo Kennard Clemency; *HA*, November 24, 1960, April 3, 1961. Hollander, "How Mississippi Southern Stayed White," 286.

35. Quoting *HA*, November 24, 1960. Evers, Report, December 20, 1960, 25-D-15, NAACP-P. *HA*, November 26, December 2, 1960, April 3, 1961, October 9, 1961; *Mississippi v. Evers* (1960), 4966,

Minute Books, vol. 21, p. 34, FCCC-H; MSSC #2-72-1-72-2-1-1 to 3-1-1-1, #10-28-0-14-1-1-1; *HA*, December 2, 1960; Hollander, "How Mississippi Southern Stayed White," 286; *Mississippi v. Kennard and Roberts* (1960), 124/5833 and 5834, *Minutes*, vol. 24, p. 16, FCCC-H.

36. Evers, Monthly Report, January 20, 1961, 25-D-15, NAACP-P; *US v. Lynd* (1962), 1646, records, 8, 33; *US v. Lynd*, in Brooks, Carrasco, Martin Jr., *Civil Rights Litigation*, 520–23; Lawson, *Black Ballots*, 273; Dittmer, *Local People*, 180–84; Earline Boyd, interview, MOPH-D; *HA*, March 6, 1962; *US v. Lynd*, 1646 (1962), A-1-60, USvTL; Report on Forrest County, March–September, 1962, SNCC-P, reel 38. See, too, Martin, *Count Them*, 45–48, 58–64, 116, 126, 132–34, 140.

37. First and second quotes, *HA*, March 2, 1962; third and fourth quotes, *HA*, March 6, 1962; last quote, *HA*, March 8, 1962. *US v. Lynd*, in *Civil Rights Litigation*, 522; *HA*, April 12, 16, 18, 30, 1962; *US v. Lynd*, 1646 (1962), records, 34-36, 60-150, USvTL; Lee Cole to file, n.d., MSSC #4-7-0-9-1-1; Dittmer, *Local People*, 179–82; Martin, *Count Them*, ix–xii.

38. Mason with Smith. *Beaches, Blood, and Ballots*. Carson, *In Struggle*, 9–54; Dittmer, *Local People*, 103–19; Chafe, *Civilities and Civil Liberties*, 71–86; 9–44; Branch, *Parting the Waters*, 413–70; Payne, *Light of Freedom*, 107–108.

39. Victoria Gray, Civil Rights Course, October 10, 2000, audiotape 1, Adams Papers, ML-USM; Adams, "They Didn't Know the Power of Women," *Hands on the Freedom Plow*, 230–35; Dittmer, *Local People*, 99–115, 179–84. COFO, *Mississippi: Handbook for Political Programs*; Forrest County Report. Watkins, interview by Rachal, MOHP-D; *HA*, September 18, 1998, Woods Guest House Collection, ML-USM; Adickes, "Hattiesburg Freedom School," Metrodome, Minneapolis, September 14, 1998, 17, Adickes Papers, ML-USM; MSSC #2-64-1-23-1-1-1, #2-64-1-18-1-1-1, #2-64-1-24-2-1.

40. Quoting Earline Boyd, interview, MOHP-D; Martin, *Count Them*, 211.

41. Zinn, *SNCC*, 81; Task Force: Freedom, November 13, 1962, CORE-P, reel 26; Second Report Special Committee On Strategy Concerned with Expanded CORE Program, March 28, 1962, Pt.20, Reel 13, NAACP-P; Dittmer, *Local People*, 116, 179. MSSC #2-55-3-69-2-1-1, #2-49-0-37-1-1-1, #2-49-0-26-1-1-1, #2-49-0-44-1-1-1, #1-70-0-14-1-1-1, #1-70-0-14-1-1-1, #2-150-1-3-1-1-1; McGill, interview.

42. Kennard Clemency Memo; Dent, "Portrait of Three Heroes," 257; Huie and Griffin, "Why They Can't Wait," 18–19; Webb, "Big Struggle in a Small Town," 221–22. Correspondence between Haynes Heslep, Fred Jones, Ross Barnett, M. L. Dalton, C. E. Brezeale, March 10, 12, 13, 1962; June 21, 25, 26 1962, all in RG 27, Ross Barnett, MDAH. *MFP*, January 26, 1963; Eagles, *Price of Defiance*, 261–318; Oshinsky, *Worse Than Slavery*.

43. *MFP*, July 28, August 4, 11, 18, September 1, 8, 15, 22, December 1, 1 5, 22, 29, 1962, January 5, 19, 26, 1963. Barnett to James Meredith, September 7, 1962, Segregation Files, George McIlheny Papers, MML-MSU; Dittmer, *Local People*, 138–41; *HA*, August 16, 1963; MSSC # 13-59-0-26-4-1-1-1; "Miss. High Court Rejects Plea," *Daily Defender*, January 15, 1963. Dorie Ladner Churnet, interviewer anonymous, n.d.; Joyce Ladner, interview by Barbara Ransby, March 23, 1990, both in Ladner Papers, TC, MDAH.

44. First, fifth, and sixth quotes, Huie and Griffin, "Why They Can't Wait," 19. Second quote, Griffin, *Black Like Me*, 67–69. Third quote, Jess Brown to Barnett, January 26, 1963. Fourth quote, Order for Indefinite Suspension of Clyde Kennard, January 28, 1963; Correspondence, Barnett, RG 27, MDAH. Dent, "Portrait of Three Heroes," 258; Dittmer, *Local People*, 83; Evers, *For Us, The Living*, 224–25; *HA*, January 30, 1963; MSSC #13-59-0-27-1-1-1; *MFP*, February 2, 1963.

45. First quote, John F. Kennedy, speech, June 11, 1963, American Experience, The Presidents, John F. Kennedy, PBS, website. *Petal Paper*, July 1963; *HA*, July 5, 1963; Evers, *For Us, The Living*, 299–304.

46. Quoting, *HA*, July 13, 1963. Dittmer, *Local People*, 199; Bob Moses to SNCC Executive Committee, n.d., Ser. [?], reel 40; "What is COFO?" COFO Publication, CORE-P, reel 25; Statement by Governor Barnett before Senate Commerce Committee, July 12, 1963, JCS. Correspondence, Colmer

and constituents in Jones and Forrest Counties, June 1963–1964, WCP. *HA*, June 14, 17, 1963; Paul B. Johnson, speech, Jackson Citizens Council, May 17, 1963, IV, PBJ.

47. *LLC*, July 17, 18, 20, 24, August 1, 8, 1963; *US v. Lynd* (1962), 1646, records 36–38, ML-USM; *HA*, July 15, 1963; Fact Sheet: Hattiesburg, Mississippi, n.d., SNCC-P, reel 38.

48. *HA*, July 15, 16, August 7, 28, October 28–30, 1963. Hattiesburg Reports, September 23, 24, 1963; Chronology of Violence and Intimidation in Mississippi Since 1951, Police Brutality Report, n.d., Mississippi Freedom Vote Campaign, all in SNCC-P, reel 38. Bob Moses to SNCC Executive Committee, Ser. [?], SNCC, reel 40. "What is COFO"; Summary of Events in Hattiesburg, Freedom Vote, October 28 and 29, 1963, CORE-P, reel 25. Sandy Leigh, interview by Anne Romaine, November 7, 1966, Michaels Papers, ML-USM; Journal of Victoria Gray, October 3, 7, 1963, November 5, 1963, transcript, Adams Papers, ML-USM; Dittmer, *Local People*, 184, 200–203; *LLC*, November 6, 1963; NAACP Voter Education Project Annual Report of Jones County (January 1963–December 1963), 25-D-14, NAACP-P.

49. First quote, Freedom Summer Journal Sandra Adickes, transcript, August 4, 1964, Adickes Papers; second quote, President Johnson, speech, November 27, 1963, American Experience, The Presidents, PBS. Dittmer, *Local People*, 211.

50. Fact Sheet: Hattiesburg, Mississippi, n.d., SNCC, reel 38; Dittmer, *Local People*, 218–21.

51. First and second quotes, McGill, interview; all other quotes, Jackson, interview, MOHP recording.

CHAPTER 3

1. Jackson, interview; "Hattiesburg Vote Push," n.d., SNCC-P, reel 38; *HA*, January 22, 1964.

2. First quote, *HA*, January 22, 1964; second quote, Zinn, *SNNC*, 111. Wade, interview. Hattiesburg Report, January 22, 1964, reel 15 and "Hattiesburg Vote Push," n.d., SNCC-P, reel 38.

3. Quoting Jackson, interview; Wade, interview; Henry with Baker, *Aaron Henry*.

4. First quote, Zinn, *SNNC*, 111; second quote, *HA*, January 22, 1964. Hattiesburg Report, January 22, 1964, SNCC-P, reel 15; "Hattiesburg Vote Push." Houck, *Rhetoric, Religion, and the Civil Rights Movement, 1954–1965*; Chappell, *Stone of Hope*; Marsh, *Beloved Community*.

5. A. D. Morgan to T. B. Birdsong and R. L. Morgan, January 22, 1964, II-10, PBJ. Hattiesburg Reports, January 22, 27, February 11, 1964, SNCC-P, reel 15. *HA*, January 22, February 8, 1964.

6. Easton and Preyor, interview. Sandy Leigh, interview by Anne Romaine, November 7, 1966, Michaels Papers, ML-USM. Sanford R. Leigh, n.d., reel 39, Comments on Hattiesburg Freedom Day, n.d., reel 38. Hattiesburg Report, January 22, 1964, reel 15, all in SNCC-P. *HA*, April 4, 1993; Wade, interview; Jeannette Smith, interview; Newman, *Divine Agitators*, 46, 48–50. "Hattiesburg Vote Push."

7. Quoting Zinn, *SNCC*, 105–106; ibid., 102–104.

8. Quoting ibid., 112–13; ibid., 111. Hattiesburg Report, January 22, 1964, SNCC-P, reel 15; "Hattiesburg Vote Push"; *HA*, January 22, 1964.

9. Quoting Violence against Oscar Chase, n.d., SNCC-P, reel 39. *HA*, January 22, 1964. COFO Report, n.d., SNCC-P, reel 38, Hattiesburg Report, January 22, 1964, SNCC-P, reel 15. Zinn, "Incident in Hattiesburg," *The Nation*, May 18, 1964, Ellin Freedom Summer Collection.

10. Quoting *HA*, January 24, 1964. Zinn, *SNCC*, 117; *HA*, January 23, 1964.

11. *HA*, January 27, 1964. Leigh interview; Hattiesburg Reports, January 22, 27, 1964, SNCC-P, reel 15; Dittmer, *Local People*, 220–21; Mississippi Student Union Pamphlet, n.d., II-9, PBJ; Wade, interview; Jackson, interview; Outlaw, interview. US Const. amend. XXIV.

12. Quoting Hattiesburg Report, February 7, 1964, reel 15; Hattiesburg Reports, January 27, 1964, February 3, 14, 22, 24, 1964, reel 15 and Leigh to Friend, February 11, 1964, both in reel 38, SNCC-P. Hattiesburg Demonstrations, MSSC, February 13, 1964, LF; File vol. 30, #44-1512-2579, DABURN-FBI-RBH; Newman, *Divine Agitators*, 50–51. Leigh, interview.

13. Hall, interview by Adams, MOHP-D; Leigh, interview. Hattiesburg Report, January 27, February [?], 11, 1964, reel 15; Leigh to Friend, February 11, 1964, reel 38. All in SNCC-P.

14. Quoting Wade, "Reminiscences," notebook, n.d., Wade Papers, ML-USM. Hattiesburg Reports, February 18, 24, 1964, SNCC-P, reel 15.

15. *HA*, January 30, 1964. COFO Report, n.d., reel 38, *Hattiesburg v. Moses* (1964), 22688, and COFO Report, reel 38; Hattiesburg Report, January 27, 1964, SNCC reel 15; all in SNCC-P. Bill 546, Antipicketing Law, CORE-P, reel 47. *HA*, January 29, 1964; Zinn, *SNCC*, 112.

16. Quoting Zinn, *SNCC*, 118, ibid., 117–21. *HA*, January 28, 1964; Hattiesburg Report, January 27, 1964, SNCC-P, reel 15.

17. Quoting Leigh, interview. News clippings and Ben-Ami Timeline, Ben-Ami Papers, ML-USM; Outlaw, interview; Wade, interview.

18. Quoting *HA*, January 25, 1962. *HA*, January 27, 28, February 24, 1964; A. James Rudin, "Freedom Trend Unstoppable," *Kansas City Jewish Chronicle*, March 6, 1964, Ben-Ami Papers.

19. Quoting *HA*, February 4, 1964. Hattiesburg Report, February 1964, SNCC-P, reel 15. *Edwards v. South Carolina* (1963).

20. James K. Dukes, interview.

21. Quoting *HA*, February 19, 1964. *HA*, February 4, 24, 1964.

22. First quote, *HA*, February 4, 1964; second quote, *HA*, February 24, 1964. *HA*, February 8, 1964.

23. *HA*, March 10, 1966; Hattiesburg Report, February 1964, SNCC-P, reel 15

24. Quoting Earline Boyd, interview by Bolton, MOHP-D. Wade, interview; *HA*, January 31, 1964. Hattiesburg Reports, January 27, 28, 29, 1964, reel 15 and COFO Report, n.d., reel 38, both in SNCC-P.

25. Quoting Jackson, interview. Adickes, *Freedom School*, 65; Hattiesburg Report, January 28, 1964, SNCC-P, reel 15.

26. Quoting Anthony J. Harris, "Personal Recollections," 2, Harris Civil Rights Memoir, ML-USM; ibid., 1–3. Biographical Information, Wade Papers; Wade, interview, by author.

27. Quoting Adickes, *Freedom School*, 70; Wade, "Reminiscences," notebook, n.d., Wade Papers.

28. First quote, Zinn, "Incident in Hattiesburg." Second quote, Cliff Vaughts to Burke Marshall, February 5, 1964; Hattiesburg Reports, January 27, February 5, 7, 12, 14, 21, 1964, all in SNCC-P, reel 15.

29. Quoting *Mississippi v. Guyot Jr.*, Docket, October 22, 1964, 20, CORE-P, reel 21. *Guyot Jr. v. Mississippi* (1964) 137/6319, Docket, vol. 5, 6, FCCC-H; *HA*, January 28, 1964. Hattiesburg Reports, January 27, February 1, 11, 21, 1964, reel 15 and COFO report, n.d., reel 38, all in SNCC-P. Hattiesburg Demonstration, MSSC Report, February 13, 1964, LF; MSSC #2-64-1-65-1-1-1 through 5-1-1; #2-64-1-63-1-1-1 to 4-1-1; #2-64-1-68-1-1-1; *HA*, January 31, 1964.

30. COFO Report, n.d., SNCC-P, reel 38. Stoner, "Experiences in Hattiesburg," January 7 to May 21, 1964, 1–3, and Stoner, "A Glimpse into the Past," Memoir, March 1998, both in Stoner Papers, ML-USM.

31. Quoting "Experiences in Hattiesburg," 3; ibid., 2–5. Hattiesburg Reports, February 6, 8, 15, 1964, SNCC-P, reel 15.

32. Quoting "Experiences in Hattiesburg," 3–5; ibid., 7–8. *HA*, May 2, 1964; Hattiesburg Report, May 23, 1964, SNCC-P, reel 15.

33. "Experiences in Hattiesburg," 6–8; *HA*, May 2, 1964; Hattiesburg Report, May 23, 1964, SNCC-P, reel 15.

34. Quoting Governor Johnson, January 21, 1964, *Mississippi Senate Journal*, 1964, 37–38. Erle Johnston to Governor Johnson, May 1, 1964, II-9; Morgan to Johnson, March 12, 1964, II-10, PBJ; Saxon, interview by Derr, MOHP-D.

35. Quoting Crespino, *Another Country*, 132; ibid., 115–17, 125–26, 143. Correspondence and Reports, II--9, 10, PBJ.

36. Quoting Nelson, *Terror in the Night*, 88; ibid., 86–87. For New Orleans base, see Bowers-FBI-RBH, vol. 1. *HA*, July 10, 1964. See too "Killed by the Klan," prod. and dir. Charles C. Stuart; Marsh, *God's Long Summer*, 27; Dittmer, *Local People*, 250; Rowe-Sims, "Mississippi State Sovereignty Commission," 29–39.

37. Quoting Marsh, *God's Long Summer*, 49; ibid., 49-81, 224n104. Files vol. 1, #157-1654, vol. 2, #157-18-115, 10, 72, Bowers-FBI-RBH; McDaniel, interview by Caudill, MOHP-D; US House, 89th Congress, *Activities of Ku Klux Klan of the United States*, index, 55, 58,59, 62, 67–69, 76–77. US House, 90th Congress, *The Present Day Ku Klux Klan Movement Report*, Pt. 2, 153–54; Bowers, interview.

38. Files vol. 2, #157-18-115, vol. 3, #157-18-249, Bowers-FBI-RBH; Bowers, interview; Marsh, *God's Long Summer*, 50–51.

39. Quoting Bowers, interview. Marsh *God's Long Summer*, 52–53; File vol. 2, #157-18-115, Bowers-FBI-RBH.

40. Marsh, *God's Long Summer*, 53. File vol. 42, #44-1512-3492, DABURN-FBI-RBH. File vol. 3, #157-5183-173, Martin-FBI-RBH. For discussion of Bowers's sexuality, see Files vol. 42, #44-1512-3492, DABURN-FBI-RBH, vol. 7, #157-18-1011; vol. 3, #157-18-282, Bowers-FBI-RBH.

41. Quoting Bowers, interview; Marsh, *God's Long Summer*, 49, 53–55; Dixon, *Clansman*.

42. Bowers, interview; Marsh, *God's Long Summer*, 50–51.

43. First quote, Marsh, *God's Long Summer*, 61; second and third quotes, ibid., 64; ibid., 50–51, 60–64. Fourth quote, "My Fellow Americans," Klan flyer, Misc. Klan Info. "Executive Lecture," March 1, 1964; *The Klan Ledger*, Early Autumn Edition, Misc. Klan Info, RBH.

44. *Constitution of the White Knights of the Ku Klux Klan of the Sovereign Realm of Mississippi*, in *State v. Nobles*, RBH.

45. Quoting ibid., 36–37. Files vol. 1, #157-18-2C, #157-18-5, #157-18-12, vol. 4, #157-18-393, Bowers-FBI-RBH. File vol. 1, #157-854-67, Sessum-FBI-RBH. File vol. 11, #44-1512-528, DABURN FBI-RBH and *Mississippi v. Bowers* (1998), 6922, vol. 3, transcript, FCCC-H. Marsh, *Last Days*, 35–37.

46. Quoting Bill No. 546, Antipicketing Law, CORE-P, reel 47. Hattiesburg Report, n.d., SNCC-P, reel 37. Plaintiff's Proposed Findings, *US v. Lynd*, n.d., 1646, 8, S.D. Miss, USvTL; *HA*, April 10, 15, 1964. Hattiesburg Reports, April 10, 11, 1964, SNCC-P, reel 15.

47. First quote, Fairley, interview by Garvey, 34, MOHP; ibid., 32–34; second quote, Charles Kershner, speech, Symposium for Social Justice, USM, November 9, 2007, 5, Kershner Papers, ML-USM; ibid., 3–6. John Frazier, speech, Social Justice Seminar, November 9, 2007, recording, Department of Mass Communications and Journalism, USM; *HA*, March 6, 10, 20, 1964. MSSC #1-70-0-20-1-1-1 through 3-1-1; #1-70-23-1-1-1, MDAH; Erle Johnson to President W. D. McCain, II-9, PBJ; *The Student Printz*, March 20, 1964.

48. Quoting *HA*, April 14–17; *US v Lynd*, 1646.

49. Statement of Charles Evers before the US Commission on Civil Rights in Jackson, Mississippi, February 17, 1965, 25-D-14, NAACP-P.

50. Carson, *In Struggle*, 96–100, 108–10; Dittmer, *Local People*, 208–10; 218–20.

51. Quoting Freedom Candidates, April 1964, CRMV. "What is COFO? Mississippi: Structure of the Movement and Present Operations," COFO Publication, 1964, CORE-P, reel 25; Leigh, interview. "Negro Woman Qualifies for Mississippi Senate Seat," April 10, 1964, SNCC, SNCC-P, reel 39; Steve Max, "The Mississippi Freedom Democratic Party: Background and Development," 6, SNCC-P, reel 41. "Mississippi: How Negro Democrats Fared (Part I)," June 16, 1964, II-5, PBJ.

52. What is COFO? Leigh, interview; "How Negro Democrats Fared"; Max, "The Mississippi Freedom Democratic Party."

53. Quoting "Imperial Executive Order," May 3, 1964, Klan Misc. Info. Files vol. 2, #157-18-115, vol. 3, #157-18-186, Bowers-FBI-RBH. Laurel Police Report, #15206, May 10, 1964, Nix and Myers to FBI Laboratory, May 11, 1964, and MBI Case Report, May 14, 1964, II-10, PBJ. *LLC*, May 11, 1964; *HA*,

April 25, 1964, June 16, 1964; A List of Mississippi Churches Destroyed or Damaged, September 16, 1964, CORE-P, reel 21.

54. First quote, *HA*, June 24, 1964; second quote, *HA*, June 19, 1964; third quote, *LLC*, May 14, 1964. *MFP*, June 20, 1964; Status of Mississippi Legislation, n.d., Zwerling Collection; *AJC*, March 8, 1964, SNCC-P, reel 38; Birdsong to All Law Enforcement Officers, June 9, 1964, Marx Papers, ML-USM.

55. Summary of Major Points in Testimony by Citizens of Mississippi, June 8, 1964, reel 38; Harold Taylor to President Johnson, June 11, 1964, reel 38; Friends of Freedom to President Johnson, n.d., reel 29, all in SNCC-P. Dittmer, *Local People*, 237–40.

56. Profiles of Typical Freedom Schools, n.d., reel 39; COFO, *Mississippi: Handbook for Political Programs*, reel 38, SNCC-P; Summary of Major Points in Testimony, SNCC-P. For interpretations of Forrest County as more racially moderate, see Dittmer, *Local People*, 179; James K. Dukes, speech, "Pursuing a Late Justice," August 29, 2000, videocassette, ML-USM.

CHAPTER 4

1. Quoting McGill, interview. WATS Report, July 11, 1964, SNCC-P, reel 15; File vol. 1, #157-433-1, DeBoxtel-FBI-RBH; USCCRLE, *A Report on Equal Protection in the South*.

2. Quoting McGill, interview; File vol. 1, #157-433-1, DeBoxtel-FBI-RBH; *A Report on Equal Protection in the South*.

3. COFO, *Mississippi: Handbook for Political Programs*, reel 38; "Citizenship Curriculum" and "Mississippi Summer Freedom School Program," reel 39, SNCC-P. McAdam, *Freedom Summer*, 33; Carson, *In Struggle*, 96, 98–100, 114.

4. First and second quotes, Joseph Ellin Journal, May 6, 1964; ibid., June 7, 21, 26, 1964, Ellin Freedom Summer Collection; third quote, Owen Letter, February 5, 1963, Owen Freedom Summer Collection; Adickes, "My Seven Year (H)itch," Conference on Radicals in the Professions, Ann Arbor, Michigan, July 14–16, 1967, Adickes Papers; Owen Letter, June 10, 1964, Owen Collection; Shaw, interview by Millet, MOHP-D. Terri Shaw, "Freedom Summer Recollections," transcript, Shaw Freedom Summer Collection, all at ML-USM. For volunteers in Mississippi in general, see McAdam, *Freedom Summer*, 3–10, 35–65; Dittmer, *Local People*, 242–46; Belfrage, *Freedom Summer*, 3–8.

5. First and second quotes, Shaw, "Recollections"; third quote, COFO, *Mississippi: Handbook for Political Programs*; Security Handbook, n.d., Zeman Freedom Summer Collection. Dittmer, *Local People*, 244.

6. Quoting File vol. 1, #157-18-34, Bowers-FBI-RBH; Files vol. 1, #157-505-15, #157-505-13, #157-505-12, Byrd-FBI-RBH. For statistics on violence, see Rothschild, *Case of Black and White*, 58.

7. Nelson, *Terror in the Night*, 86–88; Carson, *In Struggle*, 114–15; Belfrage, *Freedom Summer*, 11–12; Dittmer, *Local People*, 246–52; *HA*, July 10, 1964.

8. First quote, Nelson, *Terror in the Night*, 87–88; second quote, Carson, *In Struggle*, 115; third quote, *LLC*, June 26, 1964. *HA*, June 24, 1964; Marsh, *God's Long Summer*, 27; "Killed by the Klan," prod. and dir. Charles C. Stuart; Shaw, "Recollections." For examples of plans for Klan violence, see Files vol. 1, #157-18-34, #157-505-15, #157-505-13, Bowers-FBI-RBH. File vol. 1, #157-505-12, Byrd-FBI-RBH.

9. First quote, Joseph Ellin to [?], July 3, 1964, Ellin Collection; second quote, Joseph Schwartz to Bea and Isaac, n.d., Schwartz Letters, ML-USM. Ellin Correspondence, June 30, July 10, 1964, August 1, 1964, Ellin Collection. Shaw, "Recollections"; Glass Mississippi Diary, August 11, 12, 1964, ML-USM; Owen Letter, July 2, 1964, Owen Collection.

10. Quoting Outlaw, interview. See, too, Douglass Baker, Easton, McGill, Holloway, Preyor, interviews. Payne, *Laurel*, 25–37.

11. First quote, Glass Diary, August 13, 1964; second quote, Outlaw, interview. Ellins Correspondence, June 30, 1964, July 29, 1964, July 9, 1964, all in Ellin Collection. Shaw, "Recollections"; Easton and Preyor, Jeanette Smith, Wade, interviews.

12. First quote, Siggers, interview; second quote, Adickes Journal, transcript, July 5, 1964, Adickes Paper. Jeanette Smith, interview; Shaw, "Recollections." Johnny Magee, interview; Wade, interview.

13. Quoting Gwendolyn Simmons, interview, *Veterans of Hope Project*. Lefever, *Undaunted by the Fight*, 195–98; Simmons, "From Little Memphis Girl to Mississippi Amazon," *Hands on the Freedom Plow*, 27; COFO Volunteer Lists, MSSC #s 2-166-3-37-14-1-1 and 2-150-1-10-7-1-1.

14. First quote, Simmons interview; second quote, Spinks, interview by Adams, MOHP-D. Winston A. Grady-Willis, *Challenging U.S. Apartheid*, 62–63. "Flintridge Woman in South as Civil Rights Worker," *La Canada Valley Sun*, October 8, 1964, Owen Collection. Simmons, "Mississippi Amazon," 27–28.

15. "Flintridge Woman in South." Simmons, "Mississippi Amazon," 28; Davidson, Marion, Herbert Randall, Freedom Summer Photographs, ML-USM. For blacks outside the movement and hostilities within the black community over activism, see interviews: Johnny Magee, Wyatt, Austin.

16. Shaw, "Recollections"; Joseph Ellin to Mom and Dad, July 29, 1964, Ellin Collection.

17. Report from Hattiesburg, July 8–14, 1964, reel 38 and Steve Max, The Mississippi Freedom Democratic Party: Background and Development, reel 41, both in SNCC-P. Ellin to Editor, August 1, 1964, Ellin Collection; Owen to Mom, Pop, and Rat Fink, July 2, 1964, Owen Collection; "What is COFO?" COFO Publication, CORE-P, reel 25.

18. First quote Owen letters July 2, 9, 1964, Owen Collection; second and third quotes, McAdam, *Freedom Summer*, 103; ibid., 92, 101–15.

19. Shelia Michaels, "Freedom Is a Constant Struggle," October 20, 2001, Michaels Papers. John O'Neil, interview by Joyce Ladner, n.d., 15–20, 23, 26–27, 31, 33, Ladner Papers, TC, MDAH; July 24, 1964 entry, Adickes Journal, transcript. See, too, McAdam, *Freedom Summer*, 101–15; Dittmer, *Local People*, 242–46; 263–65, Clayborne, *In Struggle*, 111–21.

20. Austin, interview; Shaw, "Recollections"; Ellin to Editor, July 10, 1964, August 1, 1964, Ellin Collection; Michaels, "Freedom Is a Constant Struggle"; Adickes, *Freedom School*, 60–62; Owen, letters home, Owen Collection.

21. Quoting Shaw, "Recollections"; Owen to Mom, Pop, and Rat Fink, July 2, 1964, Owen Collection.

22. Quoting Rothschild, *Case of Black and White*, 105; ibid., 13, 106–107. McAdam, *Freedom Summer*, 83; Rachal, "We'll Never Turn Back," 176; Chilcoat and Ligon, "'Helping to Make Democracy," 46–48; *HA*, July 10, 1964. "Citizenship Curriculum"; Community Center Report, reel 38, SNCC-P, Adickes, "Hattiesburg Freedom Schools," September 14, 1998, 3–4, Adickes Papers. Ellin to the Editor, July 10, 1964, and Nancy and Joe Ellin to S and D, July 8, 1964, both in Ellin Collection.

23. First quote, Outlaw, interview; second quote Funchess, interview.

24. Quoting Wade, interview. "Citizenship Curriculum"; Funchess, interview; McGill, interview; Johnny Magee, interview; Jackson, interview. Chilcoat and Ligon, "Helping to Make Democracy," 64–68; Adickes, "Hattiesburg Freedom School," 4–5; Adickes, *Freedom School*, 58–59, 68, 74. Ellin correspondence, July 8, 9, 10, August [?], 1964, Ellin Collection; Community Center Report; Leigh to Bob Moses, Report from Hattiesburg, July 8–14, 1964, reel 38, SNCC-P. Glass Diary, August 11, 18, 1964.

25. Last quote, Adickes, "Hattiesburg Freedom School," 16; ibid., 4–5; all other quotes, Jackson, interview. Adickes Journal, July 14, 1964; Adickes, *Freedom School*, 58–59, 65; "Mississippi Freedom Summer School Program," SNCC-P, reel 38; Funchess, McGill, Johnny Magee, interviews.

26. First, second, and third quotes, Easton and Preyor interview; all other quotes, Wade, interview; Funchess, interview.

27. Dittmer, *Local People*, 272–74, 279–81; Adams, "They Didn't Know the Power of Women," *Hands on the Freedom Plow*, 232–233; Terry Shaw, interview, *Eyes on the Prize*.

28. Shaw, "Recollections." *Washington Post*, December 25, 1964; Robert Beech to Drew Pearson, January 4, 1965, Ben-Ami Papers, ML-USM. For Hamilton's Klan activities, see "Swift Justice," *Delta Ministry Reports*, March 1967, Delta Ministry VF, ML-USM; File vol. 11, #44-1512-528, DABURN-FBI-RBH; Nancy and Joe Ellin to S and D, July 8, 1964, Ellin Collection; WATS Report, July 8, 1964, reel 15, SNCC-P; Newman, *Divine Agitators*, 50–51.

29. Quoting Shaw, "Recollections." *HA*, June 29, 1964. "Hospitality Month in Mississippi," n.d., SNCC, reel 39. For the FBI's failure to investigate other slayings in 1964, see McAdam, *Freedom Summer*, 103.

30. US Commission on Civil Rights, *A Summary of the Civil Rights Act of 1964* ; Wayne Valentine to E. F. Ray, July 3, 1964, II-10, PBJ. "Analysis of the Civil Rights Law," *Freedom Booklet*, reel 39 and WATS Report, reel 15, both in SNCC-P. *HA*, July 2, 3, 21, 1964.

31. First and second quotes, Adickes, *Freedom School*, 54; ibid., 52–54, 57; third quote, Umoja Kwanguvu, "Picnic at Vernon Dahmer's," April 1999, Kwanguvu Freedom Summer Collection, ML-USM. Adickes Journal, July 10, 1964; Adickes, "Hattiesburg Freedom School," 3; *HA*, July 3, 1964. For the use of self-defense by locals and the debate over nonviolence, see Dittmer, *Local People*, 180–81; Payne, *Light of Freedom*, 204–206; McAdam, *Freedom Summer*, 122–23.

32. First quote, Shaw, "Recollections"; second quote, Peggy J. Connor, "A Commentary on the Civil Rights Movement in Mississippi," n.d., Connor Collection, ML-USM. In Shaw's original transcript, she referred to Connor as Mrs. Norris to protect Connor. Nancy and Joe Ellin to S and D, July 8, 1964, Ellin Collection; Joseph Schwartz to Leon and Shirley, n.d., Schwartz Letters.

33. Quoting *Report on Equal Protection in the South*, 46F; ibid., 46. WATS Report, July 11, 1964, SNCC-P, reel 15; McGill, interview.

34. WATS Report, July 5, 1964, reel 15, SNCC-P. Willie Roy Guillum Affidavit, *Mississippi Black Paper*, 72; McGill, interview.

35. Wyatt, interview, *An Oral History of Jones County*, 973; *LLC*, July 6, 7, 1964; McGill, interview; Carter, *Music Has Gone*, Kindle edition.

36. Quoting *LLC*, October 15, 1964. *LLC*, September 25, 1964. *Mississippi v. Coleman* (1964) 2636, *Minutes*, vol. 21, 473, 532–33 and *Mississippi v. Buckley* (1964), 2622, *Minutes*, vol. 21, 496–97, both in JCCC-L.

37. Quoting affidavits, in Shaw, "Recollections." WATS Report, July 6, 1964, SNCC-P, reel 15.

38. Quoting Jeanette Smith, interview; Shaw, "Recollections"; Nancy and Joe Ellin to S and D, July 8, 1964, Ellin Collection; *Mississippi v. Shinall* (1965), 6434, transcript.

39. *Mississippi v. Shinall* (1965), transcript, 810–14.

40. For the purported rape of Shinall's lover, see Adickes, *Freedom School*, 148–49 and Jeanette Smith, interview. For accusations of sexual abuse and brutality, see *Shinall v. Mississippi*, Appellant's Brief, Filed January 17, 1966, 43, 866, MSC Record, 9, MDAH; Jackson, interview; *Mississippi v. Shinall* (1965), transcript, 787–814.

41. First quote, Shaw, "Recollections"; all other quotes, Adickes, *Freedom School*, 74. Lorne Cress, affidavit, n.d., *Mississippi Black Paper*.

42. First, second, seventh, and eighth quotes, "Letter from the South," August 22, 1964, SNCC-P, reel 39; all other quotes, Lawrence Spears statement, Report #44-25913-18, Spears Collection, ML-USM; Shaw, "Recollections"; WATS Reports, July 10, 11, 1964, SNCC-P, reel 15; "3 COFO Workers Beaten," July 21, 1964, *The Voice of the Movement*, vol. 1, Ellin Collection; *HA*, July 11, 1964.

43. First quote, *HA*, July 11, 1964. Second quote, File #44-259-19; third quote, File #44-25913-42, BI-RBH. All other quotes, "Letter from the South." Owen to Mom, Pop, and Slim, August 3, 1964, and Owen to [?], n.d., Owen Collection; WATS Report, July 11, 1964, SNCC-P, reel 15; Rabbi Morris

B. Margolies, "The Dilemma of the Jew in the South," *Jewish Monitor*, July 1964, 57, Ben-Ami Papers; *NYT*, July 14, 1964, *NYT*-AA; Director to New Orleans FBI Office, July 10, 1964, Spears Collection; *A Report on Equal Protection in the South*, 53; Mississippi Summer Project—running summary of incidents, transcripts, Zwerling Collection, ML-USM.

44. Nelson, *Terror in the Night*, 86–94; "Killed by the Klan"; Correspondence, T. B. Birdsong and J. Edgar Hoover, July 13 and 17, 1964, II-10, PBJ; Dittmer, *Local People*, 249–50; Whitehead, *Attack on Terror*, 98–101.

45. Quoting *LLC*, July 17, 1964. *HA*, July 16, 27, 30, 1964; WATS Reports, July 21, 25, 1964, James Forman, Discovery of Three Bodies, August 5, 1964, SNCC-P, reel 15; File vol. 1, #157-433-1, DeBoxtel-FBI-RBH.

46. First and third quotes, Jackson interview; second and fourth quotes, Adickes Journal, August 14, 1964; ibid., August 17, 1964. August 14, 1964, Mississippi Summer Project—running summary of incidents. Adickes, letter to the Editor, '64 Civil Rights Hostess Honored, n.d., Adickes Papers. *HA*, August 14, 17, 1964, September 8, 1964.

47. Max, The Mississippi Freedom Democratic Party," II-9, PBJ; Victoria Gray Adams, interview by Blackside Inc., Freedom Registration Vote, September 1, 1964, SNCC-P, reel 4; *Convention Challenge and the Freedom Vote*, CRMV; Schwartz to Bea and Izakkk, n.d., Schwartz Letters; Lawson, *Running for Freedom*, 101–102; Carson, *In Struggle*, 125–26. Dittmer, *Local People*, 125–29, 288.

48. Quoting Adams, "They Didn't Know the Power of Women," 233–35. Governor Johnson speech in response to National Democratic Convention, n.d., 1–3, II-4, PBJ. Freedom Registration Vote, September 1, 1964, SNCC-P, reel 4; *Convention Challenge and the Freedom Vote*, Platform Mississippi Republican Party, Mississippi Republican Party Records. Lawson, *Running for Freedom*, 101–102; Carson, *In Struggle*, 125–26. Dittmer, *Local People*, 125–29, 288.

49. Quoting McGill interview. *LLC*, August 24, 1964; WATS Report, August 24, 1964, SNCC, reel 15. File vol. 8, # 44-1512-145, DABURN-FBI-RBH. Mississippi Summer Project—running summary of incidents.

50. *LLC*, August 24, 1964; "Brief of Contestants Urging the Vacating of the Contested Seats and the Holding of New Elections," Appendix, 43a, Mississippi Election Contest, 1965–1966, Abernathy Papers, JDWL-UM.

51. First quote, Funchess, interview; second quote, Glass Diary, August 25, 1964; ibid., August 18, 1964; third quote, Wade, interview; fourth quote, Jackson, interview. McGill, interview; Adickes, "Hattiesburg Freedom School," 8.

52. Quoting Shaw, "Recollections." Joseph Ellin Journal, September 1, 1964, Ellin Collection.

53. Quoting Nelson, *Terror in the Night*, 93–94.

54. For evaluations of Freedom Summer, see COFO and SNCC, "Mississippi Summer Freedom Schools Program," n.d.; Staughton Lynd, "Mississippi Freedom Schools: Retrospect and Prospect," July 26, 1964; COFO, *Mississippi Handbook for Political Programs*, n.d., all in SNCC-P, reel 38. See, too, Carson, *In Struggle*, 112–14; Dittmer, *Local People*, 264–65; McAdam, *Freedom Summer*, 116–60; Whitehead, *Attack on Terror*; Chalmers, *Backfire*, 3, 47-59; McMillen, "Street Theater"; *NYT*, July 12, August 20, 1964, *NYT*-AA; "Civil Rights and the Walls Come Tumbling Down," July 17, 1964, *Time* (magazine), online reprints. For Birmingham, see McWhorter, *Carry Me Home*, 365–95.

CHAPTER 5

1. Quoting *HA*, February 13, 1994; Dahmer interview, by Gray, MOHP-D. "Killed by the Klan," prod. and dir. Charles C. Stuart. File vol. 2, #157-5512-180, Pitts-FBI-RBH; Files vol. 9. #44-1512-342, vol. 8 #44-1512-189, DABURN-FBI-RBH.

2. Quoting Adickes, *Freedom School*, 143, ibid., 76, 145-47. Payne, *Light of Freedom*, 330-37; Dittmer *Local People*, 424; ibid., 425-26. *The Convention Challenge and the Freedom Vote*, RMV. Volunteers Remaining in Hattiesburg; Hattiesburg COFO-Very Active, February 24, [1965], SNCC-P, reel 38.

3. "Paper-perceptions on Hattiesburg Movement," n.d., reel 25, CORE-P; Betty Garman to summer volunteer, n.d., Ellin Freedom Summer Collection, ML-USM; Schwartz, interview, by Michaels, MOHP-D. Wade, interview. Hasaan, *Bloody Lowndes*; *Freedom Rights*, ed. Dittmer and McGuire.

4. H. T. Richardson, MBI Case Report: David Gelfand, August 31, 1964, II-10, PBJ. Brief of Contestants, Appendix, 41a-43a, Mississippi Election Contest, 1965-1966, Abernathy Papers, JDWL-UM [hereinafter cited as MFDP Brief]; *The Freedom Voice of the Fifth Congressional District*, 1, no. 13, September 12, 1964, Ellin Freedom Summer Collection, ML-USM.

5. *MFDP Challenge to the Democratic Convention*, CRMV; Dittmer, *Local People*, 320-25.

6. File vol. 2, #157-18-115, Bowers-FBI-RBH. Governor Johnson, press release, October 29, 1964, II-5; Charles E. Snodgrass to A. D. Morgan, November 6, 1964; FBI Press Release, n.d., II-10, PBJ. *CL*, January 23, 2000; for Meadville case, see "Ex-Miss. Sheriff's Deputy Charged in '64 deaths," *MSNBC.com*, January 24, 2007.

7. Quoting Pitts, statement, File vol. 2, #157-5512-239, Pitts-FBI-RBH. *LLC*, November 19, 1964. Claude Ramsay, memo and attached article, Pat Watters, "Workers, White & Black in Mississippi," *Dissent Magazine* 3 (Winter 1972), Mississippi AFL-CIO Records, Southern Labor Archives, Georgia State University, Atlanta.

8. First and second quotes, *CL*, November 20, 1964, Cox Collection, MSU; third quote, *LLC*, November 19, 1964.

9. Quoting File vol. 3, #157-18-282, Bowers-FBI-RBH. Whitehead, *Attack on Terror*, 179-201, 215-16, 258-59. File #44-25706-12, MIBURN-FBI, 1-12.

10. Resolutions Mississippi Sheriffs Association, December 1964, II-10, PBJ. W. F. Minor, "Concern Over State's National 'Image' Noted," *TP*, December 13, 1964, Speers Papers, ML-USM; *LLC*, November 4, 1964. T. B. Birdsong, Commending the Legislature, Paul B. Johnson, and Joe T. Patterson, December 8, 1964 and Snodgrass to Morgan, December 4, 1964, II-10 and J. Y. Thomas, MSSC Report, December 3, 1964, II-9, both in PBJ.

11. *LLC*, November 4, 1964; Governor Johnson, press release, December 16, 1964, II-5, PBJ. *HA*, July 3, December 14, 1964 and February 5, 15, 1965; Drew Pearson, "Rights Loophole Exploited," January 30, 1965, Ben-Ami Papers, ML-USM.

12. Quoting Spinks, interview by Adams, MOHP-D. WATS Reports, December 16, 17, 28, 1964, SNCC-P, reel 15. *LLC*, December 22, 1964. For Swartzfager and his family's various businesses and professional work, see *Laurel City Directory, 1945-1946* and *Laurel City Directory, 1967*, ML-USM.

13. First and second quotes, WATS Report, December 28, 1964; third quote, WATS Report, January 14, 1964, SNCC-P, reel 15. B. E. Murph to Gloster Current, January 13, 1965, 27-A-10; Ruby Hurley to Current, March 19, 1965, 25-B-4, Charles Evers to Hurley, March 3, 1965, 25-D-14, NAACP-P.

14. WATS Reports, January 21, 22, 23, 25, 29, 1964, reel 15, SNCC; Incident Summary, January 28, 1965, reel 39; James Kempfer affidavit, January 26, 1965, Emanuel Logalbo affidavit, January 27, 1965, reel 38, all in SNCC-P. Incident Summary, Hattiesburg, January 21, 1965, CORE-P, reel 23. "Swift Justice," *Delta Ministry Reports*, March 1967, Delta Ministry VF, ML-USM. *HA*, January 20, 22, 1965.

15. *Convention Challenge*; MFDP Congressional Challenge—Fact Sheet, SCLC-P, reel 9; MFDP Brief; *LLC*, February 10, 1865; Dittmer, *Local People*, 338-49; Parker, *Black Votes Count*, 26.

16. Quoting *LLC*, February 12, 1965. MFDP Brief, Appendix, 37a-38a, 40a-45a; WATS Reports, February 8, 10, 1965, SNCC-P, reel 15; *HA*, February 13, 1965.

17. Quoting USCCRLE, *A Report on Equal Protection in the South*, 45-46; ibid., 1-4, 53, 64-65.

18. First and second quotes, *LLC*, February 10, 1965. *LLC*, February 12, 1965; Maurice Danton to William Colmer, February 7, 1965 and Colmer to Judge Darwin Maples, February 22, 1965, both in WCP.

19. J. C. Fairley to Mayor Claude Pittman, February 15, 1965, HMR; *HA*, February 16, 23, 24, 1965. WATS Reports, March 5, 17, 1965, reel 15 and SNCC Incident Summary, Feb 4–March 2, 1965, reel 56, both in SNCC-P. File vol. 1, #157-505-107, Byrd-FBI-RBH. MFDP Brief, Appendix, 41a-43a. MSSC #99-28-0-42-4-1-1.

20. First quote, President Johnson, Address to Congress, March 15, 1965, American Experience, The Presidents, PBS; second quote, *New York Post*, March 29, 1965. Voting Rights Act of 1965, in *Federal Civil Rights Laws: A Sourcebook*, November 1984, 54–71, Ser. 43, JCS. Parker, *Black Votes Count*, 29.

21. *US v. Lynd* (June 16, 1965), 22477, transcript, 13, 5th Cir., USvTL; *HA*, June 9, July 8, 10, 1965; File vol. 3, #157-18-255, Bowers-FBI-RBH.

22. Carter, *Music Has Gone*, Kindle edition.

23. Maycie Gore, interview. Robert Beech, "Report and Evaluation, Hattiesburg," Delta Ministry Project, September 1964–1965, Wakeman Papers, ML-USM; Newman *Divine Agitators*, 59–61. Minutes, Eaton Precinct, April 8, 1965, Community Meeting Library Center, December 1965, Kelly Settlement Center, reel 5; CDGM Registration of Children, Wesley Center, 1965–1966 session, T. D. Brown, unaddressed letter, n.d., reel 4; Area Staff Meeting, Laurel, June 21, 30, 1966, Staff Meeting Area N, August 23, 1966, Council Meeting Minutes, August 2 and 3, September 1, 1966, Reel 7, all in CDGM Records. See, too, Carter, "Fighting for the Child Development Group of Mississippi," *War on Poverty*, ed. Orleck and Hazirjian, 281–303; Payne, *Light of Freedom*, 343. Carter, *Music Has Gone*.

24. Marsh, *God's Long Summer Stories of Faith and Civil Rights*, 71; *LLC*, July 1, 2, 1965; Running Incident Summary for July 1965, SNCC-P, reel 56; *HA*, July 2, 1965; Pickering, interview, *An Oral History of Jones County*, 795.

25. *LLC*, July 3, 1965; File vol. 4, #157-18-393, Bowers-FBI-RBH.

26. *HA*, July 16, 17, November 10, 1965; MBI Case Report, Rosa Lee Coates, July 15, 1965, II-10, PBJ; *Mississippi v. Cannon* (1965) 142/6467, *Docket*, vol. 5, 55, FCCC-H.

27. *HA*, July 16, 17, November 11, 1965; Coates MBI Report; *Mississippi v. Norman Cannon* (1965), *Docket*.

28. Quoting *HA*, November 9, 1965. Ibid., November 9–11, 1965.

29. *HA*, November 11, 1965; *Mississippi v. Cannon* (1965), *Docket*; The Fellowship of the Concerned, Southern Regional Council, "Dual Justice in the Courts—Unconcerned Community," 2–5, 8–11, Cox Collection, Addendum, 1978, MML-MSU.

30. First and second quotes, *Mississippi v. Shinall* (1965), transcript, 712, 765. Ibid., 709–15, 743, 762–66, 829–30. For appearance of Shinall, see *HA*, July 23, 1965.

31. Quoting *Shinall v. Mississippi* (1965), transcript, 831. Ibid., 715–22, 767–71, 830–32.

32. Quoting *Shinall v. Mississippi* (1965), transcript, 727, ibid., 829–32; 787–814; 726–27. For the rape of Shinall's lover, see Adickes, *Freedom School*, 148–49. For general white perception of killing, see *HA*, March 29, 30, July 14, 1965.

33. Quoting Easton and Preyor, interview.

34. *Shinall v. Mississippi* (1965), transcript, 57. Ibid., 55–65.

35. First and second quotes, *HA*, March 30, 1965; third quote, *Shinall v. Mississippi* (1965), transcript, 76. Ibid., 74–79, 100–13, 785–860. *HA*, March 29, July 14, 1965; *Mississippi v. Shinall* (1965), 141/6434, *Docket*, vol. 5, 44, 89, FCCC-H; Appellant's Brief, January 17, 1966, 18–28, *Shinall v. Mississippi* (1965).

36. Elliot Chaze, *HA*, July 19, July 20, 21, 1965; Appellant's Brief (1965), 3, 11–17, 34-35, *Shinall v. Mississippi* (1965), transcript, 519–20. For the manner in which attorneys address witnesses, see *Shi-*

nall v. Mississippi (1965), transcript, 50, 59, 64, 70, 71, 80, 82, 91, 93, 100, 103, 105, 108, 568, 601, 604, 615, 617, 649, 658, 664, 673, 678, 690, 695, 728, 756, 774, 794, 798, 804, 810, 837–39, 841. For racial etiquette in Mississippi, see McMillen, *Dark Journey*, 23–24.

37. *Shinall v. Mississippi* (1965), transcript, 568–781, 816–23.

38. *Shinall v. Mississippi* (1965), transcript, 678–93, 695–781, 787–815.

39. Quoting *Shinall v. Mississippi* (1965), transcript, 831. Ibid., 825–60, 863; *HA*, July 23, 1965.

40. Appellant's Brief, *Shinall v. Mississippi* (1965), 2–3, 11–28, 31, 40–43. For MSC decision, see *Shinall v. Mississippi* (1966), 43866, 187 So. 2d 840.

41. First quote, *Mississippi v. Shinall* (1966), 6570, transcript, 491, in MSC Record (1967), 44,352, MDAH; second quote, ibid., 509; ibid., 3, 438–44, 504–12; third quote, Scarborough, interview.

42. *Shinall v. Mississippi* (1966), transcript, 1180–1319; ibid., 766–69, 773–74, 796–806, 1180–88, 1306–19.

43. Scarborough, interview. For the verdict, sentence, and appeal, see *Shinall v. Mississippi* (1966), transcript, 1356–63. For systematic exclusion of black jurors, see ibid., 492. For many other appeals, see *Shinall v. Mississippi*, May 15, 1967, 44352, 199 So. 2d 251; *Shinall v. Mississippi*, 389 US 1014, S. Ct. 590; 18 L. Ed. 2d 660; 1967 US *Shinall v. Mississippi*, January 29, 1968, 44352, 206 So. 2d 332; 1968 Miss. *Shinall v. Breazeale*, 404 F. 2d 785; 1968 US App. For the final sentence of Shinall, see *HA*, August 6, 1971. For the release of Shinall, see Adickes, *Freedom School*, 149.

44. *Shinall v. Mississippi* (1965), 43,866, *Shinall v. Mississippi* (1966), transcript. Appellant's Brief, *Shinall v. Mississippi* (1966). For provocation defenses, see *Ex Parte Fraley*, Oklahoma Criminal Court of Appeals, 109 P. 295 (1910).

45. Quoting "Dual Justice in the Courts—Unconcerned Community," 4–5; ibid., 2–3, 8–11, Cox Collection, Addendum, 1978. *A Report on Equal Protection in the South*, 182. Ibid., 183–88..

46. Statement Opposing Confirmation of Governor J. P. Coleman, n.d., Leadership Conference on Civil Rights, Ser. 16, Reel 41; Statement of Victoria Gray on Behalf of the Executive Committee, MFDP, June 29, 1965; "James P. Coleman, Profile of a Man in the News," *Southern Reporting Service*, Bills Signed Into Law by Governor Coleman, all in SNCC-P, reel 41. Parker, *Black Votes Count*, 82–85.

47. John Perdew, "How The Civil Rights Bill Is Being Subverted In Mississippi," August 4, 1965, SNCC, reel 41; Voting Rights Act of 1965, in *Federal Civil Rights Laws*, 54–71, ser. 43, JCS; *LLC*, August 12, 23, 1965; *HA*, August 11, 14, 18, 1965; Parker, *Black Votes Count*, 29–30.

48. Quoting "Dismissing the Five Mississippi Election Contests," H.R. Report No. 1008, 89th Congress, 1st Session, September 15, 1965, 4; ibid., 1–3, 5–6 and Subcommittee on Elections, House, Contested Elections in the First, Second, Third, Fourth, Fifth Districts of the State of Mississippi, September 13 and 14, 1965, 33, 49–51, Election Contest, Abernathy Collection; McMillen, "Black Enfranchisement in Mississippi," *Journal of Southern History*, 369–72.

49. Redlich, "Toward Equal Representation," 41–43. *Connor v. Finch*, 3830(A) S. D. Miss., 419 F. Supp. 1072; 1976 US Dist. See, too, Parker, *Black Votes Count*, 61–63, 85–129; 199–205; Danielson, *After Freedom Summer*, 118–23; Nash and Taggart, *Mississippi Politics*, 104–10; Percy W. Watson, Mississippi House of Representative, Mississippi State Legislature, http://billstatus.ls.state.ms.us/members/house/watson.xml.

50. Quoting Maycie Gore, interview; Adickes, *Freedom School*, 151–52. Beech, "Report and Evaluation, Hattiesburg"; Carter, *Music Has Gone*; Branch, interview by Adams, MOHP-D; Hattiesburg COFO—Very Active; Newman *Divine Agitators*, 60; *HA*, October 1, 1965. For problems in the HPD, see *Eaton v. Hattiesburg* (1972), no. 724–30, HMR and Wade, interview. Roy K. Moore to Paul B. Johnson, September 23, 1965, and attachment, II-9, PBJ.

51. File vol. 1, #157-505-107, Byrd-FBI-RBH; File vol. 1, #44-1512-4, Pitts-FBI-RBH; Files vol. 1, #157-5183-1, #157-5183-60, Martin-FBI-RBH. NAACP News Release, September 25, 1965, 20-1,

NAACP-P; *LLC*, September 15, October 11, 1965; Nicholas Von Hoffman, "FBI Digs into Klan Secrets in Grim Mississippi Struggle," *CA*, September 14, 1964, II-9, PBJ.

52. Pickering, interview, 785, 787, 790–91, 794–98; Schardt, "A Mississippi Mayor Fights the Klan." *LLC*, October 15, 16, 1965.

53. Quoting *HA*, October 19, 1965. Schardt, "A Mississippi Mayor Fights the Klan," 39–40; *LLC*, October 19, 20, 25, 28, 1965.

54. Quoting *LLC*, October 22, 1965. *LLC*, October 22, 29, 30, 1965. Schardt, "A Mississippi Mayor Fights the Klan," 39–40; "Killed by the Klan"; Pickering, interview, 795. HUAC, *The Present Day Ku Klux Klan Movement Report*, Pt. 2, 153–54.

55. Hurley, 1965 NAACP Annual Report Southeast Region, 29-A-16, NAACP-P; *A Report on Equal Protection in the South*, 97–98, 172–73, 177–87; File vol. 1, #157-854-67, Sessum-FBI-RBH.

56. Fielders, interview, by McMillen, vol. 483, 27, MOHP. Files vol. 30, #44-1512-2579, #44-1512-2576; vol. 8, #44-1512-188, #44-1512-189, DABURN-FBI-RBH. WATS Report, December 19, 1965, SNCC, reel 38; James K. Dukes, interview.

57. First quote, *Mississippi v. Bowers* (1998), 6922, vol. 3, FCCC-H; second quote, File vol. 8, #44-1512-188, DABURN-FBI-RBH. Pitts, written confession and Pitts, typed confession, Pitts Notebook, RBH. Mordaunt William Hamilton Sr., 205–16, Supplemental Investigation Neighborhood of Dahmer Home, DABURN-FBI-RBH, 44-1512-[?]. Marsh, *God's Long Summer*, 71; *HA*, May 10, 1969, February 13, 1994; *Killed by the Klan*; J. C. Fairley, interview by Garvey, 54–55.

58. *HA*, February 13, 1994; *LLC*, January 10, 1966; Whitehead, *Attack on Terror*, 235. Pitts, written confession; Pitts, typed confession. *Killed by the Klan*.

59. Whitehead, *Attack on Terror*, 235–36. Pitts, written confession; Pitts, typed confession.

60. Quoting *HA*, February 13, 1994; Ellie Dahmer, interview; *Killed by the Klan*. Files vol. 9. #44-1512-342, #44-1512-373, DABURN-FBI-RBH.

61. First and second quotes, *Killed by the Klan*; third and fourth quotes, Whitehead, *Attack on Terror*, 236. Pitts, typed confession. *HA*, February 13, 1994; Ellie Dahmer, interview; Files vol. 9. #44-1512-342, #44-1512-373, DABURN-FBI-RBH.

62. Quoting *Killed by the Klan*. File vol. 9, # 44-1512-349, DABURN-FBI-RBH.

63. First quote, *CL*, January 11, 1966; second quote, *HA*, February 13, 1994. *Killed by the Klan*. *HA*, January 14, 1966; File vol. 9, #44-1512-373, DABURN FBI-RBH.

64. *HA*, March 13, 1994, January 13, 1966; *Killed by the Klan*; Dahmer Jr., interview, by Gray.

CHAPTER 6

1. Quoting Pitts, typed confession, 9; ibid, 7–8; Pitts, written confession, 13–14, Pitts Notebook, RBH.

2. First and second quotes, Pitts, written confession; third quote, Pitts, typed confession; fourth quote, Helfrich, speech, "Pursuing a Late Justice," August 29, 2000, videocassette, ML-USM. Dukes, speech, "Pursuing a Late Justice." File vol. 2, #157-854-82, File vol. 1, #157-854-67, Sessum-FBI-RBH; for Pitts appearance, see File vol. 1, #157-5512-19, Pitts-FBI-RBH.

3. First quote, Roy Wilkins to [?], January 11, 1966, 29-B-11, NAACP-P; second quote, Lawrence Guyot to Governor Paul Johnson, January 10, 1966, II-9, PBJ; third quote, Branch, interview by Adams, vol. 682, 8, MOHP; Roy Wilkins to Nicholas Katzenbach, January 10, 1966, 29-B-11, NAACP-P.

4. First quote, Nelson, *Terror in the Night*, 29, ibid., 72; second quote, *Local People*, 391. President Johnson to Ellie Dahmer, January 11, 1966, VFD; Whitehead, *Attack on Terror*, 238; *CL*, January 11, 1966; *Killed by the Klan*.

5. First and second quotes, Governor Johnson, press release, January 11, 1966, II-5, PBJ; last quote, Billy McGee, interview; all other quotes, *HA*, January 11, 27, 1966. MHP Reports, January 10, 1966–

September 18, 1967, PBJ; President of Forrest County Board of Supervisors and Mayor Paul Grady, press release, January 10, 1966, HMR; *CL*, January 11, 1966; *HA*, January 8, 11, 1966; Hattiesburg Area Chamber of Commerce Meeting Minutes, January 12, 1966, HACCR; Ellie Dahmer, interview by Caudill, MOHP-D.

6. Whitehead, *Attack on Terror*, 237–38; T. B. Birdsong to A. D. Morgan, January 11, 1966, PBJ; Charles E. Snodgrass to Sam Ivy, January 11, 1966, II-10, PBJ. Files vol. 9 #44-1512-1, #44-152-8, #44-1512-294, DABURN-FBI-RBH. "Killed by the Klan"; Nelson, *Terror in the Night*, 29, 72. *HA*, January 11, 12, 1966, January 6, 1991.

7. Quoting File vol. 2, #44-1512-126. Files vol. 32, #44-1512-2658, vol. 9, # 44-1512-331, #44-1512-327, #44-1512-132, #44-1512-294, #44-1512-332, #44-1512-35, vol. 8, #44-1512-246, #44-1512-230, #44-1512-231, #44-1512-225 and Giles Investigation, February 7, 8, 17, 1966, 161, 164-65, 170-171, 181-182, all in Supplemental Investigation Neighborhood of Dahmer Home, DABURN-FBI-RBH. Files vol. 1, #157-433, 39-48, #157-433-[?], 202, #157-433-35, 8, DeBoxtel-FBI-RBH. Snodgrass to Morgan, January 11, 1966 and MDPS Report, January 11, 1966, II-10, both in PBJ; Whitehead, *Attack on Terror*, 238–39.

8. File vol. 1, #157-854-67, Sessum-FBI-RBH; File vol. 46, #44-1512-4058, DABURN-FBI-RBH; Trial Notes, Revolver, Oversize Materials, RBH.

9. First quote, Wade, interview; second quote, Dahmer Memorial Program, January 15, 1966, VFD; third quote, *HA*, January 11, 1966; fourth quote, *NYT*, January 11, 1966, VFD. Snodgrass to Birdsong and Morgan, January 11, 1966, II-10, PBJ; *CL*, January 11, 1966.

10. Quoting *LLC*, January 12, 1966. *HA*, January 11, 12, 1966. Dahmer Memorial Program; Snodgrass to Birdsong and Morgan, January 11, 1966, II-10, PBJ; *NYT*, January 11, 1966, VFD; *CL*, January 11, 1966. Wade, interview, by author.

11. First quote, *HA*, January 14, 1966; second quote, *HA*, March 13, 1994; Ellie Dahmer, interview. *LLC*, January 17, 1966; Jeanette Smith, interview; Nix, interview, by Rowe, MOHP-D. E. F. Ray to Morgan, MDPS Report, January 13, 1966; MSSC #2-64-1-94-1-1-1, #10-28-0-32-1-1-1; #6-36-0-55-1-1-1; #2-64-1-94-1-1-1. *HA*, January 13, 1966.

12. Quoting Spinks, interview, MOHP-D. Austin, interview, MOHP recording; Jackson and Preyor, interview.

13. First and second and quotes, *HA*, January 11, 1966; third quote, *HA*, January 5, 1966; fourth quote *HA*, January 15, 1966. Fifth quote, *HA*, January 22, 1966. WBKH Editorial, January 14, 1966, HMR. Sixth quote, *HA*, February 2, 1966.

14. Ellie Dahmer, speech, Symposium on Civil Rights in Hattiesburg, recording, ML-USM; "Swift Justice," *Delta Ministry Reports*, March 1967, Delta Ministry VF, ML-USM. Wakeman, "Journey to Mississippi," transcript. Wakeman to Friends, June 25, 1966, July 8, 1966, Wakeman Papers, ML-USM; *HA*, January 11, 1966. McAdam, *Freedom Summer*, 257–82. For examples of police brutality, see, *Eaton v. Hattiesburg* (1972), 724–30, HMR.

15. MSSC, #10-28-0-32-1-1-1; #6-36-0-55-1-1-1. Snodgrass to Birdsong, Morgan, January 17, 1966, II-10, PBJ; *HA*, January 14, 1966; *LLC*, January, 17, 1966; *TP*, January 16, 1966.

16. Quoting *TP*, January 16, 1966. Snodgrass to Birdsong, Morgan, January 17, 1966, II-10, PBJ; *HA*, January 14, 1966; *LLC*, January, 17, 1966.

17. MSSC # 2-64-1-94-1-1-1. MDPS Memos and Reports II-10, PBJ; *HA*, January 17, 1966; Snodgrass to Birdsong and Morgan, attached reports January 18, 20, 21, 25, 1966, II-10, PBJ; Ken Dean to Mayor Grady, February 1, 1966, HMR; Newman, *Divine Agitators*, 63.

18. Files vol. 2, #44-1512-126, vol. 1, #44-1512-20, DABURN-FBI-RBH; File Byrd-FBI-RBH, vol. 1, #157-505-128. Nelson, *Terror in the Night*, 29, 72, 85–95; *Killed by the Klan*; Marsh, *God's Long Summer*, 71–72.

19. Quoting File vol. 1, #157-5183-60, Martin-FBI-RBH. Files vol. 2, #44-1512-126, vol. 11, #44-1512-508, vol. 10, #44-1512-412; vol. 1, #44-1512-20, DABURN-FBI-RBH. File vol. 5, #157-18-609, Bowers-

FBI-RBH. File #s44-31694-231 and -589, in Sealed Federal Documents, *State v. Noble*; Pitts, written confession; Summary of Dahmer Incident, HSF, RBH.

20. Quoting Dukes, interview by Caudill, MOHP-D. Nelson, *Terror in the Night*, 89, 92; ibid., 93–94. *HA*, January 6, 1991, February 11, 1990, VFD.

21. Quoting "You—And the F.BI. Lawyers Advise Citizens of Rights," Dukes Papers. Hamilton, interview by Caudill, 20–26, 31–32, MOHP. File Martin FBI-RBH, vol. 3, #157-5183-173. Richard Corrigan, "Wizard Refuses to Say If Klansmen Took Lives," *Washington Post*, February 2, 1966, vol. 4, #157-18-119, Bowers-FBI-RBH. *Mississippi v. Bowers* (1998), 6922, vol. 3, transcript, FCCC-H; US House, *Activities of Ku Klux Klan Organizations in the United States Part 4*, 2904–2908. For Hamilton, see Reports, vol. 24, #44-1512-1099 through 003; vol. 31, #44-1512-[?], 72,169, #44-1512-[?], 169; Hamilton Sr. summary of investigation, 205–216, Supplemental Investigation Neighborhood of Dahmer Home, 44-1512-[?]; Files vol. 1, #44-1512-29, # 44-1512-33A. For refusal of Klansmen to speak with agents, see Files vol. 3, #44-1512-132, 593, vol. 26, #44-1512-2020; vol. 3, #44-1512-132, 636–38, 644–47, 657–60, 696–97, 705–709; vol. 8, #44-1512-218, #44-1512-230; vol. 42, 44-1512-3492, all in DABURN FBI-RBH. See, too, Files vol. 1, #157-4387-10, #157-4387-5, Lowe-FBI-RBH. File vol. 1, #157-4361-10, #157-4361-26, Thornton-FBI-RBH; File vol. 1, #157-5512-18, #157-5512-8, #157-5512-10, Pitts-FBI-RBH.

22. First quote Whitehead, *Attack on Terror*, 241. Second quote, File vol. 1, #157-3484-55; third quote, File vol. 1, #157-3484-9. Files vol. 5, #157-3484-431, vol. 1, #157-3484-55-56, #157-3484-65, NIX FBI-RBH. Arrest of Deavours Nix, MBI Case Report, February 15, 1966; and Snodgrass to Birdsong and Morgan, February 17, 1966, II-10, PBJ. *CL*, February 17, 1966.

23. Quoting File vol. 20, #44-1512-2481; Files vol. 3, # 44-1512-132, 644-653, both in DABURN-FBI-RBH. Files vol. 1, #157-5183-12, #157-5183-35, #157-5183-60, #157-5183-78, #157-5183-5, #157-5183-6, #157-5183-22, #157-5183-3 #157-5183-45, #157-5183-60, Martin-FBI-RBH. File vol. 1, #157-433-[?], DeBoxtel-FBI-RBH.

24. File vol. 1, #157-854-67, Sessum-FBI-RBH. Files vol. 1, #157-505-142, #157-505-97, #157-505-205, #157-505-90; vol. 2, #157-505-252; Byrd Statement, vol. 1, #157-505-161, all in Byrd-FBI-RBH. File vol. 4, #157-18-432, Bowers-FBI-RBH. *HA*, March 23, 28, 1967.

25. First quote, File vol. 1, #157-3565-39, Moss-FBI-RBH; second quote, File vol. 1, #157-433-35, 24, ibid., 28–29, DeBoxtel-FBI-RBH; third quote, File vol. 1 #157-854-67, Sessum-FBI-RBH. File vol. 4, #157-18-432, Bowers-FBI-RBH. Files vol. 1, #157-433-35, #157-433-18; #157-433-16, #157-433-52, DeBoxtel-FBI-RBH. File vol. 1, #157-505-126, Byrd-FBI-RBH. Files vol. 26, #44-1512-2020, vol. 28, #44-1512-2280, DABURN-FBI-RBH.

26. Files vol. 1, #157-854-67, vol. 2, #157-854-84, Sessum-FBI-RBH. File vol. 8, #44-1512-145, DABURN-FBI-RBH.

27. First and second quotes, Sessum affidavit, Dukes Collection; third and fourth quotes, File vol. 1, #157-3484-9, Nix FBI-RBH; fifth quote, File vol. 2, # 157-3484-121, vol. 1, #157-3484-91, Nix FBI-RBH.

28. Quoting File vol. 1, #157-505-159, Byrd-FBI-RBH. File vol. 1, #157-433-52, #157-433-60, #157-433-65, #157-433-53, DeBoxtel-FBI-RBH. File vol. 1, #157-505-127, #157-505-139; #157-505-150, #157-505-152, #157-505-155, #157-505-158, #157-505-151, Byrd-FBI-RBH. File vol. 4, #157-18-440A, Bowers-FBI-RBH. Files vol. 1, #157-3565-59, #157-3565-61, Moss-FBI-RBH.

29. Quoting Title 18, USC Section 241, Voting Rights Act of 1965, Pub. L. No. 89-110, 79 Stat. 437 (1965). *HA*, March 28, 1966. Files vol. 7, #44-31694-202, #44-31694-262, FBI-RBH. Files vol. 4, #157-18-482, #157-18-459, Bowers-FBI-RBH. Correspondence Snodgrass, Birdsong, Morgan, March 30, 31, April 4, 1966, II-10, PBJ. *Harper v. Virginia* (1966).

30. Quoting File vol. 5, #157-18-609, Bowers-FBI-RBH. File, 42, #44-1512-3487, DABURN-FBI-RBH. *MS*, March 27, 1968. *Harper v. Virginia*.

31. File vol. 6, #157-18-786, Bowers-FBI-RBH; *Mississippi v. Bucklew* (1966), 2884, *Docket*, vol. 23, 109–10, 395–96, JCCC-L. *LLC*, April 20, 1966, October 20, 1966; *HA*, August 7, 1967.

32. File vol. 6, #157-18-786, vol. 7, #157-18-1009, vol. 3, #157-18-255, vol. 5, #157-18-609, Bowers-FBI-RBH. File vol. 4, #157-854-319, Sessum-FBI-RBH. File vol. 1, #157-433-65, 1, #157-433-63a & 63, DeBoxtel-FBI-RBH. File vol. 1, #157-3565-46, Moss-FBI-RBH; Elmore Greaves, press release, White Christian Protective and Legal Defense Fund, January 28, 1965, Cox Papers, MML-MSU.

33. Quoting File, August 27, 1965, vol. 3, #157-18-282, Bowers-FBI-RBH. File vol. 2, #157-3484-205, Nix-FBI-RBH; File vol. 36, #44-1512-3023, vol. 4, #157-854-319, DABURN-FBI-RBH. Files vol. 7, #157-18-1009, #157-18-1011, Bowers-FBI-RBH; File vol. 2, #157-854-185, Sessum-FBI-RBH.

34. Files vol. 5, #157-18-609, vol. 6, #157-18-786, Bowers FBI-RBH. For use of the cell structures by terrorists decades after Bowers used them, see Laquer, *The New Terrorism*.

35. Quoting Dittmer, *Local People*, 396–97; ibid., 389–402; Carson, *In Struggle*, 207–11; Fairclough, *To Redeem the Soul of America*, 318–22.

36. Fairclough, *To Redeem the Soul of America*, 254–56, 318–22, 382–83; Carson, *In Struggle*, 210–11, 215–28; Dittmer, *Local People*, 396–402; Payne, *Light of Freedom*, 398. O'Reilly, "The FBI and the Politics of the Riots, 1964–1968," 91–114, Timothy B. Tyson, *Radio Free Dixie*. For debates on black power, see the aforementioned historians. Although blacks have always understood the need for power in a white supremacist system and have used a variety of strategies and tactics including passive resistance, self-defense, and violence to achieve that power, the various interpretations of that concept reached a critical debate and shaped new conflicts and trajectories in the movement after Carmichael evoked it in Greenwood.

37. Quoting *HA*, June 22, 1966. Dittmer, *Local People*, 363–88. Governor Johnson, press release, October 10, 1966; Statement by Governor Johnson before the Senate Judiciary Committee, n.d., II-5, PBJ. Danielson, *After Freedom Summer*, 35. Carter, *Music Has Gone*; Dittmer, *Local People*, 363–88.

38. "Swift Justice," *Delta Ministry Reports*. Wakeman correspondence, June 23, 25, July 8, 1966, Wakeman, "Journey to Mississippi"; File vol. 36, #44-1512-3023, DABURN-FBI-RBH; File vol. 2, #157-3484-172, Nix-FBI-RBH. Hurley, Annual Report 1966. Hill, *Deacons for Defense*, for the Deacons in Hattiesburg, see 207.

39. First quote, Pinky Hall, "Progress Report from Hattiesburg: Eaton Center," *CDGM Newsletter*, 3, n.d. reel 13; all other quotes, "Evaluation of Children in Unit IX," reel 4; Council Meeting, August 3, 1966, reel 7; reports on various Forrest County precincts, reel 5, all in CDGM records. Hurley, Annual Report 1966 Southeast Region, 29-A-17, NAACP-P. Wakeman, "Journey to Mississippi," transcript; Wakeman correspondence, June 25, July 8, 1966, both in Wakeman Papers. Dittmer, *Local People*, 363–88; Gore, interview.

40. First quote, Carter, *Music Has Gone*. Second quote, testimony, 90th Congress, 1st Session, *Examination of the War on Poverty Hearings*, Pt. 2, 584; third quote, ibid., 867; ibid., 582–84, 676–84. Fourth quote, Payne, *Light of Freedom*, 348; ibid., 343–47. "OEO grants $5 Million to Fund CDGM Work," *CL*, January 31, 1967, reel 14, David Emmons correspondence, September 30, 1966, reel 9 and History of the Last Fight for a Grant, n.d., CDGM records, reel 8. Dittmer, *Local People*, 363–88. Danielson, *After Freedom Summer*, 35. Carter, "Fighting for the Child Development Group of Mississippi," *War on Poverty*, ed. Orleck and Hazirjian, 301–302.

41. Files vol. 5, #157-18-609, vol. 6, #157-18-786, Bowers-FBI-RBH. Bolton, *Hardest Deal*, 117–40; Hurley, 1965 NAACP Annual Report. *HA*, September 2, 1965; Robert Beech, "Report and Evaluation, Hattiesburg," Delta Ministry Project, September 1964–1965, Wakeman Papers.

42. First quote in both Gore and Bunch interviews. All other quotes Funchess, interview. Harris, "A Personal Account."

43. Kenneth Fairley, interview, May 8, 2009.

44. File vol. 2, #157-854-185, Sessum-FBI-RBH. File vol. 4, #157-854-319, DABURN-FBI-RBH. Files vol. 5, #157-18-609, vol. 6, #157-18-786, #157-18-78, Bowers-FBI-RBH. File #157-5385-35 in *State v. Noble*, RBH. File vol. 1, #157-505-207, Byrd-FBI-RBH; File vol. 1, #157-4361-61, Thornton-FBI-RBH; File vol. 2, #157-3484-205, Nix-FBI-RBH.

45. Ivy to Snodgrass, March 13, 1967; MBI Case Report, March 13, 1967, II-10, PBJ. Files vol. 3, #157-18-255, vol. 8, #157-18-1152, vol. 6, #157-18-786, vol. 7, #158-18-1009, Bowers-FBI-RBH. File vol. 1, #157-4361-96, Thornton-FBI-RBH; Nelson, *Terror in the Night*, 12, 46.

46. Quoting Whitehead, *Attack on Terror*, 252. Ibid., 253–56. File vol. 1, #157-4361-96, Thornton-FBI-RBH. Files vol. 2, #157-505-212, #157-505-252, vol. 1, #157-505-678, Byrd-FBI-RBH. File vol. 2, #157-5183-95, Martin-FBI-RBH. Files vol. 5, #157-18-609, vol. 7, #157-18-1011, Bowers-FBI-RBH. File vol. 39, #44-1512-3291, DABURN-FBI-RBH. Jack Watkins statement and *Sam Holloway Bowers Jr.* report attached to vol. 1, #157-5512-89, Pitts-FBI-RBH. *HA*, March 10, 23, 28, 1967; *LLC*, November 10, 1967.

47. File vol. 2, #157-3484-121, Nix FBI-RBH. File vol. 2, #157-505-252, Byrd-FBI-RBH. File vol. 2, #157-854-137, Sessum-FBI-RBH. *HA*, March 10, 23, 28, 1967.

48. Quoting *The Biloxi-Gulfport Daily Herald*, March 29, 1967, vol. 2, #157-5512-126, Pitts-FBI-RBH. File vol. 2, #157-5183-144, Martin-FBI-RBH; File vol. 48, #44-1512-4179, FBI-RBH. MHP Report, Travis Buckley Case (1967), 25-2496, Pascagoula, Jackson County, II-10, PBJ; *HA*, March 29, 1967.

49. First quote, *The Daily Herald*, April 10, 1967, vol. 2, #157-5512-109; File vol. 2, #157-5512-117, #157-5512-118, both in Pitts-FBI-RBH. All other quotes, *Nix v. Gray, Neil, and Thomas* (1967), 2102, Gray Papers, ML-USM. File vol. 3, #157-3484-242, Nix-FBI-RBH; File vol. 2, #157-5183-146, Martin-FBI-RBH.

50. Quoting File vol. 1, #157-6389-33; Files vol. 1, #157-6389-18, #157-6389-28, vol. 3, #157-854-258 to 260, all in Rogers-FBI-RBH. Snodgrass to Birdsong and Morgan, March 30, 1967, II-10, PBJ; *Mississippi v. Carr, White, and Sessum* (1967–1970), 1502, 1510, Docket, vol. 3, 76, Covington County Circuit Court, Collins, Mississippi.

51. Quoting *HA*, March 23, 1967. Pickering, interview, *An Oral History of Jones County*, 792, 796, 800.

52. Snodgrass to Birdsong and Morgan, April 24, May 22, May 31, and June 14, 1967; in II-10, PBJ. Files vol. 6, #157-18-78[?], vol. 7, #157-18-1009, Bowers-FBI-RBH. *LLC*, April 22–26, May 2, 5, 11, 20; June 20–23, 27, 28, July 2, 11, 12, 15, 17, 18, 1967, August 9, 1967; Gore, interview. Pickering, interview, 792, 796, 800; Marsh, *Last Days*, 135–36.

53. Quoting *LLC*, August 11, 1967. *LLC*, May 31, June 29, July 11 12, 15, 25, August 1, 12, 1967; Snodgrass to Birdsong and Morgan, May 31, 1967, II-10, all in PBJ; File vol. 6, #157-18-78[?], Bowers-FBI-RBH; "MFDP Looks at Laurel Strike," *Mississippi Freedom Democratic Party News Letter*, 3 (November 27, 1967): 3, Adams Collection.

54. *LLC*, June 11, 1969. *LLC*, June 12, 1969, August 14, 16, 1967.

55. Quoting *LLC*, August 14; *LLC*, August 16, 21, September 9, 18, 21, 1967. *Mississippi v. Stockman* (1967) 3054/3055, Docket, vol. 5, 471-472, FCCC-L; Files vol. 7, #157-18-1011, vol. 6, #157-18-786, Bowers-FBI-RBH. Nelson, *Terror in the Night*, 29–49, 64.

56. Quoting McGill, interview. *LLC*, May 29, 1967; Johnny Magee, interview; Snodgrass to Birdsong and Morgan, May 29, 1967, II-10, PBJ.

57. McGill, interview; *LLC*, May 29, 1967; Snodgrass to Birdsong and Morgan, May 29, 1967, II-10, PBJ. File vol. 2, #157-854-185, Sessum-FBI-RBH; File vol. 2, #157-5183-135, Martin-FBI-RBH.

58. Quoting McGill, interview, Payne, *Light of Freedom*, 360–79.

59. Quoting City of Hattiesburg, Forrest County Board of Supervisors, and Chamber of Commerce to Dr. C. E. Smith, July 17, 1967, HMR. Forrest County NAACP to Mayor, Hattiesburg and For-

rest County Officials, and the Chamber of Commerce, n.d., HMR; Nix, interview; Wade, interview; Newman, *Divine Agitators*, 64-65.

60. *HA*, July 19-21, August 7, 1967; Chief Herring, statement, July 24, 1967, HMR. Leland Cole, MSSC Reports, July 19, 27, 1967, II-9, PBJ.

61. Quoting *HA*, July 20, 1967. *HA*, July 19-21, 25, 27, 1967; Cole, Boycott Hattiesburg, MSSC Report, July 27, 1967, LF; Wade, interview. Nix, interview.

62. Killingsworth, MSSC file, MDAH; Quinn, interview by Henderson, Nix, interview, MOHP-D. Funchess, Douglass Baker, Denard-Delgado, Naylor, Jackson, Jeanette Smith, Easton and Preyor, interviews. MSSC # 2-112-2-17-1-1-1; # 2-64-1-113-1-1-1; #2-165-6-44-5-1-1; *HA*, July 20-22, 24, August 17, 1967; Correspondence Steve Henderson to Morgan, July 31-September 18, 1967, II-10, PBJ.

63. First quote, *HA*, July 27, 1967; second quote, *HA*, July 28, 1967; third quote, *HA*, July 29, 1967. *HA*, July 31, 1967; Mayor Grady and Chief Herring, statement on shooting of Charles Magee, n.d., HMR.

64. Quoting *Smith v. Grady* (1967), 2206, 7, HMR; ibid., 1-8; *HA*, July 24-25, August 24, 1967; Henderson to Morgan, August 31, 1967, II-10, PBJ.

65. *HA*, July 24, 25, 31, August 9, 25, 1967; Henderson to Morgan, July 31-September 18, 1967, II-10, PBJ. Jeanette Smith, interview; Earline Boyd, interview, MOHP-D.

66. *HA*, September 8, 1967; Wade, interview by author and McGuire, June 5, 2006; Jeanette Smith, interview; Adickes, *Freedom School*, 153.

67. First quote, *HA*, August 3, 1967; second quote, *LLC*, June 20, 1967, vol. 3, #157-3484-271, Nix-FBI-RBH. File vol. 5, #157-3484-455, Nix-FBI-RBH. Files vol. 7, #157-18-1011, #157-18-1009, Bowers-FBI-RBH. *HA*, 4, 7, 9, 1967; *LLC*, August 7, 9, 11, 1967. William Waller, "Attacks Klan as 'Hooded Cowards,'" speech, Laurel Rotary Club, April 25, 1967, RG 27, Governors' Papers, MDAH; The Waller Story, campaign material 1967, Mississippi Republican Party Records and Campaign Literature, Waller Collection, MML-MSU.

68. Quoting Victoria Gray, "Black Politics in Mississippi," speech, September 2, 1967; "Mississippi Delegation Position Paper," National Conference for New Politics Convention, August 29-September 4, Chicago, Adams Papers, ML-USM. *LLC*, August 7, 1967.

69. *LLC*, August 9-12, 30, 1967; *HA*, August 9-10, 1967; File vol. 5, #157-2482-455, Nix-FBI-RBH. William Winter, January 16, 1968, *Mississippi Senate Journal* (Jackson 1968), 38; ibid., 35-39. State of Mississippi General Election Returns, November 7, 1967, Gandy Papers, ML-USM; *LLC*, November 8, 1967.

70. File vol. 39, # 44-1512-3291, DABURN-FBI-RBH; File vol. 7, #157-18-1011, vol. 6, #157-18-786, Bowers-FBI-RBH; Notes FBI Files, Dennis and White Notebook, RBH. *LLC*, March 14, 1968; *Killed by the Klan;* Whitehead, *Attack on Terror*, 252-54.

CHAPTER 7

1. Pitts, written confession and typed confessions, Pitts Notebook, RBH. "Killed by the Klan," prod. and dir. Charles C. Stuart.

2. Whitehead, *Attack on Terror*, 179-201. Pitts, written and typed confessions, Pitts Notebook, RBH. File vol. 39, #44-1512-3291, DABURN-FBI-RBH. Notes FBI File, Dennis and White Notebook, RBH.

3. Quoting, File #44-31694-231 and -589, Sealed Federal Documents, *State v. Noble*, RBH. File vol. 2, #157-505-126, Byrd-FBI-RBH. File vol. 1, #157-854-67, Sessum-FBI-RBH. Files vol. 23, #44-1512-1083, vol. 40, #44-1512-3327, FBI-DABURN-RBH. File vol. 7, #157-18-1099, Bowers-FBI-RBH. Files vol. 2, #157-4387-116, #157-4387-18, Lowe-FBI-RBH.

4. Pitts, statement, Watkins Investigation, vol. 39, #44-1512-3291, DABURN-FBI-RBH; File vol. 2,

#157-5512-177, Pitts-FBI-RBH. *Mississippi v. Mosley* (1967), 3062, *Minutes*, vol. 24, 31, JCCC-L; Pickering, interview, *An Oral History of Jones County*, 791–94. *US v. Price* (1967), 5291, N.D. Miss, transcript.

5. *US v. Price* (1967); Mars, with Eden, *Witness in Philadelphia*, 250. *LLC*, December 30, 1967, vol. 6, #157-18-904; File vol. 7, #157-18-1099, Bowers-FBI-RBH. Whitehead, *Attack on Terror*, 260–84; Nelson, *Terror in the Night*, 65–69.

6. Files vol. 2, #157-5512-188, #157-5512-176, #157-5512-181, Pitts-FBI-RBH. File vol. 7, #157-18-1099, Bowers-FBI-RBH; Nelson, *Terror in the Night*, 50, 65–70; Marsh, *Last Days*, 134–35; *LLC*, November 9, 10, 13, 15, 21, 22, 1967; *CL*, November 10, 1967; MSSC #99-59-0-14-1-1-1.

7. First quote, Marsh, *Last Days*, 44; ibid., 46, 137; all other quotes *LLC*, November 15, 1967. MSSC #2-49-0-64-1-1-1. *LLC*, November 16, December 1, 1967.

8. Roy Wilkins to J. C. Fairley, January 25, 1968, Fairley Collection, ML-USM. Forrest County NAACP Minutes; Forrest County Action Notebook; Summary of Forrest County Action Committee meetings, September 24, November 30, 1967, Wade Papers, ML-USM. Lee Cole, MSSC Report, December 7, 1967, II-9, PBJ; Wade, interview by author and McGuire, MOHP recording; Jeanette Smith, interview; J. C. Fairley, interview by Garvey, 1977, 60, 63, MOHP; MSSC #2-30-0-77-1-1-1; #2-64-2-14-1-1-1; #99-2-0-41-1-1-1; #99-48-0-17-1-1-1.

9. Pickering, interview, 793–94. File, #44-1512-3291, DABURN-FBI-RBH; File vol. 2, #157-5512-177, Pitts-FBI-RBH; Notes FBI File, Dennis/White Notebook.

10. Quoting *LLC*, October 12, 1967. *LLC*, October 7, 21, 1967. Pickering, interview, 791–92; ibid., 791–94. *Mississippi v. Hendry and Lee* (1967), 3082, *Docket*, vol. 5, 486, 530, JCCC-L. *Mississippi v. Mosley* (1967) 3062, *Minutes*, vol. 24, 31; *Mississippi v. Gray, Lee, Flynt, Haigler* (1967), 3058, *Docket*, vol. 5, 473; *Mississippi v. Gray, Lee, Flynt, Haigler* (September 1968), 3058, *Minutes*, vol. 25, 486, all at JCCC-L. *Mississippi v. Stockman* (1967–1968) 5619, *Docket*, vol. 4, 157; *Mississippi v. Brady* (1967–1968), 5598, *Docket*, vol. 5, 471–72, Jones County Court, Laurel. *LLC*, November 20, 30, 1967, August 21, 1967, December 7, 8, 11, 12, 1967.

11. *HA*, December 22, 1967, January 17, 1968; *LLC*, December 29, 30, 1967; *Mississippi v. Carr, White, and Sessum* (1967–1970), 1502, 1510, *Docket*, vol. 3, 76, Covington County Circuit Court, Collins, Mississippi; File vol. 6, #157-18-867, #157-18-883, Bowers-FBI-RBH; File vol. [?], #44-1512-4799, FBI-RBH.

12. *HA*, January 25, 27, March 22, 1968; *LLC*, January 26, 27, 1968. File vol. 1, #157-4361-96, Thornton-FBI-RBH; File vol. 42, #44-1512-3487, DABURN-FBI-RBH; Marsh, *The Last Day*, 151–52, 156–57.

13. Quoting *HA*, January 25, 1968, March 22, 1968.

14. Files, vol. 2, #157-5512-211, #157-5512-212, Pitts-FBI-RBH. "Travis Buckley's Kidnap Trial," n.d., VFD; *LLC*, February 8, 9, 10, March 8, April 29, May 3, 25, 1968.

15. First and second quotes, *LLC*, March 12, 1968; third quote, *HA*, March 11, 1968. Ibid., March 12, 13, 1968, January 6, 1991. Dukes, interview by Caudill, January 23, 1973, MOHP-D. MSSC #2-30-0-77-1-1-1; #2-64-2-10-1-1-1; #2-64-2-14-1-1-1; #99-2-0-41-1-1-1; #99-48-0-17-1-1-1.

16. *LLC*, March 13, 1968; *HA*, March 13, 1968.

17. Quoting Rogers Testimony, *Mississippi v. Sessum* (1968), 45,174, 297–300, 310, ibid., 294–96, 301, HSF, RBH; *HA*, March 13, 1968; *LLC*, March 13, 1968.

18. Quoting Sessum, statement, Defense Exhibit, *Mississippi v. Sessum* (1968), 248–49; ibid., 206–21, 237–47. *LLC*, March 14, 1968.

19. Quoting Sessum, statement, 250–53; ibid., 250–57.

20. Quoting *HA*, March 16, 1968 and March 15, 1968 respectively; Pitts Testimony, *Mississippi v. Sessum* (1968) vol. 3, Awe Testimony, *Mississippi v. Sessum* (1968), 133–63, Awe, HSF, RBH. *LLC*, March 13, 14, 15, 1968; *HA*, March 13, 14, 20, 1968; Whitehead, *Attack on Terror*, 238–39.

21. First quote, *HA*, March 16, 1968; second quote, Pitts Testimony, 453; ibid., 455–78; *LLC*, March 15, 1968; *HA*, March 15, 1968.

22. Quoting *HA*, March 16, 1968; Awe Testimony, 209–16.

23. *HA*, March 16, 1968.

24. Quoting Wells, interview by Kight, MOHP, 63–69. *HA*, March 16, 1968.

25. First, second, third quotes, *CL*, HSF, RBH; fourth and sixth quotes, Wells, interview, 70–72, ibid., 68; fifth quote, *HA*, March 16, 1968.

26. First quote, *MS*, March 17, 1968, vol. 4, #157-854-35, Sessum-FBI-RBH. All other quotes, Wells, interview, 72–73; *HA*, May 31, 1998. According to the Southern Regional Council, prior to the Dahmer case, the only white person in the South convicted for murdering a black person during the civil rights era occurred in Alabama in 1956, see, *HA*, March 19, 1995. File vol. 2, #157-5512-251, #157-5512-263, both in Pitts-FBI-RBH.

27. First and second quotes, Johnny Magee, interview; third, fourth, and fifth quotes, *LLC*, March 20, 1968. Marsh, *The Last Day*, 139. Funchess, Benton, Douglass Baker, interviews.

28. First and second quotes, Harris, "A Personal Account"; all other quotes Marsh, *Last Days*, 140. Carson, *In Struggle*, 288.

29. Martin Luther King Jr., 1929–1968—Assassination, Winfred Moncrief Photograph Collection, MDAH Digital. MSSC File, May 6, 1968, MSSC# 9-31-8-12-1-1-1.

30. Quoting *Report of the National Advisory Commission on Civil Rights Disorders*, 2, 10. Report, May 6, 1968, MSSC# 9-31-8-12-1-1-1; Civil Rights Act of 1968, Pub. L 90-284, 82 Stat. 73 (1968); Paul Grady to Sadie C. Barron, May 30, 1968, HMR. Jones, *Tribe of Black Ulysses*.

31. First quote, William McCain, May 6, 1968, speech, 16–17, 20, McCain Papers, ML-USM. All other quotes, File vol. 8, #157-18-1152, 18–52, Bowers-FBI-RBH.

32. Quoting *HA*, May 22, 1968. *HA*, March 22, May 21–23, August 22, 1968; Whitehead, *Attack on Terror*, 285–302.

33. *CL*, August 22, 1998 and December 18, 1994; *LLC*, January 21, May 15–18, 1968; Marsh, *Last Days*, 185.

34. Files vol. 7, #158-18-1099, vol. 8, #157-18-1217, Bowers FBI-RBH. Nelson, *Terror in the Night*; *HA*, May 21, 1968; *Los Angeles Times*, February 13, 1970.

35. John Bell Williams, statement, August 21, 1968, RG 27, MDAH; Voter Registration in the South, Spring–Summer 1968, Voter Education Project, Cox Collection, MML-MSU.

36. Quoting *HA*, July 19, 1968. *HA*, July 9, 16, 18, 1968; *LLC*, July 19, 1968.

37. Quoting *HA*, July 29, 1968. *HA*, July 23, 27, 1968.

38. *LLC*, November 11, 15 1968, February 1, 1969; *TP*, January 23, 1969. File vol. 1, #157-3565-167, Moss-FBI-RBH. File vol. 52, #44-1512-4433, DABURN-FBI-RBH. *Tarrants v. Mississippi* (1970).

39. Quoting File vol. 51, #44-1512-4388; File vol. 52, #44-1512-4444, both in DABURN FBI-RBH.

40. First quote, File vol. 51, #44-1512-4399; last quote, vol. 51, #44-1512-4388; see too, vol. 52, #44-1512-4444, #44-1512-4453, #44-1512-4449, all in DABURN FBI-RBH.

41. Quoting *LLC*, January 24, 1969; *TP*, January 23, 1969; *HA*, January 27, 1969; *LLC*, January 25, 1969.

42. Quoting File vol. 52, #44-1512-4433, DABURN-FBI-RBH; Gore, interview; Marsh, *Last Days*, 226–30. *LLC*, January 25, 27, 1969.

43. Quoting Marsh, *Last Days*, 229; ibid., 226–30.

44. Ibid. 231, 235; ibid., 230–35.

45. Quoting *MS*, May 1, 1969, VFD. Newspaper clippings, April, 1969, VFD; *HA*, April 15, 1969; Files, #44-31694-889, FBI-RBH; vol. 54, #44-1512-4554, DABURN-FBI-RBH.

46. Quoting *TP*, n.d., and "Dahmer Witness Testifies at Miss. Conspiracy Trial," n.d., newspaper clippings, both in VFD. Summary DABURN federal trial; Ellie Dahmer, speech, Symposium on Civil Rights in Hattiesburg, recording, ML-USM; *MS*, April 29, 1969; *HA*, May 5, 1969; *TP*, May 4, 1969.

47. Summary DABURN federal trial; *MS*, May 1, 1969; *TP*, May 2, 1969; *HA*, May 8, 1969.

48. First quote, *TP*, May 8, 1969, VFD; second quote, Summary DABURN federal trial; *HA*, May 10, 1969; James H. Downey, *HA*, May 12, 1969.

49. Quoting *Killed by the Klan*. Dahmer Jr., interview by Gray; File vol. 9, #157-18-1350, Bowers-FBI-RBH; *HA*, July 23, 26, 1969.

50. Quoting Judge Hall, interview by Willis, 46, MOHP. *Mississippi v. Hendry and Lee* (1967), 3082, *Docket*, vol. 5, 486, 530; *Mississippi v. Hendry* (June 1969), 3082, *Minutes*, vol. 26, 316, 412 both at JCCCL. *LLC*, June 13, 16, 1969.

51. *LLC*, June 6, 17, 1969; *Mississippi v. Holifield* (1967–1969), 3052, *Docket*, vol. 5, 470; *Mississippi v. Lee* (June 1967), 3082, *Minutes*, vol. 26, 412, JCCC-L.

52. Quoting File vol. 54, #44-1512-4575. Files vol. 52, #44-1512-4424, vol. 56, #44-1512-4661, #44-1512-4703, #44-1512-4663, #44-1512-4689, all in DABURN FBI-RBH. *Mississippi v. Carr, White, Sessum* (1967–1970); *HA*, April 14, 1969; *Wilson v. Mississippi*, 45711, 234 So. 2d 303 (Miss.1970).

CHAPTER 8

1. Quoting McGill, interview; Johnny Magee, interview; Bunch, interview; Coleman interview.

2. Bolton, *Hardest Deal*, 117–223; Faber, *Age of Great Dreams*, 138–261; Gitlin, *Sixties*, 195–419; Forman, *Making of Black Revolutionaries*; Whitehead, *Attack on Terror*, 302–14.

3. Quoting *HA*, December 4, 1969. *Green v. Board*, 391 US 430, (1968), *Federal Civil Rights Laws*, 127 and *Alexander v. Holmes*., 396 US 1218 (1969), Ser. 43; Bill S. 2762, August 4, 1969, Congressional Record, vol. 115, Ser. 47; School Desegregation, Book I and Statistical Comparisons of Desegregation, September 22, 1970, Ser. 47, all in JCS. *HA*, November 7, December 13, 1969. For overview of massive resistance to school desegregation in Mississippi, see, Bolton, *Hardest Deal*, 117–66. For perceptions of school desegregation and massive resistance in the CPW, see McGill, Coleman, Johnny Magee, Kenneth Fairley, Funchess, and Scarborough, interviews, and Harris, "A Personal Account."

4. Quoting *HA*, December 11, 1969. Scarborough, interview; Forrest County Consolidated School District II: Recommendations for School Desegregation, 1969–1970, HMR; *HA*, December 8, 10, 13, 22, 31, 1969.

5. Quoting John Bell Williams, speech, January 3, 1970, RG 27, MDAH; *HA*, August 20, 1969.

6. Statement of Assistant Attorney General Jerris Leonard Before Select Committee on Equal Educational Opportunity, US Senate, July 13, 1970, Appendix A, Mississippi Fall 1969 Elementary and Secondary School Survey; Leonard to Mississippi State Board of Education, April 17, 1970, Ser. 47, JCS. Spinks, interview, by Adams, vol. 693, 25–26, MOHP.

7. Quoting Harris, "A Personal Account." *S. H. Blair High School L'il Miss. Yearbook*, 1969, Hattiesburg High School Library, Hattiesburg, Mississippi.

8. Quoting Kenneth Fairley interview, May 8, 2009; *L'il Miss. Yearbook, 1970*, 145–46.

9. Kenneth Fairley, interview, May 8, 2009.

10. Ibid.

11. Quoting Marsh, *Last Days*, 248; ibid., 247–53; Bolton, *Hardest Deal*, 188; Spinks, interview, 25–26; *HA*, September 8, 16, 17, 1970; Field Director's Annual Report, Mississippi State Conference NAACP 1970, 29-B-6, NAACP-P; Harris, "A Personal Account"; Denard-Delgado, interview; *HA*, September 1, 1970.

12. Quoting *HA*, February 9, 1971; *HA*, February 5, 1971, both in 29-B-9, NAACP-P. Clarence Magee, interview. Kenneth Fairley, interviews. *L'il Miss. Yearbook*, 1971.

13. *HA*, March 2, 1971; ibid., n.d., 29-B-9, NAACP-P; Clarence Magee, interview; MSSC #99-128-0-1-3-1-1; *HA*, March 3, 1971.

14. *HA*, February 5, 1971, 29-B-9, NAACP-P. Kenneth Fairley, interview, May 8, 2009; Spinks, interview, 26–30. Woullard, interview. Harris, "A Personal Account."

15. Quoting Woullard, interview. Kenneth Fairley, interview, May 8, 2009; *L'il Miss. Yearbook*, 1972, 5, 82–83. Harris, "A Personal Account."

16. Kenneth Fairley, interview, May 8, 2009; DuPree, interview; Woullard, interview; *HA*, February 15, 16, 1971, 1972, 29-B-9, NAACP-P; School Board appointments, February 14, 1972, HMR; DuPree, interview; *L'il Miss. Yearbook Yearbook*, 1972, 84–89.

17. Quoting, DuPree, interview. Billy McGee, Kenneth Fairley, Woullard, interviews; *L'il Miss. Yearbook*, 1972, 14, 24–25, 35, 67, 82, 90, 98–99.

18. Quoting Coleman, interview. Johnny Magee, Austin, interviews; Payne, *Oak Park Story*, 1998.

19. McGill, Coleman, Johnny Magee, interviews; Field Director's Annual Report, Mississippi State Conference NAACP 1970, 29-B-6, NAACP-P; Marsh, *Last Days*, 247.

20. McGill, Johnny Magee, Coleman, interviews.

21. McGill, interview; Coleman, interview; Bunch interview, Johnny Magee interview.

22. Coleman, Austin, interviews.

23. Quoting Coleman, interview. Austin, interview.

24. First quote, Coleman interview; second quote Bunch interview.

25. Quoting, Johnny Magee, interview. Bunch interview, Coleman interview.

26. Johnny Magee, interview.

27. Quoting Coleman, interview. Austin, interview.

28. Quoting McGill, interview. Johnny Magee, interview; Austin, interview by Adams, MOHP-D.

29. Johnny Magee, McGill, Austin, Coleman, interviews.

30. Wade-Seals, interview.

31. Terry Caves, interview, *An Oral History of Jones County*, 120–21; Wade-Seals, interview.

32. Quoting Marsh, *Last Days*, 260; ibid., 257–72.

33. *LLC*, May 16, 2004. Woullard, Kenneth Fairley, DuPree, Johnny Magee, interviews; *LLC*, May 15, 2004. Jones County, Laurel, Forrest County schools, Hattiesburg, and Lamar County schools, Public School Report website.

34. File vol. 56, #44-1512-4703, DABURN-FBI-RBH. *Mississippi v. Bowers* (1968) 49/6800, *Mississippi v. Buckley* (1968), 159/6801, 159/6799; *Mississippi v. DeBoxtel* (1968), 158/6796, 159/6784; *Mississippi v. Giles* (1968), 159/6802; *Mississippi v. Lyons* (1968), 156/6786; *Mississippi v. Lyons* (1968), 157/6791; *Mississippi v. Nix* (1968), 159/6801; *Mississippi v. Noble* (1968), 156/6785; *Mississippi v. Sessum* (1968), 158/6796; *Mississippi v. Smith* (1968), 158/6797; *Mississippi v. Thornton* (1968), 15/6787 and 158/6792; *Mississippi v. Wilson* (1968), 157/6788; ibid., 158/6795, all in *Docket*, vol. 5, 161–67, FCCC-H. *LLC*, October 24, 1969.

35. Files vol. 57, #44-1512-4733, #44-1512-4778, #44-1512-4785, #44-1512-4270, DABURN FBI-RBH. File vol. 2, #157-505-270, Byrd-FBI-RBH. File vol. 9, #157-18-1377, Bowers-FBI-RBH. File vol. 4, #157-854-409, Sessum-FBI-RBH. Files vol. 6, #157-3484-583, #157-3484-590, #157-3484-581, #157-3484-597, #157-3484-598, #157-3484-600, Nix-FBI-RBH. Governor Announces Policy on Emergency Leave, June 16, 1972, RG 27, MDAH.

36. *TP*, August 1, 1971, Gandy Papers, ML-USM; *MS*, June 30, 1971; Bill Waller, Press Release, May 25, 1971, HMR; Parker, *Black Votes Count*, 200–201; Waller, speech, January 17, 1972, *Mississippi Senate Journal*, 1972, 58–60, ML-USM. Thomas Espy, "Annual Report: State of Mississippi Office of Minority Business Enterprise"; "Mississippi State Penitentiary," December 10, 1975; Affirmative Action Plan Mississippi State Democratic Party, n.d., RG 27, MDAH.

37. Quoting *The Delta Democrat-Time*, July 30, 1972. Governor Announces Policy on Emergency Leave; Emergency Leaves, Charles Clifford Wilson, Parchman Records; "Mississippi: The Lifer," *Newsweek*, n.d., 20; Parchman Work-Release Program, November 28, 1972; "Mississippi State Penitentiary," RG 27, MDAH. *LLC*, November 30, 1972.

38. First quote, "Mississippi: The Lifer"; second and third quotes, *CL*, November 30, 1972; File vol. 58, #44-1512-4809, #44-1512-4808, #44-1512-480[?], #44-1512-481[?], #44-1512-4793, DABURN FBI-RBH. *LLC*, November 29, 1972; *HA*, December 7, 1942. Southeast Region NAACP Annual Report 1972, 29-A-17; 1972 Annual Report of Laurel NAACP Branch Activities, 29-B-9, NAACP-P.

39. Files vol. 59, #44-1512-4816, #44-1512-4817; vol. 58, #44-1512-4818, #44-1512-4841, all in DABURN FBI-RBH. *HA*, n.d., VFD; *CL*, April 11, 1972; File vol. 9, #157-18-1382, Bowers-FBI-RBH.

40. Quoting Richardson, statement, June 4, 1974, Flowers case file, *Mississippi v. Flowers* (1974), 4620, JCCC-L. *LLC*, June 5, 1974, November 20, 1974. For Flowers's Klan membership, see vol. 1, #157-18-5, Bowers-FBI-RBH.

41. *LLC*, June 5–7, 1974; *HA*, June 6–7, 1974.

42. *Mississippi v. Flowers* (1974), 4620, *Docket*, vol. 6, 208; Flowers case file, JCCC-L. *LLC*, November 2–22, 1974, May 19–21, 1975; *LLC*, May 21, 1975; Johnny Magee, interview.

43. First quote, Statement from the Black Community, October 20, 1969; second quote, Statements from "The Black Coalition," n.d., third quote, Black Coalition, untitled document; The Black Coalition Objectives, n.d., Dennis Lee Watson, Roe Michael Shoemake, and James Owen, statements, November 5, 1969, all in HMR. *HA*, October 24, 25, 1969, November 7, 21, 1969.

44. Quoting *HA*, November 19, 1969; *HA*, November 21, 1969; "Open Letter to the Citizens of Forrest County," n.d., HMR.

45. Quoting *HA*, November 21, 1969. *HA*, November 26, 1969. Nix, interview, MOHP-D; Fairley and Philipses, interview by Bolton, MOHP-D.

46. *HA*, March 8, 1971; Fairley, interview by Garvey, MOHP; MSSC #99-128-0-39-1-1-1, MDAH.

47. Quoting MSSC #99-128-0-39-1-1-1, MDAH; *HA*, March 23, 1971; Fairley, interview by Garvey, 50.

48. John Smith, Paul Taylor, T. J. Gordon, July 13, 1972, affidavits, *Eaton v. Hattiesburg*, (1972), 724–30, HMR; *Eaton v. Hattiesburg*, 72-30 (1972), NARA; Douglass Baker, interview.

49. Quoting Landers, interview. Kenneth Fairley, interview, May 8, 2009. Douglass Baker, interview. *Eaton v. Hattiesburg* (1972), NARA. Eaton, Smith, Taylor, Gordon, July 13, 1972, affidavits; Hattiesburg Affirmative Action Plan Police and Fire Departments, June 16, 1977; Resolution Endorsing Civil Rights Law and Executive Orders Applicable to City of Laurel, HMR.

50. Kenneth Fairley, interview, May 13, 2009; Johnny Magee, interview; *HA*, February 26, 2006, April 16, 17, 21, 1974; US Army Corps of Engineers, "Abstract," *Post Disaster Report on April 1974 Floods in Mississippi in the Mobile District*, May 1974, federal internet source.

51. *HA*, April 17, 18, 19, 1974; Forrest County Branch of the NAACP and the Flood Victims Committee, Recommendations and Petition, June 20, 1974, HMR; Johnny Magee, interview; Burns, interview, June 10, 2009; Kenneth Fairley, interview, May 13, 2009; Fairley, interview by Garvey, January 31, 1974, 375, 93-94, MOHP. J. C. Fairley to A. L. Gerrard Jr., March 19, 1980; Flood Victims Petition, HMR.

52. Burns, interviews; Kenneth Fairley, interview, May 13, 2009; Johnny Magee, interview; Siggers, interview. *HA*, February 25, 1996, Hattiesburg History, *HA*, February 26, 2006, and *HA*, April 9, 2006, Hattiesburg Revitalization, *HA*, August 1, 1993, Hattiesburg Government, all in VF, ML-USM. David Stanton Key, "Laurel, Mississippi: A Historical Perspective," 82–83. Walmart History Timeline, website. For various arguments as to the causes and perpetuation of the black underclass, see Massey and Denton, *American Apartheid*; Katz, *"Underclass" Debate*; Wilson, *Truly Disadvantaged*; Lemann, *Promised Land*; Moynihan, *Negro Family*.

53. File vol. 6, #157-3484-583, Nix-FBI-RBH. File vol. 9, #157-18-1351, Bowers-FBI-RBH; File vol. 2, #157-4387-129, Lowe-FBI-RBH. Files vol. 6, #157-3484-614, #157-3484-581, #157-3484-582, Nix-FBI-RBH. Rev. Emmett C. Burns, NAACP Youth Night Program, speech, 27th Annual Session, Turner Chapel AME Church, November 2, 1972, 29-A-6, NAACP-P; Clarence Magee to Leslie Newcomb,

November 15, 1972, NAACP-P; 1972 Annual Report of Laurel Activities, 29-B-9, NAACP-P. Marsh, *Last Days*, 240-243.

EPILOGUE

1. Quoting Janet Braswell, *HA*, May 29, 1998, Noble VF, ML-USM; Arrest Records: Bowers, #000074106X, Nix, #0000741167, Nobles #0000741175, May 28, 1998, CSF, RBH. *HA*, May 28, 29, 1998.
2. Quoting *HA*, May 29, 1998; *HA*, June 1, 1999.
3. Redlich, "Toward Equal Representation," 41–43. *Connor v. Finch*, 3830(A). See, too, Parker, *Black Votes Count*, 61–63, 85–129; 199–205; Nash and Taggart, *Mississippi Politics*, 104–10; Percy W. Watson, Mississippi House of Representative, Mississippi State Legislature, website.
4. Himelstein, "Rhetorical Continuities," 153–66. *Boykins, Phillips, and McFarlin Jr. v. Hattiesburg* (1980), H77-0062 (C), HMR. *Boykins, Phillips, and McFarland v. Hattiesburg* (1977), H77-062(N); *Clayton and Miller and the US v. Laurel* (1982), H-82-202(R); *Fairley v. Patterson*, (1967), H2205 (C); *Jones County NAACP v. Jones County* (1983), H83-0200(R), *Docket*, S.D. Miss. Senator John Stennis, Senate Floor Statement, June 12, 1982, Voting Rights Act, Ser. 33, JCS. "Winter Calls for Abolishing Voting Rights Act," n.d., William Winter, RG 27, MDAH; Parker, *Black Votes Count*, 207; Newspaper clippings, Hattiesburg and Laurel Government VF, ML-USM; *HA*, November 9, 1983; *LLC*, February 14, 1984; Elliott Andalman, Andalman & Flynn, website. For lack of black power, see Lawrence, Holloway, Kenneth Fairley, Burns, Cooley, Johnny Magee, interviews.
5. *HA*, November 1, 1986; ibid., November 6, 1986; ibid., December 3, 12, 1986. Kenneth Fairley, May 8, 13, 2009, Burns, May 12, June 10, 2009, Woullard, Jeanette Smith, Douglass Baker, Siggers, interviews. Hattiesburg School Board Minutes, October 7, 20, 1986, *Minutes*, vol. 2, Hattiesburg Mississippi School District, Hattiesburg, Mississippi; *Jones County NAACP v. Mississippi and Laurel School Districts*, 4706, H87-0245(L) S.D. Miss.
6. Quoting *NYT*, September 16, 2010. *CL*, September 15, 2010. *Dixon, Bivens v. Mississippi* (2010), case no. CI 10-0147; *Mississippi v. Dixon and Ruffin* (1979), 248/9380, *Docket*, vol. 6, 425; *Mississippi v. Ruffin* (1979–2010), 9513, *Docket*, vol. 5, 466; *Mississippi v. Dixon* (1980–2010), 9784, *Docket* vol. 6, 559; *Mississippi v. Bivens* (1980–2010) 9764, *Docket*, vol. 5, 553, all in FCCC-H.
7. Quoting *HA*, April 24, 1994. *HA*, August 26, 1993, Hattiesburg Police VF, ML-USM; *HA*, May 23, June 6, 1993, April 23, 24, 29, 1994; Burns, Woullard, Fairley, Billy McGee, interviews.
8. Quoting Alexander, *The New Jim Crow*, 13. For analyses of the struggles between black communities and police across America and various arguments as to the causes and perpetuation of black suffering in the inner cities, see Alexander, *The New Jim Crow*, 1–248; Massey and Denton, *American Apartheid*; Katz, *The Underclass Debate*; Wilson, *The Truly Disadvantaged*; Lemann, *The Promised Land*; Moynihan, *The Negro Family*.
9. Hattiesburg Police VF, ML-USM; Siggers, Fairley, Landers, Burns, Billy McGee, Woullard, Douglass Baker, Sims, Holloway, Easton and Preyor, Wade, Outlaw, Benton, Lawrence, Denard-Delgado, interviews.
10. Quoting Holloway, interview. *HA*, February 6, 1990, March 7, 1990, August 22, 1993, Hattiesburg Police VF, ML-USM; McGee, Woullard, Fairley, Burns, interview, Sims, interviews.
11. *HA*, May 8, 28, 30, and June 4, 1997, and February 18, 1998; *Advertiser News*, May 14, 1997, Hattiesburg Elections VF, ML-USM. *HA*, February 18, 1998; Kenneth Fairley, interviews, May 8, 13, 2009; DuPree, interview; Burns, interviews.
12. Quoting Kenneth Fairley, interview, May 8, 2009; Kenneth Fairley, interview, May 13, 2009; *HA*, September 27, 1997.
13. Charlie Sims, interview.

14. Quoting Kenneth Fairley, interview, May 8, 2009. Carlton Wade, *HA*, February 18, 1998; Fairley, interview, May 13, 2009; Johnny DuPree, interview; Fred Burns, interviews, May 12, June 10, 2009.

15. *LLC*, November 25, 1992, December 7, 1993; *HA*, September 19, 1992, in NAACP VF, LRM; Manuel Jones, interview.

16. *Killed by the Klan*; Christopher Sullivan, "Authorities Reopen Case of Race-related Deep South Murders," [?] November 3, 1991, *State v. Noble*, RBH. *CL*, May 28, 1991; *HA*, January 6, May 28, 1991; Vollers, *Ghosts of Mississippi*, 259–64; Kenneth Fairley, interviews.

17. City Council Meeting, March 8, 1994, *Minutes*, vol. 1994-1, 496, City Hall, Hattiesburg, Mississippi. Statements by Cecil Sessum, July 5, 1994, Delmar Dennis, August 9, 1994, Arnold Ingram, May 2, 1994; Defendants in Summary of Dahmer Incident, n.d., all in HSF, RBH. Kenneth Fairley, interviews; Carter, interview. *Killed by the Klan*; *HA*, February 7, 9, 11, 1994, March 7, 9, 12, 1994, January 8, 1995, January 7, 1996; *CL*, December 17, 1994, February 16, March 5, 14, 17, April 26, July 19, November 8, 1995.

18. Helfrich Legal Pad Notes, CSF, RBH. Carter, interview; *CL*, December 13, 1997, May 10, 22, August 15, 16, 17, 1998.

19. Quoting Sybil Nix, taped conversation, January 29, 1998, transcript, 11–13; Collection of FBI files, "Various Notes"; Lee Martin, Jury Tampering Info and Memo, February 7, 1998; Curtis Wilkie, "Ex-Klan Insider Sheds New Light on '66 Killings," *Boston Globe*, n.d, all in HSF, RBH. Roy K. Moore, to Edwin B. Zeigler, December 11, 1967, #44-31694-713; Files #s44-31694-807 through 911, Bowers 1968 murder trial, FBI-RBH, all in *State v. Bowers* Notebooks, RBH. *Killed by the Klan*; *CL*, August 2, 1998; Dahmer Jr., interview by Gray, MOHP; *TP*, August 22, 1998.

20. Billy Roy Pitts, statement, January 30, 1998, audiocassette, *State v. Noble*; Medical Report State Louisiana Hospital, HSF; Pitts, Divorce Papers and Defense Exhibits; *Smith v. Pitts*, CSF; Files vol. 57, #44-1512-4778, all in RBH. *CL*, January 17, February 7, 10, 1998.

21. Quoting Marsh, *God's Long Summer*, 63; ibid., 64. Adam Cohen, "Widow and the Wizard," *Time* (magazine), May 18, 1998, 72–75. Nix, Noble, Bowers arrest records. Helfrich, interview, October 10, 2001; Kenneth Fairley, interviews.

22. Juror Questionnaires, CSF, *Mississippi v. Bowers*, (1998), 6922, vol.1, transcript, CSF, RBH. *CL*, August 11, 17, 18, 1998, Bowers VF, ML-USM.

23. Quoting Opening Statement, *Mississippi v. Bowers*, (1998), audiocassette recording; Andy Sheldon, *Mississippi v. Bowers* trial notes, CSF, RBH. Billy McGee, interview; Sims, interview; *HA*, August 17, 19, 1998, *CL*, August 13, 21, 1998.

24. Quoting *Mississippi v. Bowers*, (1998), transcript, vol. 2, 9–29; Sheldon, Trial Notes.

25. First quote, *Mississippi v. Bowers* (1998), transcript, vol. 3, 24; second quote, vol. 3, 27; third quote, vol. 4, 19; fourth quote, vol. 4, 29. Ibid., vol. 3, 3–35, 102–5, 138–39.

26. Quoting *Mississippi v. Bowers* (1998), transcript, vol. 2, 95. Ibid., vol. 2, 34–114, vol. 3, 36–86, 91–95, 106–35; 140–49 and vol. 4, 21–24 29, 38–55. Nelson, *Terror in the Night*, 11–273. Sheldon, Trial Notes.

27. First quote, *Mississippi v. Bowers*, (1998), transcript, vol. 4, 85; ibid., second quote, vol. 4, 104; ibid., vol. 4, 66–106. US House, *Activities of Ku Klux Klan Organizations in the United States Part 4*, 2904–8, RBH.

28. First quote, *Mississippi v. Bowers* (1998), transcript, vol. 5, 22; second, third, and fourth, and quotes, ibid., vol. 5, 21; fifth quote, ibid., vol. 5, 26; sixth quote, ibid., vol. 5, 23; seventh quote, 30.

29. *Mississippi v. Bowers*, (1998), transcript, vol. 5, 30–31.

30. Quoting *CL*, August 22, 1998; *Mississippi v. Bowers* (1998), vol. 5, 34.

31. Quoting *CL*, August 26, 1998. "Killed by the Klan."

32. *HA*, September 20, 1998; Helfrich interviews. *HA*, July 21, 1998, June 10, 1999; *CL*, December

15, 1998, June 7, 9, 11, 1999. Various motions, *Mississippi v. Noble*, 6785 and 6793, MS, September 21, 1998, January 4, 1999, March 15, 1999.

33. File vol. 1, #157-433-60, Martin-FBI-RBH. File vol. 23, #44-1512-1083, DABURN-FBI-RBH; File vol. 1, #157-433-45, DeBoxtel-FBI-RBH. File vol. 2, #157-5512-207, Pitts-FBI-RBH. File, #157-5385-17, Noble-FBI-RBH, *State v. Noble*. File vol.1 #157-505-122, Byrd-FBI-RBH. For Watkins case, see *LLC*, February 6, 1968.

34. Pitts, testimony, *Mississippi v. Noble*, (1999), 6785, 6793, transcript, FCCC-H. *CL*, June 12, 1999, Noble VF, ML-USM; *Mississippi v. Bowers*, transcript, vol. 3 (1998); MDPS Report, Vernon Dahmer, January 11, 1966, PBJ. Callahan Notes, HSF; Pitts's pardon, Governor Kirk Fordice, Executive Order 799, May 21, 1999, in State v. Noble; File vol., 9, #44-1512-294, all in RBH.

35. Quoting Pitts testimony, *Mississippi v. Noble* (June 14, 1999), transcript, 106. Ibid., 107, 130–31; Defense motion for mistrial, Pitts Testimony, order for mistrial, *Mississippi v. Noble* (June 15, 1999), transcript, 2–9.

36. First quote, *CL*, June 20, 1999; second quote, *HA*, January 23, 2001. Newspaper clippings, *HA*, June 16, 1999, *CL*, June 16, 1999, Noble VF. *HA*, January 9, 2002. Interviews with Jurors in Noble Mistrial, Helfrich CSF, RBH. *Mississippi v. Noble*, Case 156/6785, January 10, 2002, *Docket*, vol. 5, 161, FCCC-H.

37. "League of the South Remembers the 'Gold Ole Days,'" Intelligence Report, Issue 99, Summer 2000, SPLC website.

38. Quoting *HA*, November 9, 2009. Kenneth Fairley, Woullard, Vincent, DuPree, James Jones, Helfrich, May 4, 2009, interviews. *HA*, May 31, June 6, 8, 30, July 3, 2001, January 30, February 18, May 18, 2006; *LLC*, June 5, 6, 14, July 3, 2001, October 1, 2008; *Chicago Tribune*, May 18, 2006. *Mississippi v. Kennard* (2006), 5833, case file, FCCC-H; Clyde Kennard website.

39. Vincent, Johnny Magee, Wheat, Cooley, Manuel Jones, interviews. Charles Pickering, Melvin Mack, interviews, *An Oral History of Jones County*, vol. 792, 678–79, 784–96, 813–14, MOHP; *HA*, February 18, 2004; *LLC*, November 5, 2003, June 14, 2005; Annexation Ordinance, June 17, 1997, *LCC Minutes*, vol. 73, 371–83, Council Meeting, March 16, 2004, *Minutes*, vol. 83, 102–3, City Hall, Laurel, Mississippi; Appellate briefs and court ruling, *Laurel v. Sharon Waterworks Association* (2009), 2007-AN-01547-SCT, JCCC-L.

40. Quoting *HA*, December 6, 1958. *Carroll, Bailey and Bradley v. DuPree* (2006), CI06-0132, FCCC-H; Scarborough, Charlie Sims, Landers, Fred Burns, Robert Helfrich, May 4, 2009, DuPree, Holloway, Billy McGee, Woullard, Kenneth Fairley, Cheryl Outlaw, Denard-Delgado, Clarence Magee, Bradley, Ware, Dukes, Naylor, Carroll, interviews. *HA*, May 24, June 9, 11, October 26, 30, 2006, December 31, 2006, January 21, 2007, March 18, 2007. See, too, Hattiesburg Police, Hattiesburg Government VF, ML-USM. *CL*, September 28, 2013. *HA*, September 16, 2010; *CL*, September 15, 16, 2010; *Mississippi v. Ruffin* (1979–2010); *Dixon, Bivens v. Mississippi* (2010). Larry Ruffin Case, Innocence Project.

Bibliography

ARCHIVAL MATERIALS

Abernathy, Thomas, Collection. J. D. Williams Library, Special Collections, University of Mississippi, Oxford.
Adams, Victoria Gray, Papers. McCain Library and Archives, University of Southern Mississippi, Hattiesburg.
Adickes, Sandra, Papers. McCain Library and Archives, University of Southern Mississippi, Hattiesburg.
Ben-Ami, Rabbi David Z., Papers. McCain Library and Archives, University of Southern Mississippi, Hattiesburg.
Bilbo, Theodore G., Papers. McCain Library and Archives, University of Southern Mississippi, Hattiesburg.
Bowers, Sam. Manuscript, December 9, 1984. Digital Archives. Mississippi Department of Archives and History, Jackson.
Bowers, Sam. Vertical File. McCain Library and Archives, University of Southern Mississippi, Hattiesburg.
Child Development Group of Mississippi Records. Microfilm. Wisconsin Historical Society. Madison.
Civil Rights Congress Papers. Microfilm. Schomburg Center for Research in Black Culture, New York, NY.
Coleman, J. P., Collection. Manuscript Papers and Special Collections. Mitchell Memorial Library, Mississippi State University, Starkville.
Colmer, William M., Papers. McCain Library and Archives, University of Southern Mississippi, Hattiesburg.
Congress of Racial Equality Archives Papers. Microfilm. Martin Luther King Center, Atlanta.
Congress of Racial Equality Archives Papers. Addendum. Microfilm. Martin Luther King Center, Atlanta.
Connor, Peggy Jean, Papers. McCain Library and Archives, University of Southern Mississippi, Hattiesburg.
Cox, Alex Eugene, Papers. Manuscript Papers and Special Collections. Mitchell Memorial Library, Mississippi State University, Starkville.
Crimes—Howard Wash Lynching. Vertical File. Lauren Rogers Museum of Art, Library and Archives, Laurel, Mississippi.
Crimes—Violent, Willie McGee. Vertical File. Lauren Rogers Museum of Art, Library and Archives, Laurel, Mississippi.

Dahmer, Vernon F., Collection. McCain Library and Archives, University of Southern Mississippi, Hattiesburg.
Dahmer, Vernon F. Vertical File. McCain Library and Archives, University of Southern Mississippi, Hattiesburg.
Elections. Vertical File. McCain Library and Archives, University of Southern Mississippi, Hattiesburg.
Dukes, James K., Papers. McCain Library and Archives, University of Southern Mississippi, Hattiesburg.
East, P. D., Collection. McCain Library and Archives, University of Southern Mississippi, Hattiesburg.
Ellin, Joseph and Nancy, Freedom Summer Collection. McCain Library and Archives, University of Southern Mississippi, Hattiesburg.
Fairley, J. C., Civil Rights Collection. McCain Library and Archives, University of Southern Mississippi, Hattiesburg.
Faulkner, Leesha, Civil Rights Collection. McCain Library and Archives, University of Southern Mississippi, Hattiesburg.
Gandy, Edythe Evelyn, Papers. McCain Library and Archives, University of Southern Mississippi, Hattiesburg.
Glass, Jinny, Mississippi Freedom Diary. McCain Library and Archives, University of Southern Mississippi, Hattiesburg.
Governor's Papers, Record Group 27. Mississippi Department of Archives and History, Jackson.
Gray, W. G., Papers. McCain Library and Archives, University of Southern Mississippi, Hattiesburg.
Guzman, Jessie Parkhurst, Vera Chandler Foster, and William Hardin Hughes, eds. *Negro Yearbook: A Review of Events Affecting Negro Life, 1944–1946*. Tuskegee, AL: Negro Yearbook Publishing Co., 1947. National Humanities Center, http://nationalhumanitiescenter.org/pds/maai3/segregation/text2/lynchingcrime.pdf. Accessed November 2010.
Hall, Robert F., Papers, 1928–1993. New York State Library, Albany, New York.
Harris, Anthony J., Civil Rights Memoir. McCain Library and Archives, University of Southern Mississippi, Hattiesburg.
Hattiesburg Area Chamber of Commerce Records. McCain Library and Archives, University of Southern Mississippi, Hattiesburg.
Hattiesburg Department of Urban Development. McCain Library and Archives, University of Southern Mississippi, Hattiesburg.
Hattiesburg Government. Vertical File. McCain Library and Archives, University of Southern Mississippi, Hattiesburg.
Hattiesburg History. Vertical File. McCain Library and Archives, University of Southern Mississippi, Hattiesburg.
Hattiesburg Municipal Records. McCain Library and Archives, University of Southern Mississippi, Hattiesburg.
Hattiesburg Police. Vertical File. McCain Library and Archives, University of Southern Mississippi, Hattiesburg.
Hattiesburg Revitalization. Vertical File. McCain Library and Archives, University of Southern Mississippi, Hattiesburg.
Helfrich, Robert B., Papers. McCain Library and Archives, University of Southern Mississippi, Hattiesburg.
Holmes, Vernon S., Collection. J. D. Williams Library, Special Collections, University of Mississippi, Oxford.
Johnson, Paul B., Sr., and Paul B. Johnson Jr., Family Papers. McCain Library and Archives, University of Southern Mississippi, Hattiesburg.

Johnston, Erle E., Jr., Papers. McCain Library and Archives, University of Southern Mississippi, Hattiesburg.
Kennard, Clyde, File. Southern Poverty Law Center, Montgomery, Alabama.
Kennard, Clyde. Pardon Docket 06-0005. Digital Archives. Mississippi Department of Archives and History, Jackson.
Kershner, Charles, Papers. McCain Library and Archives, University of Southern Mississippi, Hattiesburg.
Knight, Newt, Descendants. Vertical File. Lauren Rogers Museum of Art, Library and Archives, Laurel, Mississippi.
Kwanguvu, Umoja, Freedom Summer Collection. McCain Library and Archives, University of Southern Mississippi, Hattiesburg.
Ladner, Joyce, Unprocessed Papers of the Tougaloo Collection. Mississippi Department of Archives and History, Jackson.
Laurel History. Vertical File. Lauren Rogers Museum of Art, Library and Archives, Laurel, Mississippi.
Laurel History Founding. Vertical File. Lauren Rogers Museum of Art, Library and Archives, Laurel, Mississippi.
Laurel 1990. Vertical File. McCain Library and Archives, University of Southern Mississippi, Hattiesburg.
Laurel 1990. Vertical File. Lauren Rogers Museum of Art, Library and Archives, Laurel, Mississippi.
Laurel Politics and Government. Vertical File. Lauren Rogers Museum of Art, Library and Archives, Laurel, Mississippi.
Law Students Civil Rights Research Council Papers. Seeley G. Mudd Manuscript Library, Princeton University, Princeton, NJ.
"League of the South Remembers the 'Good Ole Days,'" Intelligence Report, 99 (Summer 2000), Southern Poverty Law Center, Montgomery, Alabama, http://www.splcenter.org/intel/intelreport/article.jsp?aid=256&printable=1. Accessed October 2001.
Mantinband, Rabbi Charles, Papers. McCain Library and Archives, University of Southern Mississippi, Hattiesburg.
Marx, Charles A., Papers. McCain Library and Archives, University of Southern Mississippi, Hattiesburg.
Mascot, USM. Vertical File. McCain Library and Archives, University of Southern Mississippi, Hattiesburg.
McCain, William D., Collection. McCain Library and Archives, University of Southern Mississippi, Hattiesburg.
McIlhenny, George Neal, Papers. Manuscript Papers and Special Collections. Mitchell Memorial Library, Mississippi State University, Starkville.
Michaels, Shelia, Papers. McCain Library and Archives, University of Southern Mississippi, Hattiesburg.
Mississippi AFL-CIO Records, Southern Labor Archives. Georgia State University Special Collections and Archives, Atlanta.
Mississippi Legislature, Record Group 47. Mississippi Department of Archives and History, Jackson.
Mississippi Republican Party, Records. Manuscript Papers and Special Collections. Mitchell Memorial Library, Mississippi State University, Starkville.
Mississippi State Sovereignty Commission Records. Digital Archives. Mississippi Department of Archives and History, Jackson.
Moncrief, Winfred, Photograph Collection. Digital Archives. Mississippi Department of Archives and History, Jackson.

NAACP. Vertical File. Lauren Rogers Museum of Art, Library and Archives, Laurel, Mississippi.
National Association for the Advancement of Colored People Papers. Microfilm. Library of Congress, Washington, DC.
Noble, Charles. Vertical File. McCain Library and Archives, University of Southern Mississippi, Hattiesburg.
Owen, David, Freedom Summer Collection. McCain Library and Archives, University of Southern Mississippi, Hattiesburg.
"Pursuing a Late Justice: The Prosecution of Mississippi's Civil Rights Murders, Then and Now." Forum. August 29, 2000, tape recording. McCain Library and Archives, University of Southern Mississippi, Hattiesburg.
Randall, Herbert, Freedom Summer Photographs. McCain Library and Archives, University of Southern Mississippi, Hattiesburg.
Register Mississippi State Penitentiary Convicts. Microfilm. 13785. Mississippi Department of Archives and History, Jackson, Mississippi.
Rue, Myrtis, African American Hattiesburg Collection. McCain Library and Archives, University of Southern Mississippi, Hattiesburg.
Schwartz, Joseph S., Civil Rights Letters. McCain Library and Archives, University of Southern Mississippi, Hattiesburg.
Shaw, Terri, Freedom Summer Collection. McCain Library and Archives, University of Southern Mississippi, Hattiesburg.
Smith, Hazel Brannon, Papers. Manuscript Papers and Special Collections. Mitchell Memorial Library, Mississippi State University, Starkville.
Southern Christian Leadership Conference Papers. Microfilm. Martin Luther King Center, Atlanta.
Spears, Lawrence D., Civil Rights Collection. McCain Library and Archives, University of Southern Mississippi, Hattiesburg.
Speer, Klaus, and Elisabeth C., Papers. McCain Library and Archives, University of Southern Mississippi, Hattiesburg.
Stennis, John C., Collection. Congressional and Political Research Center. Mitchell Memorial Library, Mississippi State University, Starkville.
Stoner, Peter, Papers. McCain Library and Archives, University of Southern Mississippi, Hattiesburg.
Student Nonviolent Coordinating Committee Papers. Microfilm. Martin Luther King Center, Atlanta.
Symposium on Civil Rights in Hattiesburg, Gonzalez Auditorium, University of Southern Mississippi, June 5, 2001, recording. McCain Library and Archives, University of Southern Mississippi, Hattiesburg.
Toller, Kenneth James, Papers. Manuscript Papers and Special Collections. Mitchell Memorial Library, Mississippi State University, Starkville.
United States Works Progress Administration. Unpublished WPA Files, Covington County. Microfilm. 2866. Mississippi Department of Archives and History, Jackson.
United States Works Progress Administration. Unpublished WPA Files, Forrest County. Microfilm, 2857. Mississippi Department of Archives and History, Jackson.
United States Works Progress Administration. Unpublished WPA Files, Jones County. Microfilm, 2870. Mississippi Department of Archives and History, Jackson.
United States Works Progress Administration. Unpublished WPA Files, Perry County. Microfilm, A769. Mississippi Department of Archives and History, Jackson.
United States Works Progress Administration. Unpublished WPA Files, Smith County. Microfilm, A749. Mississippi Department of Archives and History, Jackson.

US v. Lynd, Registrar of Voters of Forrest County, Mississippi, Legal Case, Collection. McCain Library and Archives, University of Southern Mississippi, Hattiesburg.
Wade, Daisy Harris, Papers. McCain Library and Archives, University of Southern Mississippi, Hattiesburg.
Wakeman, Jill, Papers. McCain Library and Archives, University of Southern Mississippi, Hattiesburg.
Woods Guest House/COFO. Hattiesburg Headquarters Collection. McCain Library and Archives, University of Southern Mississippi, Hattiesburg.
Zeman, Zoya, Freedom Summer Collection. McCain Library and Archives, University of Southern Mississippi, Hattiesburg.
Zwerling, Matthew, Freedom Summer Collection. McCain Library and Archives, University of Southern Mississippi, Hattiesburg.

COURT RECORDS

Boykins, Phillips, and McFarland v. Hattiesburg (1977-1984), H77-062(N). United States District Court: Mississippi Southern District Court, Eastern Division, Hattiesburg.
Brown v. Board of Education of Topeka, 347 US 483 (1954). United States Supreme Court (published).
Brown v. Mississippi, 297 US 278 (1936). United States Supreme Court (published).
Clayton and Miller and the US v. Laurel (1982), H-82-202(R). United States District Court: Mississippi Southern District Court, Eastern Division, Hattiesburg.
Divorce Records. *Minutes*, vol. 18, March 1938–March 1939. Office of the Chancery Clerk, Forrest County Chancery Court, Hattiesburg, Mississippi.
Dixon, Bivens v. Mississippi (2010), CI 10-0147. Case file. Office of the Circuit Clerk, Forrest County Circuit Court, Hattiesburg.
Cannon v. Mississippi, 44002, 190 So. 2d 848 (Miss. 1966) (published). Mississippi Supreme Court and Court of Appeals, Jackson.
Cannon v. Mississippi, 2000-CP-01828-COA, 816 So. 2d 433 (Miss 2002) (published). Mississippi Supreme Court and Court of Appeals, Jackson.
Carroll, Bailey and Bradley v. DuPree (2006), CI06-0132. Electronic file. Office of the Circuit Clerk, Forrest County Civil Court, Hattiesburg, Mississippi.
Connor v. Finch, 3830(A), 419 F. Supp. 1072 (US Dist. 1976). United States District Court for the Southern District of Mississippi Cases (published). Jackson.
Eaton v. Hattiesburg (1972), 724-30. United States District Court: Mississippi Southern District Court, Eastern Division, Hattiesburg.
Eaton v. Hattiesburg (1972), 72-30, Transfer No. 021780238, Box No. 1, Location No. 10030672, Civil Cases. National Archives and Records Administration, Atlanta.
Edwards v. South Carolina, 86, 372 US 229; 83 S. Ct. 680; 9 L. Ed. 2d 697 (1963). United States Supreme Court (published).
Ex Parte Fraley, Oklahoma Criminal Court of Appeals, 109 P. 295 (1910) (published). Oklahoma City.
Fairley v. Patterson, (1967–1977), H2205 (C). United States District Court: Mississippi Southern District Court, Eastern Division, Hattiesburg.
Gaines v. Canada, 305 US 337 (1938). United States Supreme Court (published).
Jones County NAACP, v. Mississippi and Laurel School Districts, 4706, H87-0245(L). United States District Court: Mississippi Southern District Court, Eastern Division, Hattiesburg.
Kennard v. Mississippi (1961), 41890. Transcript. Mississippi Supreme Court/Mississippi Department of Archives and History, Jackson.

Larry Ruffin Case, Innocence Project, http://www.innocenceproject.org. Accessed August 8, 2014.

Laurel v. Sharon Waterworks Association, (2009), 2007-AN-01547-SCT. Mississippi Supreme Court and Court of Appeals, Jackson.

Marriage Record. Office of the Circuit Clerk, Forrest County Circuit Court, Hattiesburg, Mississippi.

Marriage Record-Colored. Minutes. Office of the Circuit Clerk, Forrest County Circuit Court, Hattiesburg, Mississippi.

Marriage Record Colored. Office of the Circuit Clerk, Jones County Circuit Court, Laurel, Mississippi.

McGee v. Mississippi, 36166 Miss, 26 So. 2d, 680-684 (1946) (published). Mississippi Court of Appeals and Mississippi Supreme Court, Jackson.

McLaurin v. Oklahoma, 339 US 637 (1950). United States Supreme Court (published).

Mississippi v. Bivens (1980-2010) 9764. Docket. Office of the Circuit Clerk, Forrest County Circuit Court, Hattiesburg.

Mississippi v. Bowers (1968), 49/6800. Docket. Office of the Circuit Clerk, Forrest County Circuit Court, Hattiesburg.

Mississippi v. Bowers (1998), 6922, transcript. Office of the Circuit Clerk, Forrest County Circuit Court, Hattiesburg.

Mississippi v. Brady (1967–1968), 5598. Docket. Office of the Circuit Clerk, Jones County Court, Laurel.

Mississippi v. Bucklew (1966), 2884. Minutes. Office of the Circuit Clerk, Jones County Circuit Court, Laurel.

Mississippi v. Buckley (1964), 2622. Minutes. Office of the Circuit Clerk, Jones County Circuit Court, Laurel.

Mississippi v. Buckley (1968), 159/6799. Docket. Office of the Circuit Clerk, Forrest County Circuit Court, Hattiesburg.

Mississippi v. Byrd (1968), 159/6803. Docket. Office of the Circuit Clerk, Forrest County Circuit Court, Hattiesburg.

Mississippi v. Cannon (1965), 142/6467. Docket. Office of the Circuit Clerk, Forrest County Circuit Court, Hattiesburg.

Mississippi v. Carr, White, and Sessum (1967-1970), 1502, 1510. Office of the Circuit Clerk, Covington County Circuit Court, Collins.

Mississippi v. Coleman (1964), 2636. Minutes. Office of the Circuit Clerk, Jones County Circuit Court, Laurel.

Mississippi v. DeBoxtel (1968), 156/6784. Docket. Office of the Circuit Clerk, Forrest County Circuit Court, Hattiesburg.

Mississippi v. DeBoxtel (1968), 158/6796. Docket. Office of the Circuit Clerk, Forrest County Circuit Court, Hattiesburg.

Mississippi v. Dixon (1980–2010), 9784. Docket. Office of the Circuit Clerk, Forrest County Circuit Court, Hattiesburg.

Mississippi v. Dixon and Ruffin (1979), 248/9380. Docket. Office of the Circuit Clerk, Forrest County Circuit Court, Hattiesburg.

Mississippi v. Evers (1960), 4966. Minutes. Office of the Circuit Clerk, Forrest County Circuit Court, Hattiesburg.

Mississippi v. Flowers (1974/1975), 4620. Case file. Office of the Circuit Clerk, Jones County Circuit Court, Laurel.

Mississippi v. Flowers (1974/1975), 4620. Docket. Office of the Circuit Clerk, Jones County Circuit Court, Laurel.

Mississippi v. Giles (1968), 159/6802. Docket. Office of the Circuit Clerk, Forrest County Circuit

Court, Hattiesburg.
Mississippi v. Gray, Lee, Flynt, Haigler (1967), 3058. Docket. Office of the Circuit Clerk, Jones County Circuit Court, Laurel.
Mississippi v. Gray, Lee, Flynt, Haigler (1968), 3058. Minutes. Office of the Circuit Clerk, Jones County Circuit Court, Laurel.
Mississippi v. Hamilton (1968), 154-6826. Docket. Office of the Circuit Clerk, Forrest County Circuit Court, Hattiesburg.
Mississippi v. Hendry (1969), 3082. Minutes. Office of the Circuit Clerk, Jones County Circuit Court, Laurel.
Mississippi v. Hendry and Lee (1967), 3082. Docket. Office of the Circuit Clerk, Jones County, Laurel.
Mississippi v. Holifield (1967–1969), 3052. Docket. Office of the Circuit Clerk, Jones County Circuit Court, Laurel.
Mississippi v. Kennard (1959), 124/5757. Docket. Office of the Circuit Clerk, Forrest County Circuit Court, Hattiesburg.
Mississippi v. Kennard (2006), 5833. Case file. Office of the Circuit Clerk, Forrest County Circuit Court, Hattiesburg.
Mississippi v. Kennard and Roberts (1960), 124/5833 and 5834. Docket. Office of the Circuit Clerk, Forrest County Circuit Court, Hattiesburg.
Mississippi v. Knight (1948), 646. Case File. Office of the Circuit Clerk, Jones County Circuit Court, Ellisville.
Mississippi v. Knight (1948), 646. Transcript. *Knight v. Mississippi* (1949), 37,205. Mississippi Supreme Court/Mississippi Department of Archives and History, Jackson.
Mississippi v. Lee (1967), 3082. Minutes. Office of the Circuit Clerk, Jones County Circuit Court, Laurel.
Mississippi v. Lyons (1968), 156/6786. Docket. Office of the Circuit Clerk, Forrest County Circuit Court, Hattiesburg.
Mississippi v. Lyons (1968), 157/6791. Docket. Office of the Circuit Clerk, Forrest County Circuit Court, Hattiesburg.
Mississippi v. Massengale (1968), 154/6815. Docket. Office of the Circuit Clerk, Forrest County Circuit Court, Hattiesburg.
Mississippi v. McGee (1945), 1173. Minutes. Office of the Circuit Clerk, Jones County Circuit Court, Laurel.
Mississippi v. McGee (1945–1951), 1173, 3237, 1268. Case file. Office of the Circuit Clerk, Jones County Circuit Court, Laurel.
Mississippi v. McGee (1946), 3237. Transcript. *McGee v. Mississippi* (1947), 36411. Mississippi Supreme Court/Mississippi Department of Archives and History, Jackson.
Mississippi v. McGee (1948), 1268. Transcript. *McGee v. Mississippi* (1948), 36892. Mississippi Supreme Court/Mississippi Department of Archives and History, Jackson.
Mississippi v. Mosley (1967), 3062. Docket. Office of the Circuit Clerk, Jones County Circuit Court, Laurel.
Mississippi v. Mosley (1967), 3062. Minutes. Office of the Circuit Clerk, Jones County Circuit Court, Laurel.
Mississippi v. Nix (1968), 159/6801. Docket. Office of the Circuit Clerk, Forrest County Circuit Court, Hattiesburg.
Mississippi v. Noble (1968), 156/6785. Docket. Office of the Circuit Clerk, Forrest County Circuit Court, Hattiesburg.
Mississippi v. Noble (1999), 6785 and 6793. Transcript. Office of the Circuit Clerk, Forrest County Circuit Court, Hattiesburg.

Mississippi v. Pitts (1968), 152/6790. Docket. Office of the Circuit Clerk, Forrest County Circuit Court, Hattiesburg.

Mississippi v. Royals and Holliman (1948), 761. Case File. Office of the County Clerk, Jones County Court, Ellisville.

Mississippi v. Royals and Holliman (1948), 761. Minutes. Office of the County Clerk, Jones County Court, Ellisville.

Mississippi v. Ruffin (1979–2010), 9513. Docket. Office of the Circuit Clerk, Forrest County Circuit Court, Hattiesburg.

Mississippi v. Sessum (1968), 158-/6796. Docket. Office of the Circuit Clerk, Forrest County Circuit Court, Hattiesburg.

Mississippi v. Shinall (1965), 141/6434. Docket. Office of the Circuit Clerk, Forrest County Circuit Court, Hattiesburg.

Mississippi v. Shinall (1965), 6434. Transcript. *Shinall v. Mississippi* (1965), 43,866. Mississippi Supreme Court/Mississippi Department of Archives and History, Jackson.

Mississippi v. Shinall (1966), 6570. Transcript. *Shinall v. Mississippi* (1967), 44,352. Mississippi Supreme Court/Mississippi Department of Archives and History, Jackson.

Mississippi v. Smith (1968), 158/6797. Docket. Office of the Circuit Clerk, Forrest County Circuit Court, Hattiesburg.

Mississippi v. Stockman (1967), 3054/3055. Docket. Office of the Circuit Clerk, Jones County Circuit Court, Laurel.

Mississippi v. Stockman (1967), 3054, 3055, 3056. Docket. Office of the Circuit Clerk, Jones County Circuit Court, Laurel.

Mississippi v. Stockman (1967–1968), 5619. Docket. Office of the Circuit Clerk, Jones County Court, Laurel.

Mississippi v. Tarrants, (1968), 1534. Office of the Circuit Clerk, Covington County Circuit Court, Collins.

Mississippi v. Thornton (1968), 157/6787. Docket. Office of the Circuit Clerk, Forrest County Circuit Court, Hattiesburg.

Mississippi v. Thornton (1968), 158/6792. Docket. Office of the Circuit Clerk, Forrest County Circuit Court, Hattiesburg.

Mississippi v. Wash (1942), 996. Minutes. Office of the Circuit Clerk, Jones County Circuit Court, Laurel.

Mississippi v. Wilson (1968), 157/6788. Docket. Office of the Circuit Clerk, Forrest County Circuit Court, Hattiesburg.

Mississippi v. Wilson (1968), 158/6795. Docket. Office of the Circuit Clerk, Forrest County Circuit Court, Hattiesburg.

Patton v. Mississippi, 68 US 184 (1947). United States Supreme Court (published).

Peay v. Cox, 190 F. 2d 123-127 (1951). United States Court of Appeals for the Fifth Circuit (published).

Peay v. Cox, 342 US 896 (1951). United States Supreme Court (published).

Plessy v. Ferguson, 163 US 537 (1896). United States Supreme Court (published).

Powell v. Alabama, 287 US 45 (1932). United States Supreme Court (published).

Shinall v. Breazeale, 404 F.2d 785 (1968). United States Court of Appeals for the Fifth Circuit (published).

Shinall v. Mississippi, 43866, 187 So. 2d 840 (Miss. 1966) (published). Mississippi Court of Appeals and Mississippi Supreme Court, Jackson.

Shinall v. Mississippi, 44352, 199 So. 2d 251 (Miss. 1967) (published). Mississippi Supreme Court and Court of Appeals, Jackson.

Shinall v. Mississippi, 44352, 206 So. 2d 332 (Miss. 1968) (published). Mississippi Supreme Court and Court of Appeals, Jackson.

Shinall v. Mississippi, 389 US 1014, S. Ct. 590; 18 L. Ed. 2d 660 (1967). United States Supreme Court (published).

Sipuel v. Oklahoma, 332 US 631 (1948). United States Supreme Court (published).

Smith v. Allwright Election Judge, 321 US 649 (1944). United States Supreme Court (published).

Special Session of Grand Jury Report, January 10, 1929. Minutes. Office of the Circuit Clerk, Forrest County Circuit Court, Hattiesburg.

Sweatt v. Painter, 339 US 629 (1950). United States Supreme Court (published).

Tarrants v. Mississippi, 45684, 236 So. 2d 360 (Miss. 1970) (published). Mississippi Supreme Court and Court of Appeals. Jackson.

US v. Caves (1965), 1963 (H) (M). United States District Court: Mississippi Southern District Court, Eastern Division, Hattiesburg.

US v. Lynd, Mississippi, 301 F.2d 818 (1962). United States Court of Appeals for the Fifth Circuit (published).

US v. Patterson, 219 F.2d 659 (1955). United States Court of Appeals for the Fifth Circuit (published).

US v. Price (1967), 5291. Transcript. United States District Court: Mississippi Southern District Court, Northern Division, Jackson.

Wilson v. Mississippi, 45711, 234 So. 2d 303 (Miss. 1970) (published). Mississippi Supreme Court and Court of Appeals. Jackson.

LOCAL AND STATE RECORDS

City Council, *Minutes*, Hattiesburg City Hall, Hattiesburg, Mississippi.

City Council, *Minutes*, Laurel City Hall, Laurel, Mississippi. *Journal of the Proceedings of the Constitutional Convention, of the State of Mississippi*. Jackson, MS: E. L. Martin, 1890.

Li'l Miss, S. H. Blair High School Yearbooks (1969, 1970, 1971), Hattiesburg High School, Blair Center Library, Hattiesburg, Mississippi.

Mississippi Department of Corrections, Record of Sam Bowers, MDOC #R5597. Jackson, Mississippi.

Mississippi Senate Journal, Extraordinary Session, 1954–1955, *Mississippi Senate Journal*, Regular Sessions. Jackson, MS: Hederman Brothers, 1964, 1968, 1972.

Watson, Percy, legislative experience, Mississippi House of Representatives, Jackson, Mississippi, http://billstatus.ls.state.ms.us/members/house/watson.xml. Accessed January 2010.

Williams, Iola. *The Family of Charles and Laura Craft*. Unpublished genealogical and oral history family study, in author's possession.

UNITED STATES OF AMERICA GOVERNMENT RECORDS

"American Experience, The Presidents," Public Broadcasting Service. Johnson, Lyndon Baines. Speech, November 27, 1963. http://www.pbs.org/wgbh/amex/presidents/36_1 johnson/psources/ps_firstspeech.html. Accessed June 2004.

"American Experience, The Presidents," Public Broadcasting Service. Johnson, Lyndon Baines. Address to Congress, March 15, 1965. http://www.pbs.org/wgbh/amex/presidents/36_1_johnson/psources/ps_overcome.html. Accessed June 2004.

"American Experience, The Presidents," Public Broadcasting Service. Kennedy, John F. Speech, June 11, 1963, http://www.pbs.org/wgbh/amex/presidents/35_kennedy/psources/ps_civilrights.html. Accessed June 2004.

Civil Rights Act of 1968, Pub. L 90-284, 82 Stat. 73 (1968). Library of Congress, Washington, DC.
FBI File: MIBURN (Mississippi Burning). Federal Bureau of Investigation Central Records System, Washington DC. Microfilm.
FBI File: Student Nonviolent Coordinating Committee. Microfilm. Federal Bureau of Investigation Central Records System, Washington DC.
FBI File: Wash, Howard. Federal Bureau of Investigation Central Records System, Washington DC (copy in author's possession).
The MAGIC Documents: Summaries and Transcripts of the Top Secret Diplomatic Communications of Japan, 1938–1945, Microfilm. Library of Congress, Washington, DC.
Mississippi Investigation, 79th Congress, Special Committee to Investigate Senatorial Campaign Expenditures. Records of the US Senate, Record Group 46, National Archives, Washington, DC, 1946.
Roosevelt, Franklin Delano. "The Four Freedoms," Franklin Roosevelt's Annual Address to Congress, Washington DC, January 6, 1941, Franklin Delano Roosevelt Presidential Library and Museum, Hyde Park, New York, http://docs.fdrlibrary.marist.edu:8000/od4frees.html. Accessed June 2004.
United States. Commission on Civil Rights. *A Summary of the Civil Rights Act of 1964. Civil Rights Digest,* special bulletin. Washington DC: US Commission on Civil Rights, August 1964, 1–6.
United States. Commission on Civil Rights Law Enforcement. *A Report on Equal Protection in the South.* Washington, DC: US Government Printing Office, 1965. National Archives, Washington, DC.
United States Congress. House. Committee on Un-American Activities. *Activities of Ku Klux Klan of the United States.* 89th Congress. Washington, DC: US Government Printing Office, 1966. National Archives, Washington, DC.
United States Congress. House. Committee on Un-American Activities. *The Present Day Ku Klux Klan Movement Report, 90th Congress.* Washington, DC: US Government Printing Office, 1967. National Archives, Washington, DC.
United States Federal Census (database online), Provo, UT: The Generations Network, Inc., 2006, Ancestry.com.
United States Historical Census Browser, *Mississippi Total Slaves by County,* Census Data over Time, http://fisher.lib.Virginia.edu. Accessed August 2008.
United States House, 86th Congress, 1st Session, *Civil Rights Hearings Before Subcommittee No. 5 of the Committee on the Judiciary House of Representatives, 1959.* Washington, DC: GPO, 1959. National Archives, Washington, DC.
United States Senate, 79th Congress, *Hearings Before the Special Committee to Investigate Senatorial Campaign Expenditures, 1946.* December 2–5, 1946, Senate Library, vol. 808. Microfiche. National Archives, Washington, DC.
United States Senate, 85th Congress, 1st Session, *Hearings Before the Subcommittee on Constitutional Rights of the Committee on the Judiciary United States Senate, 1957.* Washington, DC: GPO, 1957. National Archives, Washington, DC.
United States House, 90th Congress, 1st Session, *Examination of the War on Poverty Hearings, PT. II.* Washington, DC: GPO, 1967. National Archives, Washington, DC.
US Army Corps of Engineers, "Abstract," *Post Disaster Report on April 1974 Floods in Mississippi in the Mobile District,* May 1974, United States Geological Survey Water Resources in Mississippi, http://choctaw.er.usgs.gov/new_web/reports/other_reports/flood/april74postdisaster.html. Accessed June 2004.
Voting Rights Act of 1965, Pub. L. No. 89-110, 79 Stat. 437 (1965). Library of Congress, Washington, DC.

Bibliography

ORAL HISTORIES, DOCUMENTARIES, MEDIA, AND FORUMS

Adickes, Sandra, interview by Stephanie Scull Millet, October 21, 1999. Digital Collection. Mississippi Oral History Program, the Center for Oral History and Cultural Heritage, University of Southern Mississippi, Hattiesburg.

Abzug, Liz, interview by Bridgette McGee-Robinson, provided to author by Radio Diaries, New York, NY.

Austin, Gladys, interview by Kim Adams, May 2, 1995. Digital Collection. Mississippi Oral History Program, the Center for Oral History and Cultural Heritage, University of Southern Mississippi, Hattiesburg.

Austin, Gladys, May 5, 2009. Oral Histories by Patricia (Buzard) Boyett. Recording. Mississippi Oral History Program, the Center for Oral History and Cultural Heritage, University of Southern Mississippi, Hattiesburg.

Birth of a Nation. Film. Prod. and dir. by D. W. Griffith, Image Entertainment, 1915. Image Entertainment, Los Angeles.

Baker, Constance, interview by Kim Adams, April 3, 1995. Digital Collection. Mississippi Oral History Program, the Center for Oral History and Cultural Heritage, University of Southern Mississippi, Hattiesburg.

Baker, Douglass, September 24, 2008. Oral Histories by Patricia (Buzard) Boyett. Recording. Mississippi Oral History Program, the Center for Oral History and Cultural Heritage, University of Southern Mississippi, Hattiesburg.

Barnes, Ariel, interview by Sarah Rowe, April 1, 1993. Digital Collection. Mississippi Oral History Program, the Center for Oral History and Cultural Heritage, University of Southern Mississippi, Hattiesburg.

Barnes, Ariel, interview by Priscilla Walker, January 6, 1995. Digital Collection. Mississippi Oral History Program, the Center for Oral History and Cultural Heritage, University of Southern Mississippi, Hattiesburg.

Benton, Clementine, September 23, 2008. Oral Histories by Patricia (Buzard) Boyett. Recording. Mississippi Oral History Program, the Center for Oral History and Cultural Heritage, University of Southern Mississippi, Hattiesburg.

Bolton, Frazier, May 6, 2009. Oral Histories by Patricia (Buzard) Boyett. Recording. Mississippi Oral History Program, the Center for Oral History and Cultural Heritage, University of Southern Mississippi, Hattiesburg.

Bowers, Sam H., interview by Deborah Spencer, October 24, 1983, January 30, 1984, November 5, 1984, January 30, 1984, MDAH Digital Collection, Mississippi Department of Archives and History, Jackson: http://mdah.state.ms.us/arlib/contents/er/bowers.

Boyd, Richard, and Earlene Boyd, interview by Charles Bolton, August 29, 1991. Digital Collection. Mississippi Oral History Program, the Center for Oral History and Cultural Heritage, University of Southern Mississippi, Hattiesburg.

Bradley, Kim, May 4, 2010. Oral Histories by Patricia (Buzard) Boyett. Recording. Mississippi Oral History Program, the Center for Oral History and Cultural Heritage, University of Southern Mississippi, Hattiesburg.

Branch, Raylawni, interview by Kim Adams, October 25, 1993. Digital Collection. Mississippi Oral History Program, the Center for Oral History and Cultural Heritage, University of Southern Mississippi, Hattiesburg.

Branch, Raylawni, interview by Patricia Buzard (Boyett) and Danielle McGuire, June 3, 2006. Recording. Mississippi Oral History Program, the Center for Oral History and Cultural Heritage, University of Southern Mississippi, Hattiesburg.

Bunch, Jamie, May 14, 2010. Oral Histories by Patricia (Buzard) Boyett. Recording. Mississippi Oral History Program, the Center for Oral History and Cultural Heritage, University of Southern Mississippi, Hattiesburg.

Burger, N. R., interview by R. Wayne Pyle, May 11, 1982. Digital Collection. Mississippi Oral History Program, the Center for Oral History and Cultural Heritage, University of Southern Mississippi, Hattiesburg.

Burns, Frederick G., May 12, 2009; June 10, 2009; April 28, 2010. Oral Histories by Patricia (Buzard) Boyett. Recording. Mississippi Oral History Program, the Center for Oral History and Cultural Heritage, University of Southern Mississippi, Hattiesburg.

Carroll, Carter, June 8, 2009. Oral Histories by Patricia (Buzard) Boyett. Recording. Mississippi Oral History Program, the Center for Oral History and Cultural Heritage, University of Southern Mississippi, Hattiesburg.

Carter, Lindsay, February 5, 2005. Oral Histories by Patricia (Buzard) Boyett. Recording. Mississippi Oral History Program, the Center for Oral History and Cultural Heritage, University of Southern Mississippi, Hattiesburg.

Caves, Terry, July 28, 2006. *An Oral History of Jones County*, vol. 792 (2006), by Patricia Buzard (Boyett). Mississippi Oral History Program, the Center for Oral History and Cultural Heritage, University of Southern Mississippi, Hattiesburg.

Coleman, Larry, June 12, 2009. Oral Histories by Patricia (Buzard) Boyett. Recording. Mississippi Oral History Program, the Center for Oral History and Cultural Heritage, University of Southern Mississippi, Hattiesburg.

The Convention Challenge and the Freedom Vote, Civil Rights Movement Veterans, http://www.crmvet.org/docs/ms_primer1_64.pdf. Accessed March 2014.

Cooley, Lula, May 13, 2010. Oral Histories by Patricia (Buzard) Boyett. Recording. Mississippi Oral History Program, the Center for Oral History and Cultural Heritage, University of Southern Mississippi, Hattiesburg.

Dahmer, Ellie, interview by Orley B. Caudill, July 2, 1974. Digital Collection. Mississippi Oral History Program, the Center for Oral History and Cultural Heritage, University of Southern Mississippi, Hattiesburg.

Dahmer, Vernon, Jr., interview by Re'Tina D. Gray, April 1, 2001. Recording. Mississippi Oral History Program, the Center for Oral History and Cultural Heritage, University of Southern Mississippi, Hattiesburg.

Delgado, Deborah Denard, June 8, 2009. Oral Histories by Patricia (Buzard) Boyett. Recording. Mississippi Oral History Program, the Center for Oral History and Cultural Heritage, University of Southern Mississippi, Hattiesburg.

Dukes, James K., May 12, 2010. Oral Histories by Patricia (Buzard) Boyett. Recording. Mississippi Oral History Program, the Center for Oral History and Cultural Heritage, University of Southern Mississippi, Hattiesburg.

Dukes, William F., interview by Orley Caudill, January 23, 1973. Digital Collection. Mississippi Oral History.Program, the Center for Oral History and Cultural Heritage, University of Southern Mississippi, Hattiesburg.

Dukes, William F., interview by Orley B. Caudill, January 23, 1973, vol. 40. Transcribed and bound. Mississippi Oral History Program, the Center for Oral History and Cultural Heritage, University of Southern Mississippi, Hattiesburg.

DuPree, Johnny, June 9, 2009. Oral Histories by Patricia (Buzard) Boyett. Recording. Mississippi Oral History Program, the Center for Oral History and Cultural Heritage, University of Southern Mississippi, Hattiesburg.

Easton, Lillie Jackson, September 26, 2008. Oral Histories by Patricia (Buzard) Boyett. Recording.

Mississippi Oral History Program, the Center for Oral History and Cultural Heritage, University of Southern Mississippi, Hattiesburg.

Eyes on the Prize: America's Civil Rights Years (1954–1965). Henry Hampton Collection, Film and Media Archive, Washington University Libraries. Washington University Libraries, St. Louis, Missouri.

Fairley, J. C., interview by Mike Garvey, January 31, February 4, 1977, vol. 375. Transcribed and bound. Mississippi Oral History Program, the Center for Oral History and Cultural Heritage, University of Southern Mississippi, Hattiesburg.

Fairley, J. C., Mamie Philips, and Charles Philips, interview by Charles Bolton, June 24, 1998. Digital Collection. Mississippi Oral History Program, the Center for Oral History and Cultural Heritage, University of Southern Mississippi, Hattiesburg.

Fairley, Kenneth, Sr., May 8, May 13, 2009. Oral Histories by Patricia (Buzard) Boyett. Recording. Mississippi Oral History Program, the Center for Oral History and Cultural Heritage, University of Southern Mississippi, Hattiesburg.

Fielder, Ben, and Mable Fielder, interview by Neil McMillen, January 29, 1994, vol. 483. Transcribed and bound. Mississippi Oral History Program, the Center for Oral History and Cultural Heritage, University of Southern Mississippi, Hattiesburg.

Frazier, John, speech. Social Justice Seminar, November 9, 2007. Compact Disc. Department of Mass Communications and Journalism, University of Southern Mississippi, Hattiesburg.

Freedom Candidates, April 1964, http://www.crmvet.org/docs/64_mfdp_candidates.pdf. Accessed March 2014.

Funchess, Glenda, September 23, 2008. Oral Histories by Patricia (Buzard) Boyett. Recording. Mississippi Oral History Program, the Center for Oral History and Cultural Heritage, University of Southern Mississippi, Hattiesburg.

Gore, Maycie, June 10, 2009. Oral Histories by Patricia (Buzard) Boyett. Recording. Mississippi Oral History Program, the Center for Oral History and Cultural Heritage, University of Southern Mississippi, Hattiesburg.

Gray, William G. "Bud," interview by Charles Bolton, March 19, 1999, vol. 728. Transcribed and bound. Mississippi Oral History Program, the Center for Oral History and Cultural Heritage, University of Southern Mississippi, Hattiesburg.

Hall, Pinky, interview by Kim Adams, December 13, 1995. Digital Collection. Mississippi Oral History Program, the Center for Oral History and Cultural Heritage, University of Southern Mississippi, Hattiesburg.

Hall, Stanton, interview by Carl Willis, April 14, 1972, vol. 3. Transcribed and bound. Mississippi Oral History Program, the Center for Oral History and Cultural Heritage, University of Southern Mississippi, Hattiesburg.

Hamilton, M. W., interview by Orley B. Caudill, February 13, 1978, vol. 464. Transcribed and bound. Mississippi Oral History Program, the Center for Oral History and Cultural Heritage, University of Southern Mississippi, Hattiesburg.

Helfrich, Robert, October 10, 2009; May 4, 2009. Oral Histories by Patricia (Buzard) Boyett. Recording. Mississippi Oral History Program, the Center for Oral History and Cultural Heritage, University of Southern Mississippi, Hattiesburg.

Holloway, Eddie, September 30, 2008. Oral Histories by Patricia (Buzard) Boyett. Recording. Mississippi Oral History Program, the Center for Oral History and Cultural Heritage, University of Southern Mississippi, Hattiesburg.

Jackson, Jimmella Stokes, January 9, 2009. Oral Histories by Patricia (Buzard) Boyett. Recording. Mississippi Oral History Program, the Center for Oral History and Cultural Heritage, University of Southern Mississippi, Hattiesburg.

Jefcoat, Douglas E., July 19, 2006. *An Oral History of Jones County*, vol. 792 (2006), by Patricia Buzard (Boyett). Mississippi Oral History Program, the Center for Oral History and Cultural Heritage, University of Southern Mississippi, Hattiesburg.

Johnson, Della Louise, interview by Bridgette McGee-Robinson, audio excerpts, provided to author by Radio Diaries, New York, NY.

Jones, James, October 1, 2008; June 9, 2009. Oral Histories by Patricia (Buzard) Boyett. Recording. Mississippi Oral History Program, the Center for Oral History and Cultural Heritage, University of Southern Mississippi, Hattiesburg.

Jones, Manuel, February 22, 2006. Oral Histories by Patricia (Buzard) Boyett. Recording. Mississippi Oral History Program, the Center for Oral History and Cultural Heritage, University of Southern Mississippi, Hattiesburg.

"Killed by the Klan," prod. and dir. by Charles C. Stuart, Discovery Channel by Stuart Television Productions, Inc., Concord, MA, 1999.

Knight, Thomas, Sr., interview by Charles Bolton, February 7, 1992. Transcribed and bound. Mississippi Oral History Program, the Center for Oral History and Cultural Heritage, University of Southern Mississippi, Hattiesburg.

Landers, Wayne, May 6, 2009. Oral Histories by Patricia (Buzard) Boyett. Recording. Mississippi Oral History Program, the Center for Oral History and Cultural Heritage, University of Southern Mississippi, Hattiesburg.

Lawrence, Charles, May 5, 2010. Oral Histories by Patricia (Buzard) Boyett. Recording. Mississippi Oral History Program, the Center for Oral History and Cultural Heritage, University of Southern Mississippi, Hattiesburg.

Lucas, Aubrey, April 29, 2010. Oral Histories by Patricia (Buzard) Boyett. Recording. Mississippi Oral History Program, the Center for Oral History and Cultural Heritage, University of Southern Mississippi, Hattiesburg.

Mack, Melvin, July 17, 2006. *An Oral History of Jones County*, vol. 792 (2006), by Patricia Buzard (Boyett). Mississippi Oral History Program, the Center for Oral History and Cultural Heritage, University of Southern Mississippi, Hattiesburg.

Magee, Clarence, September 25, 2008. Oral Histories by Patricia (Buzard) Boyett. Recording. Mississippi Oral History Program, the Center for Oral History and Cultural Heritage, University of Southern Mississippi, Hattiesburg.

Magee, Johnny, May 12, 2009. Oral Histories by Patricia (Buzard) Boyett. Recordings. Mississippi Oral History Program, the Center for Oral History and Cultural Heritage, University of Southern Mississippi, Hattiesburg.

McCarty, Oseola, interview by Shana Walton, February 22, 1996. Digital Collection. Mississippi Oral History Program, the Center for Oral History and Cultural Heritage, University of Southern Mississippi, Hattiesburg.

McGee-Robinson, Bridgette, narration, provided to author by Radio Diaries, New York, NY.

McGee, Billy, May 7, 2009. Oral Histories by Patricia (Buzard) Boyett. Recording. Mississippi Oral History Program, the Center for Oral History and Cultural Heritage, University of Southern Mississippi, Hattiesburg.

McGill, Larry, April 24, 2007. Oral Histories by Patricia (Buzard) Boyett. Recording. Mississippi Oral History Program, the Center for Oral History and Cultural Heritage, University of Southern Mississippi, Hattiesburg.

Mills, Donna, interview by Bridgette McGee-Robinson, provided to author by Radio Diaries, New York, NY.

Myers, Hulon, interview by Orley Caudill, July 11, 1979, vol. 349. Transcribed and bound. Mississippi Oral History Program, the Center for Oral History and Cultural Heritage, University of Southern Mississippi, Hattiesburg.

Naylor, Henry, June 9, 2009. Oral Histories by Patricia (Buzard) Boyett. Recording. Mississippi Oral History Program, the Center for Oral History and Cultural Heritage, University of Southern Mississippi, Hattiesburg.

Nix, James, interview by Sarah Rowe, March 7, 1993. Digital Collection. Mississippi Oral History Program, the Center for Oral History and Cultural Heritage, University of Southern Mississippi, Hattiesburg.

Outlaw, Cheryl, October 2, 2008. Oral Histories by Patricia (Buzard) Boyett. Recording. Mississippi Oral History Program, the Center for Oral History and Cultural Heritage, University of Southern Mississippi, Hattiesburg.

Pickering, Charles, September 7, 2006. *An Oral History of Jones County*, vol. 792 (2006), by Patricia Buzard (Boyett). Mississippi Oral History Program, the Center for Oral History and Cultural Heritage, University of Southern Mississippi, Hattiesburg.

Preyor, Carol Jackson, September 26, 2008. Oral Histories by Patricia (Buzard) Boyett. Recording. Mississippi Oral History Program, the Center for Oral History and Cultural Heritage, University of Southern Mississippi, Hattiesburg.

Quinn, Peter Oliver, interview by William Henderson, November 2, 1999. Digital Collection. Mississippi Oral History Program, the Center for Oral History and Cultural Heritage, University of Southern Mississippi, Hattiesburg.

Sanders, Ann, interview by Samara Freemark and Radio Diaries Staff, provided to author by Radio Diaries, New York, NY.

Saxon, George, interview by Reid Stoner Derr, June 3, 1993. Digital Collection. Mississippi Oral History Program, the Center for Oral History and Cultural Heritage, University of Southern Mississippi, Hattiesburg.

Scarborough, William K., April 25, 2007. Oral Histories by Patricia (Buzard) Boyett. Recording. Mississippi Oral History Program, the Center for Oral History and Cultural Heritage, University of Southern Mississippi, Hattiesburg.

Schwartz, Joseph, interview by Shelia Michaels, July 24, 1999. Digital Collection. Mississippi Oral History Program, the Center for Oral History and Cultural Heritage, University of Southern Mississippi, Hattiesburg.

Shaw, Terry, interview by Stephanie Scull Millet, June 7, 1999. Digital Collection. Mississippi Oral History Program, the Center for Oral History and Cultural Heritage, University of Southern Mississippi, Hattiesburg.

Siggers, Arthur, June 10, 2009. Oral Histories by Patricia (Buzard) Boyett. Recording. Mississippi Oral History Program, the Center for Oral History and Cultural Heritage, University of Southern Mississippi, Hattiesburg.

Simmons, Gwendolyn, interview, http://www.veteransofhope.org/show.php?vid=32&tid=13&sid=44#. Accessed July 2009.

Sims, Charlie, May 6, 2009. Oral Histories by Patricia (Buzard) Boyett. Recording. Mississippi Oral History Program, the Center for Oral History and Cultural Heritage, University of Southern Mississippi, Hattiesburg.

Smith, E. Hammond, interview by Orley B. Caudill, April 8, 1982. Digital Collection. Mississippi Oral History Program, the Center for Oral History and Cultural Heritage, University of Southern Mississippi, Hattiesburg.

Smith, Jeanette, May 14, 2009. Oral Histories by Patricia (Buzard) Boyett. Recording. Mississippi Oral History Program, the Center for Oral History and Cultural Heritage, University of Southern Mississippi, Hattiesburg.

Spinks, Eberta, interview by Kim Adams, Spring 1995. Digital Collection. Mississippi Oral History Program, the Center for Oral History and Cultural Heritage, University of Southern Mississippi, Hattiesburg.

Spinks, Sam, interview by Charles Bolton, September 15, 1997, vol. 693. Transcribed and bound. Mississippi Oral History Program, the Center for Oral History and Cultural Heritage, University of Southern Mississippi, Hattiesburg.

Swartzfager, Jon, interview by Bridgette McGee-Robinson, provided to author by Radio Diaries, New York, NY.

Vincent, Susan, June 12, 2009. Oral Histories by Patricia (Buzard) Boyett. Recording. Mississippi Oral History Program, the Center for Oral History and Cultural Heritage, University of Southern Mississippi, Hattiesburg.

Wade, Daisy Harris, interview by Patricia Buzard (Boyett) and Danielle McGuire, June 5, 2006. Recording. Mississippi Oral History Program, the Center for Oral History and Cultural Heritage, University of Southern Mississippi, Hattiesburg.

Wade, Daisy Harris, September 26, 2008. Oral Histories by Patricia (Buzard) Boyett. Recording. Mississippi Oral History Program, the Center for Oral History and Cultural Heritage, University of Southern Mississippi, Hattiesburg.

Wade-Seals, Cora, May 5, 2009. Oral Histories by Patricia (Buzard) Boyett. Recording. Mississippi Oral History Program, the Center for Oral History and Cultural Heritage, University of Southern Mississippi, Hattiesburg.

Ware, Dave, June 12, 2009. Oral Histories by Patricia (Buzard) Boyett. Recording. Mississippi Oral History Program, the Center for Oral History and Cultural Heritage, University of Southern Mississippi, Hattiesburg.

Watkins, Hollis, interview by John Rachal, October 23, 29, 30, 1996. Digital Collection. Mississippi Oral History Program, the Center for Oral History and Cultural Heritage, University of Southern Mississippi, Hattiesburg.

Welborn, Clint, Jr., interview by Jonathan Odell, n.d., recording, in author's possession.

Wells, Ray William, interview by Lawrence Kight, May 6, 1997, vol. 697. Transcribed and bound. Mississippi Oral History Program, the Center for Oral History and Cultural Heritage, University of Southern Mississippi, Hattiesburg.

Wheat, Anthony, May 5, 2010. Oral Histories by Patricia (Buzard) Boyett. Recording. Mississippi Oral History Program, the Center for Oral History and Cultural Heritage, University of Southern Mississippi, Hattiesburg.

Williams, Iola, interview by Brad Kavan, August 26, 2004. Recording. Mississippi Oral History Program, the Center for Oral History and Cultural Heritage, University of Southern Mississippi, Hattiesburg.

Williams, Iola, November 6, 2006. Oral Histories by Patricia (Buzard) Boyett. Recordings. Mississippi Oral History Program, the Center for Oral History and Cultural Heritage, University of Southern Mississippi, Hattiesburg.

"Willie McGee and the Traveling Electric Chair," *All Things Considered*, National Public Radio, prod. Joe Richman and Samara Freemark. May 7, 2010, Radio Diaries.

"Willie McGee Execution," Live Radio Broadcast by Jack Dick and Granville Walters, WAML and WAFL, May 7–8, 1951. Recording. Mississippi Oral History Program, the Center for Oral History and Cultural Heritage, University of Southern Mississippi, Hattiesburg.

Woullard, Roderick, May 13, 2009. Oral Histories by Patricia (Buzard) Boyett. Recordings. Mississippi Oral History Program, the Center for Oral History and Cultural Heritage, University of Southern Mississippi, Hattiesburg.

Wyatt, Jerome, July 21, 2006. *An Oral History of Jones County*, vol. 792 (2006), by Patricia Buzard (Boyett). Mississippi Oral History Program, the Center for Oral History and Cultural Heritage, University of Southern Mississippi, Hattiesburg.

NEWSPAPERS, MAGAZINES, PERIODICALS

Atlanta-Journal Constitution
Chicago Defender
Clarion-Ledger (Jackson, MS)
Commercial Appeal (Memphis, TN)
Daily Worker (New York, NY)
Delta Democrat-Times (Greenville, MS)
Hattiesburg American (MS)
Hattiesburg Daily Progress (MS)
Jackson Advocate (MS)
Jackson Daily News (MS)
Laurel Chronicle (MS)
Laurel Daily Leader (MS)
Laurel Leader-Call (MS)
Life (magazine)
Los Angeles Times
Mississippi Free Press (MS)
Meridian Star (MS)
Newsweek
New York Times
The New York Times Magazine
New York Post
Petal Paper (Petal, MS)
Pittsburgh Courier (PA)
Ralls County Record (New London, MO)
Student Printz (Hattiesburg, MS)
Time (magazine)
Times Picayune (New Orleans)

MISCELLANEOUS WEBSITES AND DATABASES

Clyde Kennard Timeline, http://www6.district125.k12.il.us/~bbradfor/kennardnytimes05.html. Accessed October 2006.

Elliott Andalman, Andalman & Flynn, Attorneys at Law, http://www.andalmanflynn.com/profiles/elliott_andalman/experience. Accessed October 2010.

The Lynching Century: African Americans Who Died in Racial Violence in the United States, http://www.geocities.com/Colosseum/Base/8507/NLPlaces1.htm. Accessed March 10, 2007.

MSNBC News, "Ex-Miss Sheriff Deputy Charged in '64 deaths," *MSNBC.com*, January 24, 2007, http://wwww.msnbc.msn.com/id/16792385/. Accessed January 2007.

Project HAL (Historical American Lynching) Data Collection Project, collected by Elizabeth Hines and Eliza Steelwater, http://usersbestweb.bestweb.net/~rg/lyncihgs/Mississippi%20Lynchings.htm. Accessed December 2010.

Public School Report, http://schools.publicschoolsreport.com/Mississippi. Accessed April 1, 2014.

Walmart History Timeline, http://walmartstores.com/AboutUs/7603.aspx. Accessed October 2010.

BOOKS, THESES, AND DISSERTATIONS

Adickes, Sandra. *The Legacy of a Freedom School*. New York: Palgrave MacMillan, 2005.

Alexander, Michelle. *The New Jim Crow: Mass Incarceration in the Age of Colorblindness*. New York: The New Press, 2010.

Austin, Curtis J. *Up against the Wall: Violence in the Making and Unmaking of the Black Panther Party*. Fayetteville: University of Arkansas Press, 2006.

Bannister, Robert C. *Social Darwinism: Science and Myth in Anglo-American Social Thought*. Philadelphia: Temple University Press, 1979.

Bartley, Numan V. *The Rise of Massive Resistance: Race and Politics in the South during the 1950's*. Baton Rouge: Louisiana State University Press, 1969.

Bates, Ruth L. *Before There Was a Mississippi*, Kearney, NE: Morris Publishing, 1999.

Belfrage, Sally. *Freedom Summer*. Charlottesville: University of Virginia Press, 1990.

Belknap, Michael R. *Federal Law and Southern Order*. Athens: University of Georgia Press, 1987.

Bolton, Charles C. *The Hardest Deal of All: The Battle Over School Integration in Mississippi, 1870–1980*. Jackson: University Press of Mississippi, 2005.

Bond, Bradley G. *Political Culture in the Nineteenth Century South, Mississippi, 1830–1900*. Baton Rouge: Louisiana State University Press, 1995.

Brooks, Roy L., Gilbert Paul Carrasco, and Gordon A. Martin Jr., eds. *Civil Rights Litigation: Cases and Perspectives*. Durham, NC: Carolina Academic Press, 1995.

Brown-Nagin, Tomiko. *Courage to Dissent: Atlanta and the Long History of the Civil Rights Movement*. New York: Oxford University Press, 2011.

Branch, Taylor. *Parting the Waters: America in the King Years, 1954–63*. New York: Simon and Schuster, 1989.

Bynum, Victoria. *The Free State of Jones: Mississippi's Longest Civil War*. Chapel Hill: University of North Carolina Press, 2001.

Cagin, Seth, and Philip Dray. *We Are Not Afraid: The Story of Goodman, Schwerner and Chaney and the Civil Rights Campaign for Mississippi*. New York: Nation Books, 2006.

Capici, Dominic J., Jr. *The Lynching of Cleo Wright*. Lexington: University Press of Kentucky, 1998.

Carson, Clayborne. *In Struggle: SNCC and the Black Awakening of the 1960s*. Cambridge, MA: Harvard University Press, 1991.

Carter, Dan T. *Scottsboro: A Tragedy of the American South*. Baton Rouge: Louisiana State University Press, 1979.

Carter, David C. *The Music Has Gone Out of the Movement: Civil Rights and the Johnson Administration, 1965–1968*. Chapel Hill: University of North Carolina Press, 2009.

Chafe, William H. *Civilities and Civil Liberties: Greensboro, North Carolina and the Black Struggle for Freedom*. New York: Oxford University Press, 1980.

Chalmers, David. *Backfire: How the Ku Klux Klan Helped the Civil Rights Movement*. Lanham, MD: Rowman and Littlefield, 2003.

Chalmers, David M. *Hooded Americanism: The History of the Ku Klux Klan*. Durham, NC: Duke University Press, 1987.

Chang, Iris. *The Rape of Nanking*. New York: Penguin Books, 1998.

Chappell, David. *A Stone of Hope: Prophetic Religion and the Death of Jim Crow*. Chapel Hill: University of North Carolina Press, 2004.

Cortner, Richard C. *A Scottsboro Case in Mississippi: The Supreme Court and Brown v. Mississippi*. Jackson: University Press of Mississippi, 2005.

Crespino, Joseph. *In Search of Another Country: Mississippi and the Conservative Counterrevolution*. Princeton, NJ: Princeton University Press, 2007.

Cronon, E. David. *Black Moses: The Story of Marcus Garvey and the United Negro Improvement Association.* Madison: University of Wisconsin Press, 1960.
Danielson, Chris. *After Freedom Summer: How Race Realigned Mississippi Politics, 1965–1986.* Gainesville: University Press of Florida, 2012.
Degler, Carl. *In Search of Human Nature.* New York: Oxford University Press, 1991.
Dittmer, John. *Local People: The Struggle for Civil Rights in Mississippi.* Urbana: University of Illinois Press, 1995.
Dixon, Thomas. *The Clansman.* New York: Gossett and Dunlap, 1905.
Dower, John W. *War without Mercy: Race and Power in the Pacific War.* New York: Pantheon Books, 1986.
Duziak, Mary. *Cold War, Civil Rights: Race and the Image of American Democracy.* Princeton, NJ: Princeton University Press, 2000.
East, P. D. *Magnolia Jungle.* New York: Simon and Schuster, 1960.
Eagles, Charles W. *The Price of Defiance: James Meredith and the Integration of Ole Miss.* Chapel Hill: University of North Carolina Press, 2009.
Evers, Myrlie. *For Us, The Living.* 1967. Reprint, Jackson: Banner Books, University Press of Mississippi, 1996.
Fairclough, Adam. *Race and Democracy: The Civil Rights Struggle in Louisiana 1915–1972.* Athens: University of Georgia Press, 1995.
———. *To Redeem the Soul of America: The Southern Christian Leadership Conference and Martin Luther King, Jr.* Athens: University of Georgia Press, 1987.
Farber, David. *The Age of Great Dreams: America in the 1960s.* New York: Hill & Wang, 1994.
Finkle, Lee. *Forum for Protest: The Black Press during World War II.* Cranbury, NJ: Associated University Presses, 1975.
Finnegan, Terence Robert. "At the Hands of Parties Unknown: Lynching in Mississippi and South Carolina, 1881–1930." PhD diss., University of Illinois, 1993.
Flynt, Wayne. *Alabama Baptists: Southern Baptists in the Heart of Dixie.* Tuscaloosa: University of Alabama Press, 1998.
Foner, Eric. *A Short History of Reconstruction, 1863–1877.* New York: Harper Collins, 1990.
Forman, James. *The Making of Black Revolutionaries.* 1972; Seattle: University of Washington Press, 1997.
Franklin, John Hope, and Alfred A. Moss. *From Slavery to Freedom: A History of African Americans.* 7th ed. 1947. Reprint, New York: McGraw Hill, 1994.
Frazier, Franklin. *The Negro Family in the United States.* New York: The Dryden Press, 1951.
Frederickson, George M. *The Black Image in the White Mind.* 1971. Reprint, Hanover, NH: Wesleyan University Press, 1987.
———. *Racism: A Short History.* Princeton, NJ: Princeton University Press, 2002.
Gates, Robbins L. *The Making of Massive Resistance: Virginia's Politics of Public School Desegregation, 1954–56.* 1964. Reprint, Chapel Hill: University of North Carolina Press, 2011.
Gellman, Erik S. *Death Blow to Jim Crow: The National Negro Congress and the Rise of Militant Civil Rights.* Chapel Hill: University of North Carolina Press, 2012.
Gerstle, Gary. *American Crucible: Race and Nation in the Twentieth Century.* Princeton, NJ: Princeton University Press, 2001.
Gilmore, Glenda. *Defying Dixie: The Radical Roots of Civil Rights, 1919–1950.* New York: W.W. Norton, 2009.
Gitlin, Todd. *The Sixties: Years of Hope, Days of Rage.* New York: Bantam Books, 1993.
Goldfield, David R. *Black, White, and Southern: Race Relations and Southern Culture, 1940 to the Present.* Baton Rouge: Louisiana State University Press, 1990.

Grady-Willis, Winston A. *Challenging U.S. Apartheid: Atlanta and the Black Struggle for Human Rights*. Durham, NC: Duke University Press, 2006.

Grantham, Dewey. *The South in Modern America: A Region at Odds*. New York: Harper Collins, 1994.

Griffin, John Howard. *Black Like Me*. 1962. Thirty-fifth Anniversary ed. New York: Signet Books, 1996.

Griffith, Barbara S. *The Crisis of American Labor: Operation Dixie and the Defeat of the CIO*. Philadelphia: Temple University Press, 1988.

Grossman, James R. *Land of Hope: Chicago, Black Southerners, and the Great Migration*. Chicago: University of Chicago, 1991.

Hall, Jacquelyn Dowd. *Revolt against Chivalry: Jessie Daniel Ames and the Women's Campaign against Lynching*. New York: Columbia University Press, 1979.

Hamlin, Francoise N. *Crossroads at Clarksdale: The Black Freedom Struggle in the Mississippi Delta after World War II*. Chapel Hill: University of North Carolina Press, 2012.

Heard, Alex. *The Eyes of Willie McGee: A Tragedy of Race, Sex, and Secrets in the Jim Crow South*. New York: Harper Collins, 2010.

Henry, Aaron, with Constance Baker. *Aaron Henry: The Fire Ever Burning*. Jackson: University Press of Mississippi, 2000.

Hill, Lance. *Deacons for Defense: Armed Resistance and the Civil Rights Movement*. Chapel Hill: University of North Carolina Press, 2004.

Hobbes, John. "Leviathan." In *Classics of Moral and Political Theory*, edited by Michael L. Morgan, 584–735. 1651; Indianapolis: Hackett Publishing, 1996.

Holsart, Faith S., Martha Prescod Noonan, Judy Richardson, Betty Gammon Robinson, Jean Smith Young, and Dorothy M. Zellner, eds. *Hands on the Freedom Plow: Personal Accounts by Women in SNCC*. Urbana: University of Illinois Press, 2010.

Houck, David E. *Rhetoric, Religion, and the Civil Rights Movement, 1954–1965*. Ed. David E. Houck and David E. Dixon. Waco, TX: Baylor University Press, 2006.

Howard, John. *Concentration Camps on the Homefront: Japanese Americans in the House of Jim Crow*. Chicago: Chicago University Press, 2008. Kindle edition.

Jeffries, Hasaan. *Bloody Lowndes: Civil Rights and Black Power in Alabama's Blackbelt*. New York: New York University Press, 2010.

Johnson, Walter. *River of Dark Dreams: Slavery and Empire in the Cotton Kingdom*. Cambridge, MA: Harvard University Press, 2013.

Jones, William P. *The Tribe of Black Ulysses: African American Lumber Workers in the Jim Crow South*. Urbana: University of Illinois Press, 2005.

Katz, Michael B. *The "Underclass" Debate: Views of History*. Princeton, NJ: Princeton University Press, 1993.

Key, David Stanton. "Laurel, Mississippi: A Historical Perspective." Master's thesis, East Tennessee State University, 2001

Kluger, Richard. *Simple Justice: The History of Brown v. Board of Education and Black America's Struggle for Equality*. New York: Alfred A. Knopf, 1976.

Knight, Anna. *Mississippi Girl: An Autobiography*. Nashville, TN: Southern Publishing Association, 1952.

Kruse, Kevin, and Stephen Tuck, ed. *Fog of War: The Second World War and the Civil Rights Movement*. Oxford: Oxford University Press, 2012. Kindle edition.

Laqueur, Walter. *The New Terrorism: Fanaticism and the Arms of Mass Destruction*. New York: Oxford University Press, 1999.

Laurel City Directory, 1945–1946. Corpus Christi, TX: C. B. Page Directory Co., 1964.

Laurel City Directory, 1967. Richmond, VA: R. L. Polk, 1967.
Lawson, Steven F. *Black Ballots: Voting Rights in the South, 1944–1969.* New York: Columbia University Press, 1976.
———. *Running for Freedom: Civil Rights and Black Politics in America since 1941.* New York: McGraw Hill, 1991.
Lee, Harper. *To Kill A Mockingbird.* New York: Warner Books, 1960.
Lefever, Harry. *Undaunted by the Fight: Spellman College and the Civil Rights Movement, 1957–1967.* Macon, GA: Mercer University Press, 2006.
Lemann, Nicholas. *The Promised Land: The Great Black Migration and How it Changed America.* New York: Vintage Books, 1992.
Lewis, David Levering. *When Harlem Was in Vogue.* New York: Penguin Books, 1997.
Locke, John. "Second Treaties of Civil Government." In *Classics of Moral and Political Theory*, edited by Michael L. Morgan, 739–815. 1690; Indianapolis: Hackett Publishing, 1996.
Litwack, Leon. *Trouble in Mind: Black Southerners in the Age of Jim Crow.* New York: Alfred A. Knopf, 1998.
Maney, Patrick J. *The Roosevelt Presence: The Life and Legacy of FDR.* Berkeley: University of California Press, 1992.
Martin, Gordon A. *Count Them One by One: Black Mississippians Fighting for the Right to Vote.* Jackson: University Press of Mississippi, 2010.
Mars, Florence, with the assistance of Lynn Eden. *Witness in Philadelphia.* Baton Rouge: Louisiana State University Press, 1977.
Marsh, Charles. *God's Long Summer: Stories of Faith and Civil Rights.* Princeton, NJ: Princeton University Press, 1997.
———. *The Last Days: A Son's Story of Sin and Segregation at the Dawn of a New South.* New York: Basic Books, 2001.
———. *The Beloved Communit7y: How Faith Shapes Social Justice from the Civil Rights Movement to Today.* New York: Basic Books, 2006.
Mason, Gilbert R., with James Patterson Smith. *Beaches, Blood, and Ballots: A Black Doctor's Civil Rights Struggle.* Jackson: University Press of Mississippi, 2000.
Massey, Douglas S., and Nancy A. Denton. *American Apartheid: Segregation and the Making of the Underclass.* Cambridge, MA: Harvard University Press, 1993.
McAdam, Doug. *Freedom Summer.* New York: Oxford University Press, 1990.
McGovern, James R. *Anatomy of a Lynching: The Killing of Claude Neal.* Baton Rouge: Louisiana State University Press, 1982.
McGuire, Danielle L. *At the Dark End of the Street: Black Women, Rape, and Resistance—A New History of the Civil Rights Movement from Rosa Parks to the Rise of Black Power.* New York: Alfred A. Knopf, 2001.
McGuire, Danielle L., and John Dittmer, eds. *Freedom Rights: New Perspectives on the Civil Rights Movement.* Lexington: University Press of Kentucky, 2011.
McGuire, Philip, ed. *Taps for a Jim Crow Army: Letters from Black Soldiers in World War II.* Santa Barbara, CA: ABC-Clio, 1983.
McMillen, Neil R. *Dark Journey: Black Mississippians in the Age of Jim Crow.* Urbana: University of Illinois Press, 1990.
———. *The Citizens' Council: Organized Resistance to the Second Reconstruction, 1954–1964.* Urbana: University of Illinois Press, 1994.
———, ed. *Remaking Dixie: The Impact of World War II on the American South.* Jackson: University Press of Mississippi, 1997.
McWhirter, Cameron. *Red Summer: The Summer of 1919 and the Black Awakening.* New York: Henry Holt, 2011.

McWhorter. Diane. *Carry Me Home: Birmingham Alabama: The Climatic Battle of the Civil Rights Revolution*. New York: Simon and Schuster, 2001.
Mississippi Black Paper. New York: Random House, 1965.
Morgan, Chester M. *Dearly Bought, Deeply Treasured: The University of Southern Mississippi, 1912–1987*. Jackson: University Press of Mississippi, 1987.
Moynihan, Daniel Patrick. *The Negro Family*. 1965. Reprint, Westport, CT: Greenwood, Reprinted 1981.
Myrdal, Gunnar. *An American Dilemma: The Negro Problem and Modern Democracy*. New York: Harper and Brothers, 1944.
NAACP. *Thirty Years of Lynching in the United States, 1889–1919*. New York: Arno Press and the New York Times, 1969.
Nash, Jere, and Andy Taggart. *Mississippi Politics: The Struggle for Power, 1976–2006*. Jackson: University Press of Mississippi, 2006.
Nelson, Jack. *Terror in the Night: The Klan's Campaign against the Jews*. Jackson: University Press of Mississippi, 1993.
Newman, Mark. *Divine Agitators: The Delta Ministry and Civil Rights in Mississippi*. Athens: University of Georgia Press, 2004.
———. *Getting Right with God: Southern Baptists and Desegregation, 1945–1995*. Tuscaloosa: University of Alabama Press, 2001. Kindle edition.
Norrel, Robert J. *Reaping the Whirlwind: The Civil Rights Movement in Tuskegee*. New York: Albert A. Knopf, 1985.
Orleck, Annelise, and Lisa Gayle Hazirjian, eds. *The War on Poverty: A New Grassroots History, 1964–1980*. Athens: University of Georgia Press, 2011.
Oshinsky, David. *"Worse Than Slavery": Parchman Farm and the Ordeal of Jim Crow Justice*. New York: Simon and Schuster, 1997.
Parker, Frank R. *Black Votes Count: Political Empowerment in Mississippi after 1965*. Chapel Hill: University of North Carolina Press, 1990.
Payne, Charles M. *I've Got the Light of Freedom: The Organizing Tradition and the Mississippi Freedom Struggle*. Berkeley: University of California Press, 1995.
Payne, Cleveland. *Laurel: A History of the Black Community, 1882–1962*. Laurel, MS: C. Payne, 1990.
———. *The Oak Park Story: A Cultural History*. Laurel, MS: National Oak Park High School Alumni Association, 1988.
Piliawsky, Monte. *Exit 13: Oppression and Racism in Academia*. Boston: South End Press, 1982.
Redlich, Edward Grobow. "Toward Equal Representation: The Connor Case and the Struggle for Reapportionment of the Mississippi Legislature." Bachelor of arts honors thesis, Harvard College, 1981.
Rolinson, Mary. *Grassroots Garveyism: The Universal Negro Improvement Association in the Rural South, 1920–1927*. Chapel Hill: University of North Carolina Press, 2007.
Roper, Eugene Albert. "The CIO Organizing Committee in Mississippi, June 1946–January 1949." Master's thesis, University of Mississippi, 1949.
Rothman, Adam. *Slave Country: American Expansion and the Origins of the Deep South*. Cambridge, MA: Harvard University Press, 2005.
Rothschild, Mary Aiken. *A Case of Black and White: Northern Volunteers and the Southern Freedom Summers, 1964–1965*. Westport, CT: Greenwood Press, 1982.
Scott, Emmett. Jay. *Negro Migration during the War*. Project Guttenberg, 2009. HTML E-book.
Silver, James. *Mississippi: The Closed Society*. New York: Harcourt, Brace and World, 1963.
Sitkoff, Harvard. *A New Deal for Blacks: The Emergence of Civil Rights as a National Issue, The Depression Decade*. New York: Oxford University Press, 1978.

Skates, John Ray. "Hattiesburg: The Early Years." In *Hattiesburg: A Pictorial History*, edited by Kenneth G. McCarty Jr., 5–11. Jackson: University Press of Mississippi, 1982.
Smead, Howard. *Blood Justice: The Lynching of Mack Charles Parker*. New York: Oxford University Press, 1986.
Stokes, Mason. *The Color of Sex: Whiteness, Heterosexuality, and the Fictions of White Supremacy*. Durham, NC: Duke University Press, 2001. Kindle edition.
Street, James. *Look Away: A Dixie Notebook*. New York: Viking Press, 1936.
Sullivan, Patricia. *Days of Hope: Race and Democracy*. Chapel Hill: University of North Carolina Press, 1996.
———. *Lift Every Voice and Sing: The NAACP and the Making of the Civil Rights Movement*. New York: The New York Press, 2009.
Van den Bergh, Pierre L. *Race and Racism: A Comparative Study*. New York: John Wiley, 1967.
Vollers, Maryanne. *Ghosts of Mississippi: The Murder of Medgar Evers, the Trials of Byron De La Beckwith and the Haunting of the New South*. Boston: Little Brown, 1995.
Ward, Jason Morgan. *Defending White Democracy: The Making of a Segregationist Movement and the Remaking of Racial Politics*. Chapel Hill: University of North Carolina Press, 2011. Kindle edition.
Webb, Clive, ed. *Massive Resistance: Southern Opposition to the Second Reconstruction*. Oxford University Press, 2005. Kindle edition.
Wells, Ida B. *A Red Record: Lynchings in the United States*. Edited by Jacqueline Jones Royster. [1894?]; Boston: Bedford Books, 1997.
White, Deborah Gray. *Ar'n't I a Woman?* New York: W.W. Norton, 1985.
White, Walter. *Rope and Faggot*. New York: Arno Press and the New York Times, 1969.
Whitehead, Don. *Attack on Terror: The FBI Against the Ku Klux Klan in Mississippi*. New York: Funk and Wagnalls, 1970.
Whitfield, Stephen J. *A Death in the Delta: The Story of Emmett Till*. Baltimore: Johns Hopkins University Press, 1988.
———. *The Culture of the Cold War*. 2nd ed. Baltimore: Johns Hopkins University Press, 1996.
Williamson, Joel. *The Crucible of Race: Black-White Relations in the American South since Emancipation*. New York: Oxford University Press, 1984.
Wilson, William Julius. *The Truly Disadvantaged: The Inner City, the Underclass and Public Policy*. Chicago: University of Chicago Press, 1987.
Woods, Jeff. *Black Struggle, Red Scare: Segregation and Anti-Communism in the South, 1948–1968*. Baton Rouge: Louisiana State University Press, 2004.
Wynn, Neil. A. *The Afro-American and the Second World War*. 2nd ed. New York: Holmes and Meir, 1993.
Zangrando, Robert L. *The NAACP Crusade against Lynching, 1909–1950*. Philadelphia: Temple University Press, 1980.
Zinn, Howard. *SNCC: The New Abolitionists*. 1964; Cambridge, MA: South End Press, 2002.

ESSAYS AND ARTICLES

Bynum, Victoria E. "'White Negroes' in Segregated Mississippi: Miscegenation, Racial Identity, and the Law." *Journal of Southern History* 64 (May, 1998): 247–76.
Cha-Jua, Sundiata Kieta, and Clarence Lang. "The 'Long Movement' As Vampire: Temporal and Spatial Fallacies in Recent Black Freedom Struggles." *Journal of African American History* 92 (Spring 2007): 265–88.
Chilcoat, George W., and Jerry A. Ligon. "'Helping to Make Democracy a Living Reality': The Cur-

riculum Conference of the Mississippi Freedom Schools." *Journal of Curriculum and Supervision* 15 (Fall 1999): 43–68.

Dalfume, Richard M. "The 'Forgotten Years' of the Negro Revolution." *Journal of American History* 55 (June 1968): 90–106.

Dent, Tom. "Portrait of Three Heroes." *Freedomways* 5 (Spring 1965), p. 257.

Eagles, Charles. "Toward New Histories of the Civil Rights Era." *Journal of Southern History* 66 (November 2000): 815–48.

Harris, Anthony. "A Personal Account of Efforts to End School Segregation in a Southern School System." *Connexions*, November 17, 2006, http://cnx.org/content/m14113/latest/. Accessed June 2010.

Himelstein, Jerry. "Rhetorical Continuities in the Politics of Race: The Closed Society Revisited." *Southern Communications Journal* 48 (1983): 153–66.

Holmes, William F. "Whitecapping: Agrarian Violence in Mississippi, 1902–1906." *Journal of Southern History* 35 (May 1969): 165–85.

Hollander, Ronald A. "One Mississippi Negro Who Didn't Go to College." *The Reporter* 27 (November 8, 1962), pp. 30–34.

Huie, Bradford Daniel, and John Howard Griffin. "Why They Can't Wait." *The Progressive* 28 (July 1964), pp. 15–19.

Kelley, Robin D. G. "'We Are Not What We Seem': Rethinking Black Working-Class Opposition in the Jim Crow South." *Journal of American History* 80 (June 1993): 75–112.

Klarman, Michael J. "How *Brown* Changed Race Relations: The Backlash Thesis." *Journal of American History* 81 (June 1994): 81–118.

Lawson, Steven F. "Freedom Then, Freedom Now: The Historiography of the Civil Rights Movement." *American Historical Review* 96 (April 1991): 456–71.

Lawson, Steven F., David R. Colburn, and Darryl Paulson. "Groveland: Florida's Little Scottsboro." *Florida Historical Quarterly* 65 (July1986): 1–26.

Martin, Charles. "Race, Gender, and Southern Justice: The Rosa Lee Ingram Case." *American Journal of Legal History* 29 (July 1985): 251–68.

McMillen, Neil R. "Black Enfranchisement in Mississippi: Federal Enforcement and Black Protest in the 1960s." *Journal of Southern History* 43 (August 1977): 351–72.

———. "Street Theater and the Collapse of Jim Crow: How the Black Freedom Movement Outsmarted Mississippi Segregationists." *Mississippi History Now, Mississippi Historical Society*, http://mshistory.k12.ms.us/articles/280/street-theater-and-the-collapse-of-jim-crow-how-the-black-freedom-movement-outsmarted-mississippi-segregationists.

Odell, Jonathan. "City Beautiful, How a Confederate Deserter, an Opera Diva, a KKK Grand Wizard, and a Traveling Electric Chair Shaped Life in a Small Mississippi Town." A series of twelve columns (August 2008–December 2008) for the *Laurel Leader-Call*. Copies in author's possession.

O'Reilly, Kenneth. "The FBI and the Politics of the Riots, 1964–1968." *Journal of American History* 75 (June 1998): 91–114.

Rachal, John R. "We'll Never Turn Back: Adult Education and the Struggle for Citizenship in Mississippi's Freedom Summer." *American Education Research Journal* 35 (Summer 1998): 167–98.

Rise, Eric W. "Race, Rape, and Radicalism: The Case of the Martinsville Seven, 1949–1951." *Journal of Southern History* 58 (August 1992): 461–90.

Rowe-Sims, Sarah. "The Mississippi State Sovereignty Commission: An Agency History." *Journal of Mississippi History* 61 (Spring 1999): 29–58.

Schardt, Arlie. "A Mississippi Mayor Fights the Klan." *The Reporter* 34 (January 27, 1966), pp. 39–40.

Schmidt, William T. "The Impact of Camp Shelby in World War II on Hattiesburg, Mississippi." *Journal of Mississippi History* 39 (Fall 1977): 41–50.

Vorspan, Albert. "The Iconoclast of Petal, Mississippi." *The Reporter* 16 (March 21, 1957), pp. 33–35.
Waldrep, Christopher. "National Policing, Lynching, and Constitutional Change." *Journal of Southern History* 74 (August 2008): 589–626.
Ward, Jason Morgan. "'No Jap Crow': Japanese Americans Encounter the World War II South." *Journal of Southern History* 73 (February 2007): 75–104.
Zaim, Craig. "Trial by Ordeal: The Willie McGee Case." *Journal of Mississippi History*, 65 (Fall 2003): 215–47.
Zarnow, Leandra. "Braving Jim Crow to Save Willie McGee: Bella Abzug, the Legal Left, and Civil Rights Innovation, 1948–1951." *Law & Social Inquiry* (Fall 2008), 1003-41.

Index

Abrams, Robert, 127
Abzug, Bella, 39, 43, 46, 47
Acheson, Dean, 47
Adickes, Sandra, 108, 116
Ainsworth, Kathy, 169, 190
Alexander, Michelle, 227
Alexander v. Holmes, 200, 212
Alford, Ellis, 228–29
Andalman, Elliott, 225
Anderson, Helen, 117
Anderson, Jack, 40
Anderson, James, 133, 135
Anti-Defamation League of B'nai-B'rith, 190, 230
Anti-Poll Tax bill, 23, 24, 25, 43
Armstrong, Elaine, 140
Armstrong, Robert, 84
Arnold, Carl, 72
Arrington, Jessie, 98, 111, 128
Arrington, Lawrence, 132, 173, 174, 182, 183, 184–85, 189, 192
Austin, Gladys, 106, 151, 208, 209–10
Awe, James, 155, 156, 157, 184–85
Axis powers, 24–25, 26, 30–31
Aycock, Herman, 216

Bailey, Kenneth, 164
Baker, Douglass, 218, 226, 230
Baker, Ella, 77
Barnes, John, 60
Barnes, Milton, 143, 179
Barnett, Ross, 49, 67, 70–71, 173
Barnette, Doyle, 125, 176
Bass, Dave, 78–79
Beal, Lillie, 132
Beard, Erlene, 59

Beckwith, Byron de la, 71, 173, 174, 213, 230, 238
Beech, Robert, 109, 161–62
Ben-Ami, David Z., 81–82
Berry, Carl, 195
Biddle, Francis, 26
Bilbo, Theodore, 17, 23, 32, 43, 44, 52
Billiot, Robert Anthony, 168, 180, 196
Birdsong, T. B., 96
Birmingham, Alabama, 77
Bivens, Phillip, 226, 241
Black Coalition, 216, 217
Black Panthers, 160, 169, 173
Blackwell, Charles, 142, 166, 173, 174
Blair, George, 201, 207
Blair High School (Hattiesburg), 201, 202–3, 204, 205, 206
Blalock, Marie, 117
Bolton, Frazier, 240
Bonney, James, 167
Bowers, E. J., 91
Bowers, Sam, 163, 173, 187, 189, 223; attacks on Jews, 168–69; DABURN investigation, 153–54, 156, 157–58, 161, 164, 177; Dahmer attack, 3, 121, 143, 149, 158, 182; Dahmer trials, 181, 182, 186, 189–90, 192–96, 230–36, 237, 238; formative years, 89–91; Freedom Summer, 93, 100; Invisible Empire, 89, 92, 93, 124, 125, 129, 131, 142, 146–47, 159–60, 164, 176, 221, 243; loss of control, 174–75; Masonite attacks, 167–68, 175; McGee case, 34; Neshoba case, 124–25, 161, 177–78, 180; release from prison, 215, 221; Watkins kidnapping, 165, 178, 213; worldview, 91–92
Bowers, Sam, Sr., 89–90, 91
Boyd, Billy, 124
Boyd, Bus, 90

Boyd, Earline, 68–69, 84
Boyd, M. W., 34, 36
Boyd, Richard, 28, 29, 43, 45, 66, 69
Boykin, James, 225
Brady, Thomas Pickens, 54
Branch, Raylawni, 140, 147
Breeland, Dan, 37, 38, 39
Brezeale, C. E., 70
Brookhaven, Mississippi, 89
Brooks, Loren C., 148
Broom, Stewart, 30
Brown, Ed, 17
Brown, J. W., 117
Brown, R. Jess, 63–64, 65, 70, 134–35, 136
Brown v. Board of Education, 52, 53–54, 55, 57, 65, 125, 150, 152, 163, 200, 212
Bucklew, Fern, 168
Bucklew, Henry, 141–42, 159
Buckley, Isaac, 212
Buckley, James Lee, 112
Buckley, Travis, 212, 213; as attorney in Dahmer trial, 233–35; Dahmer case, 181; Watkins kidnapping, 165, 166, 174, 182, 197
Burns, Fred, 225–26
Butler, Donald, 190
Butts, Lampkin, 196
Byrd, John, 24
Byrd, Lawrence, 93, 100, 164–65, 183, 197, 213, 237; DABURN trial, 194, 195; involvement in Dahmer's murder, 156, 157–58, 181, 191

Cameron, John, 83–84, 86, 95, 109
Camp Shelby Military Base, 14, 18, 27, 32, 82
Cannon, Norman, 131–32
Canton, Mississippi, 79, 160
Carlisle, Richard, 58
Carmichael, Stokely, 160
Carr, Billy, 164, 166–67, 181, 197
Carr, Julian, 168
Carson, Eugene, 84
Carter, Hodding, 55
Carter, Lindsay, 231, 232
Casey, Lunsford, 112, 168, 196
Caves, Leonard, 60, 71–72, 127, 141, 174, 211–12
Caves, Terry, 211
Caves, Tina, 212
Center for Democratic Renewal, 230
Central Intelligence Agency (CIA), 101, 234

Chandler, James, 66
Chaney, James, 101, 115, 125, 177
Chase, Oscar, 78–79, 85
Chaze, Elliot, 76, 79, 110, 134, 151, 181
Chicago Defender, 15, 25, 27, 31
Child Development Group of Mississippi (CDGM), 130, 131, 140, 160, 161, 162, 163, 167, 168
Chisolm family, 8
Citizens' Council, 54–55, 58, 60, 61, 63, 71, 116, 127, 137, 142, 200, 212; in Forrest County, 56–57, 110, 126–27; Jones County, 154; in Laurel, 159
Citizens for Justice, 230
Civil Rights Act of 1957, 60
Civil Rights Act of 1960, 60, 72
Civil Rights Act of 1964, 71, 110, 119, 123, 125, 150, 152, 169, 202, 243
Civil Rights Act of 1966, 161
Civil Rights Act of 1968, 188, 243
Civil Rights Commission, 43, 44, 129, 138, 142
Civil Rights Congress (CRC), 37, 39, 41–42, 43, 46–47, 48, 49, 50
Civil War, 6, 20, 91
Civilian Conservation Corps (CCC), 18
Clarion-Ledger, 26
Clark, Shannon, 167
Clarke County, Mississippi, 66, 162, 171
Coates, Rosa Lee, 131–32
Cobb, Charlie, 106
Cold War, 48, 49, 50
Cole, Leland, 172
Coleman, Charles, 112
Coleman, Frank, 30
Coleman, James P., 54, 61, 62, 64, 138–39
Coleman, Larry, 201, 207, 208–9
Collins, Burkitt, 21, 24, 35, 36–38, 39, 41, 44, 46, 48
Collins, E. K., 39, 128
Collins, Luther, 123
Colmer, William, 25, 46, 53, 71, 128, 139
Committee for Local Control of Education (CLCE), 200
Committee of Concern, 168, 178
Committee of One Hundred, 18
Committee on Civil Rights, 47
Communist Party, 25, 30, 37, 128; Chinese, 42

Community Improvement Association of Forrest County (CIAFC), 226, 228, 229
Compromise of 1877, 7
Confederacy, 6, 44
Congress of Federated Organizations (COFO), 67–68, 69, 82, 85, 86, 98, 114, 116, 118, 120, 140, 142, 224; attack on, 109–10, 129, 131; Freedom Days, 73, 75, 76, 77, 79–80, 86, 88, 97; Freedom Summer, 95, 97, 99, 100, 101, 103, 104–5, 106, 122; Freedom Vote campaign, 72, 73; MFDP registration, 109; sit-in protests, 111, 112–13, 126
Congress of Industrial Organizations (CIO), 24, 25, 45
Congress of Racial Equality (CORE), 22, 67–68, 76, 101, 103, 115, 138, 142, 160, 161
Connor, Dudley, 56, 61, 63, 71
Connor, Peggy Jean, 96, 111, 131, 140
Connors, Robert A., 156
Constitution of 1890, 8, 29
Cook, Grady, 36, 41
Cook, Robert Cecil, 57
Cooley, Lula, 225
Cooper, Ellis, 30
Covington County, Mississippi, 12, 166, 181, 197
Cox, Harold, 67, 116, 166, 172, 178, 180, 203, 215
Cox, Luther, 29, 56, 59, 65
Craft, Charlie, 12
Craft, Laura, 12
Crespino, Joe, 88
Cress, Lorne, 114
Crosby, Janet, 114
Cumbest, Donald, 165, 166, 177, 212
Cummings, Homer, 19
Curie, Andrew, 23, 24
Curie, Brewell, 117, 129, 141, 157, 180

Dabbs, Daniel W., 63
Dahmer, Alvin Hulon, 19, 145, 150
Dahmer, Bettie, 3, 59, 144, 145, 151, 234
Dahmer, Carroll, 19, 145
Dahmer, Dennis, 59, 144, 145, 151, 231, 236
Dahmer, Ellen, 12
Dahmer, Ellie, 3, 110, 121, 143, 144, 145, 147, 150, 154, 182, 184, 194–95, 196, 214, 231, 234, 236, 238, 239
Dahmer, George W., 12, 19, 145
Dahmer, Harold, 19, 144, 145, 154
Dahmer, Martinez, 19, 145
Dahmer, Ora Lee, 59
Dahmer, Peter, 12
Dahmer, Vernon, 67, 77, 80, 102, 110–11; family, 5, 12, 18–19, 59, 110, 150, 234; Forrest County NAACP, 49, 50, 51, 58, 59, 60, 68, 140; Klan attack, 3, 4, 143, 144–45, 146, 154, 179, 233; leadership, 3, 20, 49, 58, 68, 121, 140, 143, 242; murder, 146–48, 151, 152, 156, 161, 176, 223, 233; voter registration efforts, 29, 59, 60, 64, 65, 66, 67, 143
Dahmer, Vernon, Jr., 19, 29, 145, 223, 236
Daily Worker, 49
Dale, T. Price, 59
Dalton, M. L., 70
Daniels, Lee, 56, 62, 63
Davidson, Marion, 104
Davis, Ellie J., 59
Davis, Ray, 200
Deacons for Defense and Justice, 161
Deavours, Jack, 38, 39, 40
DeBoxtel, Henry, 124, 146, 149, 157, 164; Dahmer trials, 194–96, 235; indictments, 158, 161, 181; mistrial, 189; role in Dahmer murder, 144, 153–54, 156, 237
Dee, Henry Hezekiah, 115, 124
DeFazio, Sergeant, 168
Delta Democrat-Times, 214
Delta Ministry, 130, 140, 143, 150, 160, 161
Democrat Party, 7, 9, 10, 43–44, 45, 60, 96, 117, 122, 123, 127, 141, 158, 159, 190
Dennis, Dave, 77, 95
Dennis, Delmar, 153–54, 177, 230
Department of Health, Education, and Welfare (HEW), 200, 201, 203, 204
Department of Justice, 29, 30, 97, 185; Dahmer case, 147, 158, 176, 194, 232; lynching cases, 27, 31; police brutality complaints, 113, 127; school desegregation lawsuits, 201; voter discrimination cases, 3, 59, 60, 65–66, 67, 68, 69, 78, 86, 94, 139
Depression, 18, 19, 20
Devine, Annie, 117, 123
Dewey, Thomas E., 45
Dick, Jack, 48
Dickerson, Pat, 117
Dillard, William O. "Chet," 128, 131, 140–41, 168, 177, 180

Dixiecrat Party, 44, 45
Dixon, Bobby Ray, 226, 241
Dixon, Thomas E., *The Clansman*, 8, 39, 91
Doar, John, 66–67, 94
Dubinsky, Ed, 126
Du Bois, W. E. B., 14, 212
Dukes, Jimmy, 82–83, 87, 132, 148, 177, 185, 186, 191, 200
Dukes, William, 148, 154, 157, 165, 176, 177, 183
Dulles, Allen, 101
Dumas, Christos, 151
Dunagin, Huck, 43, 45, 66
Duncan, John, 218
DuPree, Johnny, 206, 228, 229, 239, 240–41
Dyer, Leonidas, 15

East, P. D., 55–56
Easterling, Albert, 35, 41, 46
Eastland, James O., 53, 128, 161, 174
Eaton, Alvin, 218
Edwards, Charles Marcus, 124
Edwards v. South Carolina, 83
Ellin, Joseph, 99, 101–2, 105, 108, 119
Ellington, Arthur, 17
Ellisville, Mississippi, 7; klavern, 149
Enforcement Act (1870), 7
Entrekin, Sarah, 191
Episcopal Society for Cultural and Racial Unity, 77
Evers, Charles, 149, 150, 152
Evers, Medgar, 53, 59, 65, 71, 134; murder, 173; new trial, 230

Fair Employment Practice Commission (FEPC), 22, 43
Fairley, Isaac, 163–64
Fairley, J. C., 68, 80, 94, 117, 140, 145, 149–50, 152, 179, 195, 220
Fairley, Kenneth: activism in Forrest County, 225–26, 227; confrontation with police, 228–29; reopening Dahmer case, 230–31; school integration, 163–64, 202–3, 204, 205, 206, 219
Farmer, James, 76
Faulkner, William, 43
Federal Bureau of Investigation (FBI): cooperation with local authorities, 88, 125, 131, 134, 148, 168, 181; Dahmer case, 148–49, 152, 153–57, 158, 159, 161, 165, 166–67, 174, 176–77, 182, 184, 191–92, 213, 230–31, 234–35, 236–38; Forrest County voter registration case, 66; investigation of Klan, 89, 90, 100, 109–10, 115, 118, 123–24, 159, 164; John Albert White investigation, 218; local distrust of, 30, 159, 166, 189; Mack Charles Parker investigation, 62; Neshoba County investigation, 101, 115, 116, 119, 177; police brutality reports, 79, 86, 87–88, 113; Shubuta murders investigation, 26; war against Klan, 3, 4, 119, 125, 174, 181, 197–98, 214, 216, 230; Wash lynching investigation, 26–27
Fellowship of the Concerned Southern Regional Council, 138
Fifteenth Amendment, 6, 96
Finch, Jimmy, 72, 115, 134, 143, 172, 174, 212; Dahmer case, 176, 177, 181, 182, 183, 185–86, 191; Kennard case, 63, 64, 65, 128, 132
First Amendment, 53, 81
Flowers, Maurice, 215, 216
Floyd, Lawrence, Jr., 171
Fluker, Ellis, 179
Ford, Carl, 161, 166, 196, 238
Fordice, Kirk, 237
Forman, James, 77, 78
Forrest, Nathan Bedford, 6, 9, 57
Forrest County Action Committee (FCAC), 179; Black Coalition, 216
Forrest County NAACP, 51, 58, 59–60, 64, 65, 170, 204, 214, 217, 224; Youth Council, 60
Forrest County Voters League, 68
Fourteenth Amendment, 6, 8, 30, 38–39, 45, 52, 53, 142, 158
Fowler, Inmon O., 21
Franklin, Ed, 30
Frazier, Franklin E., 188
Frazier, John, 94, 97
Free State of Jones, 6
Freedom Day demonstration (Hattiesburg), 75–76, 77, 78, 79, 80, 96, 97
Freedom Days campaign, 79–83, 86, 88, 93–94, 95, 97, 101, 104, 108, 116, 122, 242
Freedom Rides, 67, 69, 71
Freedom Schools, 95, 99, 104, 106–8, 122–23, 243; Laurel bombing, 131
Freedom Summer: challenges within the movement, 105; commencement, 100–101;

community involvement, 102–3; conclusion, 121, 122–23; Freedom Vote campaign, 72, 73, 95, 99, 123, 127; participants, 131, 134, 151, 163, 170, 199, 209, 220; planning, 95, 96, 97, 99; results, 101, 105–6, 116–17, 118–19, 122, 243; training, 99–100; violence at farewell picnic, 118, 123, 157, 180; voter registration project, 104–5
Freeman, Flip, 212
Funchess, Glenda, 107, 118, 163, 171

Gaddy, George, 225
Gaines v. Canada, 53
Gardiner, Eastman, 12
Gardiner family, 8
Gardiner Junior High (Laurel), 212
Garrett, Jimmy, 103
Gartin, Carroll, 46, 47, 128
Garvey, Marcus, 17
Gates, L. G., 16
Gavagan, Joseph, 26
Gaylor, Diane, 83
Gelfand, David, 117–18, 123, 180
Gerrard, A. L., 220
Gerrard, Eleanor, 205
Giles, Cleeburgh, 209–10
Giles, Travis, 146, 149, 153, 154, 155, 156, 157, 158, 181, 184, 209, 238; Dahmer trial, 194–96
Ginsberg, Lou, 63
Glass, Jimmy, 102, 118
Glen, Charles, 77
Goldwater, Barry, 125
Goodman, Andrew, 101, 115, 125, 177
Gordon, T. J., 218
Gore, Alvin, Sr., 167, 193
Gore, Glen, 163
Gore, Maycie, 60, 131, 140, 163, 167, 193
Grady, Paul E., 129, 148, 172, 217, 218
Grant, J. B., 19
Graves, Benjamin, 192
Gray, Joe, 16, 17
Gray, Victoria, 73, 77, 151, 242; COFO leadership, 68, 82, 114; MFDP leadership, 95, 109, 116, 117, 122, 123, 127, 139, 173–74
Gray, W. G., 58, 72, 78, 81, 82, 87, 88, 114, 132, 137, 138, 143, 155, 165, 166
Green, Ernest, 23, 26
Green v. County School Board, 200

Greenville, Mississippi, 55
Greenwood, Mississippi, 54, 68, 77, 79, 160
Gregory, Dick, 70, 80
Griffin, Joe, 18, 19
Griffin, John Howard, 70–71; *Black Like Me*, 70
Griffith, D. W., *Birth of a Nation*, 8
Grimmett, Ervin E., 204, 205
Groveland Four case, 47
Guyot, Lawrence, 72, 77, 78, 86, 87, 147

Halberstam, David, 238
Hall, Pinky, 80, 117, 130–31, 162
Hall, Robert, 17
Hall, Stanton, 64, 65, 81, 134, 136, 137, 138, 186, 189, 190, 191, 193, 196, 204–5
Hall, Toxey, 30, 31
Hamer, Fannie Lou, 77, 95, 117, 123
Hamilton, Mordaunt, 93, 109, 125, 127, 143, 154–55, 161, 194
Haralson, Luella, 84
Hardy, William H., 7
Harlem, 17, 25, 48
Harper, George, 117
Harrelson, William, 86
Harris, Anthony, 85, 163, 187, 201–2
Harris, Daisy Griffin, 19, 20, 75, 77, 79, 80, 85, 102, 108, 109, 118, 149, 179
Harris, James, 85
Harrison, Unkgang, 212
Hartfield, John, 15, 17, 20
Harvest Quarters community (Laurel), 13
Hattiesburg American, 55, 56, 61, 64, 82, 110, 147–48, 151, 161, 167, 172, 181, 200, 214, 217
Hattiesburg Interfaith Alliance, 230
Hattiesburg Minister's Project, 79–80, 130
Hattiesburg Police Department (HPD), 58, 62, 86, 140, 170, 226, 229, 240; affirmative action plan, 219; discrimination lawsuit, 218–19; police brutality charges, 216–17, 227–28
Hauberg, Robert, 194, 195
Hawkins, Troy, 33, 35, 36, 38, 40, 42, 48, 49
Hawkins, Willette, 32–38, 39–40, 41–42, 43, 48, 49, 216
Hawkins Junior High, integration, 163–64, 202
Hayes, Curtis, 68
Hayes, Rutherford B., 7
Head Start, 130, 160, 162

Heard, Alex, 42
Heidelberg, Luranie, 144
Helep, Haynes, 70
Helfrich, Robert, 231, 232, 233, 235–36, 238, 239, 240, 241
Henderson, Steve, 165
Hendry, Andre, 177, 180, 196
Henry, Aaron, 72, 77–78, 123
Hercules Plant, 18, 19, 28, 43, 66, 68
Herring, Hugh, 32, 40, 41, 84, 115, 116, 152, 172; calls for resignation, 216–17, 218; discrimination lawsuit, 219
Hess, Rudolph, 91
Hitler, Adolf, 22, 91
Hix, James, 85
Hobbes, Thomas, 5
Hobby, T. C., 63, 64
Holder, Luther, 21, 27, 29, 30
Holifield, Bob, 60
Holifield, John, 196–97
Holiman, Mack, 16
Holloway, Eddie, 225, 227–28
Holmes, Bud, 226
Holy Rosary Catholic Church (Hattiesburg), 96, 171, 187
Hoover, Herbert, 18
Hoover, J. Edgar, 26, 89, 101, 119, 189
Horne, Raymond, 34
Horton, Robert, 15
House Un-American Activities Committee (HUAC), 143, 154, 235
Hughes, Garvin, 111
Humphrey, Frederick, 113, 133, 135, 136, 137–38
Hyatt, Marjorie, 114, 115

Ickes, Harold, 17
Ingram, James, 155, 156, 157, 234–35
Innocence Project, 241
International Woodworkers of America union, 124, 167
Ivey, Robert, 161
Ivory, Ernest, 162

Jackson, Carol, 134, 151, 171
Jackson, Forrest B., 37
Jackson, Lillie, 109, 134, 151, 171
Jackson, Mississippi, 32, 34, 39, 43, 62, 66, 68, 86, 87, 90, 94, 128, 137, 162, 176, 178, 216; attacks on Jewish population, 169, 190; FBI office, 101, 147, 231; Freedom Riders, 67, 69; March Against Fear, 160; Medgar Evers assassination, 71; SNCC movement, 69, 87; Willie McGee incarceration, 41, 46
Jackson, Wharlest, 164
Jefferson Davis County, Mississippi, 66
Jeffries, Hasa Kwame, 122
John's Cafe (Laurel), 35, 155, 156, 189, 231
Johnson, Allen, 178, 187, 216
Johnson, Eckard, 82
Johnson, Hattie, 33, 42, 43
Johnson, James Weldon, 15
Johnson, Jerome, 212
Johnson, Lyndon Baines, 60, 86, 97, 101, 117, 125, 138–39, 140, 142, 147, 185, 188; Civil Rights Act, 73, 110, 123, 161, 243; Voting Rights Act, 129; War on Poverty, 130
Johnson, Paul B., Jr., 26, 97, 174; anti-picketing statute, 93; Dahmer case, 147, 148; defection to Republican Party, 117; fight against desegregation, 70, 71, 88–89, 110, 125, 128, 160–61, 174; Neshoba case, 101; opposition to Klan, 88, 174; response to Freedom Summer, 76, 96, 101, 243
Johnson, Paul B., Sr., 21, 24, 26
Johnson, Tom, 11
Johnson, Walter, 91
Johnson, Wanda, 206
Johnson, William, 24, 29, 30
Johnston, Erle, 96, 125
Jones, Arlington, 132
Jones, Barney, 24, 29, 30
Jones, Horatio, Jr., 85
Jones, J. Dale, 229–30
Jones, Jimmy, 149
Jones, Manuel, 229, 230
Jones, Print, 86, 87
Jones, William P., *The Tribe of Black Ulysses*, 11, 188
Jordan, Charles, 112
Jordan, James, 125, 176
J. P. Campbell College, 94

Katzenbach, Nicholas, 147
KC Bottom community (Laurel), 13, 111, 169; 1974 flood, 219–20
Keller, Joyce, 162

Kelly, Dick, 107
Kelly, Green, 5, 12
Kelly, Henrietta, 12
Kelly, John, 5, 12
Kelly, Richard, 127
Kelly, Steve, 203
Kelly, Warren, 12, 13
Kelly Settlement, 6, 12, 13, 57, 145, 223
Kennard, Clyde, 51, 57–58, 59, 60, 128, 132, 134, 138, 152, 241; efforts to desegregate MSC, 61–64, 97, 242; exoneration, 239; felony charge, 64–65; prison term, 69–71
Kennedy, John F., 70, 71, 72–73
Kennedy, Robert, 86
Kerner Commission, 188
Kershner, Charles, 94
Keys, Clifton Archer, 115
Keys, Kilmer Esus, 115
Killingsworth, J. C., 162, 171, 172, 179, 182, 188, 217
King, Clennon, 61
King, Edwin, 72
King, Martin Luther, Jr., 52, 70, 117, 160, 169; assassination, 187–89
Kingston community (Laurel), 13, 193
Kinsey, Paul, 135
Kitchens, Wilmer, 87, 113, 114, 133, 134, 135–36, 137, 138
Knight, Anna, 12, 13
Knight, Davis, 44–46, 126, 128
Knight, Newton, 6, 12, 44, 77, 241
Knight, Rachel, 6, 12, 13, 16, 44, 45, 77, 241
Knight, Serena, 6
Knight, Stewart, 16
Knight, Thomas, Sr., 43
Knight Company, 6
Koch, H. E., 34, 36
Kress, S. H., department store (Laurel), 98, 111
Kroen, Charles, 186
Ku Klux Klan, 6, 7, 57, 116, 127, 142, 191; Original Knights, 89. *See also* White Knights of the Ku Klux Klan

Ladner, Dorie and Joyce, 60, 70
Ladner, Herbert, 123
Landers, Wayne, 219, 227, 229
Lang, Charlie, 23, 26
Larson, Robert, 90, 125

Laurel Brace and Limb Company, 181, 213
Laurel Interdenominational Ministerial Alliance, 214
Laurel Leader-Call, 26, 27, 34, 55, 96, 101, 112, 124, 141, 178
Lawrence, Charles, 225, 227–28
Lawyers of the Constitutional Defense Committee, 224
Leaf River, 5, 8; 1974 flood, 219–20
Lee, Harper, *To Kill a Mockingbird*, 49–50
Lee, Norman, 167, 177
Lee, Robert E., 141, 142, 156, 176, 177
Lee, V. L. "Dubie," 118, 123, 167, 180
Leigh, Sandy, 77, 80, 84, 85, 104
Lelyveld, Arthur, 114–15, 128
Leonard, John, 87
Letow, M., 16
Lewis, John, 77, 101
Lewis, Robert, 66
Lexington, Mississippi, 55
Little, M. M., 29
Locke, John, 5
London, A. N., 39, 40, 41
Lotts, Mrs., 171
Lowe, Charles, 154, 158, 177, 194, 237
Lowe, Clifton, 154, 158, 194, 237
Lowenstein, Allard, 95
Lowry, Robert, 6, 7, 10
Lucas, Aubrey, 61, 62
Lunney, Robert, 79
Lynd, Theron, 56, 64; Department of Justice lawsuit, 65, 66–67, 68–69, 94; registrar, 60, 61, 64, 70, 83, 84, 97, 118, 127, 129–30, 135, 139; response to Freedom Days campaign, 75, 76, 78, 79; voter discrimination conviction, 72, 73, 129–30, 174
Lyons, Franklin, 140, 144, 154, 155, 158, 181, 191, 194, 196, 235
Lyons, Mary, 155

Mack, Melvin, 239, 240
Madison, Bama, 113, 133, 135
Magee, Clarence, 59, 204, 205, 214, 220
Magee, Johnny, 104, 107, 169, 187, 209, 211, 220
MaGee, Lonnie Charles, 171–72
Malcolm X, 71, 169
Malone, Viola, 225
Malvain, Morty, 114

Mantinband, Charles, 56, 57, 61, 63, 69, 81
Maples, Darwin, 166, 181, 182
March Against Fear, 160, 161
March on Washington Movement, 26
Marsh, Charles, 89, 187, 193, 194, 203, 212
Marsh, Robert, 178–79, 193, 203
Marshall, George, 37
Marshall, Thurgood, 52, 53, 59, 64
Martin, Charles, 66, 179
Martin, J. L., 148, 157, 183
Martin, Pete, 140–41, 154, 155–56, 157, 158, 169, 194, 237
Martin, William B., 6–7, 10
Masonite Plant (Laurel), 45, 69, 142, 149, 155; integration, 124; Klan attacks on, 167–69, 175, 176, 177, 180, 193; strike, 167–69, 173, 180, 197; trial, 196–97
Massengale, Pat, 189
Matison, Dave, 57, 63
Matthews, Otis, 124, 126
Mayberry, R. A., 149
McCain, William, 57, 58, 62, 63, 94, 189
McCallum, Manual, 16, 59
McCleskey, Donnie, 206
McComb, Mississippi, 68, 123
McCombs family, 12
McGee, Bessie, 37, 56
McGee, Billy, 148, 227
McGee, Della, 37
McGee, Willie, 32–43, 44, 45, 46–48, 49–50, 64, 91, 126, 128, 152, 216, 242
McGee, Willie Earl, 37, 49
McGill, Bertie Mae, 69, 73
McGill, Larry, 73, 74, 98, 107, 111, 117, 128, 170, 199, 201, 207–8
McGilvery, Willie, 171–72
McKenzie, Richard, 236, 237, 238
McKinley, Clarence, 218
McKinnie, Lester, 69, 103–4
McLaurin v. Oklahoma, 53
McMillen, Neil, *Dark Journey*, 22
McMinn, R. W., 118
McNair, Lonnie, 21, 27
Meadville, Mississippi, 123–24
Meharry Medical College, 52
Melvin, Harold, 128, 191
Melvin, Leonard, Jr., 128, 191
Melvin, Leonard, Sr., 191

Meredith, James, 69, 70, 160, 161
Meridian, Mississippi, 178, 180–81; DABURN trial, 194; Jewish population, 169, 190
Michaels, Shelia, 105
Milloy, Ralph, 205
Milsaps, Otis, 168
Ministerial Improvement Association (MIA), 58
Miscegenation, 8, 13, 42, 44, 54, 92, 128, 164, 185, 200, 210; laws, 32, 45
Mississippi Action for Progress (MAP), 162
Mississippi Constitution, 8, 29, 72, 94; Constitutional Convention of 1890, 10
Mississippi Council on Human Relations (MCHR), 56
Mississippi Council on Human Rights, 82
Mississippi Department of Corrections, 232
Mississippi Federation of Colored Women's Clubs, 18
Mississippi Flood Control Project, 18
Mississippi Freedom Democratic Party (MFDP), 97, 109, 131, 138, 140, 143, 147, 161, 174, 178, 216, 224, 243; Congressional Challenge, 127, 139, 141; Freedom Vote election, 123; March Against Fear, 160; National Democratic Convention, 95–96, 99, 105, 109, 116–17, 122, 190; 1967 elections, 173–74; US Civil Rights Commission hearings, 128–29
Mississippi Free Press, 70, 97
Mississippi Highway Patrol (MHP), 76, 88, 96, 123–24, 125, 131, 132, 148, 152, 155, 165, 168, 238
Mississippi Southern College (MSC), 51, 55, 57, 58, 61, 62, 63, 64
Mississippi State Penitentiary, 213–14. *See also* Parchman, Mississippi
Mississippi State Sovereignty Commission, 54, 58, 61, 62, 68, 72, 76, 86, 88, 89, 96, 125, 141, 152, 172, 179
Mississippi Supreme Court, 37, 39, 41, 43, 45, 46, 65, 70, 136, 167, 180, 197, 240
Mississippi v. Clyde Kennard, 64–65
Mize, Sidney, 47, 59, 87, 116
Mobile-Bouie community (Hattiesburg), 13; Mobile Street, 13, 68, 75, 102, 104
Montague, Frank, Jr., 83, 134
Montgomery, Jeff, 40–41
Montgomery Bus Boycott, 52
Moore, Charles Eddie, 115, 124

Moore, Michael, 223, 231, 235
Moore, Robert, 84
Moore, Roy, 3, 119, 147, 153, 155, 158, 178, 189
Moore, Willie, 82
Moore, Willie (Cheryl Outlaw's grandmother), 107
Morgan, Ed, 228, 239
Morgan, Les, 87
Morrell, Irving, 207
Morrison, Philip, 43
Morse, Wayne, 117
Moses, Robert, 68, 69, 77, 81, 95, 109
Moss, Billy, 154, 156, 157, 158, 194, 237
Moss, Bob, 87
Mott, Warnie Laura, 18
Moulds, Arlon, 219
Moynihan, Daniel Patrick, 188
Mt. Zion Baptist Church (Hattiesburg), 172, 187
Murph, Benjamin, 13, 49, 51, 58, 60, 69, 105, 140, 237, 242
Murphey (assistant attorney general), 215
Murphy, Henry, 32
Murphy, Robert A., 212
Musgrove family, 12
Myers, Hulon, 16

Natchez, Mississippi, 164
Nation, The, 85
National Association for the Advancement of Colored People (NAACP), 14, 15, 16, 17–18, 22, 25, 27, 53, 56, 67, 70, 76, 99, 134, 147, 169, 178, 191, 216, 218, 221; Black Coalition, 216, 217; desegregation of USM, 140; Flood Victims Committee, 220; Forrest County, 51, 59, 60, 63, 143, 145, 149, 150, 179, 204, 214, 217, 224, 226; Jones County, 58, 60, 140, 142, 226, 229–30; lynching investigations, 24, 26; McGee case, 47; in Mississippi, 18, 49, 55, 62, 63–64, 65, 68, 69, 72, 73, 77, 80, 94, 103, 106, 151, 152, 153, 161, 162, 164, 170, 172; 1967 elections, 173; school desegregation, 204, 205; Supreme Court cases, 43, 44, 52; violence against members, 140, 164; voter discrimination complaints, 139; Voter Education Project, 72; youth involvement, 111, 171
National Committee to Abolish the Poll Tax, 22
National Democratic Convention (1956), 59; Atlantic City, 95–96, 99, 105, 116–17, 122

National Democratic Convention (1968), 190
National Guard, 24, 35, 38, 70
National Negro Congress, 18
Nazism, 22–23, 25, 30, 50, 91
Negro Civic Welfare Association (NCWA), 28
Negro Labor Victory Committee, 26
Nelson, Jack, *Terror in the Night*, 234–35
Neshoba County, Mississippi, 101, 115, 116, 119, 148, 160, 177, 243
New Amsterdam News, 24
New Deal, 17, 18
New Orleans, Louisiana, 66, 89
New South, 8, 10, 12–13
Newsweek, 214
New York, City Hall, 26
New York Post, 129
1963 Children's Crusade, 119–20
Nix, Deavours, 140, 143, 154, 161, 164, 165, 166, 173, 174, 213; Dahmer investigation, 153, 155, 156, 157, 158, 181, 231, 232; Dahmer trials, 192, 194–96, 223, 235, 236; lawsuit against Sheriff Gray, 165–66, 175; Masonite attacks, 167; Watkins kidnapping, 177, 178, 213
Nix, Floyd, 38
Nix, James, 19, 20, 150, 153, 154, 155, 156, 157, 158, 171
Nix, L. C., 111, 128, 155, 179
Nix, Sybil, 231
Nixon, Richard, 49
Noble, Charles, 140; Dahmer attack, 144, 154, 156, 195; Dahmer indictment, 158, 164, 181, 194, 232; Dahmer trials, 194–96, 223, 232, 236–38
Norris, Mildred, 81, 83, 84, 109
Novels, Henry, 11

Oak Park High School (Laurel), 13, 179, 209; transition to elementary school, 206–7, 201
Oatis, William, 11
Obama, Barack, 239
Oberlin College, 99
Odom, Harold, 196
Office of Economic Opportunity (OEO), 130, 162
O'Kelly, J. H., 83
Ole Miss, 53; integration of, 69, 70, 71, 160
Olson, James, 86
O'Neal, Ford, 165

O'Neal, John, 72
Operation Dixie, 43, 44, 45
Operation Freedom Summer. *See* Freedom Summer
Outlaw, Cheryl, 102, 107
Owen, David, 99, 105, 107, 114, 128
Owen, James, 152, 153
Owen, Robert, 194, 195
Owen, Sam Joe, 236–38
Owens, Robert, 66

Pace, Paula, 107
Palmers Crossing, 13, 68, 73, 77, 82, 102, 104, 106, 108, 114, 133–34, 135, 137, 151
Parchman, Mississippi, 69, 70, 213
Parker, Jesse, 205
Parker, Mack Charles, 61
Parks, Rosa, 52
Patrick, Bill, 203, 216
Patterson, Eva Gail, 226
Patterson, Luke, 226
Patterson, Robert, 54
Patterson, T. W., 37–38
Patterson, William, 42, 46, 48
Patton v. Mississippi, 38–39
Payton, Eliza, 32–33, 42
Payton, Olive, 91
Pearl Harbor, 25, 28
Pearl River County, Mississippi, 61
Perez v. Lippold, 45
Perry County, Mississippi, 5, 7, 9
Petal, Mississippi, 55
Petal Paper, 55, 56
Pickering, Charles, 128, 131, 141, 142, 177, 180, 231
Pickering, Merrill, 124, 126, 168, 195
Pickett, Roscoe, 205–6
Pittman, Claude, 76, 79, 116, 127
Pittman, Homer, 35, 36
Pitts, Billy Roy, 124, 161, 231–32, 236; Dahmer attack, 144–45, 146; Dahmer indictment, 158; Dahmer investigation, 154, 155, 156, 157, 237; Dahmer trial, 182, 183–84, 186, 189–90, 191–92, 195, 197, 230, 233, 234, 235, 238; FBI informant, 174, 176–77, 178, 180, 181; release from prison, 213, 232; Watkins kidnapping, 165, 166
Pitts, Bonnie, 231
Pittsburgh Courier, 25, 29–30

Plessy v. Ferguson, 8, 52
Ponder, Annelle, 77
Ponder, L. P., 68
Poole, John, 39, 40, 41, 43, 46
Poor People's March, 187, 188
Poplarville, Mississippi, 23
Populist party, 9
Porter, Richard, 208–9, 210
Powell, J. M., 44
Pratt, John, 79
Presbyterian Church United States, 82, 83
Price, George, 207
Price, Leontyne, 207
Prine, Lucille, 232
Progressive Party, 44, 45
Pryor, Allen Welborn, 21–22, 27, 29, 30
Pugh, Urban, 169
Pyles, Dixon, 37–38, 39

Queensburg community (Laurel), 13
Quinn, Percy, 182
Quinn, Peter, 171, 182, 187

Rabbinical Association of America, 77, 82
Railroads, 7
Randolph, A. Philip, 22, 26
Rankin, John E., 23–24, 29
Rauh, Joseph, 117
Ray, James Earl, 187
Rayburn, Sam, 60
Reagan, Ronald, 225
Reconstruction, 6–7, 8, 10, 15, 20, 30, 31, 39, 107, 121, 159
Red Cross, 28, 148
Reddoch, J. Press, 21, 23, 24, 30
Redeemers, 9, 10
Redemption, 9, 10, 242
Reiter, John, 58, 62, 63
Reno, Janet, 230–31
Republican Party, 6, 7, 9, 117, 125, 129
Rice, Greek L., 45
Richardson, Carl, 215, 216
Ridgeway, W. D., 59, 60
Riggs, Evangeline Patton, 89
Riggs, Lincoln James, 91
Rives, Richard, 116
Roberson, Bobby Earl, 172
Roberts, Alton Wayne, 180

Roberts, Johnny Lee, 64–65, 239
Roberts, M. M., 66
Robeson, Paul, 42
Robinson, Gwendolyn, 103–4
Roby, Harold, 123
Rogers, Truman, 174; Klan attack on, 166–67, 181, 197; Dahmer trial, 182–83, 184, 189, 191, 195, 234, 235
Rogers family, 8
Roosevelt, Eleanor, 17
Roosevelt, Franklin Delano, 17, 22, 24–25, 26
Roper, John, 225
Ross, Charles, 16
Ross, Quitman, 20, 44, 45, 128
Rousseau, Jean Jacques, 212
Rowan High School (Hattiesburg), 13, 204; integration, 205; walkout, 204
Royals, Preston, 41, 46
Rudin, James, 82
Ruffin, Larry, 226, 241
Ruffin, Susie, 103, 161, 220
Russell, Dan, 194, 195, 219
Rustin, Bayard, 117

Saul, Luther, 23
Savage, John, 30
Scarborough, William, 136–37, 200
Schwarz, Joseph, 127
Schwerner, Michael, 101, 115, 125, 177
Scott, Andrew, 30
Scott, A. S. 104
Scott, Gladys, 20
Scott, Maddie Jones Austin, 19–20
Scottsboro Boys, 17, 49
Seale, James Ford, 124
Selma, Alabama, 129
Sessum, Cecil, 93, 117–18; Dahmer attack, 143–45, 146; Dahmer investigation, 153–54, 156–57, 158, 165; Dahmer trials, 181, 182–87, 189, 194–96, 197, 237; prison sentence, 213, 215; Rogers kidnapping, 166–67; Watkins kidnapping, 177, 178, 213
Sessum, Mary, 157
Shaw, Terry, 99–100, 104, 110, 119
Shelton, Andrew, 232
Shelton, Robert, 142
Shields, Henry, 17
Shinall, Cloudies, 113–14, 133–37, 216–17

Shinall, Lee Mae, 113, 135–36
Shirley, Jerry Wayne, 189
Shoemake, Michael, 218
Short, Eugene, 206
Shotts, Nathaniel T., 24, 29, 30
Shriver, Sargent, 130, 162
Shubuta, Mississippi, 23; murders, 26
Siggers, Arthur, 102–3, 226
Sikeston, Missouri, lynching, 24, 25, 26–27
Sims, Charlie, 228–29
Sipuel v. Board of Regents, 53
Sit-ins, 22, 67, 69, 98–99, 111, 112, 116, 119, 120, 126, 127, 128–29, 131, 169, 170, 199, 243
Smith, C. E., 77, 169, 172–73, 179, 217
Smith, Charles, 62
Smith, Douglas, 77, 122
Smith, Harvel, 189
Smith, Hazel Brannon, 55
Smith, James, 110
Smith, Jay, 148–49, 184, 186
Smith, Jeanette, 77, 103, 172, 179
Smith, John, Jr., 218
Smith, Joseph, 17
Smith, Lewis Willie, 133, 135
Smith, Ora Lee, 19
Smith, Rachel, 232
Smith, Roy, 84
Smith, William Ray, 158
Smith, William Thomas: Dahmer attack, 144–45, 146, 154, 158; Dahmer trials, 181, 184, 189, 190–91, 194–96; sentencing and prison, 196, 197, 213, 215
Smith County, Mississippi, 100
Southern Christian Leadership Conference (SCLC), 52, 76, 138, 143, 160, 230
Southern Manifesto, 53
Southern Negro Youth Congress, 18
Southern Poverty Law Center, 230
Southern Regional Council, Second Annual Report, 95
Southside community (Laurel), 13
Sparkman, Robert, 168
Spears, Lawrence, 107, 114, 115, 128
Spinks, Elberta, 103, 126, 151, 161
Stanway, W. J., 83
Steele, Ed, 205
Stegal, Jessie, 66
Stennis, John, 38, 43, 53, 161, 162, 174, 200

Stenson, Robert, 117, 161
Stevenson, George, 11
St. James Church (Hattiesburg), 149–50, 152, 153, 170
Stockman, Lavelle, 168, 180
Stokes, Jimella, 73–74, 75, 79, 84–85, 108, 116, 118, 122, 171
Stone, John M., 10
Stoner, Peter, 86–88
St. Paul's Methodist Church (Laurel), 77, 143, 178, 187, 209
Street, James, 15; *Tap Roots*, 44
Strickland, Ralph, 184
Strickland, Roy, 165–66
Stringer, Bob, 231, 234
Stringer, Harrell, 112
Student Nonviolent Coordinating Committee (SNCC), 67–68, 69, 70, 72, 80, 82, 84, 85, 86, 87, 101, 122, 127, 129, 138, 143; black power movement, 160, 161; Freedom Day, 73, 76, 77, 79, 97; Freedom Summer, 95, 99, 103–4, 106, 120
Sullivan, Charles, 213
Sullivan, Robert, 196
Swan, Jimmy, 159, 164, 173, 174, 184, 213
Swartzfager, Jon, 34
Swartzfager, Paul, 23, 24, 39, 44, 46, 126
Sweatt v. Painter, 53

Tarrants, Thomas, III, 169, 180–81, 190, 191, 197
Tatum, W. F. S., 12
Tatum family, 8
Taylor, Paul, 218
Temple Beth Israel Synagogue (Jackson), 169
Temple Beth Israel Synagogue (Meridian), 190
Temple B'nai Israel, 56, 81
Terrell, Wilson, 211
Texarkana, Texas, lynching, 24, 27
Thames Junior High, 148, 187; integration, 163, 201
Thirteenth Amendment, 6
Thomas, Barbara Ann, 86
Thornton, Lester, 140, 144, 154, 155, 158, 181, 194, 195, 196, 235
Thornton, Tommy, 124
Thurmond, Strom, 44
Till, Emmett, 55
Times Picayune, 15

Tougaloo College, 70, 72, 86
Truman, Harry, 42, 43, 44, 45, 47
Tuskegee Normal and Industrial Institute, 11
Twenty-Fourth Amendment, 79, 96, 139
Twenty-Negro Law, 6

United Klans of America (UKA), 89, 123, 124, 142, 159
United Presbyterian Church of the USA, 80, 82, 83
United Presbyterian Commission on Religion and Race, 77
Universal Negro Improvement Association (UNIA), 17, 18
University of Chicago, 57, 62
University of Mississippi, 61
University of Missouri, 18
University of Southern Mississippi (USM), 94, 96, 97, 138, 140, 239
US Civil Rights Commission, 128, 129
US Commission on Civil Rights, 60, 82
US Fifth Circuit Court of Appeals, 59, 67, 71–72, 73, 78, 87, 129–30, 138
US Southern District Court, 43, 66, 68
US Supreme Court, 8, 17–18, 38, 43, 45, 46, 47, 52, 53, 59, 65, 72, 73, 83, 125–26, 137, 158, 196, 200
US v. Lynd, 68, 69, 71, 95, 129, 135, 242
US v. Shipp, 26

Valentine, C. W., 32, 34, 36, 38, 40
Valentine, Deavours, 168
Vardaman, James P., 14
Van den Burghe, Pierre L., 9
Van Landingham, Zack, 61, 62, 63
Vietnam War, 140, 168, 169, 188, 199, 216
Vincent, Susan, 40
Vinson, Willie, 24
Voting Rights Act of 1965, 129, 139, 150, 152, 158, 242; 1982 extension, 225

Wade, Charles, 200
Wade-Seals, Cora, 60, 211
Waley, Wilma, 67
Wallace, George, 141, 173, 185
Wallace, Henry, 44
Wallace, John, 96
Waller, Bob, 63

Waller, William, 173, 194, 213–14, 215
Walters, Granville, 48
Ward, Charley, 62
War Department, 28
Ware, Dave, 241
War on Drugs, 227
War on Poverty, 130, 162
Warren, Alex, 207, 209
Warren, Earl, 52
Warren Quarters community (Laurel), 13
Wash, Annie Slee, 27
Wash, Howard, 21–22, 23, 24, 26, 27, 29, 30, 31, 56, 91, 126
Wash, Louise, 23, 27
Washington, Booker T., 11, 82
Washington, DC, 22, 23, 30, 47
Watkins, Hollis, 68
Watkins, Jack, 165–66, 177, 237. *See also* Watkins kidnapping case
Watkins, W. H., 124
Watkins, Will, 30, 31
Watkins kidnapping case, 165–66, 174, 176, 177, 178, 181–82, 195, 197, 212–13, 233, 237
Watkins Junior High School (Laurel), 211
Watkins High School (Laurel), 199, 206, 207–11
Watson, Joseph, 211
Watson, Percy, 224
Watts, Frank, 154
WBKH, 151, 164
Welborn, Clint, 21, 24, 27
Welborn, Hillyer, 23, 27
Welborn, Laura, 189–90, 192
Welborn, Sharpe, 16
Welborn Dairy Farm, 23
Welch, Louis, 21, 23
Wells, Ray William, 185–87
West, Henry, 180
West, J. W., 96
White, Glenn, 230–31, 236
White, Hugh, 54
White, Jesse, 159, 161, 166, 174, 180, 197
White, John Albert, 218

White Christian Protective and Legal Defense Fund, 159
White Knights of the Ku Klux Klan, 3, 77, 91–93, 96, 100, 101, 121, 149, 154, 166, 173, 178, 189, 190, 230, 243; crimes committed, 124, 141, 176, 216; Dahmer attack, 143–45; defections, 164, 167, 176–77, 179–80, 197; formation, 77, 89; Imperial Wizard, 3, 89, 91, 92, 93, 143, 146, 158, 159, 191, 192, 196, 197, 223, 233, 235, 238; opposition to, 141–42, 181
White Negroes, 12, 44
Wilborn, Andrew, 135
Wilkins, Roy, 59, 147, 152
William Carey College, 148
Williams, John Bell, 173, 174, 201, 213, 214
Williams, Robert Lee, 162
Wilson, Charles, 190–91; Dahmer case, 144, 154, 158, 181, 197; Dahmer trials, 191, 194–96, 213; in prison, 213, 214; release, 215
Wilson, Samuel, 11
Windham, David, 215, 216
Wingo, Earle, 30, 37, 56
Winter, William, 173, 174
Woods, Lenon, 68, 80, 85
Woodward, T. A., 148
Works Progress Administration (WPA), 18
World War II, 20, 22, 25, 32, 50
Woullard, Rod, 205, 206, 226
Woullard, R. W., 58, 61, 68
Wright, Cleo, 24
Wright, Fielding, 42, 43, 47
Wyatt, Jerome, 104, 112, 225
Wynn, David, 240

Yankees, 7, 9, 30, 31
Yarbrough, Laverne, 38
Young, Jack, 134–35
Yount, James, 184

Zibulsky, Stan, 114
Zinn, Howard, 79, 81, 85

www.ingramcontent.com/pod-product-compliance
Lightning Source LLC
Chambersburg PA
CBHW030334240426
43661CB00052B/1629